The prevention
of terrorism
in British law

The prevention of terrorism in British law

Second edition

Clive Walker

Manchester University Press
Manchester and New York
Distributed exclusively in the USA and Canada by St. Martin's Press

Published by Manchester University Press
Oxford Road, Manchester M13 9PL, UK
and Room 400, 175 Fifth Avenue, New York, NY 10010, USA

Distributed exclusively in the USA and Canada
by St. Martin's Press, Inc., 175 Fifth Avenue, New York,
NY 10010, USA

A catalogue record for this book is available from the British Library

Library of Congress cataloging in publication data

Walker, Clive, Dr.
    The prevention of terrorism in British law / Clive Walker. — 2nd
ed.
        p.   cm.
    Includes bibliographical references and index.
    ISBN 0-7190-3175-3. — ISBN 0-7190-3176-1 (paper)
    1. Terrorism — Great Britain. I. Title.
KD8039.W35 1992
345.41'0231 — dc20
[344.105231]   91-31632

ISBN 0 7190 3175-3 *hardback*
     0 7190 3176-1 *paperback*

Typeset in Hong Kong
by Graphicraft Typesetters Ltd.

Printed in Great Britain
by Bell & Bain Ltd, Glasgow

Contents

Preface to the second edition

It is customary for authors to seek to justify the costs to readers of new editions. My case principally rests upon the welter of new materials which have arisen since the first imprint in 1986 (hereafter 'P.T.B.L. (1st ed.)'). Of foremost importance is the Prevention of Terrorism (Temporary Provisions) Act 1989, which represents the fourth generation of legislation to bear that title and which incorporates the most radical changes since the original version in 1974.[1] Other important legislation includes the Aviation and Maritime Security and the Criminal Justice (International Cooperation) Acts of 1990. The courts have also provided food for thought. The Birmingham, Maguire and Guildford cases have filled many headlines.[2] The workings of the exclusion system were examined in R. v. *Home Secretary, ex parte Stitt*,[3] and broadcasting restrictions were challenged in R. v. *Secretary of State for the Home Department, ex parte Brind*.[4] Lethal shootings have also fuelled some important litigation, especially arising out of coroners' inquests.[5] As well as these domestic claims, there is the adverse decision of the European Court of Human Rights in *Brogan and others v. United Kingdom*.[6]

In addition to the legal output from Parliament and the judges, a stream of official and unofficial commentaries has steadily flowed by. Official sources primarily comprise studies by the doughty Viscount Colville. Unofficial publications have included *Political Violence and the Law in Ireland* (hereafter P.V.L.I.)[7] by Gerard Hogan and myself, to which much cross-reference will be made. Account must also be taken of present and future trends relating to terrorism. For example, incidents of foreign terrorism, such as the bombing of Pan-Am Flight 103 over Lockerbie, have become more prominent, as have the activities of animal liberationists. As expected, the campaign of Republican terrorism has persisted. Finally, consideration must be given to the likely impact on security of the implementation of the Single European Act by the end of 1992.

In summary, there is an abundance of new materials from which to manufacture a new edition. Of course, some avenues of research remain closed, as many official reactions to terrorism are highly secret and sensitive. However, the views of the security forces and other State agencies are again reflected in two ways: through my contacts with forthcoming individuals and through the evidence they have presented to official inquiries. In any event, it would be wrong to allow official secrecy to stifle discussion.

I wish to record my thanks to all those who have aided my efforts. My sources have ranged from contacts in government departments, police forces and foreign embassies to legal practitioners and fellow academics. A substantial degree of secretarial and library assistance was as usual provided here at Leeds.

The law is stated in accordance with sources available to me on 12 April 1991, by which time the Prevention of Terrorism (Temporary Provisions) Act 1989 was fully in force.[8] I have since incorporated important later developments, especially the Northern Ireland (Emergency Provisions) Act 1991, which replaces sections 21 to 24 of the 1989 Act.

Notes

1 Regrettably, the Act is now so substantial (72 pp.) that it cannot be fully reproduced here.

2 See ch. 11.

3 (1987) *Times* 3 February.

4 [1991] 2 W.L.R. 588.

5 See ch. 8.

6 Appl. Nos. 11209/84, 11266/84, 11386/85, Judgment of Court Ser. A Vol. 145-B.

7 Manchester University Press, 1989.

8 S.I. 1989 No. 1361; S.I. 1990 No. 215 (except the repeal by Sched. 9 of Sched. 7 para. 9). Sched. 9 repeals Sched. 7 para. 9 pursuant to the Land Registration Act 1988.

Clive Walker
University of Leeds
31 October 1991

Glossary of short titles of governmental documents

Baker Report	*Review of the Operation of the Northern Ireland (Emergency Provisions) Act 1978* (Cmnd. 9222, 1984)
Bennett Roport	*Report of the Committee of Inquiry into Police Interrogation Procedures in Northern Ireland* (Cmnd. 9497, 1979)
Bowen Report	*Report on Procedures for the Arrest, Interrogation and Detention of Suspected Terrorists in Aden* (Cmnd. 3165, 1966)
Cameron Report	*Disturbances in Northern Ireland. Report of the Commission appointed by the Governor of Northern Ireland* (Cmd. 532, Belfast, 1969)
Colville Annual Reports	*Reports on the Operation in 1986–90 of the Prevention of Terrorism (Temporary Provisions) Acts* (Home Office)
Colville Annual Reports on the E.P. Acts	*Reports on the Operation in 1987–89 of the Northern Ireland (Emergency Provisions) Acts* (Northern Ireland Office)
Colville Report	*Review of the Operation of the Prevention of Terrorism (Temporary Provisions) Act 1984* (Cm. 264, 1987)
Colville Report on the E.P. Acts	*Review of the Northern Ireland (Emergency Provisions) Acts 1978 and 1987* (Cm. 1115, 1990)
Compton Report	*Report of an Inquiry into allegations against the security forces of physical brutality in Northern Ireland arising out of arrests on the 9 August 1971* (Cmnd. 4828, 1972)

Diplock Report

Report of the Commission to consider legal procedures to deal with terrorist activities in Northern Ireland (Cmnd. 5185, 1972)

Gardiner Report

Report of a Committee to consider, in the context of civil liberties and human rights, measures to deal with terrorism in Northern Ireland (Cmnd. 5847, 1975)

H.O. Circular

Home Office Circular No. 27/1989: *Prevention of Terrorism (Temporary Provisions) Act 1989* (as amended by Home Office Circular No. 60/1989)

Hope Report

Royal Commission on Intelligence and Security (*4th Report* PP. 249 (Cth) (1977))

Jellicoe Report

Review of the Operation of the Prevention of Terrorism (Temporary Provisions) Act 1976 (Cmnd. 8803, 1983)

Laudau Report

Report of the Commission of Inquiry into the methods of investigation of the General Security Service regarding hostile terrorist activity (1987, Jerusalem)

McDonald Commission

Report of the Commission of Inquiry concerning certain activities of the Royal Canadian Mounted Police: Freedom and Security under the Law (2nd Report, 1981).

May Inquiry

Interim Report on the Maguire Case (1989–90 H.C. 556)

N.I.O. Guide

Northern Ireland Office *Guide to the Emergency Powers* (1990)

O'Briain Report

Report of the Committee to recommend certain safeguards for persons in custody and for members of An Garda Siochana (Prl. 7158, Dublin, 1978)

Philips Annual Reports

Reports on the Operation in 1984–85 of the Prevention of Terrorism (Temporary Provisions) Acts (Home Office)

Rabie Report

Report of the Commission of Inquiry into Security Legislation (RP90/1981, Pretoria, 1981)

S.A.C.H.R.

Standing Advisory Commission on Human Rights for Northern Ireland, *Annual Reports,* 1973–90 (House of Commons Papers)

Scarman Report

Government of Northern Ireland. Violence and Civil Disturbance in Northern Ireland in 1969. Report of a Tribunal of Inquiry (Cmd. 566, Belfast, 1972)

Shackleton Report

Review of the Operation of the Prevention of Terrorism (Temporary Provisions) Acts 1974 and 1976 (Cmnd. 7324, 1978)

S.H.H.D. Circular

Scottish Home and Health Department Circular No. 3/1989: *Prevention of Terrorism (Temporary Provisions) Act 1989* (identical to H.O. Circular unless stated otherwise)

Widgery Report

Report of the Tribunal appointed to inquire into the events on Sunday 30 January 1972 which led to loss of life in connection with the procession in Londonderry on that day (1971–72 H.C. 220)

Chapter 1

Introduction

United Kingdom laws on the subject of terrorism can be divided into three. By far the most numerous and important are those concerned with the recurring crises over the relationship between Ireland and Great Britain, the source of acute disaccord in constitutional law since the Acts of Union in 1800 and long before. What the United Kingdom Parliament has deemed to be terrorism may be viewed as but a small part of that controversy. Nevertheless, Irish terrorism has spawned a great variety and quantity of legislation, not only from Westminster, but also from Dail Eireann and the now defunct Northern Ireland Parliament. The second source of relevant laws is concerned not only with Irish terrorism but also with other sources of domestic political violence. Some examples are of great longevity (such as treason), but more recent additions deal with bomb hoaxes and food contamination. The third set of legal materials addresses the exploitation by terrorists of international frontiers.

Unfortunately constraints of space demand that only a proportion of these three sources of laws can be discussed. Detailed coverage (chapters 4 to 11) will be confined to the Prevention of Terrorism (Temporary Provisions) Act 1989, which represents the central response in British law to terrorism. An array of other relevant measures which operate domestically, including those based on international treaty, will be examined (chapter 12), and attention will be given throughout to 'normal' laws applicable to terrorism. Suggestions for improvements will also be offered and drawn together at the end (chapter 13). To complete the picture, it may be as well to detail forthwith those equally interesting fields of study which must be eschewed for present purposes.

From the foregoing remarks, it may be deduced that the main anti-terrorism codes in Ireland, the Northern Ireland (Emergency Provisions) Acts 1973–91 and the Offences against the State Acts 1939–85, will not be examined comprehensively.[1] However, given their importance in the battle against terrorism and their intimate relationship with the Prevention of Terrorism Act, it would be misleading to ignore them altogether. Consequently, they will be mentioned extensively for comparative and critical purposes. Incidentally, the same treatment will be bestowed, though on a reduced scale, upon anti-terrorism legislation used in the past in the British Isles and to current measures in foreign jurisdictions.

Next, a secondary source of some British anti-terrorism measures, namely international law, will not be closely scrutinised. This omission is dictated by lack of space, by the fact that there already exists a vast literature on the subject,[2] and by the observation that international cooperation has so far produced a rather patchy and stultified response.[3] Consequently, coverage will extend only to those international norms which have been translated into British legislation (such as extradition or multilateral conventions) or have some indirect impact (as in the case of the European Convention on Human Rights).[4] Cross-border arrangements between Britain and the Republic of Ireland fall within this scope but will be omitted since they have been described in P.V.L.I.[5]

The third important issue which is omitted is whether terrorism is justifiable historically, politically or morally.[6] So vital are these questions that the vindication of one side or the other determines the very labelling of the conflict: in the oft-repeated phrase, 'one man's "terrorist" is another man's "freedom-fighter"'. However the concern of this book is with the positive law and its role in combating terrorism, whereas the issue of justification questions not that laws are able to combat terrorism but whether they should do so at all. This is evidently an issue which the laws themselves cannot settle since it is their very authority which is in doubt.[7] It is to be hoped that this prior question will be carefully considered whenever political violence is encountered, but, for the purposes of this book, it will naively be assumed that the current hostile reaction in British law to terrorism is acceptable. Similarly, whilst recognising the moral overtones implied by its use, the label 'terrorism' will be used to describe any action correlating to the description in chapter 2. The term is not meant to convey any pejorative implication.

Finally, not all forms of terrorism are accorded equal treatment. Special prominence will be given to 'revolutionary' terrorism, which is exemplified by attacks by the I.R.A. on the security forces and involves:[8]

. . . systematic tactics or terroristic violence with the objective of bringing about political revolution.

Other forms of political terrorism encompass counter-revolutionary terrorism (perhaps by Loyalist paramilitaries in Northern Ireland), sub-revolutionary terrorism which seeks objectives within the political order (such as animal rights) and 'state' or 'repressive' terrorism, which is officially sanctioned against targets at home[9] or abroad.[10] Terrorism may equally be utilised for private ends, such as by racketeers and robbers. The Prevention of Terrorism Act was prompted mainly by revolutionary terrorism but has also been applied to counter-revolutionary, and some sub-revolutionary, terrorism. Other relevant laws focus mainly on sub-revolutionary terrorism.

Notes

1 But see P.V.L.I.
2 See ch. 12.
3 See: Judge A.D. Sofaer, 'Terrorism and the Law' (1986) 64 *Foreign Affairs* 901; A. Cassesse, *Terrorism, Politics and Law* (1989); J.F. Murphy, *State Support of International Terrorism* (1989).
4 Cmd. 8969, 1950. For its relationship with U.K. law, see: K.D. Ewing and W. Finnie, *Civil Liberties in Scotland* (2nd ed., 1988) ch. 2; *R. v. Sec. of State for the Home Dept. ex p. Brind* [1991] 2 W.L.R. 588.
5 Ch. 14 and 15.
6 See: Fifth Working Party of the Irish Council of Churches/Roman Catholic Church Joint Group on Social Questions, *Violence in Ireland* (1976); M. Waltzer, *Just and Unjust Wars* (1978); B. Paskins and M. Dockrill, *The Ethics of War* (1979); M. Hughes, 'Terrorism and national security' (1982) 57 *Philosophy* 5; C.A.J. Coady, 'The morality of terrorism' (1985) 60 *Philosophy* 47; S.D. Bailey (ed.), *Human Rights and Responsibilities in Britain and Ireland* (1988) ch. 7; T. Honoré, 'The right to rebel' (1988) 8 *Ox. J.S.* 34; H. Katchadourian, 'Terrorism and morality' (1988) 5 *Jo. of Applied Philosophy* 131; P. Hillyard and J. Percy-Smith, *The Coercive State* (1988); P. Gilbert, 'Terrorism: war or crime?' (1989) 3 *Cogito* 51; G. Wallace, 'Area bombing, terrorism and the death of innocents' (1989) 6 *Jo. of Applied Philosophy* 3; T. Honderich, *Violence for Equality* (1989).
7 The public and Government have experienced 'legitimation crises': F. Burton and P. Carter, *Official Discourse* (1979). Some soldiers have also refused to serve in Northern Ireland: P. Rowe, *Defence: The Legal Implications* (1987) p. 6.
8 P. Wilkinson, *Political Terrorism* (1974) p. 36.
9 See: E.V. Walter, *Terror and Resistance* (1969); P. Wilkinson, 'Can a state be "terrorist"?' (1981) 57 *Int. Affairs* 467; M. Stohl and G.A. Lopez (eds.), *The State as Terrorist* (1984). The Prevention of Terrorism Acts have themselves been condemned as 'terrorising efforts': A.McC. Lee, *Terrorism in Northern Ireland* (1983) p. 173.
10 Murphy, *op. cit.*

Chapter 2

Theory of terrorism and anti-terrorism

1 Nature of terrorism

Between 1969 and 1971, there was a spate of terrorist incidents around Britain ranging from the destruction of an outside-broadcast van covering the 'Miss World' contest to the planting of bombs directed against two of Her Majesty's Secretaries of State.[1] 'No revolution was ever won without violence,' proclaimed the Angry Brigade, the instigators of these attacks. However, the campaign was relatively short-lived, for, by the end of 1972, five of its members had been imprisoned and its arsenal seized.[2] Yet, given that the Irish Republican Army, one of the most effective and durable organisations ever to resort to political violence, had renewed its operations in 1970, it must have seemed that an era of terrorism had dawned in the United Kingdom. From the almost archetypal campaign of the Angry Brigade, a number of general remarks concerning the nature of terrorism may now be extrapolated.

(a) Revolutionary terrorism as a strategy

Revolutionary terrorism may be adopted as an end in itself, for example, by anarchists (such as the Angry Brigade) who wish to overthrow the existing government without advocating any alternative. However, terrorism is more frequently undertaken as a military strategy in support of political change, usually when two preconditions prevail.[3] First, the group's objectives cannot be attained by direct military force, and secondly, the group sees no point in pursuing constitutional means. In short, terrorism is said to be the weapon of the weak (and few were militarily or politically weaker than the Angry Brigade). Assuming these conditions apply, revolutionary terrorism will be employed as one strategy within a wider enterprise. For instance, in Maoist theory, terrorism is an early stage in guerrilla warfare and becomes increasingly irrelevant as rebel forces grow.[4] Alternatively, terrorism may be a constant military tactic with a variety of purposes (propaganda, discipline, funding, attrition) but is combined with guerrilla operations and political agitation. This probably describes the current operations of the Provisional Irish Republican Army.[5] Either way, the weakness of the rebels dictates their *modus operandi*. Above all, they must avoid open conflict with the government's military forces, which are overwhelmingly stronger. Hence, 'the central task of the guerrilla fighter is to keep himself from being destroyed.'[6] Next, terrorists must have good intelligence in order to undertake effective operations without detection. Finally, since constitutional methods are rejected, there must be some compensating public emphasis on the motives for their attacks in order to distance themselves from criminal banditry. This is often secured through links with overt political factions.

There are two contexts in which the weak commonly resort to revolutionary terrorism. First, it may be utilised within independent States. The rebels envisage that terrorism will trigger a spiral of governmental repression and consequent loss of popularity and authority.[7]

[The terrorists'] object is to shake the faith of the man in the street in the Government and its local representatives, especially the police, so that in the end a desperate population will seek security, not from authorities, but from the terrorist and his political allies.

There are two substantial impediments to this theoretical blueprint. First, terrorism is unlikely to succeed in the many countries where governments pay little heed to public fears or desires. Second, even if terrorism does provoke a reaction, that repression may secure the military defeat of the perpetrators. As a result, outright success has rarely been achieved by this path, the only exceptions perhaps being Cuba and Rhodesia, where terrorism was only one facet of the conflict. However, it may be counted as a partial terrorist success if governmental victory is achieved at the expense of political fragmentation or deep unpopularity, since they pave the way for future conflict. Thus:[8]

the issue is not merely survival, but the way in which society chooses to survive.

Revolutionary terrorism is secondly undertaken during campaigns for decolonisation or for the separation of a distinct territory from within an independent country. Here, the terrorists again seek to induce repression, which, they hope, will cause the 'parent' population to weary of the battle and to calculate that the costs of retaining the territory outweigh its benefits. This has proved more effective than terrorism in the first situation probably because it does not require governments to vacate their central seats of power and therefore demands less painful concessions. In the case of the United Kingdom, terrorism of this kind was a precipitating factor in its withdrawal from Ireland, Palestine, Malaya and South Arabia. In conclusion, terrorism in both contexts is designed to win acceptance for a political aim by a significant section of the population. Therefore, in liberal democracies at least, the increase or decrease in popular support may be taken to be the ultimate measure of success or failure for terrorists or governments.

(b)   Classification

Terrorism has sometimes been classified as a form of warfare, but it is submitted that even a campaign of revolutionary terrorism does not of itself normally qualify. This is because, under the Geneva Conventions and Protocols,[9] and probably also in common parlance, 'armed conflict' and 'warfare' consist of sustained and extensive military operations. By contrast, terrorism tends by its nature to be sporadic and of low intensity.[10]

   Terrorism of all categories has more frequently and accurately been designated as a 'risk to the security of the State'. For example, the concerns of the Security Service (M.I.5) are now listed in section 1(2) of the Security Service Act 1989 as including:

the protection of national security and, in particular, its protection against threats from espionage, terrorism and sabotage, from the activities of agents of foreign powers and from actions intended to overthrow or undermine parliamentary democracy by political, industrial or violent means.

Three points should be noted. The first concerns the wide-ranging nature of the remit, which does not even specify that the 'threats', 'activities' or 'means' be unlawful or amount to more than democratic dissent. Secondly, 'terrorism' is expressly mentioned, which is not surprising as it has long been a concern of the Security Service.[11] However, the term (and the same applies to 'espionage' and 'sabotage') is nowhere defined;[12] whether one should apply the definition in the Prevention of Terrorism Act (described shortly) remains to be determined. Finally, the Act governs the work of the Security Service (broadly, domestic intelligence) but probably does not affect other relevant agencies, such as M.I.6 (foreign intelligence), Army intelligence or police Special Branches. Before 1989, some security organisations were subjected to administrative restraint. For example, for the benefit of security agents attached to M.I.5, Lord Denning in his Report on the Profumo Affair advanced the restrictive guidance that their targets must threaten 'the Defence of the Realm' or be 'subversive, . . . that is . . . contemplate the overthrow of the Government by unlawful means'.[13] Under these tests, revolutionary terrorists qualify as security risks, but groups dedicated to revolution by constitutional means do not. A more expansive definition (which could include the latter) was proffered by the Home Office in 1975, which reformulated 'subversion' as 'activities . . . which threaten the safety or well-being of the State, and which are intended to undermine or overthrow parliamentary democracy by political, industrial or violent means'.[14] This 1975 formula was applied in 1984 to the work of police Special Branches. Their concerns are the widest of all and comprise threats to public order, espionage, sabotage, extremists, terrorists and subversion.[15]

A number of Commonwealth jurisdictions have likewise defined security targets as invariably including terrorists. For example, risks to security are listed in section 4 of the Australian Security Intelligence Organisation Act 1979 as espionage, sabotage, subversion, active measures of foreign intervention and terrorism.[16] In New Zealand, terrorism was specifically added to the concerns of the Security Intelligence Service by an amending Act of 1977[17] and now ranks alongside espionage, sabotage and subversion. Thirdly, the Canadian Security Intelligence Services Act 1984[18] mentions not only espionage, sabotage, clandestine or threatening foreign-influenced activities and subversive activities intended to overthrow constitutional government by violence but also the threat or use of serious violence to achieve a political objective. In summary, terrorism is widely recognised in liberal democracies as a prime threat to State security. It follows that it is seen as legitimate to pass laws against such activities and to direct the attention of the police and security services against it.

2   Definitions of terrorism

This discussion about the nature of revolutionary terrorism has proceeded as if that term had an incontrovertible meaning. In reality, this is far from true, and one might ask, for example, whether the Angry Brigade was properly characterised as terroristic. The following definition is advanced by section 20(1) of the Prevention of Terrorism (Temporary Provisions) Act 1989:[19]

'terrorism' means the use of violence for political ends and includes any use of violence for the purpose of putting the public or any section of the public in fear.

In the light of the foregoing delineation of terrorism as a strategy, this is a rather unilluminating and limited description of the phenomenon. However, its two main elements, 'violence' and 'political ends', are worthy of further examination.

(a)   Violence
The evaluative aspect of the word 'terrorism' is most pronounced in this element. 'Violence' implies force which is unjustified and unlawful[20] and usually entails criminal offences which involve a threat to, or endangerment of, personal safety. In fact, relevant legislation containing lists of terrorist offences are not always so limited, though their context should be recognised in that such laws quite properly react not only to acts of political violence

themselves but also to their background logistical and organisational support. For example, the Criminal Jurisdiction Act 1975 empowers Northern Ireland courts to try certain 'terrorist' offences committed in the Republic of Ireland. However, the crimes specified in Schedule 1 comprise not only violence to the person but also certain forms of damage to property, robbery and burglary. A similarly indiscriminate list is found in Schedule 1 of the Northern Ireland (Emergency Provisions) Act 1991, which defines those offences to be treated as relating to terrorism for criminal procedure purposes. Only the Suppression of Terrorism Act 1978, which is concerned with extra-territorial jurisdiction and extradition pursuant to the Council of Europe's Convention on the Suppression of Terrorism,[21] confines its attention to offences relating to personal attacks or endangerment. Nevertheless, it should be accepted that offences of that kind do comprise the core of terrorism since less directly threatening crimes are unlikely to terrorise. It follows that the incorporation of 'violence' into a definition of terrorism is desirable, though it may be more accurate to specify 'violence to the person' as its essence.

(b)   *Political ends or putting the public in fear*
Mention of 'political ends' in section 20 emphasises that terroristic violence is a symbolic means to ulterior objectives. In order to achieve this effect, the violence must be both well publicised and sparing, since its impact will be dulled by over-use. Thus, the common perception that terrorism is indiscriminate violence represents the intended induced reaction rather than the true situation.

The express inclusion of political motives has further significance since it enables the formula in section 20 to distinguish between 'ordinary' criminals and terrorists. The latter must commit crimes for certain reasons, though their motives need not themselves be criminal. On the other hand, reference simply to 'political ends' does not differentiate between disparate categories of terrorism. Consequently, the definition in section 20 is again somewhat imprecise and is equally applicable to revolutionary, counter-revolutionary, sub-revolutionary and state terrorism. However, the Government has recently sought to establish a distinction between 'political ends' and 'social objectives', such as might prompt animal liberationists or even factional fighting within Sikh extremist groups.[22] It is submitted that this contrast, which seeks to carve out an uncertain area of sub-revolutionary terrorism from the scope of section 20, is untenable because of the broad meaning of 'political ends'.

Violence in pursuit of the alternative objective in section 20, 'putting the public or any section of the public in fear', will often overlap with 'political ends' but may sometimes result from a non-political cause and yet still amount to 'terrorism'.[23] An example which could trigger the Act would be a visiting group of foreign football hooligans who inflict fear in order to intimidate a section of the public (supporters of the opposing British team). Similar street disorder has been interpreted as 'terrorism' in connection with criminal injuries claims in Northern Ireland.[24] In consequence, this element of the definition in section 20(1) is overbroad and should be deleted. Putting the public in fear should only be called 'terrorism' if perpetrated with a political motive, the course followed by the legal definition of terrorism in the Elected Authorities (Northern Ireland) Act 1989 (concerning the declaration of non-violence to be made by candidates in local elections).[25] Hooliganism or individual acts of aggression should not figure within a legal definition of terrorism,[26] since these offences are not sufficiently serious or so difficult to detect because of clandestine organisation as to justify special treatment.

(c)   Comment

The official verdict is that section 20 'has not given rise to any difficulties'[27] and does not, therefore, require amendment. In reality, however, the provision entails various problems (which would persist even if section 20 were modified in the ways already indicated). First, such a formula would still encompass some offenders not normally depicted as terrorists, such as persons involved in a bout of fisticuffs at demonstrations against government policy.[28] A more intractable problem is that the emphasis upon the political motives of terrorist offenders could create problems in regard to extradition[29] and has added weight to claims for an amnesty or for special prison treatment for convicted terrorists.[30]

A third possible difficulty arises from the interpretation of section 66 of the Northern Ireland (Emergency Provisions) Act 1991, which defines a 'terrorist' as:

a person who is or has been concerned in the commission or attempted commission of any act of terrorism or in directing, organising or training persons for the purpose of terrorism....

In *McKee* v. *Chief Constable for Northern Ireland*,[31] the Northern Ireland Court of Appeal decided that section 66 requires 'active' rather than 'passive' involvement in terrorism. Consequently, those guilty merely of membership of, or soliciting support for, a terrorist organisation are not 'terrorists'. It remains to be seen whether a similar view will ever be taken of 'terrorism' under section 20 of the Prevention of Terrorism Act, but various reasons suggest otherwise.[32] One is that the restrictive interpretation of 'terrorist' may itself be faulty. Not only does it strain the natural meaning of being 'concerned in' an enterprise, but it also ignores the fact that even 'passive' involvement, such as membership, must in the absence of a confession be evidenced by activities just as much as 'active' terrorism.[33] A second factor likely to discourage the spread of the Court of Appeal's view is that, on appeal, the House of Lords hinted *obiter* that the definition in section 66 should be seen as 'wide' rather than 'narrow'.[34] Finally, relevant measures in the Prevention of Terrorism Act almost invariably refer to a person's concern not only in the 'commission' of acts of terrorism but also, unlike the Emergency Powers Act, in their 'preparation or instigation', implying that the involvement may be remote from the violence.

Because of these various problems, the first two of which appear insoluble, no definition of terrorism will be attempted here, nor will any proposal be made in which the term is required.[35] The preferred method will be the 'scheduled offence' approach in which counter-terrorism provisions are designed by reference to the offences involved, making irrelevant the motives of the offender and underlining his criminal wrongdoing.[36] Offences would be scheduled (and thereby become susceptible to special treatment) if existing criminal laws or procedures are not reasonably adequate to secure the administration of justice in view of the organised and serious nature of that offence which is regularly being perpetrated against the public or any section of it.[37] However, whilst this policy of criminalisation is appropriate in regard to the direct legal response to terroristic violence, motivation should not be ignored altogether, since social, economic and political reactions must also be considered.[38]

3 Counter-strategy

(a) Methods in general

It would be misleading to single out any particular strategy in response to terrorism, as many counter-tactics have been improvised or have been reactive to outside pressures. However, an element often stressed is the importance of intelligence-gathering.[39] One reason is that governments desire, rather than wish to avoid, military confrontation since their forces are usually overwhelming. Alternatively, detection at an early stage may allow prevention and contingency planning. In addition, good intelligence will enable terrorists to be prosecuted by normal procedures. This is important since:[40]

Imprisonment after conviction by a criminal court is politically the most persuasive way of disposing of the accused, and the least likely way to provoke internal or international criticism.

An abundance of information also allows a government to criticise rebels, to gauge the strength of the political opposition it faces and to make cogent reforms.

Whilst good intelligence is important, it should be recalled that, in a liberal democracy at least, the ultimate test of success or failure of activities against terrorism is the maintenance of public support. From a government's point of view, this should trigger various considerations. First, there should be some attempt to demonstrate the legitimacy and value of the existing regime, and this should be reinforced by a willingness to meet legitimate demands for reform. The converse is to avoid policies which alienate the public. For example, it is generally preferable to deploy the police rather than the Army.[41] Soldiers are normally neither trained nor equipped to exercise minimum force and are not familiar with the close combat engaged in by terrorists. Furthermore, armed forces often lack local links from which to draw information and to which they can be made accountable. More generally, military intervention represents a disturbing departure from normality which may prompt an escalation of violence. Despite these considerations, a compromise is often reached: soldiers are deployed after special training, and policemen are equipped with militaristic powers and weaponry.[42] As well as responding to terrorism with regular police forces, their powers and tactics must be designed carefully. Measures of repression with substantial repercussions on the public should be avoided; not only will they be deeply unpopular, but also:[43]

> Few things would provide a more gratifying victory to the terrorist than for this country to undermine its traditional freedoms, in the very process of countering the enemies of those freedoms.

Unfortunately, internal strife is too often 'characterized by massive and brutal violations of human dignity'.[44]

The overall aim of the maintenance of public support within the context of a liberal democracy makes it wise to abide by a number of limiting principles. For example, in the international sphere, attention should be paid to agreements protecting human rights, including[45] the European Convention on Human Rights and Fundamental Freedoms[46] and the Paris Minimum Standards of Human Rights Norms in a State of Emergency.[47] Nationally, it is important to observe the traditions of the legal system, since 'special' measures may be seen as unfair and so will fail to produce terrorists who are viewed as legitimately convicted criminals. There are also relevant pragmatic principles for limiting derogations from existing laws. Special measures, it has been suggested,[48] should be operative only so far as necessary in the exigencies of the situation, and this should be judged factually. Second, anti-terrorist laws should derogate as little as factually necessary from 'normal' measures in extent. Third, special measures should be clear and precise, and safeguards should be provided to prevent their improper introduction or exercise, including parliamentary scrutiny. Further, their application in an individual case should be considered necessary by an objective and impartial arbiter and should be accompanied by remedies against unreasonable use. Next, special laws should be distinct

from ordinary powers, since the assimilation of the two may damage
confidence in the existing law, may hamper scrutiny of the impact of
special laws and may retard their expiration. Finally, the assimilation of
anti-terrorist measures in the United Kingdom with those elsewhere in
Western Europe could offer a guarantee against discrimination and an
impetus towards cooperation and the cross-fertilisation of ideas.
Harmonisation within Ireland is now actively considered by the Anglo-
Irish Inter-Governmental Conference.[49]

The overall effect of these limiting principles is to force the adoption
of a 'due process' rather than 'crime control' model.[50] Thus, criminal laws
and procedures can be modified in response to terrorism but only within
parameters set by fairness and basic rights. These constraints flow from a
rational response to the political and violent aspects of terrorism,[51] assuming
the aim of the maintenance of a liberal democracy.[52] Some believe that this
restrained approach cannot cope with the abnormal assault of terrorism
and will either suffer unmanageable strains[53] or will render ineffective the
State's response.[54] If this analysis is correct, 'the triumph of security over
legality'[55] will follow in substance so that:[56]

If there is a conflict between expediency and strict law, let the conflict be recognised,
and if the law ought to be changed by Parliament, then let it be changed – and the
sooner the better.

It may be conceded that restraints on official responses to terrorism will
cause severe tensions, but temptations to remove those restraints or to act
extra-legally should be discouraged by the argument that they are self-
defeating, since they are deleterious to the type of society to be preserved.

Conversely, it would be dangerous for a liberal democracy to fail to
react at all to terrorism. The State has a duty to safeguard the right to life
of its citizens and must therefore consider counter-measures.[57] Equally, the
apparent contradiction between the adoption of special measures and the
depiction of terrorism as ordinary criminals can be explained. Measures
against crimes need not be uniform. Just as variations have been adopted
against, for example, serious fraudsters and drug traffickers,[58] so terrorists
may warrant different treatment because of their atypical motivations and
methods. Provided the special code against them complies with the limiting
principles described, it may be depicted as a sensible policing and criminal
justice response which on balance upholds democracy and individual rights.
If no effective response can be made to terrorism within such bounds, then
legal repression or the application of extra-legal military force will follow
but will signal a defeat for constitutional democracy.

(b) Prevention

In view of the serious threat posed by terrorism to the public and
constitutional order, it is preferable to prevent terrorism than to combat

attacks already sustained. However, three strategic considerations suggest that it is not possible to devise a simple Act to achieve this, despite the contrary implication of the Prevention of Terrorism Act.

The first problem is that, if the terrorist campaign has any significant support, the programme against it requires the deployment of the full range of governmental resources. In short, the true prevention of terrorism is a 'task of national reconstruction'[59] rather than a matter of tinkering with criminal procedures and offences. The second impediment to the prevention of terrorism conflicts to some extent with the first. Even the most accommodating government will find it difficult to satisfy the political demands of extremists since such concessions will probably result in the substitution of the discontent of the majority for the terrorism of a minority. Consequently:[60]

> The problem of terrorism is really one of identification and control, and not, unfortunately, of elimination.

Finally, preventive strategies require advance targeting of individuals with a degree of accurate prediction which is unlikely to be attained. As a result, this book will be concerned not only with laws which prevent terrorism and so reduce the number of incidents, but also with measures of control which react to terrorism that has taken place. In reality, the Prevention of Terrorism Act follows a similar path.

Notes

1 See: G. Carr, *The Angry Brigade* (1975); R. Allason, *The Branch* (1983) ch. 11.

2 See: *R. v. Prescott and Purdie* (1971) *Times* 2 December p. 1; *R. v. Greenfield and others* (1973) 57 Cr. App. R. 849.

3 As to why terrorism is chosen in these circumstances, see: T. Gurr, *Why Men Rebel* (1970); E. Evans, *Calling a Truce to Terror* (1979) ch. 2.

4 *Problems of War and Strategy* (1938). Compare: W. Laqueur, *The Age of Terrorism* (1987) pp. 1, 5.

5 See ch. 3. This mode of attack was also adopted in Ireland during the War of Independence and in Cyprus; see: C. Townshend, 'The Irish Republican Army and the development of guerilla warfare 1916–1921' (1979) XCIV *E.H.R.* 318; G. Grivas-Dighensis, *Guerrilla Warfare* (1962).

6 Che Guevara, *Guerilla Warfare* (1961) p. 21.

7 A.M. Burton, *Urban Terrorism* (1975) pp. 5–6.

8 R.A. Friedlander, *Terrorism: Documents of International and Local Control*, Vol. I (1979) p. 108.

9 Geneva Conventions I–IV, 1949 (Cmnd. 550, 1958) Arts. 2, 3; Protocols I and II, 1977 (Cmnd. 6927) Art. 1.

10 See: *Mohammed Ali v. Public Prosecutor* [1968] 3 All E.R. 488; *American World Airways Inc. v. Aetna Casualty and Surety Co.* 358 F. Supp. 1098 (1973);

R.R. Baxter, 'Humanitarian law or humanitarian policies' (1975) *Harv. Int. L.J.* 1 at p. 20; Walker, 'Irish Republican prisoners' (1984) 19 *Ir. Jur.* 189.

11   See ch. 13. Compare H.C. Debs. Vol. 145 col. 198 17 January 1989, Mr. Allason.

12   See I. Leigh and L. Lustgarten, 'The Security Service Act 1989' (1989) 52 *M.L.R.* 801 at p. 805.

13   (Cmnd. 2152, 1963) para. 230.

14   H.L. Debs. Vol. 357 col. 947 26 February 1975, Lord Harris. See R.J. Spjut, 'Defining subversion' (1979) 6 *B.J. of L. & S.* 254.

15   Home Office, *Guidelines on the Work of a Special Branch* (1984). The definition of 'terrorism' in the *Guidelines* is taken from the Prevention of Terrorism (Temporary Provisions) Act 1984 s. 14(1).

16   See: Hope Report, paras. 35, 36; Initial Report of Mr. Justice White (S.A.), *Special Branch Security Records* (P.P. 145, 1978) para. 10.1.6.; H.P. Lee, 'The A.S.I.O.' (1989) 38 *I.C.L.Q.* 890.

17   New Zealand Security Intelligence Service Act 1977 s. 3, amending ss. 2 and 4 of the 1969 Act. The amendment followed the *Report by the Chief Ombudsman on the Security Intelligence Service* (1976, p. 31).

18   1983–84 (c. 21) s. 2. This was largely based on the McDonald Commission, Pt. V ch. 3 para. 41. See: P. Gill, 'Defining subversion' (1989) *P.L.* 617; *The Final Report of the Select Committee to study Governmental Operations with respect to intelligence activities* (U.S. Senate 94th Cong. 2d. Sess. Report No. 94–755, 1976) (Book II pp. 20, 320) also supported investigations to anticipate terroristic violence.

19   For the meaning of a 'section of the public', see: *Charter* v. *Race Relations Board* [1974] 3 All E.R. 592. The Northern Ireland (Emergency Provisions) Act 1973 s. 28 was the inspiration behind section 20: H.C. Debs. Standing Com. D. col. 352 8 December 1983, Mr. Waddington. For further discussion on the meaning and use of the term, see: chs. 12, 13; B.L. Smith, 'Antiterrorism legislation in the U.S.' (1984) *Terrorism J.* 213; G.M. Levitt, 'Is "terrorism" worth defining?' (1986) 13 *Ohio Northern L. Rev.* 97; Y. Alexander and A.S. Nanes, *Legislative Responses to Terrorism* (1986); W. Laqueur, 'Reflections on terrorism' (1986) 64 *Foreign Affairs* 80; J.F. Murphy, *State Support of International Terrorism* (1989) ch. 1; J.J. Lambert, *Terrorism and Hostages in International Law* (1990) pp. 13–23.

20   Compare: Fifth Working Party of the Irish Council of Churches/Roman Catholic Church Joint Group on Social Questions, *Violence in Ireland* (1976) pp. 9–12; A. Guelke, *Northern Ireland: The International Perspective* (1988) p. 23; S. Cronin, *Irish Nationalism* (1980) p. 225.

21   Cmnd. 7031, 1977.

22   H.C. Debs. Standing Comm. cols. 570, 571 17 January 1989, Mr. Hogg.

23   *Ibid.*, col. 565.

24   See: P.V.L.I. p. 5; A.T.H. Smith, *Offences against Public Order* (1987) p. 246. Compare: B. Dickson, 'The Prevention of Terrorism (Temporary Provisions) Act 1989' (1989) 40 *N.I.L.Q.* 250 at p. 256.

25   S. 6(1)(a), Sched. 2. See: H.C. Debs. Standing Comm. A. col. 32 20 December 1988.

26   Compare: D.P.J. Walsh, 'Reviews and Notices' (1986) 21 *Ir. Jur.* 365 at p. 368.

27   H.C. Debs. Standing Comm. D. col. 352 8 December 1983, Mr. Waddington.

28   See: H. Street, 'The Prevention of Terrorism (Temporary Provisions) Act 1974' [1975] Crim. L.R. 192 at p. 197; L.H. Leigh, 'Comment' (1975) *P.L.* 1 at p. 3, R.A. Friedlander, *Terror-Violence* (1983) p. 155.

29   See: *R.* v. *Governor of Durham Prison, ex p. Carlisle* [1979] Crim. L.R. 175.

30   See, *McFeeley, Nugent, Hunter and Campbell* v. *UK* Appl. No. 8317/78, D.R. 20 p. 44. Compare: Friedlander, *op. cit.* n. 28 p. 156; Irish Freedom Movement, *An Anti-Imperialist's Guide to the Irish War* (3rd ed., 1987) p. 173.

31   (1983) 11 N.I.J.B.

32   The Baker Report, paras. 305, 348, 440 proposed reversal in Northern Ireland.

33   See further: Walker, 'Emergency arrest powers' (1985) 36 *N.I.L.Q.* 145.

34   [1984] 1 W.L.R. 1358 at p. 1361.

35   The Baker Report (para. 441) agreed that reform is needed but was unable to suggest a remedy. The National Advisory Committee on Criminal Justice Standards and Goals advocates avoidance of the term: *Disorders and Terrorism* (1976) p. 81. To shift the definitional problem from the legislation to the discretion of law-enforcement agencies (compare: 18 U.S.C. s. 3077, 50 U.S.C. s. 1801) may avoid some pitfalls but still signals the political nature of the offence.

36   Compare: Aviation Security Act 1982 s. 10. See also the 'functional' or 'inductive' approaches in: G.M. Levitt, *Democracies Against Terror* (1988) ch. 1; Murphy, *op. cit.* ch. 1.

37   P.V.L.I. pp. 5–6.

38   Compare: Mr. Justice Hope, *Protective Security Review: Report* (1979) paras. 2.6, 2.13; A. Samuels, 'The legal response to terrorism' (1984) *P.L.* 365 at p. 365.

39   For example, F. Kitson, *Low-Intensity Operations* (1971) chs. 6, 7; R. Thompson, *Defeating Communist Insurgency* (1976) ch. 7; K.G. Robertson, 'Intelligence, terrorism and civil liberties' (1987) 7.2 *Conflict Q.* 43.

40   S. Kentridge, 'The pathology of a legal system: criminal justice in South Africa' (1980) 128 *U. Pa. L. Rev.* 603 at p. 612.

41   See: National Advisory Committee on Criminal Justice Standards and Goals, *op. cit.* p. 56; J.R. Thackray, 'Army–police collaboration against terrorism' (1983) LVI *Police Jo.* 41; C. Townshend, *Britain's Civil Wars* (1986) ch. 2; P. Wilkinson, 'British policy on terrorism' in J. Lodge (ed.), *The Threat of Terrorism* (1988) p. 35; G. Wardlaw, *Political Terrorism* (2nd ed., 1989) ch. 10.

42   See: P.A.J. Waddington, *Arming an Unarmed Police* (1988) ch. 7.

43   H.C. Debs. Vol. 833 col. 634 29 November 1974, Mr. Jenkins.

44   T. Meron, *Human Rights in Internal Strife* (1987) p. x.

45   See also the instruments discussed in N.S. Rodley, *The Treatment of Prisoners under International Law* (1987).

46   Cmd. 8969, 1953. See: C. Warbrick, 'The European Convention on Human Rights and the prevention of terrorism' (1983) 32 *I.C.L.Q.* 82. The impact of the Convention is subject to derogation under Art. 15. See: Notice of Derogation DH (89) 1 (Def.) pp. 10–14.

47   See: S.R. Chowdhury, *The Rule of Law in a State of Emergency* (1989).

48   See: W.L. Twining, 'Emergency powers and criminal process: the Diplock

report' [1973] Crim. L.R. 406; Standing Advisory Committee on Human Rights, *13th Report* (1987–88 H.C. 298) App. D. para. 3; International Commission of Jurists, *States of Emergency Powers in Peacetime* (1984) pp. 192–4; D. Bonner, *Emergency Powers in Peacetime* (1985) pp. 20–2. Instead of limiting principles, some authorities call for balance between conflicting State and individual interests: Baker Report, paras. 16, 49; Rabie Report, paras. 3.22, 10.1. However, this characterisation is facile. Individual interests in life, liberty, expression and representative government depend on national security, and democratic states are committed to maintaining civil liberties. Thus, the real conflict is between different individual rights.

49   See: *Review of the Working of the Conference* (1989) para. 19; H.C. Debs. Vol. 89 col. 1314 16 January 1986, Mr. King.

50   See: H.L. Parker, 'Two models of the criminal process' (1964) 113 *U. Pa. L. Rev.* 1.

51   Criminalisation is both a political and legal strategy. Compare Guelke, *op. cit.* p. 26.

52   See: A.S. Mathews, *Freedom, State Security and the Rule of Law* (1988) Pts. I and III.

53   See: C. Townshend, 'Putting subterfuge in place of strategy' *Times* 9 August 1989 p. 14.

54   'In situations of war, and situations of revolution, if you are to be soft and preserve meticulously liberal doctrines and principles ... take my advice, do not be a Minister in those circumstances, because it will be exceedingly dangerous for the security of the State or the success of the cause' H.C. Debs. Vol. 367 col. 868 10 December 1940, Mr. Morison).

55   K. Asmal, 'Human rights in Northern Ireland' (1990) 10 *Socialist Lawyer* Winter/Spring p. 12.

56   Lord Lowry, *Civil rights in a beleaguered society* (1987) p. 22.

57   See: *X* v. *Ireland* Appl. No. 6040/73 C.D. 44, p. 121; *W.* v. *U.K.* Appl. No. 9348/81, D.R. 32 p. 190; *W.* v. *Ireland* Appl. No. 9360/81, D.R. 32 p. 211, 5 E.H.R.R. 504, 506; *X* v. *U.K. and Ireland* Appl. No. 9825/82, 8 E.H.R.R. 49; *X* v. *U.K. and Ireland* Appl. Nos. 10019, 10020, 10023, 10024/82, 8 E.H.R.R. 71; *X and Y* v. *Ireland* Appl. Nos. 9378, 9839/83.

58   See: Drug Trafficking Offences Act 1986; Criminal Justice Act 1987.

59   B. Singh and K. Mei, *Theory and Practise of Modern Guerrilla Warfare* (1971) p. 74.

60   Friedlander, *op. cit.* n. 8, p. 40. See also: J.B. Wolf, *Fear of Fear* (1981) p. ix.

Chapter 3

Terrorism in Britain

1 Irish terrorism

By far the most important source of terrorism in the British Isles has been, and continues to be, Irish Nationalism. The ancestry of this challenge to the legitimacy of the United Kingdom State may be traced through the Irish Republican Brotherhood and Young Ireland back to the first outbreaks of Whiteboyism in 1761.[1] To a large extent, these demands for political independence were satisfied by the foundation of the Irish Free State in 1922.[2] However, that settlement left six Irish counties in a new territory called Northern Ireland, which is still firmly hitched to the United Kingdom.[3] Consequently, this partition has inspired further intermittent, irredentist campaigns of terrorism.

The mantle of Nationalist violence has now devolved upon various organisations. First and foremost is the Irish Republican Army, which originally developed from the Irish Volunteers at the beginning of the War of Independence as the *ad hoc* army of a non-existent republic.[4] Its contemporary guise takes the form of the Provisional I.R.A., which seceded from the Official I.R.A. at the end of 1969 owing to the desire of its mainly northern members to promote military above political activities. The Provisionals have undertaken most Nationalist terrorism after 1969, while the Official I.R.A. has observed a military truce since 1972 and is now insignificant by comparison.[5] Both factions are, of course, secret, armed conspiracies, though each is supported by overt, legal political parties, the Provisionals by Sinn Fein,[6] the Officials by the Workers' Party (formerly Republican Clubs). The military dormancy of the Officials prompted the formation in the mid-1970s of a second, though much smaller, band, the Irish National Liberation Army. This is almost identical to the Provisionals (and some cross-membership has occurred) apart from its greater emphasis on Marxist policies, as expressed through its political apologists, the Irish Republican Socialist Party. More recently, the Irish People's Liberation

Organisation (sometimes operating as the Catholic Reaction Force) emerged
from dissident factions within the I.N.L.A.[7]

Arguments for and against Republican terrorism have revolved around
morality, politics and the facts and myths of Irish history.[8] Therefore, it is
a gross but necessary oversimplification to represent the modern philosophy
of militant Republicanism as follows. Armed opposition to the existing
constitutional framework is justified primarily by the Irish people's right
to self-determination,[9] which necessarily involves the termination of 'British
colonial domination'.[10] Thus, the dispute over the sovereignty of Northern
Ireland is based on the alleged racial and cultural distinctiveness of the
Irish people, embodying the assumption that northern Loyalists have no
separate right to self-determination but simply form a recalcitrant minority.[11]
In addition to this main strand of theory, the desire to establish a more
socialist form of government throughout Ireland seems to be a constant,
albeit secondary, aim, and one which bolsters the rejection, primarily for
historical reasons, of the legitimacy of the established State in the Republic.[12]

Aside from attacks on the security forces in pursuance of constitutional
objectives, more immediate activities include protection from Loyalist attacks
and the imposition of informal justice.[13] As a result, the I.R.A. does not
operate solely as a remote terrorist group confined to a few hundred
activists,[14] but its relationship with its heartlands is often 'exploitive,
intimidating and underlaid with contempt'.[15]

Republicans by no means monopolise Irish terrorism, for the Loyalist
community harbours an equally savage and virulent strain.[16] For their part,
northern Loyalists have resisted by force Nationalist demands for many
centuries, ranging from the Battle of the Diamond in 1795 between
Protestant 'Peep O'Day Boys' and Catholic 'Defenders' to the present day.
Probably the strongest terrorist company currently in existence is the Ulster
Volunteer Force, formed in 1966 and claiming descent from the Ulster
Volunteers founded in 1913 to resist Home Rule.[17] Other smaller Loyalist
terror squads established during the last decade include the Ulster Freedom
Fighters, Young Citizen Volunteers, the Red Hand Commando, Tartan
Gangs and the Protestant Action Force. Traditionally, Loyalist terrorist
groups have tended to be smaller, less sophisticated and more sectarian
that their Republican counterparts.[18] Consequently, they do not have
corresponding political mouthpieces, though the Ulster Defence Association,
established in 1971 and currently not proscribed, acts as a cross between
a paramilitary force (linked to the U.F.F.),[19] a community action organisation
and a pressure group (sometimes through the Ulster Loyalist Democratic
Party or the Ulster Political Research Group).

The rationale behind Loyalist terrorism (and British resistance to Republican attacks) is based on two main arguments. First, it likewise invokes
the internationally hallowed principle of self-determination, but this time

on behalf of the Loyalist 'people'.[20] All expressions of will by this community have confirmed by massive majorities its desire for continued union with Britain.[21] Obduracy in the face of militant Nationalism is also justified by reference to the violent nature of the challenge being asserted. Thus, however receptive one may be to the concept of a united Ireland, that cause cannot excuse the choice of unconscionable methods when democratic and non-violent paths are available.[22] This second objection is predicated upon two hotly contested assumptions: that the electorate of Northern Ireland forms a homogeneous community rather than a gerrymandered constituency and that normal political debate about the constitution is possible within that constituency. Finally, military and economic considerations may bolster British commitment to the Union, though these factors seem of secondary importance in view of the dubious benefits accruing to Britain.[23] It is also conceivable that British administrators may fear the creation of a dangerous precedent for would-be separatists elsewhere in the United Kingdom.[24]

Having described the main protagonists and their views, their tactics will now be considered. Revolutionary terrorism was first undertaken in Britain as part of a sustained campaign by Irish Nationalists during the 'Dynamite War' of the Fenians between 1881 and 1885[25] and was developed further by the I.R.A. during the War of Independence.[26] Renewed bouts of terrorism from 1939 to 1945 and 1956 to 1962 likewise involved operations in Britain,[27] but the use of revolutionary violence since 1969 may be distinguished in the following respects. First, the present campaign – 'unparalleled in the Western World'[28] – has been the most extensive and prolonged of all. With the addition of Loyalist, sectarian and inter-factional terrorism and killings by the security forces, there have been in Northern Ireland alone 1,919 civilian deaths and 928 deaths amongst the security forces up to the end of 1990.[29] By contrast, only 564 soldiers and policemen were killed during the whole of the War of Independence. Inevitably, new tactics have developed since 1969, including more sophisticated methods of attack and a gradual shift from civilian to military and political targets.[30] Secondly, operations have been extended to Britain on a much greater scale than ever before, resulting in approximately 100 deaths. The reasoning behind this point of attack is the belief that terrorism in Britain has far more impact that violence in Ireland and that 'in a war of attrition the British public [will] tire first'.[31] An associated development is the extension of terrorism to Western Europe. The trend began sporadically in 1979 with the murder of Sir Richard Sykes, Ambassador to the Netherlands, but escalated considerably after 1986, with frequent attacks on targets associated with the British Army in Germany[32] and an attempted bombing in Gibraltar in 1988.[33] Just as I.R.A. operations have spread geographically, so have its sources of supply, with sympathetic groups or States in Europe and the

Middle East (especially Libya) replacing in part traditional reliance upon U.S. support.[34] Finally, the activities of Sinn Fein have gained prominence since 1981. By comparison, Loyalist terrorists have been more reactive in nature. Apart from obtaining munitions, their activities have rarely spread outside Ireland, nor have they developed any counterpart to Sinn Fein.

By way of assessment, the resilience of Irish terrorism is impressive, but its impact remains uncertain. On the one side, Loyalist terrorists may claim at least one notable success in 1974, when they were a significant force behind the Ulster Workers' Council's general strike,[35] which precipitated the resignation of the power-sharing Northern Ireland Executive and halted moves towards an All-Ireland Council. On the other side, probably the most important Nationalist achievement has been the creation of a security crisis which prompted the abolition of the Unionist domination of the province under the Government of Ireland Act 1920, though that system was replaced in 1972 by direct rule from Westminster, which has meant even closer ties to Britain.[36] Similarly the impact of Sinn Fein and the attack on Conservative politicians in Brighton in 1984 may have encouraged the Anglo-Irish Agreement in 1985. However, whilst Unionists denigrate the Agreement as a dangerous step towards Irish unity, it is also rejected by Republicans. Thus, in the short term, the I.R.A. has not achieved its main political objectives. In the long term also, though the British public has wearied of Northern Ireland,[37] there is no movement towards disengagement, nor has the issue been prominent in recent British General Elections.

In conclusion, Irish terrorism has made no unequivocal political impact in any direction. Equally however, British governments have failed to eradicate such violence and, given that it has become an almost endemic way of social life, are unlikely to do so in the foreseeable future.[38]

2   Other Nationalist terrorism

With the severe set-backs to devolution inflicted by the adverse referenda under the Scotland and Wales Acts 1978 and the reduced vote for Celtic Nationalism in General Elections ever since, preconditions have been created which favour the use of terrorism. As in Northern Ireland, there exists a fundamental issue which commands significant support but which cannot be secured through direct constitutional or military means. Accordingly, some Scottish and Welsh Nationalists have resorted to terrorism, though on an inferior scale to their more experienced Irish counterparts.

In Wales, recent serious political violence has been confined to three groups. Two of them now seem to be defunct, namely, the Free Wales Army (some members of which were prosecuted in 1969 for managing a paramilitary organisation and for munitions offences) and the Workers'

Army of the Welsh Republic (two members of which were convicted of incendiary attacks in 1981 and 1982).[39] However, the third relevant organisation, the Sons of Glendower (Meibion Glyndwr), remains vibrant and has been responsible for more than 150 incidents since 1979, consisting mainly of attacks on holiday homes, estate agencies and politicians.[40]

Amongst the correspondingly few terrorist bands recently emerging in Scotland[41] have been the Scottish Army of the Provisional Group in 1975 and the Scottish Republican Socialist League in 1980, both of which engaged in robbery and arms and explosives offences.[42] Finally the Scottish National Liberation Army has claimed responsibility for a series of letter-bombs between 1982 and 1986,[43] an explosion in 1983 at Army premises in Woolwich[44] and an explosion at a quarry in 1989.[45]

To date, nationalist terrorism in England has been virtually non-existent.[46]

3   Other terrorism originating in Britain

Non-Nationalist political violence during this century has mainly been the preserve of anarchists, extreme left-wing cells, racists and Fascists, ethnic groups and animal liberationists.

The current era of terroristic attacks by anarchists and leftist groups began, as described in the previous chapter, with the Angry Brigade. Their campaign was followed by explosions carried out by Freedom Fighters for All, two members of which were convicted in 1974.[47] The next serious incident arose in 1979, when Stewart Carr was imprisoned for conspiring to rob and to possess arms and explosives as part of an anarchist group's preparations for violence.[48] Finally, another self-styled 'Angry Brigade' planted bombs in 1983.

The post-war use of terrorism by Fascists has been similarly sporadic. First, in *R. v. Jordan and Tyndall*,[49] the defendants were convicted of organising 'Spearhead', a military company being trained to attack Jews. Next, in 1980, a gang operating in the Midlands was found guilty of the possession of firearms intended for use against Jews and coloured people.[50] An even less sophisticated band based in Coventry was sentenced in 1981 for petrol-bomb attacks on an Indian temple and club.[51] However, the importance of these particular conspiracies should not be exaggerated, since official studies have reported that, though racist attacks are frequent, no single organisation is responsible.[52]

Ethnic minority groups have rarely resorted to violence for political ends connected with the United Kingdom. One exception is the Black Liberation Front, which attempted a number of explosions in protest at a death in police custody in Wolverhampton.[53]

Animal liberationists have perpetrated rather more frequent and serious attacks, including damage to breeding facilities, abattoirs, laboratories and

fur shops, the contamination of consumer products and the despatch of
letter- and car-bombs.[54] Injuries have been few, but costly damage has
been inflicted on property, especially on department stores in Luton,
Plymouth and Cardiff and at Bristol University, the latter attracting official
condemnation as 'an act of terrorism'.[55] Various loosely knit groups, often
'rambling, contradictory and chaotic',[56] have claimed responsibility, especially the Animal Rights Militia, the Animal Liberation Leagues and the
Hunt Retribution Squads. In addition, the Animal Liberation Front, founded
in 1976 by Ronnie Lee, operates more openly as an advocate for the
movement. Although a fecund source of politically motivated crime since
1972, it was not until 1984 that the police established the Animal Rights
National Index, serviced by a small squad of detectives and a liaison
officer in each force.[57] The gathering of information has been achieved
through infiltration, scanning publications and employing informers. Although no special powers have been invoked, many successful prosecutions
have been mounted. The most notable was that of Ronnie Lee and others
in 1987 for conspiracy to commit arson and criminal damage and incitement
to criminal damage; Lee was sentenced to ten years' imprisonment.[58] Others
have been convicted of attacks on department stores in Cardiff,[59] Luton[60]
and Edinburgh,[61] of raids on laboratories[62] and of the desecration of the
graves of John Peel and the Duke of Beaufort.[63]

In conclusion, a vast expansion in non-Nationalist terrorism may be
unlikely in view of the lack of tradition supporting its use and the British
'inclination towards a non-violent, patient and judicious resolution of
differences'.[64] Nonetheless, Irish terrorism provides an example to all fanatics
with political ambitions commanding minority support, so further incidents
may be expected.

4 Foreign terrorism

The final type of terrorism perpetrated in Britain (often in London) is
'foreign' or 'international' terrorism – violence inflicted for political motives
unconnected with the U.K., which is simply the hapless *locus in quo*.

The affairs of the Middle East have long been the most fruitful source
of incidents in this category. A history may commence in 1947, when
Zionists planted a bomb in the Colonial Office, London, and sent several
letter-bombs, with fatal consequences in one case.[65] More recent outrages
have involved attacks on, rather than by, Jewish or Israeli targets, including
the fire-bombing of a Marks and Spencer store in London in 1969 and the
wounding of its President in 1973, the murder by letter-bomb of Dr
Schechori, an Israeli diplomat, in 1972 and the bombing of an Israeli bank
in 1974. In 1978, a coach carrying Israeli tourists was attacked, causing
two fatalities. Next, the Israeli Ambassador, Mr. Argov, was wounded by

Palestinians in 1982, three of whom were subsequently convicted.[66] Finally, a bomb sent to the Israeli Embassy was successfully defused in 1989.

Four countries figuring especially prominently have been Iraq, Iran, Libya and Syria. In the case of Iraq, a former Prime Minister, General al-Naifi, was murdered in 1978, and two bystanders were injured shortly afterwards when a grenade was thrown under the Ambassador's car, for which one person was convicted.[67] These events prompted the expulsion of eleven Iraqi nationals. In 1988, Rahimin Sharif Ali was poisoned, allegedly by Iraqi agents who fled the country. The most spectacular attack involving Iran was the seizure of its Embassy in 1980 by Khuzestani separatists. After one diplomat had been murdered, the building was stormed. Five terrorists were killed, and a sixth was sentenced to life imprisonment.[68] Iranian opposition groups have also been attacked; four exiles have been killed and injured.[69] Libyan participation in terrorism has likewise included the murder and attempted murder of a number of hostile journalists and politicians in exile during 1980 and 1981 and explosions in March 1984 directed against dissidents.[70] Such attacks culminated in April 1984 in an armed assault upon demonstrators outside the Libyan People's Bureau in London, killing a policewoman and wounding eleven participants, and the planting of a bomb at Heathrow Airport, which injured twenty-three people. These deeds were followed by the breaking of diplomatic relations with Libya and the expulsion of several Libyans. Relations further deteriorated in 1986 when Dr. Rasmi Awad, a Jordanian, was convicted of conspiracy to cause explosions; Libyan Arab Airlines, the courier of the explosives, had its flights suspended, and five persons were deported.[71] As regards Syria two diplomats killed themselves in a premature explosion in 1977. Even more serious, Nezar Hindawi, a Jordanian, was convicted in 1986 of attempting to plant a bomb on an El Al plane at Heathrow.[72] After it was shown that he held a Syrian passport and had been hidden by the Syrian Embassy, a number of Syrians were expelled.

Various other Middle Eastern-related incidents must be recounted. The Jordanian Ambassador was attacked in 1971. In 1977, a former Yemeni Prime Minister, al-Hajri, his wife and a diplomat were assassinated. In 1978, Said Hammani, a Palestine Liberation Organisation representative, was shot dead. Next, an unidentified Arab was killed in an explosion in 1980. Another member of a Palestinian group, Ismael Hussan Sowan, was found guilty in 1988 of the possession of weapons in Hull. A P.L.O. official was expelled, as were an Israeli diplomat and five Mossad agents when it was revealed that Sowan had acted as an Israeli informer.[73] In 1989, there were several attacks on bookshops selling the *Satanic Verses*. One assailant, Moustapha Mazeh, blew himself up; others have been charged or deported.[74] The destruction in December 1988 of Pan-Am Flight 103 over Lockerbie cost 270 lives – 'the worst single terrorist incident to take place on British soil'.[75] It is widely reported that the bombing has been attributed to cells of the Popular Front for the Liberation of Palestine in Germany and Sweden.[76] Middle Eastern terrorism has also affected British targets abroad. As well as kidnappings in Lebanon, British diplomats in Athens and Bombay were murdered by the Revolutionary Organisation of Socialist Muslims in 1984.[77]

Indian affairs provide the next most fruitful source of terrorism (categorised as 'foreign' since it is not designed to influence British policy). The first example was the murder of the Indian Assistant High Commissioner in Birmingham, Mr. Mhatre, by the Kashmir Liberation Army in 1984.[78] One Kashmiri was later deported after being cleared of explosives charges.[79] The following year a Sikh plot to murder the Indian Prime Minister on a visit to Britain was foiled, and two conspirators, Ranuana and Gill, were convicted.[80] Inter-Sikh factional fighting resulted in deaths in London in 1985 and 1986.[81] Similarly, Basra and Timlin were convicted of the murder of a member of the International Sikh Youth Federation in 1987.[82]

Foreign terrorism unconnected with the Middle East or India has been less frequent. However, amongst recent examples were the murder of Bulgarian dissident broadcaster, Georgi Markhov, in 1978, the hijacking of a Tanzanian jet to Stanstead, Essex, in 1982 (for which the hijackers were later convicted),[83] explosions and burglaries at the African National Congress offices in London in 1982, a plot to kidnap an A.N.C. official in 1987,[84] and the planned assassination of a Turkish diplomat by an Armenian (who was imprisoned for his efforts).[85] The attempted kidnapping of Umaru Dikko, a former Nigerian minister, was foiled in 1984, when he was discovered in a crate at Stanstead Airport. Four people were convicted, two diplomats were ordered to leave and the High Commissioner, temporarily in Nigeria, was advised not to return.[86] Next, Gerard Hoarau, leader in exile of the Seychelles opposition, was murdered in 1985.[87] Finally, Vinko Sindicic, a Yugoslav secret agent, was convicted of the attempted murder of an official of a Croatian group in 1988.[88]

5 Types of terrorism and legislation

Terrorism emanating from Ireland has been, and remains, by far the most threatening of all types occurring in Britain. However, the foregoing survey reveals that other sources of political violence have proliferated in recent years. This is especially true of foreign terrorism, which provoked the Earl Jellicoe to comment in 1983 that:[89]

The most notable trend ... in Great Britain has been the increasing threat posed by international terrorism. ... It seems to me an inescapable conclusion that terrorism associated with causes beyond the United Kingdom now poses a greater threat than it did several years ago, both relatively and absolutely. From the information presented to me I see no ground for believing that this threat will diminish in the short term.

Despite the wider contexts in which terrorism now takes place, British legislation opposing it has been traditionally preoccupied with the Irish variety. Nevertheless, there have been a few exceptions, such as the Explosive Substances Act 1883 (prompted by anarchist as well as Fenian bombers), and recent legislation has increasingly concentrated on foreign terrorism (including some changes in the Prevention of Terrorism Acts in response to Jellicoe's forebodings as well as measures against hijacking, hostage-taking and attacks on diplomats) and on non-Irish domestic terrorism (such as bomb hoaxes and food contamination). Two issues arise from this expansion: which forms of terrorism, if any, justify special legislation and should all categories be covered by one Act?

In regard to the first issue, it may be argued that the present focus on Irish terrorists is desirable since they alone pose a sufficiently serious problem to warrant special legislation. This would seem to correspond with the 'limiting principles' suggested in the previous chapter by ensuring that emergency measures are employed only so far as strictly necessary and are subject to legislative control. The desirability of these principles is not in doubt. Yet if, as shall be argued, they can better be secured by the passage of comprehensive provisions before, rather than after, an upsurge in terrorism, laws against a wider range of terrorism will be required. The actual invocation of such measures should still be proportionate to the contemporary level of terrorism and, judging from the foregoing survey, only Irish terrorism presently justifies special laws. By contrast, the frequency of foreign terrorism is hardly overwhelming[90] and normal police powers and immigration controls are already substantial and effective. As a result, the actual deployment of the Prevention of Terrorism Act against foreign terrorists is unwarranted since there is little evidence that existing laws, at least when unhampered by diplomatic privileges and immunities, are unable to cope, as evidenced by the steady stream of convictions and deportations related in this chapter.[91] Similarly, the activities of neither non-Irish nationalists nor animal liberationists have proved so dangerous to the public or so impenetrable to the police that special legislation appears necessary.

As to whether one code should cover all terrorism, it is true that no satisfactory legal definition has been isolated and that the perpetrators of political violence in Britain vary greatly and may require distinct treatment by the police and penal system.[92] However, it makes sense to place all special provisions in a single Act of Parliament so that they form a unified code and that safeguards can be applied effectively to all.

Notes

1 See: T.D. Williams (ed.), *Secret Societies in Ireland* (1973); J.W. O'Neill, 'Popular culture and peasant rebellion in pre-Famine Ireland' (Ph.D. Univ. of Minn. 1984); S. Clark and J.S. Donnolly Jr., *Irish Peasants, Violence and Political Unrest 1780–1914* (1983); C.H.E. Philpin (ed.), *Nationalism and Popular Protest in Ireland* (1987). Irish terrorism cannot be attributed to foreign instigation; see: C. Sterling, *The Terror Network* (1981); Defence Intelligence Staff Report ('Glover Report') in S. Cronin, *Irish Nationalism* (1980) App. 18 para. 26; M. McKinley, 'The Irish Republican Army and terror international' in P. Wilkinson and A.M. Stewart (eds.), *Contemporary Research on Terrorism* (1987); A. Guelke, *Northern Ireland, The International Perspective* (1988); G. Wardlaw, *Political Terrorism* (2nd ed., 1989) p. 56.

2 Irish Free State (Agreement) Act 1922; Irish Free State (Confirmation of Agreement) Act 1925.

3 See: Government of Ireland Act 1920; Ireland Act 1949; Northern Ireland Constitution Act 1973.

4 See: J. Bowyer Bell, *The Secret Army* (1979); P. O'Malley, *The Uncivil Wars* (1983) ch. 7; T.P. Coogan, *The I.R.A.* (3rd ed., 1987); P. Bishop and E. Mallie, *The Provisional I.R.A.* (1987); Guelke, *op. cit.* ch. 3.

5 See: W.D. Flackes and S. Elliott, *Northern Ireland: A Political Directory 1968–88* (3rd ed., 1989) p. 208.

6 See: Walker, 'Political violence and democracy in Northern Ireland' (1988) 51 *M.L.R.* 605.

7 See: Flackes and Elliott, *op. cit.* p. 160.

8 See: F.S.L. Lyons, *Ireland Since the Famine* (1973); M. Cranshaw, 'The persistence of I.R.A. terrorism' in Y. Alexander and A. O'Day (eds.), *Terrorism in Ireland* (1984). Violence itself is an intermediate cause: Guelke, *op. cit.* p. 39.

9 See: Charter of the U.N. (Cmd. 7015, 1946) Art. 1.2; U.N. International Covenant on Civil and Political Rights (Cmnd. 6702, 1976) Art. 1.

10 S. MacStiofain, *Revolutionary in Ireland* (1975) pp. vii, 269; Coogan, *op. cit.* ch. 33; P. Foot, *Ireland: Why Britain Must Get Out* (1989).

11 On the definition of 'people', see: A. Rigo Sureda, *The Evolution of the Right of Self-Determination* (1973) ch. 2; R.C.A. White, 'Self-determination: time for a reassessment?' (1981) 28 *Neths. Int. L.R.* 147; *Mandla* v. *Dowell Lee* [1983] 1 All E.R. 1062; J. Crawford, *The Creation of States in International Law* (1979); L. Henkin (ed.), *The International Bill of Rights* (1981) ch. 4; M. Pomerance, *Self-Determination in Law and Practice* (1982); A. Kiss, 'The people's right to self-determination' (1986) 7 *H.R.L.J.* 165; J. Crawford, *The Rights of Peoples* (1988); P. Thornbury, 'Self-determination, minorities and human rights' (1989) 38 *I.C.L.Q.* 807; F. Wright, *Northern Ireland: A Comparative Analysis* (1987) ch. 8.

12 The I.R.A. was defeated in the Irish Civil War 1922–3. See C. Younger, *Ireland's Civil War* (1968); M. Hopkinson, *Green against Green* (1988).

13 See: M. Morrissey and K. Pease, 'The black criminal justice system in West Belfast' (1982) 21 *Howard J.* 159; R. Munch, 'The lads and the hoods' in M. Tomlinson, T. Varley and C. McCullogh (eds.), *Whose Law and Order?* (1988); J. McCorry and M. Morrissey, 'Community, crime and punishment in West Belfast' (1989) 28 *Howard J.* 282.

14   Glover Report, *op. cit.* para. 20.

15   Bishop and Mallie, *op. cit.* p. 227. See also: J. Darby, *Intimidation and the Control of Conflict in Northern Ireland* (1986).

16   See: D. Miller, *Queen's Rebels* (1978); O'Malley, *op. cit.* ch. 8; S. Nelson, *Ulster's Uncertain Defenders* (1984); Guelke, *op. cit.* ch. 4; T. Wilson, *Ulster* (1989) ch. 16; J.F. Galliher and J.L. Degregory, *Violence in Northern Ireland* (1985).

17   See: D. Boulton, *The U.V.F. 1966–73: An Anatomy of Loyalist Rebellion* (1973).

18   Glover Report, *op. cit.* para. 5; Nelson, *op. cit.* p. 93; A. Boyd, *Holy War in Belfast* (3rd ed., 1987).

19   Guelke, *op. cit.* p. 73.

20   For consideration of their claim to be such, see: R. Rose, *Governing without Consensus* (1971); A.T.Q. Stewart, 'The mind of Protestant Ulster' in D. Watt (ed.), *The Constitution of Northern Ireland: Problems and Prospects* (1981); C. Townshend, *Political Violence in Ireland* (1983) pp. 42, 342–3; J. Bowman, *De Valera and the Ulster Question 1917–73* (1982) ch. 1; K. Kelly, *The Longest War* (1982) p. 353; E. Moxon-Browne, *Nation Class and Creed in Northern Ireland* (1983) ch. 1; G. Adams, *The Politics of Irish Freedom* (1986) pp. 124–5; T. Wilson, *op. cit.* intro, chs. 1, 21.

21   See especially: *The Northern Ireland Border Poll 1973* (Cmnd. 5875, 1975).

22   See: Gardiner Report, para. 8.

23   See: A. Morgan and B. Purdie, *Ireland: Divided Nation, Divided Class* (1980); P. Bew and H. Patterson, *The British State and the Ulster Crisis* (1985); Irish Freedom Movement, *The Irish War* (3rd ed., 1987) ch. 1.

24   See: Foot, *op. cit.* p. 68.

25   See: K.R.M. Short, *The Dynamite War* (1979); P. Quinlivan and P. Rose, *The Fenians in England 1865–1872* (1982); R. Allason, *The Branch* (1983) ch. 1; M. Hartigan, A. O'Day and R. Quinault, 'Irish terrorism in Britain' in Y. Alexander and A. O'Day (eds.), *Ireland's Terrorist Dilemma* (1986).

26   See: C. Townshend, 'The I.R.A. and the development of guerrilla warfare 1916–1921' (1979) XCIV *E.H.R.* 318; Allason, *op. cit.* pp. 76, 85–6; *R. v. Governor of Wormwood Scrubs, ex p. Foy* [1920] 2 K.B. 305; *R. v. Cannon Row Police Station (Inspector), ex p. Brady* (1922) 91 L.J. K.B. 98; *R. v. Sec. of State for Home Affairs, ex p. O'Brien* [1923] 2 K.B. 361.

27   This is especially true of the former; see: *R. v. Barnes and Richards* (1938–1940) 27 Cr. App. R. 154; L. Fairfield, *The Trial of Peter Barnes and Others* (1953); Allason, *op. cit.* ch. 7.

28   H.C. Debs. Vol. 143 col. 207 6 December 1988, Mr. Hurd.

29   Source: Colville Annual Report on the E.P. Acts for 1989.

30   See: H. Arnold, 'More and more a battle of the R.U.C. and the I.R.A.' (1985) 227 *Fortnight* 7; Wilson, *op. cit.* ch. 16.

31   J. Bowyer Bell, 'Strategy, tactics and terror: an Irish perspective' in Y. Alexander (ed.), *International Terrorism* (1976) p. 71.

32   See: D. Pluchinsky, 'Political terrorism in Europe' in Y. Alexander and K.A. Myers (eds.), *Terrorism in Europe* (1982); *Times* 18 June 1990 p. 2.

33   See: J. Adams, R. Morgan and A. Bambridge, *Ambush* (1988) Chs. 8–11.

34   See ch. 7.

35   See P.R. Maguire, 'Political general strikes' (1977) 28 *N.I.L.Q.* 269.

28 *The prevention of terrorism in British law*

36 See especially: House of Commons (Redistribution of Seats) Act 1979.

37 An opinion poll has suggested 63 per cent wish to end the Union: *Sunday Times* 22 December 1980 p. 1. See also: Guelke, *op. cit.* p. 101.

38 Glover Report, *op. cit.* para. 3. However, sectarian violence is unlikely to spread to Britain. See: T. Gallagher, *Glasgow: The Uneasy Peace* (1986), *Edinburgh Divided* (1987); F. Neal, *Sectarian Violence: The Liverpool Experience 1819–1914* (1988).

39 R. v. *Evans and others* (1969) *Times* 2 July p. 2; R. v. *Ladd and Rees* (1983) *Times* 15 November p. 2., 16 November p. 2.

40 See: S. Jones, P. Smith and P. Thomas, *Operation Fire* (1980) *Times* 29 March 1989 p. 12, 2 June 1990 p. 2. For earlier incidents, see: Z. Bankowski and G. Mungham (eds.), *Essays in Law and Society* (1980) ch. 4.

41 See also: H.M. Advocate v. *MacAlister and others* (1953) *Times* 30 October p. 2, 26 November p. 5; *MacAlister* v. *Associated Newspapers* 1954 S.L.T. 14.

42 H.M. *Advocate* v. *Smith and others* (1975) *Times* 9 April p. 4, 19 April p. 3, 24 May p. 2; H.M. *Advocate* v. *Wardlaw and others* (1980) *Times* 23 September p. 3, 4 October p. 4.

43 *Times* 19 April 1986 p. 1, 17 July p. 3.

44 *Times* 12 December 1983 p. 2.

45 *Times* 15 May 1989 p. 2.

46 There was one attack in Cornwall by 'An Gof': *Guardian* 9 December 1980 p. 2.

47 R. v. *Ladd and Tristram* (1974) *Times* 15 October p. 7; R. v. *Ladd* [1975] Crim. L.R. 50.

48 (1979) *Times* 20 December p. 1.

49 [1963] Crim. L.R. 124.

50 R. v. *Roberts and others* (1980) *Times* 20 June p. 2.

51 R. v. *Campbell, Westhead and Smith* (1981) *Times* 17 June p. 3.

52 Home Office Study (*Times* 18 November 1981 pp. 1 and 4); Home Affairs Committee, *Racial Attacks and Harassment* (1985–86 H.C. 409) para. 46; *Report into the Rise of Fascism and Racism in Europe* (European Parliament, Doc. A 2-160/85).

53 *Times* 8 April 1988 p. 24, 1 August p. 3.

54 See: P. Windeatt, 'They clearly now see the link' in P. Singer (ed.), *In Defence of Animals* (1985); D. Henshaw, *Animal Warfare* (1989); K. Hyder, 'Animal lovers who are ready to kill' (1990) 98 *Police Review* 1440.

55 *Times* 24 February 1989 p. 2.

56 Henshaw, *op. cit.* p. ix.

57 *Ibid.*, ch. 14.

58 R. v. *Lee and others*, R. v. *Rogers* (1987) *Times* 13 January p. 3, 5 February p. 3, 6 February pp. 1, 3.

59 R. v. *Carr and Lane* (1988) *Times* 4 June p. 4.

60 R. v. *Sheppherd and Clark* (1988) *Times* 14 June p. 5, 18 June p. 2.

61 R. v. *Barr and Mohammed* (1988, reported in Henshaw, *op. cit.* p. 182).

62 R. v. *Nunn and others* (1985) 4 December p. 5; R. v. *Smith and Callander* (1985) *Times* 12 July p. 2.

63 R. v. *Holsby and Curtin* (1984), R. v. *Huskisson* (1987), both reported in Henshaw, *op. cit.* pp. 57, 98. See also: R. v. *McIvor* [1987] Crim. L.R. 409.

64 T.E. Hachey, 'Political terrorism: the British experience' in Y. Alexander (ed.), *International Terrorism* (1976) pp. 91–2.

65 See: Allason, *op. cit.* pp. 126–9; *Times* 17 April 1947 p. 4, 5 June p. 4, 6 June p. 4, 7 June p. 4, 10 June p. 3, 24 February 1948 p. 2, 4 May p. 4, 12 May p. 4.

66 *R. v. Al-Banna (Marwan) and others* (1983) *Times* 7 March p. 4; (1984) 6 Cr. App. R. (S) 420.

67 *R. v. Al Mograbi* (1979) 70 Cr. App. R. 24.

68 *R. v. Nejad* (1981) *Times* 23 January p. 1, 5 February p. 3.

69 These events occurred mainly between 1986 and 1988. Premature explosions claimed two further lives in 1981.

70 Three Libyan students were convicted of causing the explosions in Manchester: *R. v. Mansour and others* (1985) *Times* 21 February p. 3.

71 (1986) *Times* 17 September 1986 p. 1, 27 September p. 1; H.C. Debs. Vol. 110 cols. 264–5 10 February 1987.

72 (1986) Times 25 October pp. 1, 4; (1988) 10 Cr. App. R. (S) 104.

73 (1988) *Times* 8 June p. 3, 16 June p. 3, 30 June p. 3, 25 July p. 1.

74 (1989) *Times* 26 December p. 2, (1990) 10 February p. 1, 26 May 1990 p. 3, 3 April 1991 p. 2.

75 H.M.C.I.C. *Report for 1988* (1988–89 H.C. 449) para. 8.2.3. See *Times* 23 December 1988 p. 1.

76 *Observer* 30 July 1989 p. 8, *Times* 1 November 1989 p. 7; *Report of the President's Commission on Aviation Security and Terrorism* (1990).

77 See: Colville Report, para. 2.1.3.

78 Six men were convicted, two of murder: *R. v. Riaz, Raja and others* (1985) *Times* 15 January p. 2, 5 February p. 3, 8 February p. 2.

79 (1980) *Times* 27 November p. 2. Five others had been arrested under the Prevention of Terrorism Act: (1986) *Times* 6 September p. 3, 7 September p. 2.

80 Twelve suspects were arrested, and four originally charged, but the first trial was aborted when the identity of an undercover policeman had to be revealed: (1985) *Times* 12 October p. 1, 14 October p. 1, 18 October p. 4. A second trial of two defendants was then mounted: (1986) *Times* 20 May p. 3, 23 May p. 3, 24 May p. 3, 21 November p. 5, 20 December p. 3, 21 December p. 3, (1987) 10 January p. 3, [1989] Crim. L.R. 358. Plans to murder a member of the Indian Overseas Congress Party resulted in a conviction in *R. v. Gill* (1987) *Times* 30 October p. 5.

81 *R. v. Batth and Sunder* (1987) *Times* 13 November p. 2, 14 November p. 2, (1990) 11 April (Court of Appeal set aside convictions).

82 (1987) *Times* 30 October p. 3, 31 October p. 4.

83 *R. v. Moussa Membar and others* [1983] Crim. L.R. 618.

84 See: H.C. Debs. Vol. 120 col. 1095 23 October 1987, Vol. 122 col. 1069 18 November 1987. Aspinall was convicted in 1982 of the burglary and one South African diplomat was not allowed to return; see: Foreign Affairs Committee, *The Abuse of Diplomatic Immunities and Privileges* (1984–85 H.C. 127), Minutes of Evidence p. 65.

85 *R. v. Bedros* (1983) *Times* 25 July p. 1.

86 *Times* 7 July 1984 p. 1, 12 July p. 2, 13 July p. 1; *R v Barak and others*

(1985) *Times* 13 February p. 3; *R.* v. *Lambeth JJ., ex p. Yusufu* (1985) *Times* 20 February.

   87   Two private detectives and a telephone engineer were convicted of peripheral offences: *R.* v. *Underwood, Coghland and Richards* (1987) *Times* 20 February p. 3.

   88   (1989) *Times* 22 April p. 3, 28 April p. 3, 5 May p. 3; *H.M. Advocate* v. *News Group Newspapers Ltd.* 1989 S.C.C.R. 156.

   89   Jellicoe Report, para. 23.

   90   Colville Report, paras. 2.1.4, 2.1.5, 2.2.1.

   91   Compare: J. Dellow, 'Political violence and the response' in R. Clutterbuck (ed.), *The Future of Political Violence* (1986) p. 176.

   92   Compare: R. Spjut, 'Book review' [1987] Crim. L.R. 591.

Chapter 4

The Prevention of Terrorism Acts: history and structure

1 The birth of an Act

The Prevention of Terrorism (Temporary Provisions) Act 1974 had a swift but painful public birth. On 21 November 1974, bombs planted by the Provisional I.R.A. caused explosions in two public houses in Birmingham; twenty-one people were killed and 184 injured. The nation was horrified. *The Times* condemned the catastrophe as an 'Act of War',[1] The public bayed for official vengeance, and, with sizeable Irish communities in Glasgow, Liverpool and London, the appalling prospect of sectarian reprisals in the cities of Britain was said to loom.

The reaction of Parliament was influenced by two conflicting considerations. On the one hand, there was the unavoidable truth that terrorism could not be abolished by legislative fiat and that much could already be achieved by the fullest application of the regular criminal law. On the other hand, there was a strong desire to respond to what was perceived as 'the greatest threat [to the country] since the end of the Second World War'.[2] In short, as one Member observed, 'The House wants blood.'[3] It was by means of the Prevention of Terrorism Bill that blood was to be spilt, and arguments for a more balanced approach, involving reviews of existing laws, security measures and the political situation, received scant attention.

The conception of the Bill was announced on 25 November, when the Home Secretary warned that:[4]

The powers ... are Draconian. In combination they are unprecedented in peacetime. I believe these are fully justified to meet the clear and present danger.

However, Parliament was fanatically enthusiastic and had passed the Bill by 29 November, virtually without amendment or dissent.[5] This process has been summarised as follows:[6]

Bombs in Birmingham public house. Result: immediate enactment of the Prevention of Terrorism (Temporary Provisions) Act 1974. Had there been no bombs in
Birmingham, presumably there would have been no Act.

Yet the picture thus portrayed, of a Bill drawn up and passed with aston-
ishing alacrity in response to a single horrific incident, is misleading in two
respects.

First, the Act should not be viewed solely as a response to the Birmingham
bombings, since numerous terrorist attacks had previously occurred. For
example, in February 1972, bombs planted by the Official I.R.A. in Army
barracks at Aldershot killed seven civilians. A more sustained campaign of
violence had been initiated by the Provisionals in 1973, when there were
no fewer than eighty-six explosions resulting in one death and over 380
injured. In the first ten months of 1974, there were ninety-nine further
incidents, producing seventeen deaths and 145 other casualties. Indeed, in
November 1974 alone, there had already been eleven attacks with four
dead and thirty-five injured. With this background in mind, the Home
Office drew up contingency plans during 1973, including a draft Bill to
proscribe the I.R.A., exclude suspects and restrict movement from Ireland.[7]
Indeed, the Government would rightly have been condemned if it had
ignored the continuing mayhem and had not considered counter-measures.
What was objectionable was not this stage of preparedness but the secrecy
in which it was undertaken and the cynicism with which it was revealed
only when the vigilance of Parliament was at its lowest ebb.[8] Given its hidden
period of development, the Prevention of Terrorism Act was in a sense 'not
a panic measure'.[9] Indeed, some apologists positively argue that the Act's
timing was both politically slick and objectively necessary in view of the
public disquiet.[10] In response, the Act can still legitimately be called panic
legislation, since Parliament and the public were allowed to participate
only in the final stages of its creation. Democracy surely demands more
than consideration of a Bill at leisure behind a veil of official secrecy
followed by a legislative stampede. As for the dangers of hysteria and
disorder, a few fights in pubs and building sites and petrol-bombings did
occur[11] but hardly amounted to a breakdown in communal harmony. In
any event, those prepared to mount unlawful attacks were hardly likely to
be satisfied by the passage of remote legislation.

The second respect in which the Prevention of Terrorism Act was a
measured, rather than a panic, response concerns the existence of close
precedents for such legislation. The designs produced by the Home Office
were almost certainly based on three sources. The model for proscription
and the six-monthly renewal period was the special anti-terrorist legislation
then in force in Northern Ireland, the Northern Ireland (Emergency
Provisions) Act 1973.[12] The second precursor was the Prevention of Violence

(Temporary Provisions) Act 1939, which had reacted to an earlier I.R.A. campaign in Britain and contained the ideas of exclusion and special police powers. Finally, controls in the 1974 Act on travellers from Ireland were simply adaptations from the Immigration Act 1971.[13]

It may be concluded that the appearance given in 1974, of a Bill being conjured out of thin air, does not conform to reality, as preparations were well in hand for such legislation. Unfortunately, the Home Office did not perform this task very efficiently, and, given the total absence of forewarning or time for debate, neither Parliament nor interested bodies were able to remedy its deficiencies. As a result, various faults may be attributed to the process of parturition of the Act, many of which persist today. First, measures were included which not only failed to prevent terrorism but probably hindered that objective, as will be argued in regard to proscription and exclusion. Conversely, devices which might have been more pertinent, such as identity cards and electronic surveillance, were not even mentioned. Another defect was that the Act had to be limited to Irish terrorism, since there was no time to devise a more comprehensive statute. Finally, there was no concerted effort to include the 'limiting principles' mentioned in chapter 2 – in other words to ensure that the Act respected civil liberties and existing legal traditions as far as possible. Indeed, the Draconian nature of the Act was flaunted as one of its chief virtues, illustrating perfectly the warning of Lord Scarman that:[14]

When times are normal and fear is not stalking the land, English law sturdily protects the freedom of the individual and respects human personality. But when times are abnormally alive with fear and prejudice, the common law is at a disadvantage: it cannot resist the will, however frightened and prejudiced it may be, of Parliament.

Some shortcomings have been ameliorated over time. For example, the legislation has been widened to international terrorism, original thinking has produced measures against terrorist finances and extra safeguards have been inserted for those affected by the Act. Nevertheless, many original design defects persist.

2 Renewals, reviews and re-enactments

(a) 1974–1976
The 1974 Act was due to expire on 28 May 1975 unless continued in force by statutory order. However, there were further explosions in February 1975, and a policeman had been shot. Consequently, Parliament was easily persuaded to renew the Act for a further six months.[15] Terrorist incidents became even more frequent during that period. Between August and November, attacks had resulted in nine deaths and approximately 151

injuries. In those circumstances, renewal was readily granted[16] but was limited to four months, pending the passage of a replacement Act which would allow the sort of full and free debate wholly absent in 1974.

The innovations contained in the Bill introduced in November 1975 were both minor and few but included the amendment of the renewal period from six months to one year. This longer interval was said to be justified on the basis that the provisions in the Bill were much less extreme than those in the Northern Ireland (Emergency Provisions) Act 1973.[17] Amendments during passage were equally scarce but included two important additions, namely the offences of making contributions to, and withholding information concerning, terrorism. The latter followed backbench pressure at the Committee Stage, and it is also notable that both offences extended rather than curtailed the Act, which is perhaps indicative that the atmosphere of November, 1974 had not yet dissipated.

(b) 1976–1984

With the pretence of a fundamental review successfully completed in 1976, there was little danger of any immediate challenge to the Act, and this immunity was reinforced in December 1977, when the Home Secretary announced that Lord Shackleton was to carry out a 'Review into the operation of the Prevention of Terrorism (Temporary Provisions)' Acts 1974 and 1975'.[18] Unfortunately, the Review turned out to be flawed in four important respects.[19] The first related to its terms of reference, which were as follows:[20]

Accepting the continuing need for legislation against terrorism, to assess the operation of the Prevention of Terrorism (Temporary Provisions) Acts 1974 and 1976, with particular regard to the effectiveness of this legislation and its effect on the liberties of the subject. . . .

In this way, the investigation was confined to the working of, rather than the scope of, or need for, the existing legislation. Lord Shackleton actually supported the assumption,[21] but one looks in vain for any reasoned discussion, particularly of the alleged deficiencies in 'normal' laws. These terms entailed the further drawback that closely related emergency laws in Northern Ireland could not be examined. A third inherent defect was that the study was commissioned following, rather than prior to, the passage of the 1976 Act. Having recently taken the trouble of piloting the legislation through Parliament, the Government was unlikely to accept major changes. The final flaw was that, although Lord Shackleton held lengthy discussions with the police and other observers, this evidence was not published, so there was a dearth of information to support his conclusions or on which to base alternatives.[22] Given these handicaps, the Report made little impact, and its single major proposal, that the offence of withholding information be allowed to lapse, was rejected during the renewal debate in 1979.

The annual debates between 1980 and 1984 exhibited two characteristics. One was the general lack of parliamentary interest, with the result that the debates tended to be short, poorly attended and conducted late at night. The second trend was that the passage of time tended to harden official support for the Act. Two considerations may account for this interest in continuance. From the point of view of the security forces, time and effort has been expended on becoming familiar with the statute, so changes would be inconvenient. For their part, politicians fear an unfavourable reaction were terrorist incidents to happen just after a partial or total repeal of the Act. Only in 1981 did the offical Opposition begin to express concern but confined itself to proposing another review of the Act rather than abolition.[23] The Government acceded to this demand during the renewal debate in March 1982 and apointed the Earl Jellicoe to undertake the task.

The prospects for a successful review were not good, since all the impediments which had plagued Lord Shackleton reappeared. For example, Jellicoe's terms of reference incorporated the assumption that there is a 'continuing need for legislation against terrorism', reinforced by a ministerial direction that the Review 'ought not to focus on whether or not we need the Act'.[24] As a result, the Review failed to question the need for emergency laws, nor did it examine very thoroughly the principles on which they should be based.[25] The constitution of the Review also forbade the examination of corresponding Northern Ireland emergency legislation.[26] Finally, the Review came ten years after the inauguration of the original Act and therefore faced even deeper entrenchment than the Shackleton Report.

Within these substantial barriers, the Report was meticulously argued and contained many worthwhile suggestions for reform.[27] Possibly the most eye-catching change was that the special police powers were to be expanded to cover international, but not domestic, non-Irish terrorism.[28] As for structure, the Report proposed, following the precedent of section 1 of the Armed Forces Act 1981, that the legislation should have a maximum life of five years and that reenactment after that period should be preceded by another full review.[29] At the same time, Jellicoe advocated the removal of 'Temporary Provisions' from the title of the Act, recognising that the epithet 'rings increasingly hollow ...'.[30]

The Government implemented immediately most recommendations requiring administrative changes and presented a Bill in July 1983 to replace the 1976 Act with a suitably amended version. Two features quickly emerged. The first was that most of Jellicoe's proposals were to be adopted with few additions or subtractions. The second point was that, for the first time, the official Opposition objected to reenactment even in this ameliorated form. Nevertheless, a new Prevention of Terrorism (Temporary Provisions) Act emerged in March 1984, amended to the extent desired by the Earl Jellicoe and the Government but almost in no respects beyond. The only exceptional area where Parliament did exert significant influence concerned the Act's structure, as shall now be described.

The Bill as introduced faithfully reproduced the Jellicoe proposals: its title was the 'Prevention of Terrorism Bill', and clause 17 provided for annual reviews subject to a maximum life of five years. The envisaged change of title was reversed easily. During the Committee Stage, the view was expressed that the original citation should be reinstated to emphasise the desirability of dispensing with the Act as soon as possible,[31] and this proposal secured a majority on a free vote. On balance, this was probably the wiser course. It can no doubt be predicted that the Act will exist for some years and is therefore somewhat more immutable than the beguiling qualification 'temporary provisions' would suggest. However, this legislation was never designed as a permanent, comprehensive reply to terrorism, with effective mechanisms against overuse, and changes pursuant to the Jellicoe Report have not rendered it otherwise.[32]

The five-year guillotine was welcomed as ensuring that the Act would eventually have to be considered 'in detail and de novo'[33] with the onus on its sponsors. However, it was pointed out that the new system would probably devalue still further the annual reviews of the Act during the five-year operative period. To counteract this tendency, two important devices were proposed by backbenchers,[34] which the Government implemented administratively after 1984.

The first was that a single Commissioner was appointed to review the legislation in a concentrated period just before each renewal. His role is as follows:[35]

First, he would not be an appellant authority. . . . It would be his task to look at the use made of the powers under the Act. To consider, for example, whether he saw emerging any change in the pattern of their use which required to be drawn to the attention of Parliament.

The Commissioner has access to documents and officials, and his findings take the form of a published exchange of correspondence between himself and the Secretary of State.

The second way in which the annual debates were to be encouraged was by the governmental promise that:[36]

on any occasion when we lay an order to renew this piece of legislation, we shall do so in ample time for [Parliament] to be able to debate it at a date which will permit the Government . . . to withdraw the order and replace it with another. . . .

By this method, the Government was first to test the parliamentary temperature so that a revised order could be tabled which singled out any sections giving rise to concern. This combated the problem that draft statutory orders effecting renewal cannot be amended but must be accepted or rejected *in toto*.

(c) 1984–1989

The impact of the structural innovations inserted in 1984 has been uneven. On the one hand, the multiple renewal scheme failed entirely. The Government consistently refused to lay more than one order, despite criticisms directed at specific provisions.[37] On the other hand, the Commissioner system has proved worthwhile but cannot be counted a resounding success for several reasons. One concerns the personnel who have been appointed. The two reviewers to date (Sir Cyril Philips, 1984–85, and Viscount Colville, 1986 onwards) have been independent and knowledgeable but a panel of reviewers would reflect a wider range of perspectives. Next, their terms of references are narrow. They must not look beyond the confines of the Act,[38] and even the appointment of Colville in 1988 as reviewer of the Northern Ireland (Emergency Provisions) Acts has hardly encouraged cross-references or forages into 'normal' laws. Furthermore, the Commissioners have developed some self-denying ordinances. For example, Colville did not invite representations or look beyond written documentation during his review for 1988 because legislation was then pending.[39] This reticence seems misguided, since it came at a time when Parliament and the Government were most receptive to change. Colville has also admitted that his review of exclusion considers the system as a whole rather than specific orders.[40] One redeeming feature is that Colville does at least assume against renewal of each provision 'unless the case for it is clearly established'.[41] Aside from terms of reference, the *modus operandi* of Commissioners has been unsatisfactory. No attempt has been made to keep the Act under constant review or to respond to events or complaints as they arise.[42] Nor is adequate notice always given so that representations can be made.[43] Finally, publication of the reviews is quite unsatisfactory. Parliament is sometimes informed at a late stage,[44] so that Members often fail to notice or digest scraps of information tossed their way, and there is no official publication at all to the public. It would be wrong to belittle the hard work undertaken by the Commissioners. However, their impact has been modest. The only significant reform attributable to a Commissioner's report has been the addition of a new confiscation code as Part VII of the Northern Ireland (Emergency Provisions) Act of 1991 (discussed in chapter 7).

Returning to the history of the Prevention of Terrorism Acts, their pending expiration in 1989 prompted another major review in 1987 by Viscount Colville, who, as just described, was acting as a Commissioner. Regrettably, he was required to labour under the same constraints as previous appointees,[45] but, in the event, his Report was well argued and took evidence (though revealed little of it) from a broad range of sources. Fundamental changes in substance proposed included that exclusion and the offence of withholding information be abolished and that investigative powers (especially into financial matters) be expanded. Other radical proposals concerned the structure of the Act. Colville viewed temporary status as fuelling controversy, increasing uncertainty, impeding the allocation of resources and as factually unrealistic.[46] Consequently, 'core controls' were to be put on a permanent footing, subject to annual Commissioner review and, probably, annual parliamentary debate but not annual legislative renewal. The 'core' was to include the special policing powers and financial offences; exclusion, proscription and withholding information were to remain temporary.[47] Permanence was thus accorded to provisions which might apply to foreign terrorism, the point being that the Government might eventually settle the problems of Northern Ireland but not those of the whole world.[48] Colville also seemed to relegate to temporary status any measures viewed as peripheral, Draconian or untenable. It followed from these changes that 'temporary provisions' was to be dropped from the title, and Colville was equally anxious to find another name instead of 'Prevention of Terrorism'.[49]

The subsequent changes effected by the Prevention of Terrorism Act of 1989 represent the most thorough revision since 1974. The Act has doubled in size, partly because measures previously in delegated legislation[50] are now scheduled, but mainly owing to new passages concerning financial assistance and investigative powers. By contrast, Colville's recommendations concerning exclusion and the withholding of information were rejected. The opposition parties in Parliament equally secured no major changes despite sustained efforts which resulted in later stages being guillotined.[51]

As for structural refinements, the Colville Report has again not been slavishly followed. The idea of core controls has resulted in the Act becoming permanent in the sense that the five-year limit has been dropped. Yet its claim to embody 'temporary provisions' retains a scintilla of truth, since all measures (whether core or not) must be renewed annually under section 27(6) as follows:[52]

The Secretary of State may by order made by statutory instrument provide –
(a) that all or any of those provisions which are for the time being in force (including any in force by virtue of an order under this paragraph or paragraph (c) below) shall continue in force for a period not exceeding twelve months from the coming into operation of the order;
(b) that all or any of those provisions which are for the time being in force shall cease to be in force; or
(c) that all or any of those provisions which are not for the time being in force shall come into force again and remain in force for a period not exceeding twelve months from the coming into operation of the order.

A notable temporary complication is that the annual continuance of Part VI of the Act was linked to the timetable of the Northern Ireland (Emergency Provisions) Acts;[53] this linkage was largely broken by the Emergency Provisions Act 1991, which subsumes Part VI.[54] Another structural change adopted in 1989 concerns the withdrawal of the promise to table multiple renewal orders. The Government believes that a tidier solution would be for objectors to table a hostile resolution on the same day as, and in advance of, the renewal order; if it received support, the Government would withdraw and modify its own order.[55] However, this procedure is unlikely, as it requires relatively scarce opposition time in Parliament and forces opposition parties into a negative stance, leaving them open to the charge of 'being soft on terrorism'.[56] By contrast, the Commissioner system survives, but attempts to enshrine it within the Act were rebuffed.[57] Finally, there was no response to Colville's proposals as to nomenclature.

The most significant issue arising from the structural changes in 1989 is whether the return to pre-1984 permanence is desirable. The reasons in favour include those rehearsed by Colville and also the view that the legislation has now been fully debated four times.[58] Contrary arguments include, firstly, that points raised before may not have been convincingly answered and that circumstances change. Secondly, Colville never recommended that all provisions should become permanent, so the 1989 Act has assumed a degree of entrenchment which even he considered unwise. Thirdly, the Prevention of Terrorism Act is now inconsistent with the Emergency Provisions Act, which remains subject to a five-year limit. Of course, it would be as logical to amend the Emergency Provisions Act, but, either way, the structures of these two related codes should be compatible. Finally, and most important of all, a switch to permanence can only safely be supported if it is accompanied by sufficient safeguards against overuse. Regrettably, essential features such as explicit justificatory criteria, a searching review system and independent consideration of the application of the Act to individuals have not been incorporated. In their absence, a five-year limit may not solve all problems,[59] but it does eventually force Parliament to reconsider every measure and prompts the holding of a major inquiry. Without an overall deadline, the present system is too dependent on the vagaries of political life. In conclusion, until effective safeguards are conceded within a permanent, comprehensive code, it would be better to observe a five-year limit.

(d) Comment

The Prevention of Terrorism Act has evolved considerably since 1974. There is now a more permanent and comprehensive code with more safeguards for the individual. Two questions arise from these developments: which agency has been most influential in bringing them about, and what motivations lie behind them?

The leading actors may be the easier to discern. On the evidence of the present chapter, the independent reviewers have originated most changes. However, their influence has, of course, been dependent on the support from the governments which appointed them and then selected only sympathetic recommendations. Official secrecy makes it impossible to be sure what other factors are at work within government, but it may be assumed that the police and security services are very influential.[60] Aside from these sources, Parliament has forced only a few minor amendments, while the judges (as shall be shown) have been largely quiescent. The European Convention on Human Rights has set important parameters within which the legislation must exist, but neither of the two adverse decisions under the Convention resulted in amendment.[61] Finally, any influence from pressure groups and the like has been channelled through the reviewers, Parliament or court cases.

The rationales behind the changes since 1974 are more difficult to pinpoint, and both 'motivating' and 'constraining' factors have been at work.[62]

Firstly, the demands of anti-terrorist strategy have tended in both directions. On the one hand, the growing international and financial dimensions of terrorism have prompted new legislative measures. On the other hand, the general policies of 'normalisation' and 'criminalisation' and the need to adhere to the 'limiting principles' described in chapter 2 may be illustrated by extra safeguards for individuals, an emphasis on police powers and the decline of exclusion.

Motivating and constraining influences have also flowed from the second broad consideration, namely the Government's political policies towards Ireland:[63]

Anti-terrorism policy does not only have a security dimension, but also a crucial political or 'hearts and minds' one, composed of policies designed to reduce support for terrorism and enhance support for the Government and those willing to work solely by constitutional means.

As a result, there has been in the Prevention of Terrorism Act 'a clear movement towards the restoration of the rule of law'.[64] However, as the recent derogation from the European Convention reminds us, not all the Act's provisions are as limited as they might be, and there is also concern that the security forces are frustrated by their more limited powers. Thus, as powers become more acceptable on paper, it becomes less certain that they are observed in practice.

Thirdly, international relations may have had some influence. Several relevant considerations have already been catalogued, including the European Convention and the new financial measures. Cooperation between European police forces has also strengthened.[65] More generally, it is claimed that an international consensus in favour of a United Ireland has had 'a powerful impact'.[66] Yet any such impact on security has been at most indirect. In other words, diplomatic pressures may have helped to shape attempted political initiatives in Northern Ireland, and the British desire to maintain good relations with interested parties may have tempered security policy. Even so, the refusal to amend the Diplock court system in 1987[67] suggests that foreign policy is secondary.

3   Comparisons and assessment

Before considering possible improvements to the structure of the Prevention of Terrorism Act, one should note that very similar problems of precipitate enactment, lackadaisical review and aversion to repeal have been encountered in relation to most other emergency laws in Britain during this century.[68] The closest analogue is the Prevention of Violence (Temporary Provisions) Act 1939. This measure was introduced into Parliament on 19 July 1939 and was hastened to Assent nine days later by over one hundred explosions during the intervening period. By section 5(2), the Act was to subsist for two years, but, though I.R.A. violence in Britain petered out during 1940, the Act was extended in July 1941 to the end of that year and was renewed thereafter annually until the end of 1954.[69] Only after 1950 did the charmed life of the Act become a matter of controversy, and, even under pressure, it was maintained until a Home Office review discovered it was largely spent.[70] In summary, the emergency had lasted approximately one year; the Act had lingered for just over fifteen – a *tour de force* in legislative indulgence. The lesson to be drawn is surely that, unless care is taken to ensure that forms of review and limitation are enshrined within counter-terrorism legislation from the start, Parliament will be unable to exert tight control.[71]

Turning to the current Prevention of Terrorism Act, three problems arise from its structure. The first is that just mentioned, namely that neither the existence nor actual application of any particular measure conforms to desirable limiting principles. This creates the dangers that the Act as a whole will remain in force too long and in the meantime may be used repressively. The second difficulty is that the Act overlaps confusingly with the Northern Ireland (Emergency Provisions) Act.[72] The third drawback is that the Act is primarily limited to Irish terrorism with some adaptations in relation to international terrorism. This courts the danger that, if terrorism arises from other sources or if existing political violence changes its form or intensity, the present legislation will be irrelevant, and new emergency laws will be rushed through Parliament, thereby repeating all the mistakes made in 1974.

The Offence against the State Acts 1939–85[73] may provide some answer.

These Acts, the principal legislation against terrorism in the Republic of Ireland, form a permanent, comprehensive collection of measures which are not confined to a particular emergency but can operate at different levels of severity. However, all are subject to parliamentary and judicial controls, which ensure that much of the code has remained dormant for long periods. If this precedent were followed, the inherent danger of overuse could be solved by requiring that the employment of each provision be strictly justified by the exigencies of the situation. To achieve this end, the actual application of a particular measure, such as proscription or arrest, should, where possible, be reviewable judicially. However, such control is less appropriate for the bringing into force of any measure, since the courts are not suited to the wide-ranging factual and political, as well as legal, investigations which would be required. Consequently, the overall necessity for the invocation of the anti-terrorism code or any part of it must remain a matter for Parliament, which should be helped to fulfil this task in three ways.

First, an investigative standing committee should be instituted. This would differ from ephemeral investigations, such as those conducted by Shackleton and his successors in that it would keep the Act under continual review and would involve a range of viewpoints. Such a body would also be able to take the initiative in uncovering relevant evidence rather than relying, as the courts must do, on complainants to come forward. It would equally have various advantages over a parliamentary select committee, including freedom from party political constraints, fewer disruptive changes of membership, the inclusion of experts and greater confidentiality.[74] The main functions of this proposed committee would be two-fold.[75] One would be to produce published reports which would form ammunition for renewal debates. Secondly, the body should have extensive fact-finding powers. Evidence garnered would not only form the basis of its own proposals but would also be extremely beneficial to Members of Parliament and other interested observers. Apart from publishing bare statistics on the working of the Act,[76] the committee should consider and, so far as is consistent with security, disclose details of rules of practice or guidelines affecting the operation of the legislation, reports of cases decided by the courts and Secretaries of State and submissions from interested parties, including the police. It would be pointless to strengthen independent scrutiny if its findings fall upon deaf ears. Thus, its pronouncements should be referred not only to the Secretary of State but also to the Home Affairs (Select) Committee of the House of Commons,[77] whose reports will in turn evince by convention a written response from the Secretary of State and might somewhat reduce the marginalisation of Parliament in security matters.[78] The Secretary of State's attention might be further heightened by adopting the precedent of the Boundary Commission.[79] Thus, the Secretary of State should lay the committee's report before Parliament together with a draft renewal order. If the order departs at all from the Committee's views, the Secretary of State should also table a statement of reasons (and perhaps an alternative order faithful to the committee's proposals).

The third way in which parliamentary scrutiny might be strengthened would be by dividing the counter-terrorism code into different parts, each dependent upon specified standards of justification for their use.

In conclusion, the best way to avoid the structural defects in the Prevention of Terrorism Act is to enact instead of all existing special legislation a permanent and comprehensive anti-terrorist statute which embodies limitations and reviews. The details of such an Act will be discussed further in chapter 13. For the present, attention must now be turned to the contents of the Prevention of Terrorism Act.

Notes

1   *Times* 23 November 1974 p. 15.

2   H.C. Debs. Vol. 882 col. 743 28 November 1974, Mr. Lyons.

3   *Ibid.* col. 672, Mr. Litterick.

4   *Ibid.* col. 35 25 November 1974, Mr. Jenkins.

5   The only amendment (by consent) was the dropping of cl. 1(6): see ch. 5.

6   H. Street, 'The Prevention of Terrorism (Temporary Provisions) Act 1974' [1975] Crim. L.R. 192 at p. 192.

7   See H.C. Debs. Vol. 1 col. 360 18 March 1981, Mr. Lyons; H.L. Debs. Vol. 504 col. 22 13 February 1989, Lord Harris.

8   The avoidance of opposition also determined the timing of the introduction of the Emergency Powers (Defence) Act 1939: N. Stammers, *Civil Liberties in Britain during the Second World War* (1983) p. 10.

9   P. Wilkinson, *Terrorism and the Liberal State* (2nd ed., 1986) p. 169.

10   P. Wilkinson, Book review (1987) 7 *L.S.* 236; Hilliard, *loc. cit.*

11   Petrol-bombings of the home of an Irish family and an Irish pub occurred in Birmingham: *Times* 27 November 1974 p. 2, *R.* v. *Roberts and others* 11 August 1984, p. 3. For other incidents, see: P. Hilliard, 'The time bomb goes off' (1989) 97 *Police Rev.* 2174.

12   For earlier precedents, see P.V.L.I. Pt. I.

13   These had been considered in 1939, see: O.G. Lomas, 'The executive and the anti-terrorist legislation of 1929' (1980) *P.L.* 16 at pp. 20–1, 26.

14   *English Law – The New Dimension* (1974) p. 15. Compare: *Liversidge* v. *Anderson* [1942] A.C. 206 at p. 222.

15   S.I. No. 874.

16   S.I. No. 1955.

17   H.C. Debs. Vol. 927 cols. 1474–88 19 March 1977, Mr. Rees. Reinstatement of the original rule has twice been defeated: H.C. Debs. Vol. 904 cols. 580–6 28 January 1976; H.C. Debs. Standing Comm. B col. 660 19 January 1989.

18   Cmnd. 7324, 1978.

19   See: D.N. Schiff, 'The Shackleton Review of the operation of the Prevention of Terrorism Acts' (1978) *P.L.* 352.

20   Compare: Diplock Report, Gardiner Report, Baker Report, Colville Report on the E.P. Acts.

21   *Loc. cit.* para. 160.

22   See: C. Warbrick, 'The protection of human rights in national emergencies' in F.E. Dowrick (ed.), *Human Rights* (1979) at p. 104.

23   This was rejected by 189 to 141 votes: H.C. Debs. Vol. 1 cols. 336–74 18 March 1981.

24   H.C. Debs. Vol. 20 col. 1052 16 March 1982, Mr. Whitelaw. The Jellicoe Report supports this assumption: para. 1.

25   Jellicoe Report para. 9.

26   *Ibid.* para. 6.

27   See: D. Bonner, 'Combating terrorism – the Jellicoe approach' (1983) *P.L.* 224; Walker, 'The Jellicoe Report on the Prevention of Terrorism (Temporary Provisions) Act 1976' (1983) 46 *M.L.R.* 484.

28   *Loc. cit.* paras. 12, 23, 76, 77, 144.

29   *Ibid.* para. 14. See also: Baker Report, para. 444; Northern Ireland (Emergency Provisions) Act 1987 s. 13 (now see 1991/Act s. 69).

30   Jellicoe Report, para. 18.

31   H.C. Standing Comm. D col. 362 8 December 1983, Ms. Harman.

32   Compare: Baker Report, para. 27.

33   H.C. Debs. Vol. 47 col. 56 24 October 1983, Mr. Brittan.

34   See: H.C. Debs. Vol. 52 cols. 932–9 25 January 1984, Messrs. Carlisle and Powell.

35   H.L. Debs. Vol. 449 col. 405 18 March 1984, Lord Elton.

36   H.L. Debs. Vol. 448 col. 945 23 February 1984, Lord Elton.

37   See, for example: Philips Annual Report for 1985, para. 21; H.C. Debs. Vol. 92 col. 427 19 February 1986.

38   See: Colville Annual Report on the E.P. Acts for 1988, para. 2.4.

39   Colville Annual Report for 1988, para. 1.1.

40   *Ibid.* para. 4.3.

41   *Ibid.* para. 3.1.

42   See: Colville Annual Report on the E.P. Acts for 1988, para. 2.3.

43   See: H.C. Debs. Vol. 110 col. 274 10 February 1987.

44   See: H.L. Debs. Vol. 73 cols. 1303–24 21 February 1985.

45   The Colville Report supported continuance, again without examining alternatives: para. 1.1.2, 3.1.7.

46   *Ibid.* para. 3.1.8.

47   *Ibid.* paras. 3.1.7, 7.1.5, 8.1.2, 14.1.8 (core); 11.7.1, 13.1.10, 15.1.6.

48   *Ibid.* paras. 3.1.6, 3.1.7. The same argument has been applied to anti-hijacking measures: H.C. Debs. Vol. 852 col. 495 4 April 1973. Another inference may be that aliens are less deserving of protection.

49   Colville Report, para. 3.1.9.

50   See the Prevention of Terrorism (Supplemental Temporary Provisions) Orders 1984 S.I. Nos. 417, 418.

51   H.C. Debs. Vol. 145 cols. 692–742 23 January 1989.

52   The powers in s. 27(6)(b) and (c) have not so far been employed. For orders under s. 27, see ch. 10.

53   See s. 27(10)–(12).

54   The renewal dates under both Acts now diverge. See: n. 72 infra; P.V.L.I. pp. 28–9. Pts. III and V remain linked: s. 28(10).

55   H.L. Debs. Vol. 504 cols. 993–4 28 February 1989, Earl Ferrers.

56   D. Bonner, 'Combating terrorism in the 1990's' (1989) *P.L.* 440 at p. 476.

57   H.C. Debs. Standing Comm. B col. 661 *et seq.* 19 January 1989.

58   *Ibid.* col. 10 13 December 1988, Mr. Hogg.

59   It may delay interim reform and much depends on the expertise available during renewal: *Special Report from the Select Committee on the Armed Forces Bill* (1985–86 H.C. 170) para. 3.2.

60   Compare during wartime, Stammers, *op. cit.* pp. 233–4.

61   *McVeigh, O'Neill and Evans* v. *U.K.* Appl. Nos. 8022, 8025, 8027/77, D.R. 25 p. 15; *Brogan and others* v. *U.K.* Appl. Nos. 11209, 11266/84, 11386/85, Judgment of Court Ser. A Vol. 145-B. But see ch. 8 n. 158.

62   Stammers, *op. cit.* concl.

63   Bonner, *loc. cit.* n. 56 p. 475.

64   A.S. Mathews, *Freedom, State Security and the Rule of Law* (1988) p. 267.

65   See ch. 13.

66   A. Guelke, *Northern Ireland: The International Perspective* (1988) p. 2.

67   See P.V.L.I. ch. 4.

68   Stammers, *op. cit.* p. 222.

69   See: Emergency Powers (Defence) Reg. 18AE (S.R. & 0. 1941 No. 1088); Expiring Laws Continuance Acts 1941–53.

70   See H.C. Debs. Vol. 520 col. 580 26 November 1953.

71   See: Paris Minimum Standards, Section B para. 4(6).

72   See: Baker Report, ch. 8, para. 444; Standing Advisory Committee on Human Rights, *13th Report* (1987–88 H.C. 298) App. D. para. 58, *14th Report* (1988–89 H.C. 394) Annex E p. 106, Annex F p. 115; Colville Report on the E.P. Acts, ch. 20. A self-contained code for Northern Ireland could cause complications on the transfer of prisoners: H.C. Debs. Standing Committee B cols. 75–76 18 December 1990. Some consolidation has been undertaken in the Northern Ireland (Emergency Provisions) Act 1991 (see Preface n. 8).

73   See: P.V.L.I. Pt. III.

74   Compare: Jellicoe Report, para. 17; Baker Report, para. 445; Standing Advisory Committee on Human Rights, *9th Report* (1983–84 H.C. 262) paras. 6, 9. The Parliamentary Ombudsman might act as its investigator: Colville Report on the E.P. Acts, para. 19.4.

75   The closest parallel in existence is the Standing Advisory Committee on Human Rights; see: P.R. Maguire, 'The S.A.C.H.R. 1973–80' (1981) 32 *N.I.L.Q.* 31. However, the Committee is confined in jurisdiction and fears that review and advisory roles might conflict: H.C. Debs. Standing Comm. B col. 335 31 January 1991.

76   Since 1979, the Home and Northern Ireland Offices have published quarterly bulletins of statistics.

77   Similarly, that committee now considers reports from the Police Complaints Authority: (1987–88 H.C. 583) para. 14.

78   See: P. Hillyard, 'The normalisation of special powers' in P. Scraton (ed.), *Law, Order and the Authoritarian State* (1987) p. 307.

79   Parliamentary Constituencies Act 1986 ss. 3, 4.

Chapter 5

Proscribed organisations

1 Provisions

(a) Powers

Part I of the Prevention of Terrorism (Temporary Provisions) Act 1989 contains two processes by which organisations can be proscribed. Firstly, by section 1(1):

Any organisation for the time being specified in Schedule 1 to this Act is a proscribed organisation for the purpose of this Act; and any organisation which passes under a name mentioned in that Schedule shall be treated as proscribed, whatever relationship (if any) it has to any other organisation of the same name.

Two groups currently appear in Schedule 1: the I.R.A. (with no distinction between Officials and Provisionals) and the I.N.L.A. A second path to proscription is indicated by section 1(2)(a):[1]

The Secretary of State may by order made by statutory instrument . . . add to Schedule 1 to this Act any organisation that appears to him to be concerned in, or in promoting or encouraging, terrorism occurring in the United Kingdom and connected with the affairs of Northern Ireland. . . .

Conversely, organisations may be removed by order from Schedule 1 under section 1(2)(b). These are potentially very wide powers. Subsection (6) defines 'organisations' as including 'any association or combination of persons', which means that bans are not confined to disciplined or structured associations.[2] Nor is the Secretary of State (in practice the Home Secretary) prevented from proscribing a named group 'and like organisations', no matter how sweeping the resulting order.[3] Furthermore groups which support terrorists either politically or materially but do not themselves engage in terrorism (or even set foot in Northern Ireland)[4] may be proscribed as 'promoting or encouraging', though it is not government policy to invoke those wider grounds.[5]

The process of proscription is wholly 'an executive exercise'[6] unsullied by any statutory appeal.[7] It may therefore be questioned whether the powers to make subordinate legislation at least can be curtailed by the courts. The Act does not expressly exclude judicial review, and the Government has adverted to its availability to persons charged with membership.[8] However, review is likely to be extremely limited in the circumstances[9] and mainly confined to the mechanics of issuing the order.

In the first place, the requirements of natural justice probably have no relevance. Not only would procedural safeguards be viewed as a hindrance to 'prompt preventative action'[10] and a danger to the security of sensitive information, but they would also conflict with the wishes of Parliament by providing suspected terrorists with a public platform.[11]

A second possible heading of review, illegality, might arise through improper purpose or bad faith on the part of the Home Secretary. The overwhelming problem in this connection is proof. For example, in *Ningkan* v. *Government of Malaysia*,[12] a proclamation of an emergency was challenged as fraudulent, the allegation being that it was promulgated for political convenience rather than to diffuse an emergency. The Privy Council advised that, assuming the issue to be justiciable, there was a heavy onus on the appellant to demonstrate abuse which had not been met. Similarly, in the context of the Prevention of Terrorism Act, it will be very difficult to prove that a group has been banned for its political, rather than criminal, activities. The definition of terrorism in section 20(1) refers to objectives ('political ends') which both terrorists and political parties may share. Only the methods are different, and the Secretary of State may support his decision by claiming he has evidence (which need not be divulged in detail), say, of intimidation on behalf of the political group.

Next, there is a possibility, albeit remote, that a proscription order could be challenged in court as irrational. For example, in *McEldowney* v. *Forde*,[13] the Minister of Home Affairs in Northern Ireland made an order in 1967 which banned 'republican clubs or any like organisation howsoever described'.[14] The first part of the instrument, whilst highly controversial, was at least clearly directed against the political society called 'Republican Clubs'. However, the House of Lords generously interpreted the second part as outlawing:[15]

any organisation having similar objects to those of a republican club or of any organisation whose objects included the absorption of Northern Ireland in the Republic of Ireland.

This was an 'alarming and remarkable' verdict,[16] since it potentially suppressed all Nationalist political parties. However, it is also notable that such startling results did not convince the court that the order was *ultra vires*. Lord Diplock, for instance, suggested he would intervene only if proscription were extended to obviously innocuous and apolitical bodies, such as the Automobile Association or the Athenaeum.[17]

The more recent case in the Irish Republic of *The State (Lynch)* v. *Cooney*[18] presents a slightly more hopeful picture of judicial vigilance. A statutory order was made in 1982 banning party political broadcasts on behalf of Provisional Sinn Fein on the basis that they were in the Minister's opinion 'likely to promote, or incite to, crime or would tend to undermine the authority of the State'. The Supreme Court held that the opinion of the Minister 'must be one which is . . . factually sustainable and not unreasonable'.[19] In this way, the issue of reasonableness was relevant and could no longer be settled simply by examining the terms of the order itself; instead, brief indications of the evidence justifying it had to be (and were) produced. However, the Irish understanding of 'unreasonableness' in administrative law probably differs from the English equivalent,[20] and comparable cases in Britain (especially *R.* v. *Secretary of State for the Home Department, ex parte Brind*)[21] suggest a lesser degree of detail will still suffice.

Applications under the European Convention on Human Rights may have more impact than domestic review, especially as, unfettered by parliamentary sovereignty, they can question both forms of proscription. The banning of an organisation appears *prima facie* to contravene Articles 9 (freedom of thought and conscience), 10 (freedom of expression) and 11 (freedom of association), but there may be three arguments to justify proscription.

In respect of Article 9, a distinction was drawn in *Arrowsmith* v. *U.K.*[22] between a belief (pacifism) and activities in pursuit of it (handing out literature to soldiers). Only the former receives protection. The same contrast may be drawn between the policy of militant Republicanism (the private harbouring of which is not illegal) and its expression through action.

Secondly, both Articles 10 and 11 allow limitations 'prescribed by law' and 'necessary in a democratic society' in the interests of, *inter alia*, 'public safety', 'public order', 'the protection of the rights and freedoms of others', 'the prevention of disorder and crime' and (under Article 10 only) 'national security' and 'territorial integrity'. For example, offences in Austria directed against the revival of National Socialism were upheld by the Commission.[23] Similarly, the proscription of revolutionary or sub-revolutionary paramilitary groups (such as the I.R.A.) could fall within the margin of appreciation allowed under Article 10(2).[24] However, it may be less confidently asserted that the systems actually adopted under the Prevention of Terrorism Act, substantially unreviewable powers wielded by politicians, are 'necessary in a democratic society'. Thus, some degree of independent oversight and periodical review[25] might be required.

The third possible argument in favour of proscription is based on Article 17:

Nothing in this Convention may be interpreted as implying . . . any right to engage in any activity or to perform any act aimed at the destruction of any of the rights and freedoms set forth herein or at their limitation to a greater extent than is provided for in the Convention.

In *Lawless* v. *Ireland*,[26] the Court held that Article 17 did not preclude an I.R.A. internee from demanding procedural justice, since his fate did not directly affect the I.R.A.'s campaign. However, were the I.R.A. as an organisation to make complaints about its rights under Articles 9 to 11, then Article 17 might well bite. Though the I.R.A.'s political aims may not be inimical to Convention rights and freedoms,[27] its methods would probably be so construed.

In conclusion, while the European Convention may be useful as a last resort, there remains a case for a speedier domestic appeal to act as a safety valve for aggrieved groups and to encourage public discussion. The preferred form of such an appeal will be considered later.

(b) Offences

Section 2 contains various offences connected with proscribed organisations. First, by section 2(1)(a), it is an offence if any person 'belongs or professes to belong to a proscribed organisation'. Proof of belonging – 'being a member'[28] – is formidably difficult. The I.R.A. does not issue membership cards, so this offence will probably be evidenced by a confession from the defendant or a colleague.[29] The profession of belonging is more readily capable of proof. To 'profess' means 'to declare openly, announce, affirm . . . acknowledge or confess . . . [some] positive intentional act',[30] though it is precisely membership rather than sympathy or support which must be demonstrated, either orally or physically.[31] For example, Gerry Adams, now leader of Sinn Fein, was charged in 1978 with membership under corresponding Northern Ireland legislation arising from his participation in paramilitary displays in the Maze Prison and from voicing support for violence at meetings. He was acquitted:[32]

Fighting talk and military metaphor are the current coin of politics, especially revolutionary politics, and, going even further, support for violence is not equivalent to actual membership.

It is immaterial whether the profession is an idle boast or not, for section 2 is concerned with stemming public offence and disorder as much as catching genuine I.R.A. members.[33]

By section 2(3) the accused has a defence if he can show, presumably on the balance of probabilities:[34]

(a) that he became a member when it was not a proscribed organisation . . .
(b) that he has not since he became a member taken part in any of its activities at any time while it was a proscribed organisation. . . .

It follows that it is not an offence to have been an active member before proscription[35] (thus avoiding a retrospective crime contrary to the European Convention), but even passive membership is unlawful if one joined after the Acts commenced. This defence is of diminishing importance since it mainly protects I.R.A. members whose attachment derives from pre-1974 conflicts and has become *pro forma*. Furthermore, the defence carries the penalty of an admission of membership which may prejudice claims that it is passive and will certainly excite close police attention.[36]

Offences in section 2(1)(b) are committed when a person:

solicits or invites support for a proscribed organisation, other than support with money or other property. . . .

The 'soliciting' or 'inviting'[37] of 'support' comprehends non-financial material aid, such as supplies of services (including 'transport, board and lodging, food and so on').[38] It may also comprise intangible activities (such as soliciting people to attend I.R.A. meetings),[39] provided they evince active support rather than mere passive approval.[40] Thus, it is probably not an offence *per se* to shout, 'Up the I.R.A.' but could be in the context of a pending collection or meeting. Equivalent offences in earlier versions of the Act also dealt with money and property, but such support is now consigned to Part III (described in chapter 7). This otherwise sensible relocation has had the probably unintended and unsupportable consequence that contributors in response to requests under section 2(1)(b) are no longer mentioned. The prosecution need not prove that the proscribed organisation had authorised the defendant to act on its behalf (the same applies under section 2(1)(c), *infra*).[41] It is also no defence to show that some consideration was given for the support.[42]

The next offences, in section 2(1)(c), are committed if any person:[43]

arranges or assists in the arrangement or management of, or addresses, any meeting of three or more persons (whether or not it is a meeting to which the public are admitted) knowing that the meeting is –
(i)   to support a proscribed organisation;
(ii) to further the activities of such an organisation; or
(iii) to be addressed by a person belonging or professing to belong to such an organisation.

The defendant or hostile spectators may count as one of the 'three or more persons'. However, a radio or television audience of millions would probably not suffice for three reasons.[44] First, section 2 is designed to prevent disorder at Republican demonstrations; this cannot arise directly via the electronic media. Secondly, the word 'meeting' suggests requirements of physical presence and the possibility of interaction. Thirdly, most programmes on behalf of terrorists are already expressly forbidden by broadcasting law,[45] so section 2 is superfluous. However, though members of the public are not participants at a meeting in a broadcasting studio, other contributors to the programme, a studio audience and technicians will be eligible.[46] Assuming that a meeting of the requisite size is planned,[47] it need not actually occur, nor must it be open to the public or in a public place. Under subsections (c)(i) and (ii), the purpose of the meeting must be to support or advance the organisation and not just to promulgate its aims or activities.[48] However, under subsection (c)(iii), provided the meeting is addressed by an actual or self-confessed member, the matters discussed need not even be connected with the organisation or Irish affairs. The Act's message is that they are not to be trusted with public platforms.

As for the *mens rea* of all offences in section 2, the core activities of belonging, soliciting and arranging presumably require intention,[49] though they are unlikely to happen otherwise. The defendant need not know either the facts which have caused the proscription of the organisation or its status in law as a proscribed organisation.[50]

The penalties for offences in section 2 are, on summary conviction, imprisonment not exceeding six months, a fine not exceeding the statutory maximum or both, or, on indictment, imprisonment not exceeding ten years, a fine or both.[51]

The final offence in Part I is section 3(1). This penalizes[52]

Any person who in a public place –
(a)   wears any item of dress; or
(b)   wears, carries or displays any article, in such a way or in such circumstances as to arouse reasonable apprehension that he is a member or supporter of a proscribed organisation. . . .

Public places are defined in section 3(3) in terms identical to section 9(1) of the Public Order Act 1936 (as amended). This definition differs slightly (but probably not materially) from that in section 16 of the Public Order Act 1986.[53] The behaviour must imply membership or support and not just sympathy with its political beliefs. Thus:[54]

general political or social objections or programmes, which are not peculiarly or specially identified with a banned organisation, are not put under quarantine. . . .

However, the distinction between message and message-bearer is in practice lost on many British courts. In any event, apprehension of support must actually be aroused as well as being a reasonable reaction.[55] Verbal expressions of support (unless displayed on banners) are not forbidden by section 3 but may breach section 2(1)(b), as may some of the displays which are covered by section 3. As for *mens rea*, the defendant must intend to 'wear' or 'display' the relevant item but need not intend or foresee the apprehension of membership.[56] Thus, a pro-I.R.A. T-shirt worn purely as a fashion trend would still infringe section 3. A power of arrest without warrant attaches to this offence in Scotland but no longer in England.[57]

2 Comparisons

(a) Sections 1 and 2

By section 28(2)(a), Part I of the Prevention of Terrorism Act does not extend to Northern Ireland. However, proscription under section 28 of the Northern Ireland (Emergency Provisions) Act 1991[58] exhibits close similarities to Part I, which is not surprising as the latter was modelled on earlier versions of special laws in Northern Ireland. Only four differences are worthy of note. Two obvious distinctions are that seven organisations in addition to the I.R.A. and I.N.L.A. are proscribed in Northern Ireland[59] and the penalties for the various offences differ in practice because of parole and remission rules in Northern Ireland.[60] Next, there is no equivalent in section 2 to section 28(5), whereby the possession of certain documents is evidence of membership. This matter will be discussed shortly. The fourth contrast is that there is no equivalent in the Prevention of Terrorism Act to section 28(1)(c), which makes it an offence to solicit or invite any person to join a proscribed organisation or to carry out its orders. This subsection was enacted in 1975 in order to catch terrorist 'godfathers' who avoid direct participation in violence.[61] However, the innovation is modest, since most activities forbidden by section 28(1)(c) will be unlawful under section 28(1)(b) or, in Britain, under section 2(1)(b).[62]

The 'godfather hypothesis'[63] also lies behind the offence adopted in section 27 of the Northern Ireland (Emergency Provisions) Act 1991, by which any person who 'directs, at any level, the activities of an organisation which is concerned in the commission of acts of terrorism' is liable to life imprisonment. Section 27 is wider than section 28(1)(c) and may even encompass the giving of desirable orders to observe a ceasefire or to pay money to prisoners' wives. Aside from these difficulties, it would politically be preferable to prosecute for the regular crimes involved commonly in 'directing'.

There are far more striking differences between Part I and proscription under the Republic's Offences against the State Act 1939.[64] The preliminary suppression order under section 19 remains a matter for the executive. However, the relevant criteria are fully stated in section 18, which allows greater opportunity for parliamentary scrutiny, and, by section 20, the courts may be asked to review whether the power has been properly exercised. The offences relating to members and supporters (contained in section 21 of the 1939 Act and section 3 of the Criminal Law Act 1976) are similar to those in section 2(1)(a) and (b) of the Prevention of Terrorism Act, but the remaining effects of suppression are much more extensive. Under section 22 of the 1939 Act, all the group's property can be forfeited, and section 25 allows the closure of buildings suspected of being used for its purposes. Further powers to seize tainted funds held in bank accounts are granted by the Offences against the State (Amendment) Act 1985, which will be considered in chapter 7.

Three further provisions ease the burden of proving the offence of membership under the 1939 Act. First, by section 24, the possession of documents relating to, or from, a suppressed organisation is automatically evidence of the possessor's membership. There exists a very similar formula in section 28(5) of the Emergency Provisions Act, which in turn inspired clause 1(6) of the original Prevention of Terrorism Bill in 1974. However, this measure has the distinction of being the only part of the legislation lost during its passage because of fears that evidence would be 'planted'.[65] The next relevant device is section 3(1) of the Offences against the State (Amendment) Act 1972, by which any statement or conduct leading to a reasonable inference that the accused was a member of an unlawful organisation (including a failure to deny published accusations) shall be admissible evidence. This is sometimes used cumulatively with section 3(2), which provides that the statement of a senior police officer that he believes the defendant was a member of an unlawful organisation shall be evidence of such. However, both Parliament and also the Diplock Report have criticised these evidentiary short cuts.[66] Section 3(1) has been rejected on the basis that most relevant statements or activities are already admissible, while the concept of culpable non-denial would raise both practical difficulties in defining what constitutes an accusation which should be answered and theoretical difficulties by condemning a person for espousing a cause. Equally, section 3(2) has the drawback that police opinions are open to cross-examination as to the sensitive investigative methods and sources of information which justify them and could also, especially if applied in Northern Ireland, give rise to accusations of police bias and sectarianism.

Section 2 may finally be compared with section 2(1) of the Public Order Act 1936.[67] This makes it an offence for any person to take part in the control, management, organising or training of an association whose members or adherents are:

(a) organised or trained or equipped for the purpose of enabling them to be employed in usurping the functions of the police or of the armed forces of the Crown; or
(b) organised and trained or organised and equipped either for the purpose of enabling them to be employed for the use or display of physical force in promoting any political object, or in such a manner as to arouse reasonable apprehension that they are organised and either trained or equipped for the purpose....

The similarities with the Prevention of Terrorism Act are obvious, and some I.R.A. members were prosecuted under the Public Order Act before

November 1974.[68] However, a notable difference is that mere membership is forbidden under the Prevention of Terrorism Act but not the Public Order Act.[69] It would surely be feasible to amend section 2 in relatively minor ways so as to make section 2 of the Prevention of Terrorism Act redundant. This would conform to the limiting principles suggested in chapter 2, that resort to the permanent criminal law is preferable to emergency legislation. However, a Home Office Green Paper, entitled 'Review of the Public Order Act 1936 and related legislation', complaisantly concluded in 1980 that 'there seems no need for change . . .',[70] and the issue passed without comment in the subsequent White Paper, 'Review of Public Order Laws',[71] in 1985.

(b) Section 3
Section 3 of the Prevention of Terrorism Act may be compared, firstly, with section 29 of the Northern Ireland (Emergency Provisions) Act which prohibits dressing or behaving in a public place like a member of a proscribed organisation.[72] Section 29 was redrafted in 1987 to reflect section 3, but its maximum penalty remains higher.[73] Closely connected is section 33 of the Emergency Provisions Act, by which the wearing of hoods or masks in public places is unlawful, even if such dress does not imply affiliation to any organisation or amount to a uniform. This is not a significant problem in Britain, so the Prevention of Terrorism Act contains no counterpart.

Public meetings and processions in support of a suppressed organisation can be prohibited by the police in the Republic under section 27 of the Offences against the State Act 1939 subject to review by the courts. In contrast to section 2, it should be noted that a demonstration is unlawful under section 27 even if it is confined to verbal, rather than physical, support. In addition, the support must be exhibited under section 27 in the context of a public demonstration, whereas a public place is the *locus in quo* for section 2.

Finally, section 1(1) of the Public Order Act 1936 states that:[74]

any person who in any public place or at any public meeting wears uniform signifying his association with any political organisation or with the promotion of any political object shall be guilty of an offence. . . .

The only significant difference between section 3 of the Prevention of Terrorism Act and section 1(1) concerns the extent of the display of support. Whilst any item of dress or any article suffices under section 3, there must be a 'uniform' for section 1. However, the most recent interpretation of the latter, in *O'Moran* v. *D.P.P.* and *Whelan* v. *D.P.P.*,[75] suggests that this distinction may be trivial. These twin prosecutions concerned Republican demonstrations during June and August 1974 in which the leading participants wore black berets, dark glasses and dark clothing. The Divisional Court affirmed their convictions under the 1936 Act on the basis that they had worn a political 'uniform'. In the view of Lord Widgery, a beret alone would suffice, since:[76]

Subject always to the *de minimis* rule, I see no reason why the article or articles should cover the whole of the body or a major part of the body....

Despite this interpretation, the 1989 Act remains wider in two respects. Firstly, it prohibits small badges and emblems, which cannot realistically be designated as the wearing of a uniform.[77] Secondly, section 3 outlaws displays other than items of wearing apparel, especially the carrying of banners.[78] Notwithstanding these remaining differences, public displays of support for terrorist groups will usually infringe the 1936 Act. Thus, there seems little justification for the intervention of the Prevention of Terrorism Act, especially when account is taken of other relevant public order offences. For example, breach of the peace was directly substituted for charges under section 3 in *Duffield and Crosbie* v. *Skeen*,[79] a prosecution in 1980 for selling papers and chanting slogans supporting the I.R.A. outside Glasgow Celtic's football ground. Similarly, processions concerned with Northern Ireland have been banned under forerunners to section 13 of the Public Order Act 1986 in Coventry in 1974 and 1982, in Glasgow in 1980 and 1981, in Aberdeen and Kilburn in 1981 and in Luton in 1982. Additional powers of regulation exist under section 63 of the Civic Government (Scotland) Act 1982 and various predecessors, which were invoked to prohibit Loyalist marches in Hawick in 1978 and Aberdeen in 1988.[80] As well as these statutory provisions, there lurk even broader common law powers (and, in Scotland only, an offence) to suppress breaches of the peace, which may be used to disperse paramilitary[81] or sectarian[82] displays. Regrettably, the Home Office's Green and White Papers mentioned earlier failed to consider the overlap[83] with public order law, while the Commons' Home Affairs Select Committee expressed approval for the retention of Part I of the Prevention of Terrorism Act.[84]

3   Assessment

(a)   Purpose

The main purpose of Part I of the Act, as was admitted by the Home Secretary from the outset, is to reduce 'affront' to the public.[85] The Jellicoe Report made this point even more forcefully. Proscription may have some practical side-effects, including the prevention of public disorder and the stemming of the flow of funds and support. However, it is the 'presentational' effect – that 'it enshrines in legislation public aversion' – which is the clearest.[86] Unfortunately, to achieve this goal, proscription must be sufficiently broad to suppress all public emanations relating to outlawed groups, even if this means confusing Republican violence with Republican politics.[87]

If the maintenance of public order is the objective, it may next be considered whether Loyalist terroristic outfits should also be unlawful, as many are in Northern Ireland.[88] In support of this proposition, it may be pointed out that they also have perpetrated acts of violence in Britain. Loyalists were involved in attacks upon Irish public bars in London in 1975 and in Glasgow in 1979,[89] and activities in Liverpool have included attempts to injure a U.V.F. renegade and to import arms from Canada.[90] Moreover there have been numerous incidents involving the supply of munitions, fund-gathering and military training, mostly in Scotland. Reported cases have included *Hamilton* v. *H.M. Advocate*[91] (U.D.A. activities in Dumfries), *Sayers* v. *H.M. Advocate*[92] (a U.V.F. unit in Glasgow, with important evidence being given by a former commander), *Walker, Edgar and others* v. *H.M. Advocate*[93] (a 'gun-kitty' for the U.V.F. in Glasgow, again with a former member turning informer), *H.M. Advocate* v. *Copeland, Robertson and others*[94] (U.D.A. involvement in Glasgow), and *Forbes* v. *H.M. Advocate*[95] and *Reid* v. *H.M. Advocate*[96] (U.D.A. members based in Perth, with evidence again provided by an informer). The detection of these cells is attributable either to infiltration and informers or to the routine surveillance of suspects. The special policing powers in the Prevention of Terrorism Act sometimes assisted by allowing interrogation and the monitoring of contacts in Belfast, but the fact that the U.D.A. and U.V.F. are not proscribed seems to have made no difference to the police or the conspirators.

Despite this catalogue of crimes, Lord Shackleton dismissed proposals to extend proscription:[97]

The Protestant extremist groups are not engaged in violence against the community in Great Britain and . . . their activities are not in any way comparable to those of the I.R.A. . . .

This reasoning is dubious, since the incidents cited indicate that Loyalist terrorists are prepared to execute violent attacks in Britain. For his part, the Earl Jellicoe correctly rejected the need for symmetry in Britain and Northern Ireland as a sufficient reason for augmenting the list in Schedule 1[98] but then failed to recognise the case for proscription because of the 'open and avowed use of violence' by groups such as the U.V.F.[99] In any event, the reasoning adopted in both Reports is somewhat misleading. The true basis for proscription under Part I is the prevention of public offence and disorder. Thus, it is not the paramilitary activity in Britain *simpliciter* which justifies listing but the degree of resultant public outrage. In fact, Loyalist criminality in Britain has not provoked public condemnation to the same degree as Republican misdeeds, probably because it has been relatively isolated and usually directed against other Irishmen. On that basis, there is no justification for further proscription. This conclusion may appear irreconcilable with the application of the broadcasting ban to Loyalist groups in 1988, especially as it is partly based on the historical accident that two statutes impose proscription according to geographical area whereas broadcasting law is universal. Nevertheless, Loyalist paramilitaries hardly enjoy a 'safe haven'[100] in Britain, for they are subject to the remainder of the Act as well as normal criminal offences.

Is there a stronger case for proscribing Sinn Fein? Ample evidence exists of its close relationship with the Provisional I.R.A.,[101] and it frequently evinces public outrage in Britain through its public utterances. However, proof that it is 'actively and primarily engaged in the commission of terrorist acts' as a matter of organisational policy is absent.[102] While Sinn Fein may not be 'concerned in' terrorism under section 1(2), it might more realistically be accused of 'promoting or encouraging' it. However, aside from general doubts about the efficacy of proscription, caution should be, and is in practice, exercised before action is taken on such grounds. One reason is that proscription might wastefully divert police attention towards thousands of innocent supporters. Next, it would curtail expression, close a possible avenue of dialogue, reduce the legitimacy of elections in Northern Ireland[103] and exclude a method of gauging support for Republicanism. Thirdly, it is surely desirable to encourage the I.R.A. to expend its resources on the political efforts of Sinn Fein rather than, say, munitions. In summary, the option of proscription of Sinn Fein was rejected by the Northern Ireland Office in its paper, 'Elected Representations and the Democratic Process in Northern Ireland', mainly because of the absence of direct involvement in terrorism.[104] Yet many of the attributes of proscription have been applied, including the arrest or exclusion of its leaders,[105] the refusal to allow its representatives access to government ministers, civil servants (except on constituency matters) or some governmental premises (such as prisons),[106] disqualification from office and the requirement of a declaration of non-violence as a condition of local office,[107] and restrictions on media appearances.

Aside from Irish candidates,[108] the Colville Report also considered the extension of bans to foreign terror groups. The idea was rejected for two reasons.[109] One was the difficulty of monitoring 'all manner of foreign quarrels and their manifestations in the United Kingdom', though one would hope that such an exercise is attempted even without proscription. Secondly, proscription was said to be 'too blunt and inflexible a weapon to use against international terrorism', as the recent transmogrification of S.W.A.P.O. from terrorist band to government party may testify.[110] Apart from Colville's reasons, summary executive action against foreign trouble-makers may already be taken under the Immigration Act 1971, and, more generally, one doubts whether proscription could have much impact on overseas-based groups.

The list of proscribed groups could alternatively be shortened by the removal of the Official I.R.A., which has observed a ceasefire since 1972, and, indeed, may no longer exist. The case seems unanswerable in Britain at least and has even attracted remarkable support from the Official Unionist spokesman.[111] Perhaps confused by this role reversal, the Home Office has conceded that the Official I.R.A. has not recently engaged in violence and can maintain its proscription only on the basis that it represents itself 'as a Republican Army'.[112] One hopes that the same logic will not be applied to the Salvation Army or the Church Army.

(b) Use in practice

Proscription seems to have had a marked effect in deterring displays of support for the I.R.A. which, by and large, have not taken place since 1974. However, this has been achieved through the threat of, rather than by actual, prosecutions. Thus, up to the end of 1990, official statistics recorded just three charges under section 3 (two were later withdrawn)[113] and a further seven prosecutions resulting in two convictions under section 2. One of the latter concerned James Fegan,[114] convicted at the Glasgow Sheriff Court in February 1975 for selling posters 'to support the boys' which bore such picturesque captions as 'Brit Thugs Out' and 'Victory to the I.R.A.' Although Fegan was a member of Provisional Sinn Fein and no evidence appears to have been adduced to show that the proceeds of sale were destined not for it but for the I.R.A., he was convicted and sentenced to six months' imprisonment. No charges have been officially recorded since 1981, but three further cases have been unofficially reported. The first concerned Jan Taylor, a Sinn Fein official who was fined £150 for selling the '1984 Republican Resistance Calendar' in a Hammersmith pub contrary to section 3(1)(b).[115] The second defendant was James Maley, who was charged with distributing Republican leaflets, entitled 'Ireland's War', but was not brought to trial, unlike the third defendant, Factna O'Ceallaigh, who was fined £75 for wearing a badge proclaiming, 'Out of the ashes arose the Provisionals'.[116] It may be noted that all cases were tried without a jury possibly to avoid creating a platform for 'offensive' views.[117]

The dearth of charges under Part I contrasts sharply with Northern Ireland practice and may be explained by two factors: fewer I.R.A. members in Britain and different prosecution policies. The latter may arise from a lack of familiarity with the offence, a desire not to confuse juries with minor counts, and the wish to avoid an offence which tends to emphasise the political nature of paramilitarism.

Aside from its effects in practice, the value of proscription should be assessed from two further angles. Firstly, are there any positive claims which can be made on its behalf? Alternatively, are there any criticisms which either derogate from these advantages or even totally outweigh them?

(c) Advantages

The central positive claim made in favour of proscription is that it operates as a legislative safety valve by expressing public feelings of anger. Nor is this simply a matter of satiating fevered passions; the implication in November 1974 was that there would have been attacks on the Irish community in Britain if legislation had not been forthcoming.[118] However, even if private retribution is a real threat which has occasionally reached fruition, one reply is that persons prepared to undertake unlawful attacks are the least likely to be mollified by the vicarious revenge of proscription. Thus, as many acts of revenge have been perpetrated since the passage of the Act as before it.[119]

A second claim is that proscription displays political strength by acting as a 'useful token of the Government's determination to crack down on terrorist organisations'.[120] In response, it might be argued that this is better demonstrated by substantive security and political policies, whereas the passage of presentational legislation damages confidence and arouses anger when it is found to be ineffective in practical terms, hardly signals that it was 'politically well judged'.[121]

A third advantage is said to be that proscription intimidates and discourages supporters of terrorist groups.[122] This is a sustainable, though limited, claim. In practice, proscription is likely to achieve this effect only at the fringes of an organisation, since those most deeply involved will not be deterred by the threat of prosecution for membership.[123]

Next, proscription would be justified if it could be shown that it remedied defects in the 'regular' law. However, in the light of the comparisons made earlier, it must be recognised that the supporters of terrorism could be and have been prosecuted or regulated under the Public Order Acts or, alternatively, for being a party to a criminal conspiracy or for substantive offences involving, for example, munitions. The belief that, before the Act, the I.R.A. was 'permitted' to 'meet, raise funds and recruit support'[124] is ludicrous.

A closely related ground for supporting proscription is that, even if it does not extend existing law in any way, it might usefully short-circuit it. This argument was advanced in the Diplock Report:[125]

It relieves the prosecution of the necessity to prove in court each time that an individual member of one of the named organisations is charged that its objects or the means by which it seeks to attain them are unlawful. On a charge of criminal conspiracy at common law, the evidence to establish this, though it be common knowledge, would have to be repeated in each case brought before the courts.

An illustration may be *Sayers* v. *H.M. Advocate*.[126] The defendant was charged with 'conspiracy to further by criminal means the purpose of an association known as the U.V.F.', and the criminal means specified were the attempted acquisition of munitions. The jury convicted him of conspiracy but deleted the reference to the criminal means.[127] Their verdict was overturned on appeal. The deletion meant that the defendant had in effect been convicted of helping the U.V.F. 'by unspecified criminal means',[128] but such a count of conspiracy was bad as inadequately specified and as not disclosing a known crime. However, had the U.V.F. been proscribed, there would have been no need to identify any additional crimes. Proscription would have implied that any involvement in its affairs was, by its nature, bound to involve criminal activities and so be unlawful without further proof. A second, less important, sense in which proscription acts as a short-circuiting device is that it provides a much simpler alternative to the offence of seditious conspiracy, which prosecutors might otherwise be tempted to invoke.[129]

Taking the last point first, it is certainly desirable to avoid resort to archaic and politically charged offences such as sedition. However, the enactment of proscription was not really necessary to attain that goal, since there already existed in 1974 a host of viable alternatives, especially under the Public Order Act 1936.[130] As for the main purpose of avoiding proof of the criminal nature of the organisation or a defendant's precise role in it, this may be a justifiable lightening of the prosecution's burden, but only if achieved in an acceptable manner. In order to ensure that the membership of a proscribed organisation is generally viewed as a legitimate criminal offence and does not contravene the European Convention on Human Rights, it is imperative that there should be judicial findings at regular intervals[131] that the group is concerned in criminal activities. By contrast, an unreviewable declaration to this effect, almost amounting to a Bill of Attainder, by Parliament or a Secretary of State is the procedure laid down by the Prevention of Terrorism Act. Whether proscription is by its nature a suitable case for judicial resolution turns upon its classification as justiciable or non-justiciable. Two considerable obstacles to arriving at an answer are that no issue is inherently justiciable and no authoritative test exists for isolating matters which should be placed before judges.[132] Therefore, it is intended to tackle this matter tangentially – by considering what advantages or difficulties flow from judicial scrutiny. This cannot logically prove or disprove that proscription is a justiciable issue, but it can provide rational and persuasive arguments for and against.

Some of the principal advantages of judicial adjudication are that it conveys the appearance of decision-making on the basis of objective fact and allows participation by those potentially affected.[133] These two factors are of some importance in the context of proscription, since it is desirable to disabuse the public and the association of any impression that a ban was imposed by reason of emotion or political distaste rather than because of criminal involvement.

A further consideration in favour of judicial resolution is that it tends to increase consistency and certainty, since the judicial method is to proceed on the basis of established rules and precedents.[134] However, this advantage is obviously dependent upon the ability of the legislature to translate its desired policy into 'sufficiently clearly defined standards to operate the judicial process efficiently by keeping discretion within narrow limits'.[135] Applying this matter to proscription, the criterion in section 1(2) of the Prevention of Terrorism Act[136] (read together with the definition of 'terrorism' in section 20) does provide a relatively definite test which essentially turns on factual matters. Thus, the making of an order could be made to depend on wholly objective evidence such as convictions of members, claims and admissions emanating from the group and statements from expert witnesses such as the police.[137]

The most common factor precluding scrutiny by judges is the presence of 'policy' considerations. The view that proscription is non-justiciable for this reason was asserted by Lord Pearson, who stated in *McEldowney* v. *Forde* that 'the decision is in the sphere of politics . . .'.[138] Such a categorisation tends to rule out the courts on a number of grounds. One is that it makes it difficult to formulate rules for their guidance. Another is that it renders participation by the parties less meaningful, since the adjudicator may have to base his decision on considerations of policy which have not been revealed to those affected. Two reasons might be given for secrecy in the context of proscription. First, it might be necessary to suppress sensitive information, such as the identities of informers or methods of investigation.[139] Yet relevant evidence could also include, as mentioned earlier, such publicly known facts as the convictions of members and statements issued on behalf of the organisation concerned. A second reason would be that the issues arising are so wide-ranging and polycentric that allowing them to be disputed would make the litigation unmanageable. However, compared to the proclamation of an emergency[140] or the institution of special courts or internment,[141] the proscription of a specific organisation is a much narrower issue, especially as section 1(2) makes no reference to such vague concepts as the 'public interest'.[142]

By way of summary, it would seem that there are no insuperable obstacles to submitting the issues arising in connection with proscription to some form of judicial process and, therefore, abolishing legislative proscription under section 1(1) of the Prevention of Terrorism Act and amending substantially subsection (2). Indeed, opponents of judicial involvement appear to have overlooked the existence of two partially judicial powers of proscription in section 2 of the Public Order Act 1936. Before convicting under subsection (1) or forfeiting property under subsection (3), a court must first determine the nature of the group concerned. Judicial condemnation of the I.R.A. has also been possible in the United States. In the case of *U.S. v. Megahy*,[143] it was held that whether that body could be defined as engaged in 'international terrorism':

hardly call[s] for sensitive determinations fraught with ... policy implications. Rather, [it calls] for findings of objective fact not unlike those made in courtrooms every day.

An even more direct precedent for judicial proscription is embodied in the Offences against the State Act 1939, as described previously.

It may be concluded that only when proscription is based on factual proof in the regular courts, as it clearly can be, is it a justifiable short cut in the criminal law. By contrast, the system currently in operation under the Prevention of Terrorism Act does not conform to that desirable limiting principle.

(d) Disadvantages

Proscription embodies two serious drawbacks, the first of which counterbalances the claim that suppression deters[144] sympathisers at the margins of an unlawful association. It may be replied that, to the extent that it does deter, proscription actually hinders police investigations, since fringe supporters are a more accessible source of information than dedicated terrorists. Consequently, even the Government felt reservations about the introduction of proscription and admitted that:[145]

it will in many ways be rather more than less difficult as a result of the banning to apprehend the terrorists.

The second deleterious effect is that proscription tends to suppress public expressions of support for Republicanism, since it is easy to accuse members of legitimate political groups of providing material support for terrorists whose political aims they share.[146] As a result, Republican groups once active in Britain, such as Clann na h'Eireann, have had to curtail their activities, as members have been arrested for raising money and selling newspapers,[147] refused access to meeting places[148] and excluded under Part II of the Act. These censorious tendencies, which are arguably intended byproducts, are extremely damaging. The curtailment of discussion renders the Republican viewpoint far less comprehensible to the people and politicians of Britain, who may thereby be misled into mistakes in their treatment of Northern Ireland. This danger was recognised by the Jellicoe Report:[149]

there is a potential problem here. It is asking a lot of the police to apply these provisions fully in relation to proscribed organisations themselves, while not affecting the free expression of views about Northern Ireland.

However, the suggested remedy, guidance to the police, was implemented half-heartedly by a Home Office Circular in 1983, which simply warns that police officers 'should take care to ensure that members of the public do not feel inhibited from the free expression of views about Northern Ireland'.[150] Yet there is no explanation as to what effect this advice should have on the enforcement of the Act, and so it is unlikely to have much impact.

Proscription finally entails two less fundamental drawbacks. First, it is counter-productive from a propaganda point of view in that it strengthens I.R.A. claims that its inability to operate lawfully justifies resort to violence. In response, the Government is unable under the present defective system in section 1 to point to any judicial confirmation that, on the facts, the I.R.A. adopted violent means before its proscription and, therefore, ignored the democratic avenue open to it. Thus, even Lord Lowry recognised it as a 'political offence' in *R. v. Adams*.[151] The final defect is the difficulty of proving the various offences connected with proscription, which makes them peripheral as a restraint upon terrorism.

(e)   Conclusions

Proscription is a cosmetic part of the Prevention of Terrorism Act, divorced from the mainstream of either preventing or combating terrorism. Its original purpose was modest and short-term: to remove the I.R.A. from public sight. On that limited basis, the Act has been successful, though, on further analysis, this achievement may be counter-productive, since it impedes criminal investigations and political discussion. Indeed, it might be asked whether the public would welcome the balm for their feelings of outrage provided by the Act if they realised that this luxury probably makes it more difficult to eradicate terrorism.[152] Furthermore, even if they did, the present system of proscription still warrants rejection, since it breaches the guiding principles that regular law should take precedence over special measures where possible and that effective safeguards should be incorporated. Consequently, its main effect is now to confine to Northern Ireland the expression of extreme Republicanism and to maintain the pretence in Britain that it neither exists nor represents a significant strand of political opinion.

In the light of all these criticisms of proscription, even Viscount Colville expressed himself as 'happy to get rid of it altogether'[153] but then resiled from recommending repeal because he feared that it would be interpreted as 'a recognition . . . that the leading merchants of Irish terrorism were no longer disapproved'.[154] The answer to his fear is to pass deproscription as part of a reform package. The Public Order Act 1986 was one such missed opportunity; the reenactment of the Prevention of Terrorism Act in 1989 was another.

In conclusion, proscription can be a justifiable evidential short cut which depicts membership as shorthand for criminal involvement. It is not acceptable on presentational grounds, and, given the extent of paramilitary activities and the impact of other laws, is probably not required at present in Britain.

Notes

1 This was invoked to proscribe the I.N.L.A.: S.I. 1979 No. 746. No indication is provided of the degree of 'concern' necessary (see: A. Cassesse, *Terrorism, Politics and Law* (1989) ch.7), but it should be an activity known to the group (see *Sweet v. Parsley* [1970] A.C. 132).

2 See: J.C. Smith and B. Hogan, *Criminal Law* (6th ed., 1988) p. 844.

3 See: D.R. Lowry, 'Draconian powers' (1976–77) 8–9 *Col. H.R.L. Rev.* 185 at p. 189; C. Scorer and P. Hewitt, *The Prevention of Terrorism Act: The Case for Repeal* (1981) p. 20.

4 See: P. Hall, 'The Prevention of Terrorism Acts' in A. Jennings (ed.), *Justice under Fire* (2nd ed., 1990) pp. 148–9.

5 H.C. Debs. Standing Comm. B col. 151 17 January 1991.

6 H.C. Debs. Standing Comm. B col. 36, 13 December 1988, Mr. Hogg.

7 Compare: *South African Defence and Aid Fund and another v. Minister of Justice* 1971 (1) S.A. 263 (A.D); H. Street, 'Quasi-judicial and the maxim audi alteram partem (1967) 87 *S.A.L.J.* 385.

8 H.C. Debs. Standing Comm. B col. 176 22 January 1991.

9 It cannot challenge scheduled organisations, and most charges will arise long after the limitation period in administrative law.

10 *South African Defence and Aid Fund and another v. Minister of Justice, loc. cit.* at p. 273 *per* Botha J.A.

11 See: H.C. Debs. Standing Comm. D col. 29 3 November 1983, Mr. Waddington.

12 [1970] A.C. 379. Compare: [1968] 1 *M.L.J.* 119.

13 [1971] A.C. 632.

14 S.I. No. 42 (N.I.).

15 *Loc. cit.* at p. 650 *per* Lord Guest; compare Lord Pearson at p. 657. See also: *Ndabeni v. Minister of Law and Order* 1984 (3) S.A. 500 (D. + C.L.D.); *S. v. Ramgobin and others* 1986 (1) S.A. 68 (N.P.D.).

16 D.N. MacCormick, 'Delegated legislation and civil liberties' (1970) 86 *L.Q.R.* 171 at p. 177. See also: H.G. Calvert, 'Special powers extraordinary' (1969) 20 *N.I.L.Q.* 1.

17 *Loc. cit.* at p. 662.

18 [1982] I.R. 337. See: C. Gearty, 'Judicial review of Ministerial opinion' (1982) 4 *D.U.L.J.* 95.

19 *Loc. cit.* at p. 361 *per* O'Higgins C.J. *Bona fides* was also pertinent

but was not disputed (at p. 366). Natural justice was not seen as applicable (at p. 465).

20 See: G. Hogan and D. Morgan, *Administrative Law* (1986) pp. 310–16; M. Forde, *Constitutional Law of Ireland* (1987) p. 744.

21 [1990] 2 W.L.R. 787. See also: *Secretary of State for Defence* v. *Guardian Newspapers Ltd.* [1985] 1 A.C. 359.

22 Appl. No. 7050/75, D.R. 19 p. 5. See also: *X* v. *U.K.* Appl. No. 6084/73, D.R. 3 p. 63.

23 Appl. No. 1747/61, 6 Y.B.E.C. 424.

24 See: R. Higgins, 'Derogations under human rights treaties' (1976) 48 *B.Y.I.L.* 281.

25 Compare *Becker* v. *Belgium* Appl. No. 214/56, 5 Y.B.E.C. 320.

26 Appl. No. 332/56, (1961) 1 E.H.R.R. 15.

27 Compare: *German Communist Party* v. *F.R.G.* Appl. No. 350/57, 1 Y.B.E.C. 222; *Retimag* v. *F.R.G.* Appl. No. 712/60, 4 Y.B.E.C.

28 *R.* v. *Adams* [1978] 5 N.I.J.B. (B.C.C.) at p. 2 *per* Lord Lowry.

29 Charges of membership should not be artifically split over different periods, but the renewal of the Act may result in multiple counts. Compare: *R.* v. *Harris* [1969] 1 W.L.R. 745; *R.* v. *Gibson and Lewis* [1986] 17 N.I.J.B. 1 (C.A.).

30 *R.* v. *Adams, loc. cit.*

31 H.C. Debs. Standing Comm. D col. 12 3 November 1983, Mr. Waddington. The profession must be 'serious' and not 'in jest'; *ibid.* col. 9.

32 *Loc. cit.* p. 8.

33 H.C. Debs. Standing Comm. D col. 71 15 December 1988, Mr. Hogg.

34 See also s. 2(4) and (5).

35 H.C. Debs. Vol. 882 cols. 823–6 28 November 1984.

36 Hall, *op. cit.* p. 153.

37 The distinction between the two is unclear, but both presumably cover incitements and less direct forms of persuasion. Compare: Criminal Law Act 1976 (Ir.) s. 3. Soliciting may be by threats: Smith and Hogan, *loc. cit.* p. 844.

38 H.C. Debs. Standing Comm. D col. 18 3 November 1983, Mr. Waddington.

39 *Ibid.* col. 19. This interpretation may be firmer since the 1989 Act clearly diverts into s. 10 gifts of money or property.

40 *Ibid.* cols. 21, 22. Provisional Sinn Fein often sails close to the wind under this fine distinction. The Baker Report, para. 417 calls for clarification of this point. See also: *Cane and another* v. *Royal College of Music* [1969] 2 Q.B. 89.

41 See: *S.* v. *Mabitselo* 1985 (4) S.A. 61 (T.P.D.); *S.* v. *Moloi* 1987 (1) S.A. 196 (A.D.).

42 Smith and Hogan, *op. cit.* p. 845.

43 This overlaps with subsection (b) since such a person will usually be soliciting or inviting 'support'. However, backroom helpers who have no direct contact with the public are probably only caught by subsection (c), and those employed by organisers to perform very menial tasks may escape s. 2 altogether if such work is not referable to arranging or managing the meeting. Compare: *Dunrose* v. *Wilson* (1907) 96 L.T. 645; *Gorman* v. *Standen* [1964] 1 Q.B. 294: *Abbott* v. *Smith* [1965] 2 Q.B. 662.

44 Compare: Smith and Hogan, *op. cit.* p. 845.

45 See ch. 13.

46 A specific offence of broadcasting support for a proscribed organisation was rejected by the Gardiner Report, para. 74.

47 Arranging or managing implies pre-planning, but one may address a casual gathering. Compare: Smith and Hogan, *op. cit.* p. 845.

48 L.H. Leigh, 'Comment' (1975) *P.L.* 1 at p. 2. This exempts academic discussion.

49 This includes recklessness: *R.* v. *Adams, loc. cit.* at p. 3.

50 This point is discussed in the first edition of this book (pp. 38–9) and seems now to be generally accepted: Smith and Hogan, *op. cit.* p. 846; Stannard, *op. cit.* p. 171; A.T.H. Smith, *Offences against Public Order* (1987) p. 247.

51 The maximum sentence on indictment was doubled in 1989 to bring it in line with Northern Ireland legislation (Baker Report, para. 426) and as a mark of disapproval. The lower penalty remains relevant to offences (or related conspiracies) committed before the change: *Reid* v. *H.M. Advocate* 1990 S.C.C.R. 83.

52 The maximum penalties (which were doubled in 1976 to bring them in line with section 2) are six months' imprisonment, a fine not exceeding level 5 (Criminal Justice Act 1982 ss. 37, 75) or both. The Baker Report (para. 433) recommended a hybrid offence in Northern Ireland so as to avoid separate trials, but this problem does not arise in Britain.

53 It might be sensible to extend the *locus* to the curtilage of a dwelling (Baker Report, para. 433) or even to any place other than within a dwelling (compare: Public Order Act 1986 s. 4).

54 A.S. Mathews, *Freedom, State Security and the Rule of Law* (1988) p. 51. See also: *Ndabeni* v. *Minister of Law and Order* 1984(3) S.A. 500(D); *S.* v. *Ntshiwa* 1985 (3) S.A. 495 (T); *Mokoena* v. *Minister of Law and Order* 1986 (4) S.A. 42 (W).

55 P.V.L.I., pp. 140–1; *McCaffrey* v. *Loughran and McGurk* [1972], N.I.J.B. (C.A.); *Castorina* v. *Chief Constable of Surrey* (1988) *Times* 15 June.

56 H.C. Debs. Standing Comm. D col. 63 8 November 1983, Mr. Waddington. Compare: *S.* v. *Mkhwanzi* 1987 (4) S.A. 171 (T.P.D.).

57 S. 3(2). The previous power in England and Wales was repealed by the Police and Criminal Evidence Act 1984 s. 26(1), but alternative powers are available under s. 25 or at common law for breach of the peace.

58 See P.V.L.I. pp. 138–43.

59 See: Sched. 2.

60 See: Baker Report, paras. 425–30.

61 Gardiner Report, paras. 52–3.

62 Following the Baker Report (para. 408) s. 28(1)(d) was added in 1987 as an equivalent to s. 2(1)(c).

63 H.C. Debs. Vol. 187 col. 401 6 March 1991 Mr. McNamara.

64 See P.V.L.I. pp. 245–53.

65 H.C. Debs. Vol. 882 cols. 797–823, 939–42 28 November 1974. Compare: Baker Report, para. 417. Such evidence is, however, probably admissible under the normal rules of evidence: Smith and Hogan, *op. cit.* p. 844. Inferences from writings and speeches by officers about the nature of an organisation are legitimate in deciding whether it should be proscribed: Public Order Act 1936 s. 2(4).

66 H.C. Debs. Col. 882 cols. 826–35 28 November 1974; Diplock Report, paras. 22–6. Compare: N.I. Assembly Debs. Vol. 4 p. 87 22 November 1982, Mr. Graham.

67 See: J. Baker, *The Law of Political Uniforms, Public Meetings and Private Armies* (1937) chs. 1, 6; Smith, *op. cit.*, ch. 14.

68 See: *R. v. Fell, Stagg and others* (1973) *Times* 9 October p. 2, [1975] Crim. L.R. 673; *R. v. Kneafsey* (1973) *Times* 23 October p. 2.

69 Compare: Public Order (N.I.) Order 1987 Art. 21.

70 Cmnd. 7891, para. 99.

71 Cmnd. 9510, paras. 2.13, 6.2.

72 See P.V.L.I. pp. 140–1.

73 See: Baker Report, para. 433; H.C. Debs. Standing Comm. B col. 196 22 January 1991.

74 See: Baker, *op. cit.* preface, ch. 1; A. Sherr, *Freedom of Protest, Public Order and the Law* (1989) ch. 7. Compare: Public Order (N.I.) Order 1987 Art. 21.

75 [1975] Q.B. 864.

76 *Ibid.* at p. 873.

77 The precise coverage of both Acts is left to local justice: H.C. Debs. Vol. 317 col. 1353 16 November 1936; H.C. Debs. Standing Comm. B col. 87 15 December 1988.

78 See: H.C. Debs. Standing Comm. B cols. 84, 89 15 December 1988.

79 1981 S.C.C.R. 66.

80 *Loyal Orange Lodge No. 493, Hawick First Purple* v. *Roxburgh D.C.* 1981 S.L.T. 33; *Aberdeen Bon-Accord Loyal Orange Lodge* v. *Grampian R.C.* 1988 S.L.T. (Sh. Ct.) 58.

81 See: K. Ewing and W. Finnie, *Civil Liberties in Scotland* (2nd ed., 1988) pp. 425–6.

82 See: *McAvoy* v. *Jessop* 1989 S.C.C.R. 301.

83 *Loc. cit.*, para. 97; *loc. cit.*, paras. 2.13, 6.2.

84 The Law Relating to Public Order (1979–80 H.C. 756) para. 85.

85 H.C. Debs. Vol. 882 col. 636 28 November 1974, Mr. Jenkins.

86 Jellicoe Report, paras. 207, 208. See also Shackleton Report, para. 28; Baker Report, para. 414; Irish Freedom Movement, *An Anti-Imperialist's Guide to the Irish War* (3rd ed., 1987) p. 169.

87 Lowry, *op. cit.* at p. 202.

88 The U.D.A. is not proscribed but has been called a criminal organisation: *R. v. Payne* (1990) 6 B.N.I.L. n. 72.

89 *Times* 13 October 1976 p. 4; H.C. Debs. Standing Comm. D col. 58 8 November 1983, Mr. Waddington.

90 *R. v. Cull* (1979) 70 Cr. App. R. 24; *R. v. Cubben and Watt* (1987) *Times* 19 December p. 2.

91 1980 S.C. 66 (nine persons charged, six convicted).

92 1982 J.C. 17 (eleven were charged). See also *Kemp and others, Petitioners* 1982 J.C. 29.

93 *Times* 14 March 1986 p. 2. See also *H.M. Advocate* v. *Seawright* (1986).

94 1987 S.C.C.R. 232. Their arrests are described by the Colville Report, App. C, but in fact only nine were charged and two convicted.

95 1990 S.C.C.R. 69.

96 1990 S.C.C.R. 83.

97 *Loc. cit.* para. 110. See also: Colville Report, para. 13.1.88.

98 Compare: Hall, *op. cit.* p. 146; S.D. Bailey (ed.), *Human Rights and Responsibilities in Britain and Ireland* (1988) p. 171.

99 Jellicoe Report, para. 211. Compare: Baker Report, para. 407; Colville Report, para. 13.1.8.

100 Hall, *op. cit.* p. 149.

101 See: *State (Lynch)* v. *Cooney*, *loc. cit.*; *In re Curran and McCann's Application* [1985] 7 N.I.J.B. 22; Glover Report, *op. cit.* para. 29; Bishop and Mallie, *op. cit.* p. 304.

102 H.C. Debs. Standing Comm. B cols. 151, 188 17 January 1991, Dr. Mawhinney. Compare Baker Report, paras. 422–3.

103 *Times* 12 August 1985 p. 2, *per* Mrs. Thatcher.

104 Para. 8. See: Walker, 'Political violence and democracy in Northern Ireland' (1988) 51 *M.L.R.* 605. Similarly, the Home Office regards endorsement of the I.R.A. as merely 'reprehensible and distasteful': H.C. Debs. Standing Comm. B col. 77 15 December 1988, Mr. Hogg.

105 See Walker, 'Members of Parliament and executive security measures' (1983) *P.L.* 537.

106 See *In re McCartney's Application* [1987] 11 N.I.J.B. 94 (C.A.).

107 Elected Authorities (N.I.) Act 1989.

108 Note also calls for the proscription of the I.P.L.O. which were fairly rejected on the ground that it is not viewed as a threat in Britain: H.C. Debs. Standing Comm. B col. 65 15 December 1988, Mr. Hogg.

109 Para. 13.1.9.

110 See: H.C. Debs. Vol. 92, col. 422 19 February 1986, Mr. Kaufman.

111 H.C. Debs. Standing Comm. B col. 61 15 December 1988, Mr. Maginnis.

112 *Ibid.* col. 64, Mr. Hogg.

113 See: n. 79 *supra*. Source: Home Office Statistical Bulletins.

114 See: C. Scorer, *The Prevention of Terrorism Acts 1974 and 1976* (1976) pp. 6, 7. Two co-defendants were acquitted.   ·

115 *Guardian* 10 May 1984 p. 3.

116 Irish Freedom Movement, *The Irish War* (3rd ed., 1987) pp. 169–70.

117 H.C. Debs. Vol. 882 col. 838 28 November 1974, Mr. Lyon.

118 Shackleton Report, para. 118; Jellicoe Report, para. 207. See also ch. 4 n. 11.

119 See: *R.* v. *Bosley and others* (1975) *Times* 12 March p. 2. Forty-eight arrests resulted from rival Irish Freedom Movement and British National Party marches in Islington in March 1989; *Times* 7 August 1988 p. 2.

120 P. Wilkinson, *Terrorism and the Liberal State* (2nd ed., 1986) p. 170.

121 *Ibid.*

122 Shackleton Report, para. 31; Colville Report, para. 13.1.6.

123 Jellicoe Report, paras. 207, 208.

124 Wilkinson, *op. cit.* n. 116.

125 Para. 21. Compare: *McEldowney* v. *Forde*, *loc. cit.* at p. 643; H.C. Debs. Standing Comm. D col. 50 8 November 1983, Mr. Brittan.

126 1982 J.C. 17.

127 *Ibid.* pp. 18–9.

128 *Ibid.* p. 19.

129 See: *R.* v. *Callinan, Quinn and Marcantonio* (1973) *Times* 20 January p. 2.

130 The defendants in *R.* v. *Callinan* (*ibid.*) were also convicted under the Public Order Act 1936 s. 2.

131 Triennial review is suggested: H.C. Debs. Standing Comm. B col. 41 15 December 1988, Mr. Sheerman.

132 See: G. Marshall, 'Justiciability' in A.G. Guest (ed.), *Oxford Essays in Jurisprudence* (1961).

133 See: R.S. Summers, 'Justiciability' (1963) 26 *M.L.R.* 530 at p. 533; L.L. Fuller, 'The forms and limits of adjudication' (1978) 92 *Harv. L.R.* 353.

134 *Prentis* v. *Atlantic Coastline Co.* 211 U.S. 210 (1908) at pp. 226–7.

135 R.B. Stevens 'Justiciability – the Restrictive Practices Court reexamined' (1964) *P.L.* 227 at p. 237.

136 Proscription by legislative fiat under s. 1(1) is obviously wholly inconsistent with judicial processes.

137 Compare the basis for a policy decision: G. Ganz 'Allocation of decision-making functions' (1972) *P.L.* 215, 299 at p. 307.

138 *Loc. cit.* at p. 655.

139 The need to resort to trial *in camera* itself weakens claims to justiciability: Summers, *op. cit.* at p. 536.

140 It has generally been held that this is either not justiciable or reviewable only if there is very clear and unmistakable evidence: H.P. Lee, *Emergency Powers* (1984) ch. 7; S.R. Chowdhury, *Rule of Law in a State of Emergency* (1989) ch. 1.

141 See: Offences against the State Act 1939 Pt. V; Offences against the State (Amendment) Act 1940.

142 Compare: Northern Ireland (Emergency Provisions) Act 1991 Sched. 3 paras. 7, 8.

143 553 F. Supp. 1180 (1982) at p. 196 *per* Sifton J. See also: *U.S.* v. *Flavery* 540 F. Supp. 1306 (1982).

144 Some argue that it has the opposite effect by conferring 'romance': H.C. Debs. Standing Comm. D col. 36 3 November 1983, Mr. Soley.

145 H.C. Debs. Vol. 882 col. 746 28 November 1974, Mr. Lyons. Compare the guarded statement in the Shackleton Report (para. 39).

146 This effect is far less pronounced in Northern Ireland: Baker Report, para. 416.

147 See: Scorer, *op. cit.* p. 7.

148 This especially applies to Trafalgar Square,: H.C. Debs. Vol. 833 cols. 1497–8 22 March 1972.

149 Para. 212. See also: Colville Report, para. 13.1.5.

150 See H.O. Circular (No. 90/1983) and SHHD Circular (No. 121/1983) para. 8. These circulars were not consolidated in 1989.

151 *Loc. cit.* p. 7.

152 Compare: Jellicoe Report, para. 210.

153 Para. 13.1.4.

154 Para. 13.1.6.

Chapter 6

Exclusion orders

1 Provisions

(a) Orders

Three types of exclusion order are delineated in Part II of the Prevention of Terrorism Act. First, under section 5(1), the Home Secretary may prohibit a person[1] from being in or entering Great Britain if satisfied that s/he:

(a)   is or has been concerned in the commission, preparation or instigation of acts of terrorism to which this Part of this Act applies; or
(b)   is attempting or may attempt to enter Great Britain with a view to being concerned in the commission, preparation or instigation of such acts of terrorism. . . .

The terms 'preparation' and 'instigation' are wider than the more technical 'attempt' and 'incitement',[2] so relevant evidence can range from mere planning and encouragement of, to direct involvement in, terrorism. Furthermore, persons attempting to enter need only harbour 'some vague intention of terrorism' in the future.[3]

The second type of exclusion order was added in 1976 as a mirror-image to section 5. By section 6(1), the Secretary of State for Northern Ireland has identical powers to exclude suspected terrorists from the Province. In some ways, section 5 is anomalous. Not only is the Prevention of Terrorism Act mainly intended to protect, rather than put at risk, residents of Britain, but also terrorism in Northern Ireland is comprehensively counteracted by the Northern Ireland (Emergency Provisions) Acts. As exclusion has never figured in these Acts, it may be inferred that it is irrelevant to that part of the United Kingdom. In reality, section 6 resulted from objections by Loyalist Members of Parliament to 'one way' exclusion and their demands for 'reciprocity'.[4] The Government resisted this pressure in 1974 on two grounds: that the power was inappropriate since most terrorists in Northern Ireland are not outsiders, and that exclusion to an area as large as Britain is pointless. Undeterred, the Loyalists maintained their objections and induced the Government to change its mind in 1976, presumably not out of conviction but in the hope that it would mollify the troublesome Ulstermen at no real cost.[5]

The third type of exclusion order, under section 7(1), protects the whole of the United Kingdom from terrorists originating abroad – 'substantially – although not exclusively' in the Irish Republic.[6] This power has existed since 1974, though the complicated drafting of the original version suggests it was added at the last minute.[7]

In regard to the potential clientele of all three orders, section 4(1) provides that the Secretary of State may[8] invoke Part II 'as appears to him expedient to prevent acts of terrorism to which this Part of this Act applies'.[9] However, a Home Office Circular warns that exclusion will not be ordered if a successful prosecution is feasible; exclusion should be unavoidable rather than merely advantageous.[10] Section 4(2) defines relevant acts of terrorism as those 'connected with the affairs of Northern Ireland'.[11] As a result, a Middle Eastern terrorist could not lawfully be excluded,[12] but terrorism committed outside the United Kingdom is relevant provided it is referable to Northern Ireland.[13]

Further restrictions on the potential subjects of exclusion differ according to the type of order involved, though the onus of proving exemption is always on the person asserting it.[14] There are three qualifications to section 5

(3) ... the Secretary of State shall have regard to the question whether [the] person's connection with any country or territory outside Great Britain is such as to make it appropriate that such an order should be made.
(4)   An exclusion order shall not be made ... against a person who is a British citizen and who –
(a)   is at the time ordinarily resident in Great Britain and has then been ordinarily resident in Great Britain throughout the last three years; or
(b)   is at the time subject to an order under section 6 below.

The three years' residence exemption for British citizens[15] in subsection (4)(a) is the most important and controversial. Until amended in 1984, the relevant period, based on that in the Prevention of Violence (Temporary Provisions) Act 1939, was twenty years. However, the Jellicoe Report[16] recognised that this tended to relegate Northern Ireland into a 'terrorist dustbin' and to cause upheavals in the family lives of those affected. Therefore, Jellicoe concluded that suspects ordinarily resident for just three years or more should not be excluded, despite some danger that the I.R.A. will resort to terrorist 'sleepers'.[17] The concept 'ordinarily resident' is not defined by the Act,[18] but detailed rules as to calculating the period of residence are contained in Schedule 2.[19] The residence exemption makes the pejorative epithet 'internal exile' somewhat inaccurate, since it ensures that exclusion ensures confinement to, rather than displacement from, home territory.

The further immunity in subsection (3) provides residual relief to a suspect whose circumstances are such that exclusion would return him not to his 'natural home' but to a location where 'he is a complete stranger'.[20]

The final qualification, in subsection (4)(b), prevents the issuance of an order if the result would be to exclude a British citizen from the whole of the United Kingdom because he has already been excluded from Northern Ireland under section 6. Such total banishment would probably contravene international law.[21]

Exactly the same three exemptions apply *pari passu* to orders under section 6. However, section 7 may never be invoked against British subjects, nor is it limited by the three years' residence rule. Two points may be made concerning the latter. First, although no set period of residence confers immunity, the longer the period the less 'appropriate' exclusion will become. Second, foreigners may reduce their exposure to exclusion by becoming British citizens under the British Nationality Act 1981. This is particularly easy for citizens of the Irish Republic who have been settled in the United Kingdom for a substantial period, since many can register as British citizens as of right.[22]

Assuming exclusion is applicable to a suspect, the first step towards obtaining an order in Britain is the referral of potential cases by the relevant police force to the National Joint Unit (consisting of Special Branch officers) at New Scotland Yard.[23] If favourable to exclusion, a report will be forwarded to the Home Office, where it is considered by 'a number of officials up to Deputy Secretary level before it is put first to the Minister of State and then to the Secretary of State'.[24] The Northern Ireland Secretary deals with cases in the Province, but applications from Scottish police forces are routed through the Home Office.[25]

The relevant Secretary of State will base his decision on the original police reports and comments thereon by the National Joint Unit and his officials. Three categories of information will emerge.[26] First, there will be personal particulars (nationality, place and length of residence, dependants, past conviction). Second, there will be relevant background information (connections with terrorist or related organisations and suspect individuals). Third, and most important of all, there must be evidence of involvement in terrorism. In practice, indications of 'active personal involvement' are demanded,[27] such as the planning of terrorism by carrying out reconnaissances or preparing plans, or by providing money, materials or facilities. Conversely, the following examples of 'passive' involvement are insufficient: being seen in the company of terrorists, harbouring terrorists,[28] expressing support for terrorists or even being a member of a terrorist group. Aside from personal particulars, most of the information will derive from intelligence sources such as informers and police officers. Much of this will be hearsay and low-grade information about the person's associations and views which, Lord Shackleton warned, should be treated with caution, for:[29]

It has no evidential value in the judicial sense. Its value depends upon the careful gradings and assessment made of it, and the way it is used. It may reveal a good deal about a person, but any conclusions drawn from it have to be carefully judged.

Another source of information will be the report of any police interrogation of the suspect. One rather startling disclosure in this regard is that silence may be used as evidence against a suspect on the basis that it is evidence of training in 'anti-interrogation techniques'.[30] This alarming inference would seem to place the suspect in an unenviable position for, if they choose to exercise their legal privilege against self-incrimination, they still run the risk of being excluded. It is submitted that such evidence should be irrelevant even to the Secretary of State, since the police's interpretation of silence is wholly speculative and, therefore, of very low value. The final source will be the results of any forensic tests.[31] These will rarely be present, as their availability would lead to prosecution rather than exclusion.

An exclusion order may be revoked at any time by order of the Secretary of State.[32] This may occur before or after removal and for a variety of reasons.[33] Apart from these random revocations, a periodic review must be conducted, as follows:[34]

(2)   An exclusion order shall, unless revoked earlier, expire at the end of the period of three years beginning with the day on which it is made.
(3)   The fact that an exclusion order against a person has been revoked or has expired shall not prevent the making of a further exclusion order against him.

A three-year period is designed to be long enough for a repentant excludee 'to mend his ways . . . and for the Secretary of State to be reasonably certain that he had done so'.[35] An informal system of review existed after 1979 pursuant to a recommendation of the Shackleton Report.[36] However, the statutory scheme established pursuant to the Jellicoe Report[37] represents an improvement in several respects. First, it transforms a mere administrative concession only triggered by a request into a legal right to an automatic review. Second, since orders must be positively renewed, the burden of proof has been transferred to those wishing exclusion to continue. Next, a system for hearing objections (described hereafter) is available. Finally, in order to prevent the police applying for renewals under subsection (5) as a matter of routine, thereby nullifying the effect of subsection (4), the Home Secretary promised that:[38]

if the events during the three years . . . indicate that nothing fresh has occurred . . . if all that is being relied on is material which led to the initial application – I envisage making a fresh exclusion order only in the rarest of circumstances.

Conflicting interpretations of this promise have been offered. The Minister of State referred in 1988 to the need for a 'fresh intelligence assessment' rather than new evidence,[39] whereas the current Home Office Circular discounts 'intelligence more than 3 years old'.[40] The latter (which seems to mean both facts and assessments of those facts) is to be preferred.

The triennial renewal procedure[41] commences by sending a questionnaire to the subject.[42] The questionnaires ask for any new information such as present employment, references, reasons why exclusion should not continue and whether an interview is desired. The form is returned to the National Joint Unit, which will make inquiries (especially of police forces in Ireland) and may arrange for an interview with the police and the Home Secretary's Adviser (described below). Regrettably, unlike on the original exclusion, there is no right to an interview. The police's assessment, any representations and any other relevant information are then forwarded to the Home Secretary.

Exclusion orders may be revoked entirely but cannot be suspended. Such a concession was suggested by the Colville Report[43] and might usefully allow subjects to attend events such as funerals or to transit through the forbidden territory.

(b)   Representations
Once an exclusion order has been made or renewed, a notice must be served on the suspect under section 7(1) '[a]s soon as may be'.[44] The notice shall:

(a)   set out the rights afforded to him [under this Act]; and
(b)   specify the manner in which those rights are to be exercised.

In practice, the person will also be given a copy of the exclusion order, and the terms of the notice should be explained and arrangements for removal discussed.[45] However, the executive is relieved of its statutory obligations in the case of the exclusion of a person who is outside the United Kingdom,[46] while subjects who are not in detention may be notified by letter to their last-known address.[47]

Following service, Schedule 2 paragraph 3(1) states that:

If . . . the person against whom [the exclusion order] is made objects to the order he may –
(a)   make representations in writing to the Secretary of State setting out the grounds of his objections; and
(b)   include in those representations a request for a personal interview with the person or persons nominated by the Secretary of State. . . .

Full details of the person's objections need not be revealed at this stage, but the request must be made within the statutory time-limit.[48] This is seven days from the service of the notice, unless the person consents to removal during that period to another territory within the United Kingdom or to the Republic of Ireland or is already in the required part of the United Kingdom, in which case interviews may be requested within fourteen days of removal.[49] The current time-limits are considerably more generous than those specified in pre-1984 versions of the Act. The improvement is designed to encourage suspects to make representations after removal, thereby avoiding the considerable disincentive of further incarceration pending review.[50] This objective has been secured to a significant extent,[51] but it is arguable that Advisers should intervene automatically, whether or not a request or representations have been made.

If a valid request is made, the matter shall be referred for the advice of one or more persons nominated by the Secretary of State.[52] Persons detained within the United Kingdom have a legal right to a 'personal interview' with the Secretary of State's Adviser,[53] but those who have been removed with consent may be denied an interview if it does not appear to the Secretary of State to be 'reasonably practicable to grant him such an interview in an appropriate country within a reasonable period . . .'.[54] The appropriate territories and country comprise Northern Ireland or the Republic of Ireland (for section 5), Great Britain or the Republic (for section 6) and the Republic (for section 7).[55] Any choice between them is in the gift of the Secretary of State,[56] who may also determine the venue (which is usually at a police station for Northern Ireland interviews or the British Embassy in Dublin for Irish Republic interviews).[57]

When an interview is granted, a single Adviser is delegated to form an independent view of the merits of the case.[58] His report will usually be based on two pieces of evidence.[59] Firstly, he sees all the materials placed before the Secretary of State. Secondly, he holds an interview with the suspect.[60] It is not clear how far a system of precedent operates, but it would be strange if Advisers did not find it helpful to refer to earlier cases, especially as most have been lawyers[61] and the Home Office makes available to each a file containing all his earlier reports.[62] There is no right to legal representation, but it is often permitted.[63] Regrettably, Advisers have no investigative facilities and do not even conduct interviews with other relevant witnesses, including police officers, though they do take account of written submissions tendered by suspects.[64]

Following an interview, the Adviser makes a report on receipt of which the Secretary of State is enjoined to:[65]

(1) . . . reconsider the matter as soon as is reasonably practicable . . .
(2) . . . take into account everything which appears to him to be relevant and in particular –
(a) the representations relating to the matter made to him [by the subject] . . .

(b) the advice of the person or persons to whom the matter was referred by him . . . and

(c) the report of any interview [with an Adviser] relating to the matter. . . .

The word 'reconsider' is meant to imply that the Secretary of State need not accept the recommendations of the Adviser, which form just one of three pertinent considerations. In practice, however, the Home Secretary has, with one exception, always followed a recommendation to revoke and has even cancelled some orders contrary to an Adviser's wishes.[66]

After reconsideration,[67] the Secretary of State must give written notice of his final decision 'if it is reasonably practicable to do so . . .'.[68] This proviso differs from that relating to the original notice in that it may apply to persons remaining within the United Kingdom. The notice specifies the relevant statutory authority and terms of the order, but security considerations inevitably preclude the giving of explanations.[69] Finally, assuming the order is confirmed (or if the person consents or has made no representations), Schedule 2 grants powers physically to remove the person.[70]

(c) Ancillary matters

Save for those already outside the relevant territory or country when excluded,[71] the implementation of exclusion invariably entails detention as a preliminary step. This may be secured in two ways. First, travellers may be 'examined' at a 'designated port' to see if they are concerned in terrorism and therefore liable to exclusion or if already subject to an order.[72] If the former applies, they may be detained 'pending consideration by the Secretary of State whether to make an exclusion order';[73] if already subject to an order, they may be detained pending removal.[74] Secondly, there is no specific detention power at inland locations solely because exclusion is contemplated, but most candidates will be arrestable as suspected terrorists under section 14(1)(b); those already subject to orders can be held under section 14(1)(c).[75] The maximum period of a detention of those not subject to an order is seven days.

Once an order is made, detention will continue pending any review by an Adviser, the giving of directions for removal by the Secretary of State and then the physical removal of the person.[76] Normally, the subject will be held in a police station for seven days and will then be transferred to a prison, unless removal is to occur within twenty-four hours.[77] During detention, the person is liable to be photographed and measured for record purposes.[78] The period of detention is reviewed under Schedule 3; a review officer (a senior policeman) must be satisfied as soon as detention begins and at twelve-hourly intervals thereafter that removal is being arranged 'diligently and expeditiously'.[79] This review system was introduced in 1989 and is to be welcomed, but it is odd that it extends for a far longer period than for more vulnerable detainees under sections 14 or 16.[80] Other safeguards under the Police and Criminal Evidence Codes do not apply to detainees,[81] save that custody records are recommended by circular.[82]

Directions for the removal of persons subject to exclusion orders may oblige ship or aircraft owners, agents or captains to provide a berth or may refer to 'arrangements to be made . . .', which allows flexible use to be made of regular transport links with Ireland.[83] Removal by land may alternatively be ordered for exclusion from Northern Ireland to the Republic. Legislative authority to issue specific directions for removal is also conferred on examining officers in respect of persons detained at ports, but these powers are in practice 'convenient' only against persons already subject to an order, whose summary removal is desired.[84]

Whichever method is adopted, the destination of the person must be a country or territory:[85]

(a) of which the person in question is a national or citizen;
(b) in which he obtained a passport or other document of identity; or
(c) to which there is reason to believe that he will be admitted.

A person to be removed after examination at a port may also be returned to the country or territory from which he embarked.[86] In other respects, the person's connections with a country or territory or his expressed wishes as to his destination need not be considered.[87] However, there is a proviso that British and certain Commonwealth citizens may not be displaced to a place outside the United Kingdom, unless they are nationals or citizens of, or have indicated their willingness to be removed to, that country or territory.[88] This creates the possibility of British citizens with dual nationality being removed against their wishes, which would appear to conflict with section 7(4) of the Act.[89]

In view of the fact that an excludee suffers from the effects of an executive security measure which is never (unlike, say, binding over or many deportations) subject to judicial authorisation, a strong case for compensation may be made. Accordingly, the costs of physical removal are met by the Secretary of State,[90] but the only other concession to the welfare of the person is that he should not be returned to Northern Ireland after 7.30 p.m. If a later arrival time is envisaged, the person is penniless and has no easily accessible home address, an *ex gratia* payment of £15 should be made.[91] However, losses in terms of relocation or unemployment are not recoverable.

Finally, a variety of offences under section 8 deal with breaches of exclusion orders:

(1) A person who is subject to an exclusion order is guilty of an offence if he fails to comply with the order at a time after he has been, or has become liable to be, removed under [this Act].

(2) A person is guilty of an offence

(a) if he is knowingly concerned in arrangements for securing or facilitating the entry into [the relevant country or territory] of a person whom he knows, or has reasonable grounds for believing, to be an excluded person; or

(b) if he knowingly harbours such a person. . . .

The wording of section 8(1) ensures that a person commits no offence until he has been served with an order and has had a chance to make representations. Equally however, the Act does not allow for access to an Adviser by a person who has not yet been served.[92] Even an excluded person who is in transit through a forbidden United Kingdom port to a foreign destination is liable to arrest and prosecution.[93] 'Knowingly' in subsection (2) probably imports a requirement of *mens rea* as to all the elements of the offence save that it is sufficient merely to believe on reasonable grounds that the person aided has been excluded.[94]

By the end of 1990, there had been twenty-three charges under section 8(1) in Great Britain resulting in twenty convictions; six persons were fined and thirteen imprisoned.[95] Under subsection (2), there had been four charges, three convictions, one sentence of imprisonment and two fines. In Northern Ireland, there have been just eight charges, all under subsection (1) and all before 1984. The offences may be tried either way and carry penalties ranging from five years' imprisonment to a fine. In the case of Jude Charles Arbuckle in 1981,[96] it was held that imprisonment rather than a fine is appropriate for an offence under section 8(1).

2 Comparisons

(a) Position under general law of citizens of the Irish Republic

The treatment in British immigration law of Irish citizens is significantly better than that accorded to most foreigners. For example, their entry and residence is virtually unrestricted because the Republic and United Kingdom form a 'Common Travel Area' under section 1(3) of the Immigration Act 1971. This means that travellers on a 'local journey'[97] within the Area can enter the United Kingdom without permission, and refusal is possible under section 9(4) only on the grounds of a previous refusal to enter or because of national security interests.[98]

The powers to deport Irish citizens are also curtailed. Section 3(5) and (6) of the Act provide that a person other than a British citizen may be deported if he does not observe his conditions of entry, if another member of his family is deported, if he is convicted of an imprisonable offence for which the court recommends deportation or if the Secretary of State deems it to be conducive to the public good. The first ground does not apply to any Irish citizens, and, by section 7, those who were ordinarily resident on 1 January 1973 and, at the time of the Home Secretary's decision to order deportation or at the date of conviction in the case of a court's recommendation, have been so resident for the previous five years, are wholly exempted from deportation. Thus, only Irish citizens not falling within section 7 can be deported as suspected terrorists. In practice all Irish citizens are excluded rather than deported.[99]

Entry into the United Kingdom by Irish citizens is also safeguarded by Article 48(1) of the Treaty of Rome, which states that '[f]reedom of movement for workers shall be secured within the Community . . .'.[100] However, this Article does little to prevent the banning or removal of Irish terrorists[101] for two reasons. First, Article 48 benefits only 'workers' or those genuinely seeking work[102] and not persons whose purpose of entry is to perpetrate political violence. Of course, an entrant's intentions may be far from obvious, and a terrorist may also enter as the spouse or dependant of a genuine worker. Therefore, removal will usually occur after entry pursuant to Article 48(3), by which the movement and residence of Community nationals is 'subject to the limitations justified on grounds of public policy, public security or public health . . .'.[103] Most suspected terrorists will readily fall under the 'public security' exception.[104] Thus, exclusion cannot easily be impugned either because of its substantive effects[105] or even because of its scant regard for due process.[106]

The refusal of entry or removal under the Immigration Act 1971 of non-E.E.C. aliens suspected of terrorism is even more unassailable, as illustrated by the examples in chapter 3 and by the arrest with a view to deportation of 160 Iraqis and 12 others during the Gulf War in 1991.[107] The Court of Appeal dismissed a legal challenge in *R.* v. *Secretary of State for the Home Department, ex parte Cheblak*[108] on the ground that the weighing of national security considerations was exclusively for the Home Secretary and his Advisory Panel. Consequently, the Government has dismissed the extension of exclusion to foreign terrorists.[109] Furthermore, concessions in favour of refugees and stateless persons are subject to expulsion on national security grounds,[110] the application of which to a Palestinian asylum-seeker with alleged terrorist links was upheld in *R.* v. *Secretary of State for the Home Department, ex parte NSH*.[111]

(b) Position under general law of British citizens

Apart from the uniquely privileged treatment of Irish citizens, legal controls on movement are absent in two further directions.

First, there are no statutory restrictions concerning rights of entry, exit or place of residence of British citizens. As regards departure, it may be possible to withdraw or refuse to issue a passport under the royal prerogative,[112] which could hinder the movement of British citizens suspected of involvement in terrorism. However, no such attempt has yet come to light. Similarly, there are no direct legal powers to restrict on security grounds the place of abode of a British citizen. Again, this objective might be achieved indirectly through the attachment of residence conditions to binding orders,[113] but two features make it unlikely. First, a binding-over order is normally imposed following proof in open court of criminal or other misbehaviour. Second, the subject must consent to entering into a recognisance with the condition that he leaves a part or the whole of the country.[114] Consequently, there has been no report of any suspected terrorist being despatched in this fashion.

(c) Past special controls
The various spheres where controls are lacking in regular law, in regard to entry and exit by both Irish and British citizens and travel within the United Kingdom, have all been the objects of attention of earlier legislation during this century.[115] For example, the Defence of the Realm Regulation 14E, made in August 1916,[116] restricted travel between Britain and Ireland by non-British subjects or by British subjects (of the ilk of Sir Roger Casement) who had returned from abroad recently. Restrictions were reimposed in 1939 by the Defence (General) Regulation 18(2).[117] The Home Secretary's permit was thereafter required for travel between Britain and Northern Ireland.[118] This was primarily to prevent travellers contacting German diplomats in Dublin or evading national service,[119] though the Regulation also served to hinder the I.R.A. campaign in Britain which had begun in 1939. Additional measures in Northern Ireland reinforced Regulation 18(2) by requiring persons entering the Province from Britain to satisfy the police or a court that their presence was proper.[120]

Enacted shortly before these Second World War restrictions was the Prevention of Violence (Temporary Provisions) Act 1939, the most direct forebear of Part II of the Prevention of Terrorism Acts. 'Expulsion' under section 1(2) of the 1939 Act allowed the Home Secretary to make an order removing suspected terrorists from Britain, though there was no power to deport even non-citizens from the whole of the United Kingdom. Orders of 'prohibition' under section 1(4) prevented suspected terrorists entering Britain from both parts of Ireland, though again no protection was given to Northern Ireland. Residents of twenty years' standing were exempted from both powers, and section 2 also provided for objectors to be interviewed by advisers of the Secretary of State. During the fifteen years of the Act's existence, 190 exclusion, and 71 prohibition, orders were made, almost all in 1939 and 1940.[121]

Since terrorism in Ireland is indigenous, exclusion has rarely been adopted,[122] and no comparative measures exist at present in the Republic.

(d) Summary
Part II of the Prevention of Terrorism Act, like the forerunners just described, is explicable by reference to lacunae in British immigration and travel

laws. However, it could be argued that a simpler remedy than exclusion, and one more in keeping with the principle of minimising reliance upon special laws, would have been to abrogate the exemptions under section 7 of the Immigration Act in respect of Irish citizens suspected of being terrorists. This would have made redundant section 7 of the Prevention of Terrorism Act, since such persons could instead be deported. However, the Government has maintained that exclusion is preferable for two reasons.[123] First, Part II carries heavier penalties and so is more likely to be obeyed. Second, exclusion expires after three years and so is less Draconian than deportation, which lasts indefinitely. Yet both these points could easily be incorporated within temporary amending legislation to section 7 of the Immigration Act. This alternative approach would be marginally preferable to the present special measures if it were necessary to restrict only citizens of the Republic. However, it should be recalled that travel within the United Kingdom and by British citizens generally is relevant but wholly beyond the purview of the Immigration Act. Therefore, it must next be considered whether Part II is justified in filling those gaps and whether it does so in a satisfactory manner.

3 Assessment

(a) Use in practice
Before embarking upon that inquiry, Table 1, which indicates how exclusion has actually been implemented, will first be discussed.

The powers in Part II were frequently invoked in Britain during the early days of the Act's life, suggesting that the Special Branch had made preparations well before enactment. There followed a lull in 1976 and 1977 which was probably attributable not to any sharp decrease in terroristic activity but to the fact that the police had already removed the most obvious suspects, so finding evidence against new candidates was more painstaking. The variable pattern of use since 1977 demonstrates there is no close correlation between new exclusion orders and overt terrorist activity. An explanation for this might be that police monitoring remains constantly at a high level, even when violent incidents are few.

The figures for the extant totals are revealing. A peak of 248 orders in 1982 has shrunk to a depleted figure of 97 by 1990. The reasons for this trend are two-fold. The statutory reviews undertaken since 1984 have had the most direct impact. Four hundred and thirty-three orders have been revoked or have expired,[124] and only 150 (35 per cent) renewed. The renewal rate is increasing (51 per cent for 1988–90, compared to 36 per cent for 1985–87), as might be expected when the review exercise is repeated. Next, police tactics may also have been influential. It seems that exclusion was used as a palliative in the early years – to remove suspects en masse;

Table 1 The operation of exclusion in Great Britain

Year	Applications	Orders made	Location of subject			Removal to		Already outside GB	Orders ended		Orders renewed	Cummulative total in force
			Detained at port	Detained elsewhere	Not detained	Northern Ireland	Republic of Ireland		Revocation of expiry	Death		
1974	22	19	1	11	7	7	5	4	3	–	–	16
1975	61	50	25	21	4	32	12	1	5	–	–	62
1976	28	24	15	8	1	17	6	–	1	–	–	84
1977	18	18	12	5	1	16	1	–	1	–	–	99
1978	57	53	40	9	4	49	3	1	1	1	–	150
1979	58	53	42	6	5	44	4	4	6	1	1	196
1980	59	49	42	3	4	43	5	–	4	–	–	241
1981	17	11	8	2	1	10	1	–	8	–	–	244
1982	17	15	9	2	4	12	–	3	10	1	1	248
1983	16	15	11	2	2	13	2	–	18	1	–	244
1984	6	3	1	–	2	2	1	–	8	1	–	238
1985	7	7	1	1	5	3	4	–	46	1	16	214
1986	11	9	1	6	2	8	1	–	161	–	54	116
1987	22	19	10	5	4	16	3	–	40	1	17	111
1988	25	20	9	7	4	13	7	–	22	–	13	122
1989	10	9	7	2	–	8	1	–	60	1	24	94
1990	17	16	4	11	1	12	4	–	37	–	24	97
Total	451	390	238	101	51	305	60	13	431	7	150	

Source: Home Office.

in later years, the police have preferred to gather evidence and to prosecute and so consider exclusion only when that fails. This trend may be reflected in the location of the subjects. Ignoring 1974 and 1975, when there was a hurried clearing of long-standing suspects, most removals between 1976 and 1980 (77 per cent) followed detentions at ports and were therefore interceptions at source. Since 1980, only 49 per cent followed port detentions. Incidentally, it is clear that few subjects (4 per cent) are already outside Britain; thus, it is not the practice to issue orders unless there is firm evidence of an intention to visit Britain.

The destination of those removed is usually Northern Ireland (78 per cent). This proportion was somewhat lower in the early years when long-term residents were being processed.

Some pointers are also provided as to how effectively applications are being scrutinized. A significant number of applications (14 per cent) are refused by the Secretary of State on advice from the National Joint Unit or his officials. Thereafter, the recommendations of Advisers in the eighty-nine cases so referred have accounted for twenty-nine revocations (33 per cent).

Exclusions ordered in Northern Ireland have been few by comparison – see Table 2. Even taking into account the orders made by the Home Secretary banning Irish citizens from the whole of the United Kingdom, exclusion has been employed very sparingly in Northern Ireland. The obvious reason for this paucity is that most terrorism in that location is perpetrated by residents who are exempt from exclusion.[125] Further, the value of excluding Irish citizens is dubious in view of the insecurity of the border.[126] Only four persons (all suspected Loyalist terrorists) have been excluded to Britain,[127] confirming that reciprocity has, as predicted by the Government in 1976, turned out to be a red herring. Reviews have also made less impact than in Britain on the first triennial scrutiny in 1986, but the second round in 1989 was more stringent. Advisers now have an increasing influence; four out of the ten cases referred to them between 1987 and 1990 have resulted in revocation; whereas there were only two referrals with one revocation to the end of 1982.

Adding further flesh to these bare statistics, a number of trends may be detected in the employment of exclusion orders in Britain. The first is that persons who have fallen foul of security laws in Northern Ireland will immediately become possible candidates for exclusion should they arrive in Britain. This used to be the practice in regard to former internees. For example, Charles Anthony Devine[128] was released from internment in December 1974 on condition that he left Northern Ireland. Devine found a job in Germany, but, while lodging en route with relatives in Liverpool, was arrested and returned to Northern Ireland.

Similar treatment is accorded to ex-convicts from Northern Ireland. For

Table 2   The operation of exclusion in Northern Ireland

Year	Excluded from N.I.	Excluded from U.K.	Total orders	Orders revoked/ expired	Orders renewed	Cumulative total in force
1974	–	–	–	N/A	N/A	–
1975	–	1	1	N/A	N/A	1
1976	–	1	1	N/A	N/A	2
1977	–	–	–	N/A	N/A	2
1978	–	2	2	N/A	N/A	4
1979	–	4	4	N/A	N/A	8
1980	1	2	3	N/A	N/A	11
1981	6	5	11	N/A	N/A	20
1982	–	2	2	N/A	N/A	22
1983	N/A	N/A	4	N/A	N/A	26
1984	N/A	N/A	2	N/A	N/A	28
1985	N/A	N/A	–	–	–	26
1986	N/A	N/A	–	–	–	26
1987	N/A	N/A	1	3	25	22
1988	N/A	N/A	1	2	1	22
1989	N/A	N/A	1	1	1	23
1990	N/A	N/A	–	14	6	9
Total	7	17	33	20	33	

Source: N.I. Office, Colville Annual Reports on E.P. Acts. *Note*: N/A = figures not available.

example, Patrick O'Hagan, on leave from Belfast Prison, was excluded after he visited his brother in Yorkshire, albeit with the Governor's consent.[129] Irish people convicted of terrorist offences in Britain are likewise often excluded on their release (notably the 'Winchester Three'),[130] and this practice also extends to defendants who have been cleared of charges[131] and even to suspects who have been arrested but not charged.[132]

A second trend in the use of exclusion is its invocation against Republican activists.[133] Thus, many of the early victims of exclusion were prominent members and officials both of Sinn Fein and of Clann na h'Eireann (the Republican movement in Britain).[134] Probably the most notorious illustration in this category occurred in December 1982, when Gerry Adams, Danny Morrison and Martin McGuiness, all leading figures in Provisional Sinn Fein, were confined to Northern Ireland.[135] The Prime Minister claimed that the orders were justified 'on the basis of intelligence about the men's involvement in terrorist activity'.[136] However, doubt was cast on this assertion by subsequent events. Following the election of Adams to Parliament in June 1983, the Government immediately revoked his exclusion order. Since this was not required as a matter of parliamentary privilege, it seems probable that the lifting of the ban was predominantly motivated by political considerations, such as avoiding adverse publicity. However, this finding must bring into question the propriety of the original imposition of exclusion. If the Home Secretary genuinely made the orders because he was convinced of the suspect's involvement in terrorism, the lifting of the order in respect of Adams becomes incomprehensible.[137] That election, by giving this supposedly dangerous terrorist ready access to prime targets, such as the Houses of Parliament and prominent public figures, surely increased rather than reduced the need for exclusion. Consequently, it may be inferred that political rather than security considerations also weighed heavily in the decision to make the order in the first place.

It is vehemently denied in official circles that a person's political allegiances ever justify exclusion. According to one Home Secretary:[138]

I can assure the House that nobody . . . has been excluded because of his views, however extreme they may be. I have been concerned with gelignite, not with ideology.

However, involvement in 'extremist' organisations, such as Sinn Fein and the Ulster Defence Association, does often prompt exclusion, even though such groups are not proscribed anywhere in the United Kingdom. This is a most disturbing feature of the use of exclusion powers, since its effect is to shield the people of Britain not so much from violence as from unpalatable political viewpoints.

A third trend in the exercise of exclusion is the lack of importance attached to family and community ties. To say, as Lord Shackleton did, that 'welfare considerations cannot override the needs of the security of society as a whole',[139] presents a false dichotomy. Taking such matters into account is consistent with the rationale of exclusion, for police investigations most prosper when a suspect has firmly established contacts and habits. However, these arguments have in practice carried little weight, and residents of long standing have been excluded.[140] Fortunately, the reduction to three years of the qualifying period for exemption from exclusion has alleviated this problem, though not in so far as it affects citizens of the Republic.

(b) Purpose
The basic objective of, and justification for, each exclusion order is that it prevents terrorism:[141]

First . . . exclusion has rid Great Britain of dangerous terrorists. Second . . . terrorists have found their effectiveness in general substantially impaired by the fact that they were no longer able to travel legally between Northern Ireland and the mainland or between the Republic of Ireland and the United Kingdom as a whole.

The system may be unfair to the suspect compared to a criminal trial, but this is felt to be more than outweighed by the likely reduction in terrorism, which, by reason of its extreme violence and threat to the general public, is distinguishable from other serious crimes.[142] As is conceded by the Home Office Circular on the Act,[143] criminal charges are preferable if sufficient evidence is available to sustain them, for imprisonment is a more effective method of prevention. However, exclusion does have some countervailing attractions. First, it allows disruptive intervention at an earlier stage, since an order may be based on inadmissible evidence and may be granted even when the level of proof does not reach the criminal standard. Second, the police may prefer to resort to exclusion in order to avoid disclosing in open court the names of informers or methods of investigation.

This goal of prevention is likely to be achieved if three conditions are met. The first is that, in respect of each person excluded, there is evidence to suggest that he is likely to engage in terrorism in the future (past actions are only relevant to predicting future conduct, since exclusion is not intended as a punishment). The second condition is that it is reasonable to predict that exclusion will diminish the suspect's ability to commit terroristic violence in his new abode. The third condition is that, since exclusion is 'the most extreme of the Act's powers',[144] it follows, as one of the principles enunciated in chapter 2, that it should derogate as little as factually necessary from civil rights. As part of this consideration, it should also be clear that the police are unable to ensure that the person is not engaging in terrorism at his present residence by normal methods of police investigation but removal makes this more feasible.[145]

It is extremely difficult to demonstrate empirically that exclusion has, or is ever likely to, prevent terrorism, as deterrence resulting in inaction is not susceptible to direct measurement. However, if it is accepted that the three conditions just set out must be satisfied in order to achieve that objective, exclusion is probably a failure.

The problem in relation to the first condition is that too little is done to ensure convincing evidence that the person is likely to engage in terrorism in the future. Relevant material is of dubious quality, and the suspect has little opportunity to cast doubt on the case against him. How far alternative procedures would be more searching and, at the same time, better secure civil liberties, as required by the third condition, will be considered later in this chapter.

As for the second condition, of ensuring that the suspect's change of abode hinders any potential involvement in terrorism, advocates of exclusion seem to ignore the detrimental effects of removing a suspect to Ireland. For instance, a person returned to the Republic is beyond the scrutiny of United Kingdom police forces, and the Irish police will also encounter difficulties in investigating him, as his contacts and habits are bound to have changed. Even if the person is excluded only as far as Northern Ireland, the Royal Ulster Constabulary face these same problems as well as the drawback that exclusion provides an added grievance and terrorist groups in Northern Ireland offer bountiful opportunities for satiating such resentment.[146] In consequence, one can understand why the British police are 'ardent supporters' of exclusion:[147]

With one accord they say that they would not be able to provide surveillance for all the Irish terrorists who might arrive. Any one of these could and probably would travel through the areas of several forces. In terms of the number of officers and vehicles needed for a full surveillance operation, there would be a consequent drain on resources and ability to perform other policing duties.

However, the overall effect on terrorism, if any, will be displacement rather than prevention, while the impact on policing will be 'to add to the heavy load already borne by the RUC and the armed forces'.[148] The inference is that terrorism in Northern Ireland is not as politically important as terrorism in Britain.[149] This may have been less obvious in November 1974, when internment in Northern Ireland offered the possibility of removing excluded persons from circulation. However, it was officially denied that this devious scenario was ever contemplated,[150] nor was it achieved in practice, as the view was taken that suspicious activities in Britain were irrelevant to detention in Northern Ireland.[151] Any lingering plans to intern excludees were, of course, totally scotched by the ending of internment in 1975, and the Royal Ulster Constabulary have not even bothered to question most arrivals since then,[152] though they do maintain some special scrutiny.[153]

Criticisms that Northern Ireland is used as a dumping ground for terrorists were taken to heart by the Jellicoe Report, which recommended two remedies. The first was that the residence exemption should be extended, as already described. Second, the Home Secretary was to consider the possible deleterious effects for Britain and Northern Ireland before making an order.[154] In response, the Home Secretary has promised to canvass the views of the police in both relevant territories.[155] It is claimed that exclusion on this reformed basis will disrupt terrorist lines of communications and reduce the suspect's usefulness by virtue of the overt police interest in him and that these benefits will enure to all parts of the United Kingdom.[156] However, logic would suggest that these goals are more likely to be attained by ordering Irish terrorists to remain in, or even to move to, Britain where the police are able to operate more effectively and where there are fewer opportunities to engage in terrorism. Despite this logic, it is reported that the R.U.C. 'has accepted that it is easier to prevent terrorism if it can be contained in Northern Ireland, where the security forces are better equipped to deal with it'.[157] Yet facts such as a lower crime clear-up rate and

communities more supportive of paramilitaries do not tally with this acceptance. One must agree that 'it is enormously costly to keep constant
surveillance on people who are themselves trained to evade it, and it is an
extremely risky approach when people's lives are at risk'.[158] However, are
the costs and risks any less in Northern Ireland? The only convincing
counter-argument is perhaps that exclusion saves police time since there is
no need to build up a painstaking forensic case against the suspect.[159]
However, this reasoning would only be acceptable if terrorism were
overwhelming police resources in the territory benefiting from exclusion,
which has never been the situation in Britain.

In conclusion, just as Part II is an excessive response to terrorism from
the Republic, so its effectiveness against terrorists from Northern Ireland
seems highly dubious. Such doubts will be increased in so far as the present
system fails to require objective proof of future involvement in violence
or to minimise derogations from civil rights. These matters will now be
examined.

(c) *Criticisms of the exclusion system*
Two criticisms may be raised concerning the 'inherently arbitrary and
oppressive'[160] system prevailing under Part II. First, it makes it less certain
that the incriminating evidence is truthful, because it is by no means as
rigorously examined as it would be in a criminal trial. This is a drawback
in that the firmer the evidence the more likely the suspect is, based on past
behaviour, to reengage in terrorism, thereby securing the objective of the
prevention of terrorism. The second consequence is that it derogates still
further from the civil rights of the suspect. Not only is he subjected to a
system of 'internal banishment'[161] (or 'summary deportation' in the case of
citizens of the Republic), but he must endure it stripped of most rights of
due process and natural law.

These connected defects lead to two further issues, also raised in relation
to proscription. The first is how far the courts can at present control the
procedures under Part II. This is of vital interest, as it would render the
shortcomings under the Act less important if there existed effective checks
outside it. The second issue is how far judicial control should extend and
whether this corresponds to the currently prevailing degree of review.

(i) *Current degree of judicial review*   In reply to the first question, it has
been asserted that exclusion is 'not subject to review by the courts . . .'.[162]
The issue arose in *R. v. Secretary of State for Home Affairs, ex parte
Stitt*,[163] when Sean Stitt, a community worker from Belfast, sought to
overturn an order against him. Three principal arguments against judicial
review may be relevant.

The first is that the statutory Adviser system under section 7 provides 'a comprehensive package of rights'[164] which renders common law judicial review impliedly unnecessary. Though the courts are often reluctant to accept this argument 'particularly when the statutory remedy is in the hands of an administrative body . . .',[165] it received some support in Stitt's case. In the leading judgment of Watkins L.J., three grounds advanced by the respondents were examined: the 'package' argument, a claim that national security and confidentiality made review inappropriate, and concern about delay in bringing the application. The second ground prevailed as 'powerfully persuasive' and 'the central issue';[166] delay was said to be unimportant, but no comment was offered on the strength of the 'package' argument. The judgment of MacPherson J. is more forthright:[167]

. . . I agree that Parliament prescribed in the [Prevention of Terrorism Acts] a defined package of rights for those who might be or have been excluded from this country.

Yet delay and confidentiality are also cited for his rejection of review. Thus, the issue of sensitive information is the common basis for the decision, but this consideration, though relevant to many orders, need not arise in all challenges or prevent review without consideration of the evidence. However, the balance of *obiter* remarks also points towards acceptance of the 'package' argument, which is a more fundamental obstacle.

Arguments about the sensitivity of information and the existence of statutory appeals were echoed in *ex parte Cheblak*, in which the further point was raised that the Home Secretary is accountable to Parliament and so judicial review is largely superfluous.[168]

Another line of reasoning against review (not raised in *ex parte Stitt*) is based on the subjective wording of the Secretary of State's powers. Phraseology which requires a Minister to be 'satisfied' as to vague criteria is a 'commonplace technique in emergency legislation',[169] but its interpretation has been less constant. Nevertheless, it is now received wisdom that the courts retain a supervisory jurisdiction.[170]

In summary, any decision by a Secretary of State to exclude may be treated as non-justiciable, but it is arguable that the reluctance of the courts to intervene extends only to the reasons for the decision by the Minister and not to other matters (such as preconditions or procedures). Assuming that some review remains possible (as it did in *ex parte Cheblak*), its application will now be determined.

There are various forms of error affecting jurisdiction[171] which may trigger judicial intervention, such as where the competent authority has misdirected itself by applying the wrong legal test or by misunderstanding a matter in respect of which it must be satisfied.[172] This form of review is relevant to exclusion, but, as shall be described later, will be constrained by judicial unwillingness to seek out sensitive information. Thus, as in

Stitt's case, there will be no effective inquiry into whether the suspect can properly be labelled a 'terrorist'. However, four other issues may be examinable.[173] The first two – whether the person is 'ordinarily resident' and whether residence has endured for three years or more – are relevant to sections 5 and 6, and a court might act if a suspect complains that either term has been misinterpreted. A third area where intervention may arise is whether the person qualifies as a 'British citizen' under the British Nationality Act 1981. Finally, the 'appropriateness' of an order may be challenged but is less likely to be impugned, as it is difficult to show that the interpretation of such a vague term is wholly mistaken in law.

As well as errors of substance, certain procedural errors may be reviewable.[173] Thus, the courts might ensure that an order has actually been made and has been approved by the proper authority.[174] Next, the formal requirements under Schedule 2, such as the giving of the relevant notices, allowing representations, requiring reference to an Adviser and conferring a right to a personal interview, must all be considered mandatory.[175] Questions may also be raised when the Secretary of State reconsiders the case, though proof that he did not genuinely apply his mind will be difficult to find. Finally, the right of non-removal pending reconsideration is also enforceable.

Judicial review may next be triggered by abuses of discretion. By and large, evidential difficulties will ensure that challenges on the basis of irrationality[176] have little impact or are non-justiciable, subject to three exceptions.

First, if, contrary to its common practice, the executive reveals the information on which it acted, these reasons can be scrutinised. For example, in the *Attorney General of Saint Christopher, Nevis and Anguilla* v. *Reynolds*,[177] when an order for the detention of the respondent was challenged, counsel for the Crown made the extraordinary admission that:[178]

I have no evidence against [him] . . . I will speak to the authorities.

Clearly, proof that the order was unreasonable was available in those exceptional circumstances. However, the judges emphasised that they would have been accommodating towards the authorities had they chosen to rebut the respondent's allegations:[179]

Naturally, the Governor would not have been obliged to furnish anyone with his sources of his information if he considered that it was contrary to public policy to do so.

A second area where reasonableness is relevant concerns the duration of exclusion orders. In *Teh Cheng Poh* v. *Public Prosecutor of Malaysia*,[180] the Privy Council opined *obiter* that the decision whether to revoke a proclamation of a state of emergency 'is not entirely unfettered'. This suggests that executive security measures must be reconsidered after the lapse of a reasonable period, otherwise the relevant powers of revocation will have been abused. However, the statutory triennial review is probably sufficient to meet any challenge of this kind.

A third line of attack on grounds of unreasonableness concerns the time which elapses before any final decision to exclude. The Act specifies no deadline by which the Secretary of State must confirm or revoke an order following referral to an Adviser. However, a requirement as to reasonableness would be judicially imposed, especially as the person may in the meantime be incarcerated.[181]

The next forms of abuse of discretion are disregarding legally relevant, or taking into account legally irrelevant, considerations. For example, it would be improper for the Home Secretary to deploy his powers against Arab terrorists whose activities are unrelated to Northern Ireland. A further abuse would occur if the Home Secretary signed an order without reflection of any kind. However, the processing of a large number of applications in a short time does not raise such an inference.[182] Failure to specify any reasons for exclusion will certainly not be deemed to be evidence of abuse in view of the sensitive nature of the evidence involved.[183]

Problems of proof are also the main hindrance to the third form of abuse of discretion, namely bad faith on the part of the decision-maker. The following hypothetical facts may provide an illustration:[184]

A bank in Cork is relieved of a large sum of money by a gunman ... gossip ... points to a particular man who abandoned his usual haunts shortly before the robbery, and who surfaced shortly after it in Liverpool, where he now lives in adequate comfort without visible means of support.

Rather than troubling the courts under the Backing of Warrants (Republic of Ireland) Act 1965, the Home Secretary might be tempted simply to make an exclusion order which can deliver the suspect, provided he is not a British citizen, to the Republic. The Secretary of State might reply to any allegations of improper purposes that, given the I.R.A.'s propensity for financing itself by robbery, he had a genuine suspicion that the person was a terrorist and not a bank-robber *simpliciter*. Unless the authorities let it slip that exclusion is a sham, it will be impossible to find any other damning evidence.[185]

The final basis for judicial review is failure to comply with natural justice. It is unlikely that the initial making of an order by the Secretary of State is at all affected. One reason is that the statutory Adviser system rather than natural justice is available to remedy any errors at the earlier stage.[186] A second reason is that such prior notification of a suspect would make it difficult to investigate, apprehend or remove him, thereby defeating the preventive aim of the Act.[187]

By contrast, natural justice may be applicable to the Adviser system. The interests affected by the process are vital and basic, and the procedures are designed to be impartial and objective.[188] Furthermore, procedural safeguards at this stage will not endanger the objectives of exclusion, as the police's interest will already have been revealed to the suspect who is already in detention.[189] Amongst the requirements of natural justice could be the giving of adequate notice of the interview with the Adviser, so that the suspect may prepare his case. Similarly, reasonable requests for adjournments should be granted, for example, if a person wishes to obtain the statement of a material witness. However, the recurrent problem of sensitive information makes it unlikely that the present practice of suppressing the adverse allegations or reasons for the Secretary of State's decision could be impugned.[190] Natural justice will also have a restricted impact on the procedures followed at the interview itself. For example, the suspect may probably be denied a right to call or cross-examine witnesses. Aside from the risks to security, the Act grants only a 'personal' interview,[191] which seems to debar third parties. Equally, legal representation is not required in most cases, since the procedure is meant to be inquisitorial and informal. The same may apply to accompaniment by a friend, but if the purpose of such assistance is merely to take notes or to act as a mouthpiece, the attendance of such a person, even if a lawyer, is not in conflict with the concept of a 'personal' interview. A similar view was taken in Northern Ireland concerning representations before the Advisory Committee reviewing internment orders. In *Re Mackey* in 1972,[192] it was held that only in complex or special cases would it be unfair to forbid full legal representation. The court reserved its judgment on how far lawyers could act as mere 'agents', but their use was subsequently allowed in practice.[193] In *ex parte Cheblak*, the court emphasised that the Advisory Panel was to be viewed as inquisitorial in nature, and so it, rather than the subject, should take the lead in amassing information.

An obstacle to most forms of judicial review mentioned hitherto is the sensitive nature of the information involved:[194]

It is intelligence information, whose disclosure may involve unacceptable risks. Information which is specific about a person's participation in an act of terrorism may be known to only two or three people. It could, without difficulty, be traced back to its source if it became known to the subject of the exclusion order or to a wider circle of his associates and friends. From this might follow the death of the informant. The flow of information which can lead, and in many cases has led to convictions in the courts would be endangered.

The problem of disclosing security information is common to many contexts other than exclusion, but the almost universal reaction of the judges has been 'sympathetic to the decisions of the executive'.[195]

Judicial aversion to security matters was the rock on which review in Stitt's case foundered. He complained that he had not been given 'the gist or the substance of the objection which is made to his presence' in Britain,[196] so it was impossible to make cogent representations to the Adviser. However, Watkins L.J. held that reasons could not imparted since '[n]ational security is very much at stake in matters of this kind . . .', especially the need to protect confidential sources.[197]

Similar judicial reactions have been observed in response to challenges to analogous security measures. Thus, in *Re Mackey*,[198] an internee in Northern Ireland sought an order of mandamus against the Advisory Committee that he supplied with a statement of the condemnatory evidence. Gibson J. (as he was then) accepted that, if the applicant was to make relevant and effective representations, he must be entitled as a matter of natural justice to a written summary of the case in front of him. However, his entitlement did not extend to information the disclosure of which would in the opinion of the Minister be contrary to public safety because it might prejudice the work of the security forces by indicating any source of information or the identity of any informant, by enabling the nature or extent of the knowledge of the security forces to be ascertained or by revealing intelligence methods adopted by the security forces. Next, in *R. v. Secretary of State for the Home Department, ex parte NSH*,[199] a Palestinian, who had been refused entry and asylum because of alleged links with terrorism, questioned whether the decision was rational. In response, Dillon L.J. stated as follows:

Where considerations of national security are said by the Home Secretary to arise, the courts cannot expect, and do not expect, that all details of evidence of matters concerning national security will be put before the courts in civil proceedings.

From this experience, it may be predicted that judicial review of Part II of the Prevention of Terrorism Act will be largely sacrificed to the totem of security interests. So long as the Home Office answers any complaints with an affidavit rehearsing satisfaction of the statutory grounds and setting out any reasons which can be disclosed without endangering security sources, the courts will not require more.[200] Consequently, proof of a breach of administrative law in the exclusion process will be a 'formidable task'.[201] Therefore, the criticisms that exclusion is inherently arbitrary and oppressive are sustained and remain unremedied by administrative law. In the light of this conclusion, one might now examine the justiciability of the making of an exclusion order to determine whether a greater degree of judicial control could be instituted.

(ii) Justiciability of the exclusion process The current system of exclusion is meant to be unashamedly executive in character on the basis that:[202]

Either there must be a fully judicial process or an executive process with responsibility resting upon the Home Secretary.

However, an infusion of judicial method into this executive device is desirable in principle, since it would verify to a higher degree of certainty that suspects have been involved in terrorism whilst securing greater respect for their procedural rights. The relevant factors which help determine whether a judicial approach is suitable in practice (already rehearsed in regard to proscription) will now be applied.

Amongst the advantages to be gained are the tendency of the judicial method to divorce the decision from political influences and the engendering of participation by the suspect, which is likely to result in a better-reasoned decision. Judicial processes also conduce to increased certainty, provided the relevant considerations can be reduced to definite rules and principles. This should be attainable, since an exclusion order essentially depends upon proof of past actions, a traditional forensic task, rather than vague policy considerations such as the 'public safety'.[203]

The factor most often cited as hampering a switch to a judicial system is the sensitive evidence involved.[204] One solution to this problem, a trial *in camera*, was suggested as the *deus ex machina* by Lord Atkin in *Liversidge* v. *Anderson*.[205] Unfortunately, this device may be unsuitable for exclusion hearings as, unlike at the end of an internment case, the suspect will remain free to contact colleagues. Therefore, a more appropriate solution would be to adopt a rule whereby the security forces could request that evidence be given in the absence of the suspect if there is a reasonable suspicion that its disclosure might aid the commission of criminal offences.[206] A more radical solution would be simply to allow a security witness to refuse to answer questions about methods or sources. However, as that evidence would then be lost, this proposal means that some cases would have to be dropped by the police for fear of revealing too much, thereby reducing the value of exclusion.

Though judicial scrutiny is both desirable and feasible, a special judicial tribunal should be preferred to the regular courts.[207] One reason is that a trial might confuse exclusion with criminal guilt, which is contrary to the suspect's interests and also conflicts with the limiting principle that special measures be distinct from ordinary laws. Next, special rules of evidence will be required to deal with the admission of, and weight accorded to, hearsay evidence, unsubstantiated opinions and testimony heard in the absence of the suspect. Balancing these concessions to security interests, an inquisitorial procedure should be adopted in order to provide reassurance for suspects (and public) that all relevant evidence has been thoroughly examined even in their absence.[208] No doubt, adjudicators operating under special rules risk the 'danger of being seen to make an executive rather than a judicial decision ... they inherit the mantle of politicians ...'.[209] However, the difficulties of altering the outward appearance of the process should not preclude the enhancement of fairness by legally trained, independent arbiters rather than abdication to politicians and a totally 'Kafkaesque' system.[210] After all, if judicial tribunals can operate under the Interception of Communications Act 1985 and the Security Service Act 1989, why should exclusion orders not be subject to similar scrutiny? Finally, a special tribunal is desirable since its adjudicators would have the opportunity of building up the necessary expertise and would also secure the necessary consistency between decisions.[211]

(*iii*)   *Other Criticisms*   A further consequence of the absence of judicial oversight is that exclusion is a propaganda liability. There is no convincing day in court to answer the complaints of its victims, so it amounts to an admission that terrorists are unlike ordinary criminals.

A related point concerns the effects of exclusion on human rights which not only excite political 'criticism and turmoil'[212] but may also seriously damage employment prospects and the physical security of persons returned to Northern Ireland.[213] The possible complications for human rights may be considered by reference to the European Convention.

Exclusion will not *per se* breach Article 5 (the right to personal liberty). In regard to removal to the Republic, it is well established that the Convention does not guarantee a right to reside in a particular country.[214] Likewise, the degree of confinement engendered by exclusion to Northern Ireland is insufficient to amount to a deprivation of liberty.[215] However, it is strongly arguable that any detention pending the making of an order violates Article 5[216] (unless for a very short time),[217] as do the meagre possibilities of legal challenge by way of judicial review.[218]

The effect of exclusion on family life (protected by Article 8) was raised in *Ryan* v. *U.K.*[219] A citizen of the Republic was ordered to return there from Britain. His wife and three children accompanied him, but four other children were left behind. This split did not in the Commission's view breach Article 8. His family life could be established in Ireland, where his four eldest children, all of full age and independent, could freely visit. Similarly, in *Mooney* v. *U.K.*[220] a U.K. citizen with Irish parents living in Dublin was excluded from Britain. Again, his family life could adequately continue in the Republic according to the Commission. Thus, only if family contacts are made practically impossible, such as by the exclusion of different relatives to different locations or when dependent family members have to be left behind,[221] will exclusion breach Article 8.

Finally, exclusion does not amount to inhuman or degrading punishment contrary to Article 3, since the process does not engender the requisite suffering; nor does the subject's likely treatment on return to Ireland cause any concern.[222] Equally, the denial of due process does not infringe Article 6, since exclusion is not a criminal penalty,[223] nor does it directly affect civil rights and obligations.[224]

(d)   Conclusions

Part II is the principal preventive measure in the Prevention of Terrorism Act, and both the Shackleton and Jellicoe Reports concluded that it has successfully attained its objective.[225] However, hard evidence for their verdicts is not forthcoming, and they must be weighed against the obvious defects in both design and application which have been detected. Consequently, informed commentators have turned against exclusion.[226] The tide began[227] with Commissioner Phillips' Annual Report for 1985, wherein he noted that the use of exclusion was declining, coordination between British and Irish police forces had improved, and English forces had increased powers under the Police and Criminal Evidence Act 1984 to deal with suspects *in situ*.[228] Thus, he cautiously suggested a moratorium on new orders against British citizens.[229] The Colville Report in 1987[230] more firmly recommended that exclusion should not be renewed at all. In response, the Government has agreed that exclusion should be the first part of the Act to lapse,[231] but it is not likely to happen until the declining level of current orders renders police surveillance of suspects a clearly viable option.[232]

It should not be concluded that the regular criminal law must always suffice to suppress suspected terrorists, for a country might conceivably be so threatened by terrorism that its existing laws are overwhelmed. However, this precondition has not been satisfied in Britain either in November 1974 or since, as evidenced by the relative trickle of excluded persons. Furthermore, even if it were demonstrated that special measures were justified, the resort to exclusion could nevertheless be criticised as an excessive response. Registration with the police might, for instance,[233] be more appropriate for two reasons. First, and in contrast to exclusion, it would tend to increase information available to the police. Suspects could still be observed in their known haunts and would have to provide additional information as part of the registration process. Second, registration allows the police to keep a close check on individuals merely by restricting their right to liberty in a given territory rather than by totally removing it.[234]

In view of these considerations, the fact that exclusion alone was adopted in 1974 and ever since leads to the suspicion that, as for proscription, it is the appearance, rather than the reality, of prevention that most impresses Parliament and the executive when combating terrorism. Thus the continuance of exclusion may now be located in the desires to be seen to be taking overt action against, and to 'Ulsterise' Republican terrorism.

Notes

1   Orders under ss. 5 and 6 need not be confined to British citizens, but they are in practice the exclusive targets: Home Office Circular, para. 2.2; compare No. 26/1984. Circulars are notified to the R.U.C., and there are identical S.H.H.D. Circulars.

2   D.R. Lowry, 'Draconian powers' (1976–77) 8–9 *Col. H.R.L.Rev.* 185 at p. 192.

3   Colville Report, para. 11.8.1.

4   H.C. Debs. Vol. 882 cols. 849–51 28 November 1974, Mr. Powell.

5   See: H.C. Debs. Vol. 904 cols. 441–5 28 January 1976.

6   H.C. Debs. Standing Committee B col. 173 20 December 1988, Mr. Hogg.

7   See: s. 6 of the 1974 Act; 1974 S.I. No. 2037.

8   This signifies that the powers may be exercised or not rather than that their use in connection with Northern Ireland does not exhaust their ambit. Compare: D. Bonner, 'Combating terrorism in Great Britain: the role of exclusion orders' (1982) *P.L.* 262 at p. 266 n. 25.

9   'Expediency' is a less demanding test than 'necessity': H.C. Debs. Standing Comm. D. col. 90 10 November 1983, Mr. Waddington.

10   H.O. Circular, para. 2.8. Compare: D. Bonner, 'Combating terrorism in the 1990s' (1989) *P.L.* 440 at p. 454.

11   Compare: 1984 Act s. 3(6); P.T.B.L. (1st ed.) p. 83 n. 9.

12   But powers under the Immigration Act 1971 are expressly preserved: 1989 Act s. 20(3).

13   H.C. Debs. Vol. 52 col. 972 25 January 1984, Mr. Waddington; H.O. Circular, para. 2.4.

14   Sched. 2 para. 9(1). The standard of proof is the balance of probabilities: H.C. Debs. Standing Comm. B col. 155 20 December 1988, Mr. Hogg.

15   See: British Nationality Act 1981 Pt. I.

16   Jellicoe Report, paras. 181, 182.

17   D. Bonner, 'Combating terrorism: the Jellicoe approach' (1983) *P.L.* 224 at pp. 231–2. But only twenty-seven orders were made before 1984 against persons resident between three and twenty years (H.C. Debs. Standing Comm. D col. 115 15 November 1983), and most terrorists convicted since 1986 have not been long-term residents (ch. 11 *infra*.)

18   But see: *Levene* v. *I.R.C.* [1928] A.C. 217; *I.R.C.* v. *Lysaght* [1928] A.C. 234; *R.* v. *Barnet L.B.C., ex p. Shah* [1983] 2 A.C. 309.

19   Para. 9(2)–(5).

20   H.C. Debs. Standing Comm. D col. 164 16 November 1983, Mr. Waddington.

21   See: R. Plender, *International Migration Law* (2nd ed., 1988) ch. 4.

22   Ss. 4, 7. Compare: s. 6.

23   H.O. Circular, para. 2.10. Applicants should allow at least forty-eight hours for processing: paras. 2.10, 2.11. See also: *H.O. Guidelines on the Work of a Special Branch* (1984) para. 15.

24   Shackleton Report, paras. 38, 39. If the Home Secretary is unavailable, another Secretary of State will deal with the application: Jellicoe Report, para. 162.

25　S.H.H.D. Circular, paras. 2.10, 2.11.
26　H.O. Circular, para. 2.9.
27　H.C. Debs. Vol. 110 col. 267 10 February 1987, Mr. Hurd.
28　H.O. Circular, para. 2.4.
29　Para. 41.
30　*Ibid.*
31　*Ibid.* para. 39.
32　Sched. 2 para. 2(1).
33　See, for example, the case of Thomas McAllister: C. Scorer, *The Prevention of Terrorism Acts 1974 and 1976* (1976) pp. 20–1.
34　Sched. 2 para. 2.
35　H.C. Debs. Vol. 52 col. 972 25 January 1984, Mr. Waddington. Therefore, a two-year review period suggested by the Colville Report (para. 11.10.1) has not been adopted.
36　Para. 127.
37　Para. 198.
38　H.C. Debs. Standing Comm. D col. 144 15 November 1983, Mr. Brittan. Attempts to enshrine this promise in legislation have been defeated: H.C. Debs. Standing Comm. B cols. 135–9 20 December 1988.
39　H.C. Debs. Standing Comm. B col. 138 20 December, Mr. Hogg.
40　Para. 2.9.
41　See: *R. v. Sec. of State for Home Dept., ex p. Stitt* (1987) *Times* 3 February; Colville Annual Report for 1987, para. 4.4.1.
42　Suspects are often difficult to contact: Colville Annual Report for 1986, paras. 4.1.1, 4.2.1.
43　Para. 11.12.1. See also: S.A.C.H.R., *14th Report* (1988–89 H.C. 394) Annex F p. 114.
44　Sched. 2 para. 2(1).
45　H.O. Circular, para. 2.15.
46　Sched. 2 para. 2(2). But the notice must be served if the person attempts to enter the U.K.; Jellicoe Report, para. 196.
47　Sched. 2 para. 2(3).
48　The time-limits have not always been applied strictly; Shackleton Report, para. 49. Compare the cases of Smith and Megahy: Scorer, *op. cit.* p. 13.
49　Sched. 2 para. 3(3), (4). Para. 3(4) is a new concession but does not extend to persons excluded from the U.K. whilst in the Irish Republic (compare: Colville Report, para. 11.11.1). The day of service is excluded: *Goldsmith's Co. v. West Met. Ry. Co.* [1904] 1 K.B. 1; *Stewart v. Chapman* [1951] 2 K.B. 792; *In re Figgis* [1969] 1 Ch. 123. Compare: *Dodds v. Walker* [1981] 2 All E.R. 609.
50　Jellicoe Report, para. 195.
51　Between 1974 and 1986, 51 out of 326 persons excluded from Britain made a request (16 per cent). Between 1987 and 1990, representations were made in 27 out of 54 (50 per cent) of new cases but only 19 out of 119 (16 per cent) renewals. Source: Colville Annual Reports, Home Office Statistics.
52　Sched. 2 para. 3(5). S. 7(4) of the 1976 Act (concerning 'frivolous' requests) has not been renewed. See: Jellicoe Report, para. 197.
53　Sched. 2 para. 3(6). This legal right was introduced by s. 7(5) of the 1976

Act, but no such request had been refused under the 1974 Act: Scorer, *op. cit.*
p. 14.
    54 Sched. 2 para. 3(7).
    55 Sched. 2 para. 3(8).
    56 Sched. 2 para. 3(9).
    57 Sched. 2 para. 3(10). Colville Annual Report for 1986, para. 4.3.1., and for
1988, para. 4.1, and for 1989, para. 4.2. Surprisingly, no public objection has been
voiced by the Irish Government; compare: P.T.B.L. (1st ed.) p. 62.
    58 Shackleton Report, para. 47. A panel of Advisers might be preferable to
avoid case-hardening; compare: *ibid.* para. 54.
    59 No burden of proof is relevant: letter from the Home Office 20 October
1982.
    60 This is sometimes conducted before, sometimes after, the consideration of
the police evidence: Shackleton Report, para. 47. A two-stage interview, partly
before and partly after reading the relevant material, might be the best solution,
but Advisers are not given detailed guidance as to procedures: H.C. Debs. Standing
Comm. D col. 210 22 November 1983.
    61 Neither policemen nor civil servants are disqualified; compare: Prevention
of Violence (Temporary Provisions) Act 1939 s. 2(1). Advisers are paid at Crown
Court Recorder rates: s. 26: H.C. Debs. Vol. 143 cols. 281–2 6 December 1988.
    62 Shackleton Report, para. 48.
    63 H.C. Debs. Standing Comm. D col. 200 22 November 1983, Standing
Comm. B col. 118 15 December 1988. Legal aid under the Green Form Scheme
is available: col. 199.
    64 *Ibid.* col. 200.
    65 Sched. 2 para. 4.
    66 Jellicoe Report, para. 169.
    67 No time limit is specified in Sched. 2 para. 4, but most elect to leave within
twenty-four hours pending reconsideration: H.C. Debs. Standing Comm. B col.
118 15 December 1988.
    68 Sched. 2 para. 4(3). It will not be possible if the subject 'has done a bunk':
H.C. Debs. Standing Comm. B col. 145 20 December 1988, Mr. Hogg.
    69 *Ibid.* col. 142. Comparisons with reasons given for a refusal of parole are
unfair; a prisoner refused parole remains imprisoned whereas an excludee is removed
but then set free and can react to the information imparted.
    70 Para. 5. After removal, the original order is endorsed by the police and
returned to the Home Office: H.O. Circular, para. 2.15.
    71 See, for example, the cases discussed in Walker, 'Members of Parliament
and executive security measures' (1983) *P.L.* 537.
    72 Sched. 5 para. 2(1). See ch. 9.
    73 Sched. 5 para. 6(1)(b).
    74 Sched. 2 para. 7.
    75 See ch. 8.
    76 Sched. 2 para. 7(1). Persons liable to detention (but who have escaped or
have never formally been detained at a port) may be arrested without warrant by
an examining officer and search warrants may be issued to aid arrest: paras. 7(2),
8(1)–(3).

77 Sched. 2 para. 8(4); H.O. Circular, para. 2.16, Annex A, and Annex B (Places of Detention) Direction 1989. There remains a residual power to take the person elsewhere to establish nationality, to arrange admission to another county or for any other purpose connected with the Act: Sched. 2 para. 8(6). See also: Police and Criminal Evidence Act 1984 s. 30(12).

78 Sched. 2 para. 8(5).

79 Sched. 3 para. 1.

80 See ch. 8, 9.

81 H.C. Debs. Standing Comm. B col. 151 20 December 1988.

82 S.H.H.D. Circular, Annex A para. 23.

83 Sched. 2 para. 6. Once a person has been placed on board, the captain may be directed to prevent disembarkation and may detain the person for that purpose; failure to take reasonable precautions is an offence: Sched. 2 para. 7. The subject also commits an offence by failing to comply with directions without reasonable excuse; para. 6(8). 'Reasonable excuse' may arise if directions are not notified or are unclear.

84 H.O. Circular, para. 2.17.

85 Sched. 2 para. 6(4).

86 Sched. 2 para. 6(5).

87 Expressed wishes will be 'considered in the light of the circumstances of the case': H.O. Circular, para. 2.14.

88 Sched. 2 para. 6(4).

89 This has never occurred: H.C. Debs. Standing Comm. D col. 117 15 November 1983.

90 H.O. Circular No. 51/1987, para. 2.

91 *Ibid.*

92 See the case of Greally: Scorer, *op. cit.* pp. 19–20.

93 An undertaking to that effect is denied by the Home Office (letter of 8 August 1990). Compare: C. Scorer and P. Hewitt, *The New Prevention of Terrorism Act: The Case for Repeal* (1985), pp. 21–2.

94 See: J.C. Smith and B. Hogan, Criminal Law (6th ed. 1988) pp. 120–2, *Lim Chin Aik* v. *R.* [1963] A.C. 160. The belief should be actual: *Castorina* v. *Chief Constable of Surrey* (1988) *Times* 15 June. For interpretations of 'harbours' see: *Marshall* v. *Fox* (1871) L.R. 6 Q.B. 370; *Darch* v. *Weight* [1983] 1 W.L.R. 659. An exclusively subjective test would be 'too high a hurdle' H.C. Debs. Standing Comm. B col. 179 20 December 1988, Mr. Hogg. The present phrase follows the Immigration Act 1971 s. 24: H.L. Debs. Vol. 504 col. 997 28 February 1989, Earl Ferrers.

95 Source: Home Office and Northern Ireland Office. The names of excludees are circulated to ports and immigration services: H.O. Circular, para. 2.2.1.

96 *Guardian* 10 February 1981 p. 3 (Horseferry Road, Mag. Ct.). The R.U.C. tried determinedly to arrest Martin Galvin, publicity director of NORAID, for breaching the Immigration Act 1971, and one man was killed during the operation; *Times* 30 July 1984 p. 1, 13 August 1984 p. 1.

97 S. 11(4). There are restrictions if the journey begins outside the Republic: Immigration (Control of Entry through Republic of Ireland) Order 1972 S.I. No. 1610 (as amended).

98   Sean Kenny, a member of Official Sinn Fein, was refused entry on the latter ground at Manchester Airport in 1973: B. Rose-Smith, 'Police powers and the terrorism legislation' in P. Hain (ed.), *Policing the Police* (1979) Vol. 1 p. 126.

99   Out of thirty-seven people excluded from Britain to the Republic up to the end of 1982, eleven were not deportable: H.C. Debs. Standing Comm. D col. 159 17 November 1983. Statistics are not kept concerning the use of powers under the Immigration Act 1971 against suspected Irish terrorists or those believed to be connected with them. However, one example was the refusal of entry for the public good (see Immigration Rules (1982–83) H.C. 169 para. 85) of Martin Galvin (see n. 96 *supra*). But when Galvin became a joint U.S.–Irish citizen, an exclusion order was issued (but later lifted): *Times* 16 August 1989 p. 2.

100   See also: Dir. 68/360, 64/221; Regs. 1612/68, 1251/70. The rights of residence of specified non-workers have been expanded by Dir. 90/364-6, but these contain limitations akin to those under Art. 48.

101   Community law does not affect restrictions on British citizens or, according to the Divisional Court, the implementation of domestic criminal law against even non-citizens: *R. v. Saunders* [1979] 3 W.L.R. 359; *Re the Habeas Corpus Application of Narinder Singh Virdee* [1980] 1 C.M.L.R. 709; *R. v. Governor of Pentonville Prison, ex p. Healy* [1984] 3 C.M.L.R. 575.

102   See *R. v. Secchi* [1975] 1 C.M.L.R. 383.

103   This is further explained by Dir. 64/221. See: *Van Duyn v. Home Office* [1975] 3 All E.R. 190; *Bonsignore v. Oberstadtdirektor of the City of Cologne* [1975] E.C.R. 297; *Rutili v. Minister of the Interior* [1975] E.C.R. 1214; *R. v. Bouchereau* [1978] Q.B. 732; *R. v. Pieck* [1980] 3 C.M.L.R. 220; *R. v. Sec. of State for Home Affairs, ex p. Santillo* [1980] 2 C.M.L.R. 308, [1981] 2 W.L.R. 362; *R. v. Kraus* [1982] Crim. L.R. 468; *Monteil v. Sec. of State for the Home Dept.* [1984] 1 C.M.L.R. 264; *Astrid Proll v. E.C.O., Düsseldorf* [1988] 2 C.M.L.R. 387. The demand for proof of 'active involvement' in terrorism does much to ensure that exclusion will comply.

104   T.C. Hartley, *E.E.C. Immigration Law* (1978) p. 232.

105   The application of ss. 5, 6 to Irish citizens could be discriminatory contrary to the judgment in *Rutili v. Minister of the Interior* (*loc. cit.*) since the three year residence exception does not apply: Hartley, *op. cit.* pp. 232–3. In practice, s. 7 is always invoked.

106   By Dir. 64/221, the requirement to give reasons (Art. 6) is subject to the interests of State security, and the decision need be referred only for the opinion of a 'competent authority' (Art. 9) rather than be subject to a wholly distinct judicial process able to impose binding decisions (compare: D. Bonner, *Emergency Powers in Peacetime* (1985) p. 82).

107   *Times* 24 January 1991 pp. 1, 7.

108   [1991] 2 All E.R. 319.

109   H.C. Debs. Standing Comm. D col. 131 15 November 1983, Standing Comm. B col. 167 20 December 1988. But there is no expressed policy to use the 1971 Act when a foreigner is suspected of Northern Ireland terrorism: letter from Home Office of 8 August 1990.

110   See: Convention Relating to the Status of Refugees 1951 and Protocol 1967 (Cmnd. 3096); Convention on the Status of Stateless Persons 1954 (Cmnd. 1098).

111   (1988) *Times* 24 March.

112   See: H.C. Debs. Vol. 209 col. 860 16 January 1958. This is now subject to E.C. Dir. 68/360 and to domestic judicial review. (See: *R.* v. *Secretary of State for F.C.O., ex p. Everett* [1989] Q.B. 811.

113   See: *R.* v. *Flaherty* [1958] Crim. L.R. 556; *R.* v. *MacCartan* (1958) 42 Cr. App. R. 262; *R.* v. *Hodges* (1967) 51 Cr. App. R. 361; *R.* v. *Saunders, loc. cit.*

114   *Veator* v. *Glennon and others* (1981) 72 Cr. App. R. 331; *R.* v. *Williams* [1982] 1 W.L.R. 1398.

115   For more distant precedents, see: U.N., *Freedom from Arbitrary Arrest, Detention and Exile* (1959); A.G.L. Shaw, *Convicts and the Colonies* (1966); P. O'Higgins, 'English law and the Irish Question' (1966) 1 *Ir. Jur.* 59.

116   S.R. & O. No. 927. Regulation 14 (S.R. & O. 1941 No. 1699) allowed directions as to residence, but this was not prompted by Irish political violence. Internment in another territory was later used as a way of removing suspects from England until it was declared unlawful in 1923: *R.* v. *Governor of Wormwood Scrubs, ex p. Foy* [1920] 2 K.B. 305; *R.* v. *Cannon Row Police Station (Inspector), ex p. Brady* (1922) 91 L.J. K.B. 98; *R.* v. *Sec. of State for Home Dept., ex p. O'Brien* [1923] 2 K.B. 361.

117   S.R. & O. No. 927. Regulation 18A (No. 1681), restricting residence within Britain, was again not directed against terrorists.

118   Strict criteria were applied. See: H.C. Debs. Vol. 374 col. 1249 14 October 1941, Mr. Peake.

119   *Ibid.* col. 1715 21 October 1941, Mr. Morrison.

120   S.R. & O. (N.I.) 1940 Nos. 54, 61.

121   H.C. Debs. Vol. 493 col. 1209 15 November 1951.

122   But see: The Pardon Act 1798 (38 Geo. 3 c. 55 (Ir.)); Public Safety Act 1927 (No. 31) s. 13(1) (repealed by No. 38 of 1928); Civil Authorities (Special Powers) Act (N.I.) Regs. 23A, 23B (S.R. & O. (N.I.) 1922 No. 36 (see P.V.L.I. p. 96).

123   H.C. Debs. Standing Comm. D col. 180 22 November 1983, Mr. Waddington.

124   Applications for renewal are made for most orders about to expire; Colville Annual Report for 1987, para. 4.4.1.

125   See: Shackleton Report, para. 56.

126   This is evidenced by the relative frequency in Northern Ireland of convictions under s. 8, described *supra.*

127   D. Bonner, 'Combating terrorism – the Jellicoe approach' (1983) *P.L.* 224 at p. 231 (up to the end of 1982).

128   See: Scorer, *op. cit.* pp. 18–19; *Times* 6 January 1975 p. 2. See also the cases of Brian Morgan (*ibid.* p. 19), Frank Hamill (*Times* 8 May 1975 p. 2), and Tom Maguire (*Times* 3 February 1987 p. 4, 18 February p. 3).

129   H.C. Debs. Vol. 1 cols. 391–2 18 March 1981, Mr. Cryer. See also the cases of Albert O'Rawe (C. Adam, 'Exclusive Irish mysteries' (1975) 89 *New Statesman* 65); Martin McAllister (*Times* 23 December 1983 p. 1); Sean Stitt (*Times* 3 February 1987); 'John Smith' (see: Scorer, Spencer and Hewitt, *op. cit.* pp. 25, 26).

130   See: *Times* 28 April 1990 pp. 1, 4. See also: C. Scorer and P. Hewitt, *The Prevention of Terrorism Act: The Case for Repeal* (1981) pp. 34–5; H.C. Debs.

Standing Comm. D col. 158 17 November 1983; case of Patrick Guilfoyle (see: S. Huey, 'Excluding terrorists' (1985) 236 *Fortnight* 12); case of *Mooney* v. *U.K.* (Appl. No. 11517/85); case of O'Donnell, *Times* 7 March 1991 p. 3, 16 March p. 3. These cases entail acute timing problems. The police cannot apply for exclusion too far ahead of the release date otherwise it will be difficult to prove a real threat, but the release date is often moved at the last moment; Phillips Annual Report for 1985, para. 22. There is also an inherent problem of staleness of evidence where a prisoner has been out of circulation for a long period: Colville Report, para. 11.8.2.

131   See the cases of Robert Storey (Scorer and Hewitt, *op. cit.* p. 52; C. Ryder, *The R.U.C.* (1989) pp. 277–80); Daniel McBrearty (*Times* 9 January 1990 p. 2); Shanahan *et al.* (*Times* 28 April 1990 p. 1); Desmond Ellis (*Times* 31 October 1991 p. 3).

132   See the cases of John McKenna (*Sunday Times* 12 March 1978); Edward Forest (Scorer, *op. cit.* p. 12); Kenneth Hagan (*Times* 20 May 1987 p. 2); Deidre Whelan (sister of Shanahan) (*Times* 9 March 1988 p. 22).

133   A rare example of a Loyalist exclusion is the case of Freddie Weatherall (Scorer, *op. cit.* p. 17).

134   Case of David Ryan and others (see: Rose-Smith, *loc. cit.* p. 128; Scorer, *op. cit.* p. 16; *Times* 22 January 1975 p. 2). This trend continues: cases of Boyle and McAllister (*Guardian* 31 October 1980 p. 2); *Times* 9 December 1981 p. 3; case of Pamela Kane (*Times* 9 March 1988 p. 22).

135   See: Walker, 'Members of Parliament and executive security measures' (1983) *P.L.* 537.

136   H.C. Debs. Vol. 33 col. 982 9 December 1982, Mrs. Thatcher.

137   The only official explanation is that continued exclusion was 'thought wrong': H.L. Debs. Vol. 448 col. 906 23 February 1984, Lord Elton.

138   H.C. Debs. Vol. 892 col. 1085 19 May 1975, Mr. Jenkins.

139   Para. 61.

140   See the cases of Gerry Docherty (*Times* 20 February 1975 p. 4) and James Martin (Scorer and Hewitt, *op. cit.* pp. 33–4). The Shackleton Report (para. 128) recommended payments for family visits, but this was rejected on the 1980 renewal. See also Colville Annual Report for 1986, para. 2.3.10.

141   Jellicoe Report, para. 176. A third advantage, that no other legal means are available, has been considered *supra*. Compare: Colville Report, para. 11.6.1.

142   Shackleton Report, para. 115.

143   Para. 2.8.

144   Jellicoe Report, para. 175.

145   Much vaguer criteria are suggested *ibid.* para. 178.

146   Fifteen persons excluded to Northern Ireland have been convicted of terrorist offences, thirty-one of other offences: H.C. Debs. Vol. 52 col. 967 25 January 1984.

147   Colville Report, para. 11.5.1.

148   *Ibid.* para. 11.4.1.

149   See: Standing Advisory Commmission on Human Rights, *9th Report* (1983–84 H.C. 262), para. 7.

150   H.C. Debs. Vol. 882 col. 749–50 28 November 1974, Mr. Lyons.

151 See the cases of Tony Devine and Brian Morgan (Scorer, *op. cit.* pp. 18–19) and James Flynn, Noel McCombe and Albert O'Rawe (Rose-Smith, *op. cit.* p. 129).

152 See: Rose-Smith, *op. cit.* p. 129. Persons excluded to the Republic are also not automatically arrested: Dail Debs. Vol. 305 col. 275 6 April 1978.

153 H.C. Debs. Vol. 52 col. 967 25 January 1984.

154 Jellicoe Report, para. 189.

155 H.C. Debs. Vol. 38 col. 637 7 March 1983, Mr. Waddington. The H.O. Circular is silent about this promise.

156 Jellicoe Report, para. 183; Colville Report, para. 11.6.1; H.C. Debs Vol. 146 col. 50 30 January 1989, Mr. Hogg.

157 H.L. Debs. Vol. 504 col. 40 13 February 1989, Earl Ferrers.

158 H.L. Debs. Vol. 504 col. 953 28 February 1989, Earl Ferrers.

159 H.C. Debs. Standing Comm. D col. 143 15 November 1983, Mr. Brittan.

160 Shackleton Report, para. 50. The Colville Report (para. 11.5.2) views it as 'fair and reasonable'.

161 H.C. Debs. Vol. 47 col. 65 24 October 1983, Mr. Hattersley.

162 Smith and Hogan, *op. cit.* p. 851.

163 (1987) *Times* 3 February (Q.B.D.), reported fully on LEXIS. See also: P. Hillyard and J. Percy-Smith, *The Coercive State* (1988) p. 274; J. Conroy, *War as a Way of Life* (1988) p. 207.

164 LEXIS, p. 8.

165 H.W.R. Wade, *Administrative Law* (6th ed., 1988) p. 716. See also: S.A. de Smith, *Judicial Review of Administrative Action* (4th ed. by J.M. Evans, 1980) p. 360.

166 LEXIS, pp. 9, 10.

167 *Ibid.* p. 10.

168 *Loc. cit.*

169 De Smith, *op. cit.* p. 362.

170 See P.T.B.L. (1st ed.) p. 76. Compare: *Hurley* v. *Minister of Law and Order* 1986 (3) S.A. 568 (A); H.P. Lee, *Emergency Powers* (1984) ch. 7; R.J. Sharpe, *The Law of Habeas Corpus* (2nd ed., 1989) p. 93.

171 Review within jurisdiction because of an error of law on the face of the record is unlikely since the 'record' consists of the notices under section 7 and the exclusion order itself. Evidence and reasons are not recorded in these short, formal documents.

172 See: *Anisminic Ltd.* v. *Foreign Compensation Commission* [1969] 2 A.C. 147; *S.E. Asia Fire Bricks Sdn. Bd.* v. *Non-metallic Mineral Products Mfg. E.U.* [1981] A.C. 374.

173 Compare: *Eshugbayi Eleko* v. *Officer Administering the Government of Nigeria* [1931] A.C. 662.

173 For the appropriate remedy, see Sharpe, *op. cit.* pp. 107–8.

174 Ministers of State can probably approve on behalf of their Secretary of State; compare: de Smith, *op. cit.* p. 308. *Govt. of Malaysia* v. *Mahan Singh* [1975] 2 M.L.J. 155; *Najar Singh* v. *Govt. of Malaysia* [1976] 1 M.L.J. 203; *In re Golden Chemical Products Ltd* [1976] Ch. 30; *McKernan* v. *Governor of Belfast Prison and another* [1983] N.I. 83. It is probable that civil servants can also act: *R.* v. *Sec.*

of State for the Home Dept., ex p. Oladehinde [1991] 3 W.L.R. 797 (and see also ch. 8). Orders served should correspond with orders signed by the Minister: *R. v. Home Sec., ex p. Budd* [1941] 2 All E.R. 749, [1942] 1 All E.R. 373, [1943] 2 All E.R. 452.

175 Compare: *El-Karbutli v. Minister of Defence* (1948) 2 P.D. 5; *Kawasma v. Minister of Defence* (1981) 35 (3) P.D. 113.

176 *Associated Provincial Picture House Ltd. v. Wednesbury Corp.* [1948] 1 K.B. 223; *R. v. S.S.H.D., ex p. Cheblak, loc. cit.*

177 [1980] A.C. 637.

178 *Ibid.* at p. 650.

179 *Ibid.* at p. 661.

180 [1980] A.C. 458 at p. 473. However, Malaysian proclamations of emergency declared in 1964 and 1969 remain in force. Compare: *Johnson Tan Han Seng v. Public Prosecutor* [1977] 2 M.L.J. 66.

181 This may also be treated as a matter of statutory interpretation. See: *R. v. Governor of Durham Prison, ex p. Singh* [1984] 1 All E.R. 983.

182 *Stuart v. Anderson and Morrison* [1941] 2 All E.R. 665.

183 *Ex p. Stitt, loc. cit; ex p. Cheblak, loc. cit.; Padfield v. Minister of Agriculture* [1968] A.C. 997; *R. v. Sec. of State for Trade and Industry, ex p. Lonrho* [1989] 1 W.L.R. 525.

184 R.N. Petty, 'Jurisdiction and the traveller' (1980) 77 *L.S. Gaz.* 200.

185 Compare: *Little v. Commonwealth* (1947) 75 C.L.R. 95; *R. v. Governor of Brixton Prisoner, ex p. Soblen* [1963] 2 Q.B. 243; *Sebe and others v. Government of Ciskei* 1983 (4) S.A. 523 (C.K.S.C.).

186 See: P. Jackson, *Natural Justice* (2nd ed., 1983) p. 141.

187 See: de Smith, *op. cit.* p. 190; *A.G. (Eastern Cape) v. Blom* 1988 (4) S.A. (A.D.)

188 Compare: *R. v. Board of Visitors of Hull Prison, ex p. St. Germain and others* [1979] Q.B. 425.

189 But see: *Omar v. Minister of Law and Order* 1987 (3) S.A. 859 (A.D.).

190 Compare: *R. v. Lewes JJ., ex p. Home Sec.* [1973] A.C. 388; *Uganda v. Commissioner of Prisons, ex p. Matovu* [1966] E.A. 514; *Nkondo and Gumede v. Minister of Law and Order* 1986 (2) S.A. 756 (A.D.); *Minister of Home Affairs v. Austin* 1986 (4) S.A. 281 (Z.S.C.); *ex p. Cheblak, loc. cit.*

191 Sched. 2 para. 3.

192 (1972) 23 *N.I.L.Q.* 173. See: S.A. de Smith, 'Internment and natural justice', *ibid.* at p. 331; *R. v. Home Sec., ex p. Tarrant* [1984] 1 All E.R. 799.

193 See now *R. v. Board of Justices of H.M. Prison, The Maze, ex p. Hone and McCartan* [1986] 11 N.I.J.B. 34 (C.A.), [1988] A.C. 379 (H.L.).

194 Shackleton Report, para. 52, quoted with approval in *ex p. Stitt, loc. cit.* p. 9. But as the final burden of proof in habeas corpus proceedings is on the detaining authority, a claim of public interest immunity could actually damage the Minister's case: Sharpe, *op. cit.* p. 124.

195 D.G.T. Williams, *Not in the Public Interest* (1965) p. 191. See: *Kavanagh v. Chief Constable of Devon and Cornwall* [1974] 1 Q.B. 624; *Neilson v. Laugharne* [1981] Q.B. 736; *Hehir v. M.P.C.* [1982] 1 W.L.R. 715; *R. v. Gaming Board for G.B., ex p. Benaim and Khaida* [1970] 2 Q.B. 417; *D. v. N.S.P.C.C.* [1978] A.C.

171; *Payne* v. *Lord Harris* [1981] 1 W.L.R. 754; *Schmidt* v. *Secretary of State for Home Affairs* [1969] 2 Ch. 149; *R.* v. *Home Sec., ex p. Hosenball* [1977] 1 W.L.R. 766; *Church of Scientology Inc.* v. *Woodward* (1983) 57 A.L.J.R. 42; *Council of the Civil Service Unions* v. *Minister for the Civil Service* [1985] A.C. 374; *In re Hardy's Application* [1988] 12 N.I.J.B. 66.

196 *Loc. cit.* p. 8.

197 *Ibid.* at pp. 8, 9.

198 *Loc. cit.* Compare: *Nkondo and Gumede* v. *Minister of Law and Order*, *loc. cit.*; *Minister of Home Affairs* v. *Austin*, *loc. cit.*

199 *Loc. cit.* See also *ex parte Cheblak*, *loc. cit.*

200 *R.* v. *Sec. of State for the Home Dept., ex p. Stitt*, *loc. cit.* p. 9. Compare: *R.* v. *Sec. of State for Home Dept., ex p. N.S.H.*, *loc. cit.* (Neill L.J.); *Sec. of State for Defence* v. *Guardian Newspapers Ltd.* [1985] A.C. 339; *Beransa* v. *Commander of Central Front* 1982 30 (4) P.D. 247; *Dahar* v. *Minister of the Interior* 1986 40 (2) P.D. 701. 'Reasons' mean more than a recitation of statutory authority: *ex parte Cheblak*, *loc. cit.*

201 *R.* v. *Sec. of State for Home Dept., ex p. Stitt*, *loc. cit.* p. 5.

202 H.C. Debs. Vol. 904 col. 511 28 January 1976, Mr. Jenkins.

203 Evidence as to the security situation and the danger posed by the person may be relevant but is also essentially factual. Compare: Jellicoe Report, para. 191.

204 The Colville Report (para. 12.1.4) also suggests that the loss of ministerial answerability to Parliament is important, but, since details are kept secret from Parliament as well as suspects, the mechanism is hardly important.

205 [1942] A.C. 206 at pp. 241–2. See also: Official Secrets Act 1920 s. 8(4); Emergency Powers (Defence) Act 1939 s. 6.

206 Compare the civil service purge procedure (see: R. Norton-Taylor, *In Defence of the Realm* (1990) pp. 34–9) and the Immigration Appeals Act 1969 (now repealed) (see: B.A. Hepple, 'Aliens and administrative justice' (1971) 34 M.L.R. 501). Procedures for interim injunctions and arrest and search warrants illustrate that 'judicial' hearings are not necessarily *inter partes*; compare: H.C. Debs. Standing Comm. B col. 124 20 December 1988, Mr. Hogg.

207 Compare the 'Exclusion Review Board' (suggested by D. Bonner, 'Combating terrorism in Great Britain: the role of exclusion orders' (1982) *P.L.* 262) and the 'Exclusion Tribunal' (H.C. Debs. Vol. 52 cols. 942–3 25 January 1984; H.C. Debs. Standing Comm. B cols. 96–7 15 December 1988). This issue is considered further in ch. 13.

208 The respective merits of adversarial and inquisitorial procedures are considered in the Gardiner Report, paras. 150–8; P.P. Craig, *Administrative Law* (2nd ed., 1989) pp. 121–2.

209 Colville Report, para. 12.1.4.

210 H.C. Debs. Standing Comm. B col. 111 15 December 1988, Ms. Mowlam. Compare: A.S. Mathews, *Freedom, State Security and the Rule of Law* (1988) p. 183.

211 Compare: Colville Report, para. 12.1.5.

212 *Ibid.* para. 11.4.1.

213 H.C. Debs. Standing Comm. B col. 100 15 December 1988, Mr. Mallon.

214 Compare: *De Becker* v. *Belgium* Appl. No. 214/56, 2 Y.B.E.C. 214; *X* v.

U.K. Appl. No. 3325/67, 10 Y.B.E.C. But see: *Bozano* v. *France* Appl. No. 9990/82, Judgment of Court Ser. A. No. 111.

215   Compare: *Guzzardi* v. *Italy* Appl. No. 7367/76, Judgment of Court Ser. A. No. 39.

216   Compare: *Ciulla* v. *Italy* Appl. No. 11152/84, Judgment of Court Ser. A. No. 148; D. Bonner, *Emergency Powers in Peacetime* (1985) pp. 200–4.

217   *X and Y* v. *Sweden* Appl. No. 7376/76, D.R. 7 p. 123.

218   Compare: *Caprino* v. *U.K.* Appl. No. 6871/75, 4 E.H.R.R. 97; C. Newdick, 'Deportation and the European Convention' (1982) 2 *Ox. J.L.S.* 151.

219   Appl. No. 9292/80.

220   Appl. No. 11517/85.

221   Compare: *X and Y* v. *U.K.* Appl. No. 5269/71, C.D. 39 p. 104; case of John McLoughlin (see Scorer, Spencer and Hewitt, *op. cit.* p. 27).

222   Compare: *Agee* v. *U.K.* Appl. Nos. 7729/76, 7917/77, D.R. 7 p. 167; *Gallagher* v. *Neths.* Appl. No. 8088/77; *Kelly and McFarlane* v. *Neths.* Appl. No. 12543/86; *X* v. *F.R.G.* Appl. No. 7216/75, D.R.5 p. 137.

223   *Mooney* v. *U.K.*, *loc. cit.* para. 5.

224   *X and others* v. *U.K.*, *loc. cit.*, *Agee* v. *U.K.*, *loc. cit.*, *Hosenball* v. *U.K.* Appl. No. 7902/77, D.R. 9 p. 224; A. Boyle, 'Administrative justice, judicial review and the right to a fair hearing under the European Convention' (1984) *P.L.* 89.

225   Shackleton Report, para. 130; Jellicoe Report, para. 176.

226   Compare: P. Wilkinson, *Terrorism and the Liberal State* (2nd ed., 1986) p. 170.

227   See also: Bonner, *op. cit.*; S.A.C.H.R., *10th Report* (1984–85 H.C. 175) paras. 22–5, 40.

228   Para. 20.

229   Para. 21.

230   Para. 11.6.1.

231   H.C. Debs. Vol. 92 col. 434 19 February 1986, Mr. Waddington.

232   There were fifty-seven orders at the time of the repeal of the Prevention of Violence (T.P.) Act 1939. H.C. Debs. Vol. 520 col. 580 26 November 1953.

233   Further alternatives are considered in ch. 13. Port controls could remain for similar reasons: Colville Annual Report for 1986, paras. 2.3.6, 2.3.7.

234   Registration was permitted by the Prevention of Violence (Temporary Provisions) Act 1939 s. 1(3). Twenty-nine orders were made: H.C. Debs. Vol. 493 col. 1209 15 November 1951.

Chapter 7

Special offences and penalties

1 History

The special offences described in this chapter relate to financial assistance for terrorism (in Part III of the Act) and withholding information about terrorism (section 18). Their origins may be traced to the 1976 version of the Act. The forerunners to sections 9 and 10 were introduced on the Government's initiative, probably because of police concern about Loyalist activities in Scotland. Section 18 was generated by backbench pressure. The offences against financial assistance were substantially expanded in 1989, and detailed powers to forfeit property were also then added (as Schedule 4).

2 Financial assistance: provisions

(a) Offences

Section 9 outlaws contributions to terrorism. The instigation or acceptance of a contribution is forbidden by section 9(1):

A person is guilty of an offence if he –
(a) solicits or invites any other person to give, lend or otherwise make available whether for consideration or not, any money or other property; or
(b) receives or accepts from any other person, whether for consideration or not, any money or other property, intending that it shall be applied or used for the commission of, or in furtherance of or in connection with, acts of terrorism to which this section applies or having reasonable cause to suspect that it may be so used or applied.

The donation of contributions is caught by section 9(2):

A person is guilty of an offence if he –
(a) gives, lends or otherwise makes available to any other person, whether for consideration or not, any money or other property; or
(b) enters into or is otherwise concerned in an arrangement whereby money or

other property is or is to be made available to another person knowing or having reasonable cause to suspect that it will or may be applied or used as mentioned in [section 9(1)].

Consideration for the contribution is irrelevant. Thus, arms deals, the sale of flags or raffle tickets or the rattling of a collection tin are all forbidden.

Compared to its predecessor (section 10 of the 1984 Act), section 9 imports four changes. First, the *mens rea* of both subsections has been harmonised with contrasting results. On the one hand, an instigator or receiver need only reasonably suspect (rather than intend) the relevant purpose, thereby easing the prosecution's burden of proof. On the other hand, it is sufficient that a reasonable man would suspect the destination in the light of the donor's knowledge;[1] the genuine disbelief of the actual donor is no longer conclusive. Neither offence requires absolute or subjective certainty as to the beneficiary, nor need the assistance be referable in the accused's mind to 'any particular or identifiable act of terrorism . . .'.[2]

The second change is that it has become unlawful under section 9(2) to engage in arrangements for the benefit of terrorists. This may penalise financial agents (bankers or accountants) who realise, for example, that a payment from a suspect account is to purchase weapons or is to be made available to a lawful business whose profits are diverted towards terrorist purposes.[3]

The third innovation followed the detection in 1986 of a well-financed Abu Nidhal cell in London[4] and consequent prompting by the Colville Report.[5] As a result, section 9(3) applies the foregoing offences not only to Northern Ireland terrorism but also to terrorism 'of any other description, except acts connected solely with the affairs of the United Kingdom or any part of the United Kingdom other than Northern Ireland'. However, so that the police and courts do not become too embroiled in overseas politics, section 9(4) requires a domestic connection: the foreign terrorism being aided must either be committed in the U.K. or, if committed abroad, must constitute an offence triable in the U.K.[6]

Given the limited extent of such offences,[7] most groups supporting liberation movements outside Europe will not be affected. Furthermore, legitimate arms dealers can probably continue with their overseas trade, since their sales are vetted in advance.[8] In any event, solicitation or donation must occur in the U.K. As regards acts of foreign terrorism committed abroad, section 9(5) provides that the prosecution need not show that the defendant had knowledge or reasonable suspicion that the acts would infringe U.K. law, though proof of the absence of awareness will constitute a defence.

The fourth amendment is that the definition of 'property' has been reformulated by section 20(1) to include 'property wherever situated and whether real or personal, heritable or moveable and things in action and other intangible or incorporeal property'.[9] The main effect is to catch property 'wherever situated' rather than any new forms of property.

Section 10 deals with contributions to organisations proscribed under the Act itself or under the Northern Ireland (Emergency Provisions) Act 1991. The latter are included since section 10 applies in Northern Ireland but also so that British support for Loyalist groups can be suppressed. By section 10(1):

A person is guilty of an offence if he –
(a)   solicits or invites any other person to give, lend or otherwise make available, whether for consideration or not, any money or other property for the benefit of a proscribed organisation;
(b)   gives, lends or otherwise makes available or receives or accepts, whether for consideration or not, any money or other property for the benefit of such an organisation; or
(c)   enters into or is otherwise concerned in an arrangement whereby money or other property is or is to be made available for the benefit of such an organisation.

One reason for separating sections 9 and 10 is historical: section 9 derives from section 10 of the 1984 Act, section 10 from section 1. However, there are two more important differences. The first is that the assistance under section 10 is simply 'for the benefit' of the group, which may be referable to acts of terrorism but may also extend to support for prisoners' families, the maintenance of 'front' businesses[10] or payments for publicity. The latter does not necessarily mean that Sinn Fein commits an offence under section 10(1)(c) by relaying I.R.A. policies and statements. Unless there is proof of an 'arrangement' (whether express or implied), it is no more unlawful for Sinn Fein to publicise or comment on the affairs of terrorists than it is for the B.B.C. to do so.

The second difference is that the prosecution need not prove that the defendant knew or reasonably suspected his assistance would benefit a proscribed group. However, by section 10(2), donors and arrangers (but not instigators) are relieved from liability if they can show that they neither knew nor reasonably believed that their actions related to a proscribed organisation. However, a mistake in law as to the proscribed status of the organisation will presumably not count. Thus, financial managers are expected to know Northern Ireland, as well as British, law.

Section 11(1) introduces a more novel offence:

A person is guilty of an offence if he enters into or is otherwise concerned in an arrangement whereby the retention or control by or on behalf of another person of terrorist funds is facilitated, whether by concealment, removal from the jurisdiction, transfer to nominees or otherwise.

The offence is aimed at managing or laundering funds by financial aids and may be committed by a wider range of involvement than under section 9 and 10.

The 'arrangement' need not be legally enforceable,[11] so the presence or absence of consideration is as irrelevant as under sections 9 and 10. There is no definition of 'arrangement', though it suggests some definite step involving 'a fairly . . . active participation',[12] rather than negotiations which may lead to assistance.[13] Thus, it may include 'commercial dealing, informal understandings, trusts or settlements and almost anything else'.[14]

By contrast, section 11(3) does explain 'terrorist funds' as meaning:

(a)   funds which may be applied or used for the commission of, or in furtherance of or in connection with, acts of terrorism to which section 9 above applies;
(b)   the proceeds of the commission of such acts of terrorism or of activities engaged in in furtherance of or in connection with such acts; and
(c)   the resources of a proscribed organisation.

This formula reflects the differences between sections 9 and 10. Accordingly, involvement with the 'resources' of a proscribed organisation covers a broader field than assisting with the funding of 'acts of terrorism'. For instance, a defendant may be liable under section 11 if he handles welfare payments or publicity accounts, knowing or reasonably believing that the finance derives from a proscribed organisation, even though the result is not to further acts of terrorism as would be required for assisting non-proscribed terrorist funds.[15] There may also be some divergence in the types of holdings covered by the term 'funds', which is variously referred to as 'funds', 'proceeds', and 'resources'. 'Funds', in section 11(3)(a), may comprise liquid assets – money, securities or negotiable instruments.[16] 'Proceeds', section 11(3)(b), are said by section 11(4) to include also 'any property which in whole or part directly or indirectly represents such proceeds . . .'. The implication is that money and so on can be traced through various transactions and conversions into real or personal property. Similarly, 'resources' in section 11(3)(c), encompass under section 11(4) 'any money or other property which is or is to be applied or made available for the benefit of a proscribed organisation'. Finally, 'proscribed organisation' has the same meaning as in section 10. Thus, it is unlawful for a banker in, say, Glasgow, to handle an account on behalf of the U.V.F., even if the purposes of the funds are quite lawful.

The motives of the assistant may be purely commercial; section 11 requires no ulterior intent to benefit terrorism. However, section 11(3) offers a defence for anyone who can show on the balance of probabilities no knowledge nor reasonable cause to suspect that the arrangement related to terrorist funds. This switch in the onus of proof is similar to that in section 10. The reasonable suspicion may arise from the nature of the transaction, the nature of the client or both. The defendant will be judged on the facts actually known to him.[17] Conversely, if the defendant wrongly suspected that he was handling terrorist funds which turned out to be legitimate, he may be guilty of an attempt.[18]

The detection of offences under sections 9 to 11 is assisted by section 12(1):

A person may notwithstanding any restriction on the disclosure of information imposed by contract disclose to a constable a suspicion or belief that any money or other property is or is derived from terrorist funds or any matter on which such a suspicion or belief is based.

A 'suspicion' is usually interpreted as less firmly grounded than a belief.[19] This distinction may explain the inadequacy of the common law exception to the duty of confidence owed by bankers[20] which allows disclosures in the public interest though not the relaying of mere suspicions.[21] Whilst section 12 may be broader than the common law, its own limitations should be noted. There is no immunity from a suit in equity based on breach of confidence,[22] from the demands of professional discipline codes or from statutory restrictions on disclosure (say under the Official Secrets Act 1989). However, it is arguable that an employee may not be disciplined or dismissed by his employer, for any such action would be based on breach of the contract of employment which is overridden by section 12(1).

Section 12(2) allows 'sting' operations by providing that if a person informs the police under subsection (1) and they expressly[23] consent to the commencement or continuance of the transaction or arrangement, no offence under sections 9 to 11 is committed. The employment of *agents provocateurs* as a tactic is, however, limited by the fact that section 12(2) operates as a defence and not on the police's initiative. The financial assistant is also excused from liability under sections 9 to 11 if he contacts the police after the suspicious transaction or arrangement has commenced, provided notification is made 'on his own initiative and as soon as it is reasonable . . .' and provided he withdraws as soon as he is directed to do so. This defence is again designed to encourage public-minded citizens or those in fear of liability under section 9 to 11. Even if the police intervene before the agent contacts them, it is still a defence under section 12(3) to prove that he intended to disclose and his delay was reasonable.[24] Acting on one's own 'initiative' primarily demands that there has been no prompting by the police;[25] disclosure after questioning will be counted as an incriminating confession rather than a defence. Advice from one's solicitor or pressure from family or friends should not vitiate the defence.[26] Delay may be 'reasonable', for example, because the information-holder fears reprisals and needs to arrange his safety or because he is seriously ill.[27]

The penalties for offences under sections 9 to 11 are, on indictment, imprisonment not exceeding fourteen years, a fine or both and, on summary conviction, six months' imprisonment, a fine not exceeding the statutory maximum of £2,000 or both.[28] The maximum penalty on indictment was substantially increased in 1989 and exceeds that under section 2. The change is partly explained by the need for comparability with related offences in other legislation[29] and partly because sentences in Scotland for similar conspiracy offences had exceeded in a number of cases the previous limits, implying that they were inadequate.[30]

(b) Forfeiture

The second prong of attack mounted by the Prevention of Terrorism Act on terrorist funds is forfeiture. The tainted assets of a terrorist financier or launderer can be frozen, seized and forfeited by reference to section 13 and Schedule 4. The following measures represent the most important reforms in the 1989 Act and follow support by the Colville Report[31] and pressure from the R.U.C.[32]

Various conditions triggering forfeiture are set by section 13.[33] First, forfeiture can operate only when a person has been convicted of an offence under sections 9 to 11; offences such as blackmail do not count, and actions *in rem* are not permitted. Second, forfeiture applies to money or other property which, at the time of the offence, the person had in his possession or control (contrary to sections 9(1), 9(2)(a), 10(1)(2) or 10(1(b)) or had dealt with (contrary to sections 9(2)(b), 10(1)(c) or 11). The money or property may be the direct fruits of terrorism (such as from a robbery or ransom) or may be indirect assets (as when a ransom is invested and interest accrues or is spent on a business which produces profits).[34] There is unlikely to be any discount for expenses.[35] Third, only 'money or other property' can be forfeited, so a court cannot forfeit a sum of money equivalent to services rendered. Fourth, in regard to offences under section 9 but not section 10, the person must be shown to have intended, known or reasonably suspected the application or use of each asset under scrutiny for terrorist purposes. This reiterates the requirements of *mens rea* in section 9 and applies them to the forfeiture of assets held at the time of the offence. Fifth, forfeiture should not be ordered unless the court considers that the money or property would otherwise be applied for terrorist purposes. However, by section 13(5), the court may assume such a purpose in the absence of contrary evidence. This reversal in the burden of proof is subject to the establishment in the first place of an offence under sections 9 to 11. The court may be convinced otherwise in the case of the repentant or those who turn Queen's evidence. Finally, third parties who claim a title or interest shall be given 'an opportunity to be heard' (section 13(6)). Pointedly, there is no guarantee of immunity or compensation even for a *bona fide* purchase for value without notice.[36]

The detailed rules governing forfeiture are explained in Schedule 4, with variations for England and Wales, Scotland and Northern Ireland. Further implementation is by way of court rules.[37]

The initiative for raising the issue of forfeiture in Scotland rests solely with the prosecutor (section 13(7)). Elsewhere, forfeiture may be raised either by the prosecution or at the behest of the judge.

If so minded, a court may make an order:[38]

(a)   requiring any money or other property to which the forfeiture order applies to be paid or handed over to the proper officer or to a constable designated for the purpose by the chief officer of police of a police force specified in the order;
(b)   directing any such property other than money or land to be sold or otherwise disposed of in such a manner as the court may direct and the proceeds to be paid to the proper officer;
(c)   appointing a receiver to take possession, subject to such conditions and exceptions as may be specified by the court, of any such property which is land, to realise it in such manner as the court may direct and pay the proceeds to the proper officer;
(d)   directing as specified part of any money, or of the proceeds if the sale, disposal or realisation of any property, to which the forfeiture order applies to be paid by proper officer to or for a specified [third party];
(e)   making such other provision as appears to the court to be necessary for giving effect to the forfeiture order or to any order made by virtue of paragraph (a), (b), (c) or (d) above.

These overlapping powers may be ordered in any combination but may not be acted upon until the normal time-limits for an appeal have expired.[39] While the forfeiture is under way, both the prosecution and defence may apply at any time for a written certificate as to progress.[40] The costs of any sale, disposal or realisation must be deducted from the proceeds,[41] including the fees and expenses of any receiver (administrator in Scotland).[42] Once the forfeiture order has been executed, the balance is held for six months and is then paid into central funds.[43]

It will often be time-consuming either to prove that financial transactions have benefited terrorists or, having made a forfeiture order, to realise the assets. Consequently, Schedule 4 allows interim 'restraint orders' so as to prevent the dissipation or removal of funds.[44] A restraint order may be issued by the High Court (Court of Session in Scotland) where:[45]

(2)(a)   proceedings have been instituted against a defendant . . . for an offence under Part III . . . ;
(b)   the proceedings have not been concluded; and
(c)   either a forfeiture order has been made or it appears to the court that there are reasonable grounds for thinking that a forfeiture order may be made in those proceedings. [Or]
(3)(a)   the court is satisfied that, whether by the laying of information or otherwise, a person is to be charged . . . with an offence under Part III . . . ; and
(b)   it appears to the court that a forfeiture order may be made in proceedings for the offence.

An application is made by a prosecutor (the Lord Advocate in Scotland) *ex parte* to a judge in chambers by originating motion, which must provide for notice to affected persons if an order is made.[46] The motion must be supported by an affidavit which shall explain the relevant criminal proceedings, the grounds for forfeiture and particulars of the property sought.[47] The grounds should embrace 'statements of information or belief with the source and grounds thereof',[48] including hearsay evidence, but sensitive information may be omitted.[49] In Northern Ireland, and contrary to constitutional principles, restraint orders may alternatively emanate (under paragraph 25A, inserted by the Emergency Provisions Act 1991, Schedule 7) from the Secretary of State if necessary, to avoid danger or prejudice.

Once granted, a restraint order may 'prohibit any person, subject to such conditions and exceptions as may be specified in the order, from dealing with any property liable to forfeiture . . .'.[50] The conduct prohibited and property affected should be specified.[51] 'Dealing' expressly includes the repayment of debts or removal of property from the jurisdiction[52] and may otherwise be taken to mean disposals, grants, transfers and destruction.[53] Breach is a civil contempt (except in Northern Ireland),[54] and a constable may seize property to prevent its removal from the jurisdiction.[55] No account need be taken of any conflicting rights or obligations in respect of the property owed by the holder,[56] so that earlier contrived dealings will not put assets out of reach.[57]

An application for the discharge or variation of a restraint order may be made by the prosecution or any person affected; an order shall in any event be discharged when the criminal proceedings are concluded[58] or if pending proceedings are not instituted within a reasonable time.[59] Otherwise, there is no limit in the life of a restraint order.[60] A restraint order may be subject to conditions and exceptions, including, according to the court rules, the indemnification of third parties (but not the defendant) and the payment of living and legal expenses incurred by the defendant.[61] A court may also order the discovery of documents to aid forfeiture, subject to an undertaking not to use the information in the prosecution.[62]

Persons subject to restraint orders may suffer loss and inconvenience which will be particularly unfortunate if an order is not followed by a prosecution or conviction or if a conviction is quashed or pardoned. However, the rights to compensation in those circumstances are severely drawn.[63] No recompense at all is conceded if an inquiry has proved ultimately fruitless and no criminal proceedings have been instituted. Even when an unsuccessful prosecution has been undertaken, compensation for the effects of any restraint (or forfeiture) order is highly circumscribed. Not only must there have been some 'serious default on the part of a person concerned in the investigation or prosecution . . .', but that 'serious default' must have been instrumental in motivating the institution of proceedings. It must also be shown that the applicant has suffered loss in relation to the property; 'indirect' loss such as mental distress is not recoverable[64] but economic loss could be. Furthermore, the court must consider compensation 'appropriate' in the circumstances, inviting it to disqualify applicants whom the judge believes lucky to be acquitted. Assuming all these hurdles can be surmounted, the amount of compensation will be whatever the High Court (Court of Session in Scotland) 'thinks just in all the circumstances of the case'.[65] As a warning to future conduct, compensation will be paid out of police or prosecution funds. In conclusion, the statutory compensation rights are so minimal that an action for negligence[66] or malicious prosecution will often be more appropriate. Compensation is so miserly because the Government feared that more generous rules would benefit 'otherwise unmeritorious characters who have been acquitted for either trivial reasons or against the weight of the evidence . . .'.[67] The rules seem particularly unfair to businesses whose affairs are disrupted by Schedule 4 and compare unfavourably with compensation given for miscarriages of justice.[68]

The money or property which is referable to offences under sections 9 to 11 may have to be traced through various jurisdictions. Therefore, Schedule 4[69] provides for the reciprocal enforcement of restraint and forfeiture orders made elsewhere in the British Islands or made under comparable legislation in designated foreign countries.[70] For example, an application to enforce a British Islands (meaning Scotland, Northern Ireland, the Isle of Man or the Channel Islands) order in England and Wales will be made to the High Court.[71] If the order is registered, it may be enforced as if made in England and Wales.[72] The procedures in relation to 'external orders' from designated countries will be specified in the relevant Order in Council and are likely to be similar (none has yet been issued).

Finally, if a person against whom a forfeiture order has been made becomes subject to insolvency proceedings, priority between the conflicting court actions is settled by Schedule 4.[73] Provided written notice of the insolvency is given by the insolvency practitioner (the liquidator or trustee in bankruptcy) within six months following the making of the forfeiture order, the property or proceeds of sale subject to forfeiture shall cease to be so subject and shall fall to be dealt with in the insolvency proceedings.[74] However, the forfeiture order is not entirely forgotten, as the Secretary of State is recognised as a creditor in the insolvency proceedings, though his debt ranks after all others. Furthermore, any expenses incurred in the forfeiture process to date are deductible.[75] If the insolvency is nullified after six months, then forfeiture takes priority. However, if an insolvency practitioner seizes or disposes of property subject to forfeiture reasonably believing he is entitled to do so, he is not liable for any loss or damage except through negligence.[76]

These provisions relating to insolvencies may protect, for example, the suppliers or employees of a building contractor operated by a paramilitary

E

group which is closed by the police.[77] However, this commendable concern makes the treatment of the *bona fide* purchaser for value without notice outside an insolvency situation seem even more cavalier.

3 Financial assistance: comparisons

(a) Offences: contributions

The previous overlap between offences in Parts I and III has been considerably diminished by the 1989 Act, but the following differences persist.

One is that sections 9 and 11 forbid contributions not only to proscribed organisations but also to any Northern Ireland or foreign terrorists, thereby extending the law in three ways. First, they permit action to be taken against bodies acting as 'fronts' for proscribed groups but not themselves proscribed.[78] Secondly, they facilitate prosecutions when a contribution is not referable to any specified terrorist body. Thirdly, they curtail aid in Britain for groups (especially of the Loyalist variety) which are proscribed only in Northern Ireland. Only the last feature affects section 10, but other pertinent contrasts can be found in relation to that offence.

Accordingly, a second difference concerns the activities prohibited by the respective Parts. Thus, it is not unlawful under Part III to belong to a terrorist group or to arrange, or address its meetings, though arranging or addressing a fund-raising meeting could infringe both sections 2 and 10. Next, the soliciting of 'money or other property' is expressly excluded from section 2 and therefore falls under section 10 alone. Conversely, other forms of 'support' are uniquely mentioned in section 2(2)(b), and these may include the soliciting of services which do not involve the transfer of money or property (such as driving a car or acting as a look-out) or the soliciting of support (by displaying posters). Although the demarcation between sections 2 and 10 has been clarified, it has also left a substantial gap, since the actual rendition (as opposed to solicitation or display) of 'support' is no longer an offence under the Act, though the performer may become a secondary party to crimes committed by others.[79]

The only relevant measures concerned with financial assistance in the Northern Ireland (Emergency Provisions) Act 1991 are those (equivalent to section 2 of the Prevention of Terrorism Act) relating to proscribed organisations.[80] It is not unlawful in the Republic of Ireland to make contributions to an illegal organisation (unless referable to specific offences).[81] However, an incitement or invitation to support an unlawful group constitutes an offence under section 3 of the Criminal Law Act 1976.[82] This is narrower than section 10 of the Prevention of Terrorism Act since it does not penalise donors but is wider in that it prohibits supportive activities which do not involve money or property.[83]

(b) Offences: laundering and disclosure
The laundering offence in section 11 of the Prevention of Terrorism Act
derives from section 24(1) of the Drug Trafficking Offences Act 1986.[84]
The forms of assistance covered by both Acts are very similar,[85] but the
respective *mens rea* differ significantly. On the one hand, it is sufficient
under section 24 for the defendant to know or suspect that the client has
at some time benefited from drug trafficking. Under section 11, there must
be some awareness that the actual transaction relates to terrorist funds; the
nature of the client is relevant but not conclusive as to the nature of his
funds. On the other hand, the defendant under section 24 must be shown
to have known or actually suspected the drugs involvement of the client;
the merely inadvertent are not punished.[86] However, the defendant under
section 11 not only has the burden of proof as to his lack of awareness
but must prove his ignorance was reasonable as well as real.[87] The
requirement of reasonableness has excited much opposition from professional associations,[88] but the Government has resisted change on the
basis that terrorists create more pressure to turn a blind eye than ordinary
criminals.[89] However, the effect is to penalise the careless as well as the
committed assistant whose links with terrorism are rather less direct than
those in sections 9 and 10. Consequently, the only special feature of the
mens rea in section 11 should be the switch in the burden of proof. However,
some of the more recent offences against drug trafficking, in sections 14(2)
and (3) of the Criminal Justice (International Cooperation) Act 1990,
adopt the alternative compromise of leaving the burden of proof entirely
with the prosecution but allowing conviction on the basis of reasonable
suspicion of the nature of the transaction.
   A close blueprint for section 12 of the Prevention of Terrorism may be
found in section 24(3) and (4) of the 1986 Act, which was also copied by
section 98 of the Criminal Justice Act 1988.
   Account must next be taken of yet another confiscation code, Part VII
of the Northern Ireland (Emergency Provisions) Act 1991. By section 53,
it is to be an offence to assist another to retain or invest the proceeds of
terrorist-related activities. Section 54 penalises not only the concealment,
conversion or transfer of such proceeds for the purposes of avoiding prosecution or the enforcement of confiscation but also the acquisition of
such proceeds for no, or inadequate, consideration. Both offences apply
throughout the U.K. and differ from section 11 of the Prevention of
Terrorism Act as follows. Firstly, the proceeds from 'terrorist-related
activities' relevant to section 53 are even more extensive than 'terrorist
funds' under section 11. They include any property derived from relevant
offences certified by the police, regardless of the holder or his intentions
as to beneficial enjoyment. Secondly, activities outlawed by clause 54
may not necessarily facilitate the enjoyment of illicit proceeds, so long as

they are designed to thwart investigation or prosecution. These extensions, which could usefully be copied by the Prevention of Terrorism Act, derive from section 14 of the Criminal Justice (International Cooperation) Act 1990, which relates to similar activities by the inter-mediaries of drug traffickers. Section 53 fits in with extensive confiscation measures in Part VII of the 1991 Act, described later.

More distant precedents which may have influenced British legislation are the laundering[90] and racketeering enterprise offences[91] in the U.S.'s Racketeering Influenced and Corrupt Organisations Act. Terrorists groups have been indicted under the latter,[92] but it is doubtful whether such an offence should be replicated in the United Kingdom. It seems wrong in principle in create extra offences based wholly on predicate crimes, and the practical result is often vague and unwieldy prosecutions.[93] Overseas laws which demand the automatic reporting of banking transactions have also been rejected in the U.K. 'after considerable thought'[94] for good reasons. For example, the U.S. Currency and Foreign Transactions Reporting Act[95] has been found to be easily avoided or ignored, shifts responsibility from financial institutions and produces too much data.[96] However, a workable compromise, as adopted in Australia,[97] might be the issuance of monitoring orders by which banks are required to notify the authorities only about specified suspect accounts. Finally, Australian and Canadian legislation may also be preferable in the extent of the immunity given to those who report transactions.[98]

(c) Forfeiture

The provenance of forfeiture is, like the foregoing offences, directly traceable to the Drug Trafficking Offences Act 1986, Criminal Justice (Scotland) Act 1987 and Criminal Justice Act 1988.[99] The 1986 and 1988 Acts have since been reproduced in Northern Ireland as the Criminal Justice (Confiscation) (Northern Ireland) Order 1990.[100] In the background lurk more distant U.S. influences. However, other precedents must first be mentioned.

Perhaps the closest relative in British law is section 2(3) of the Public Order Act 1936, which allows the forfeiture by order of the High Court[101] of the property of paramilitary groups. Section 2(3) is more far-reaching than the Prevention of Terrorism Act in that orders are not confined to property held by a defendant before the courts nor are they necessarily linked to any conviction. Similarly broad powers are available in the Republic of Ireland. Section 22 of the Offences against the State Act 1939 allows the forfeiture of property held on behalf of unlawful organisations, section 25 allows the closure of buildings used by them, and the Offences against the State (Amendment) Act 1985 grants powers to seize tainted funds in bank accounts.[102] Though the latter Act lapsed in 1985, its passage (and that of other European precedents) excited the attention of the Colville Report.[103]

Returning to the 'confiscation' codes under the 1986, 1987 and 1988 Acts, their bulk rules out detailed comparisons with the Prevention of Terrorism Act. Therefore, discussion herein will be confined to two points: in what respects, if any, can the Prevention of Terrorism Act be claimed to be uniquely necessary in accordance with the limiting principles in chapter 2; secondly, might any features from the 'confiscation' codes be adopted by the Act?

The necessity for forfeiture under the Prevention of Terrorism Act is not immediately apparent, since Part VI of the Criminal Justice Act 1988 can apply to any serious offence.[104] Indeed, many features in Schedule 4 were undoubtedly modelled on the 1988 (and 1986) Acts, including restraint orders, minimal rights to compensation and trans-jurisdictional enforcement.[105] The principal objections to reliance upon the 1988 Act and the corresponding 1990 Order are that they do not extend to Scotland,[106] they lack laundering offences and that confiscation bites only when the defendant derives a benefit of at least £10,000.[107] This limit is inappropriate in the context of terrorism, where any funds left with terrorists represent a danger to the public and where the concept of personal 'benefit' is misplaced. Nevertheless, it might have been possible to have extended the 1988 Act to 'involvement in' (rather than benefit from) offences under sections 9 to 11 of the Prevention of Terrorism Act, no matter what amount is involved, and thereafter to follow the 1988 Act scheme.

Assuming that forfeiture in the Prevention of Terrorism Act will persist as a separate source of powers, one might next consider whether any of the divergent formulations in the confiscation codes should be adopted. In some respects, the confiscation codes are actually more Draconian, though it is doubtful whether they are preferable. For example, the confiscation codes allow enforcement as if confiscation were a fine, so that a period of imprisonment for default will be imposed.[108] The only sanction under the Prevention of Terrorism Act would seem to be contempt proceedings if there is evidence of obstruction rather than inability to pay. However, given the absence of personal benefit, the lack of a default penalty is appropriate. Next, the assumption as to the criminal origins of property held are more far-reaching under the Drug Trafficking Offences Act but, at the same time, seem unnecessarily close to outlawry.[109] Next, the definition of drug trafficking allows investigations to be conducted on behalf of foreign states;[110] the Prevention of Terrorism Act rightly requires designation by order before any reciprocal enforcement since terrorism involves sensitive political considerations. Finally, the confiscation codes allow insolvency proceedings to be overridden more readily,[111] about which the Scottish Law Commission has commented that:[112]

the reason for these different approaches is not immediately apparent. However, the reason may be that, in cases falling under the 1989 Act, the assets which are to be used to fund terrorist organisations may themselves have been honestly acquired, and, as such, could legitimately be viewed by creditors as being available to meet their claims. By contrast, the proceeds or profits of crime would never have that character, and consequently should not be made available to meet the demands of creditors.

This reasoning will not hold. In the first place, the Government believed that the drafting of the Prevention of Terrorism Act was similar to the confiscation codes,[113] and so any differences are probably unintentional. Secondly, the broad offences in Part III of the Act make it unlikely that most assets at risk have been honestly acquired or transferred. Nevertheless, the Prevention of Terrorism Act is correct in conferring greater priority upon creditors. Money owed to them can hardly amount to the 'fruits' of crime in need of forfeiture.

As might be expected, the confiscation codes display in other respects greater concern than the Prevention of Terrorism Act for the defendant and third parties. Thus, the interests of third parties must (rather than may) be deducted from property liable to confiscation.[114] The confiscation codes also employ the more flexible weapon of charging orders as well as restraint orders, which are especially helpful if property is held in common.[115] As for the treatment of the defendant, the Drug Trafficking Offences Act is likely to give greater forewarning of the possibility of confiscation and of the assets at risk, since statements to these effects will be served.[116] Unless preceded by a restraint order, a defendant under the 1989 Act need not be put on notice until the matter of forfeiture is raised on conviction.[117]

The relationships between the Prevention of Terrorism Act and the established confiscation codes have been described by Viscount Colville as 'a legislative shambles'[118] with overlapping powers and disturbing lacunae. The latter are said to include: the confinement of forfeiture to offences under sections 9 to 11, thereby ignoring involvement in extortion, breaches of copyright and tax evasion; the failure to replicate the assumptions and statements as to benefit in the 1986 Act; and the absence of effective investigative powers.[119] These criticisms provoked an early response in the shape of the 'severe'[120] confiscation measures in Part VII of the Emergency Provisions Act 1991.

A Crown Court in Northern Ireland may make an order if the following conditions in section 47 are met. The person must have benefited from terrorist-related activities engaged by him or another, have been convicted of a 'relevant offence' and have been convicted of, or shown to have committed, another relevant offence within the previous six years. The person must have held 'realisable property' worth more than £20,000, and the making of an order must not be unfair or oppressive. 'Realisable property' means the value of proceeds from terrorist-related activities or the value of realisable property actually held, whichever is less. The assumptions and tendering of statements, as in the 1986 Act, apply.

The implementation of confiscation (by Schedule 4 of the Act) also contains some innovations. The sum confiscated can be enforced as a fine and can be increased if the value of the property held rises or if the court orders interest on unpaid sums.[121] Charging orders make an appearance, but rather less familiar is the power granted to the Northern Ireland Secretary of State to use restraint and charging orders where it appears to him that an application to a court could cause danger or prejudice the investigation. This extraordinary assault on the separation of powers mirrors some search powers in Schedule 7 of the Prevention of Terrorism Act (discussed in chapter 8) and has also been replicated in Schedule 4 paragraph 25A (described earlier). Finally, section 57 allows an R.U.C. superintendent to apply to the Secretary of State for the appointment of an 'authorised investigator' to assist with investigations anywhere in the UK into the existence of:

(a)   the resources of a proscribed organisation;
(b)   funds which may be applied or used for the commission of, or in furtherance of or in connection with, acts of terrorism connected with the affairs of Northern Ireland; or
(c)   the proceeds of the commission of such acts of terrorism or of activities engaged in furtherance of or in connection with such acts.

Authorised investigators may then apply under Schedule 7 of the Prevention of Terrorism Act for search warrants, production orders and explanations of materials seized thereunder. They may also, under Schedule 5 of the 1991 Act, require a person to attend as specified to furnish oral information or to produce documents and explanations. If the investigator suspects written details are being suppressed, a search warrant may be obtained (including from the Secretary of State in Northern Ireland). The powers of the investigator under Schedule 5 are reminiscent of those of the Director of the Serious Frauds Office under the Criminal Justice Act 1987 (which does not extend to Northern Ireland),[122] but at least the Director is a public officer who is independent of the police and reports to Parliament. Perhaps more comparable are the 'nominated officers' acting under section 51 of the Criminal Justice (Scotland) Act 1987. However, they are appointed by the Lord Advocate (who will be answerable for their activities),[123] will be civil servants or procurator fiscals, and cannot directly apply for search warrants.

Confiscation under the Emergency Provisions Act can operate in Britain but can only be invoked by the R.U.C.; the Government intends to wait and see whether it needs to be extended to British forces.[124] However, it seems doubtful whether most of Part VII should be replicated in Britain or is even worthwhile in Northern Ireland. Its purpose is to ensnare 'the major players'[125] whose involvement in paramilitary activities may be for personal gain rather than to further any political cause. Thus, Part VII is concerned as much with rescuing the Northern Ireland economy from the clutches of organised crime as with the defeat of terrorism. The same dangers do not arise in Britain. Furthermore, this overblown and complex scheme may not assist in Northern Ireland without substantial extra resources for enforcement and without independent oversight of its application. Only a few features – the extension to further offences, charging orders, the forfeiture of increases in property values, the levying of interest on sums outstanding, and extra investigative powers – are worth considering further.

Another comparative exercise might be conducted in relation to the United States' Racketeering Influenced and Corrupt Organisations Act and the Continuing Criminal Enterprises Act[126] which have in turn exerted some influence over corresponding U.K., Australian and Canadian legislation.[127] The U.S. Acts are broader than the Prevention of Terrorism Act in three respects, the desirability of which should be considered.

First, forfeiture following a criminal conviction is more extensive since the defendant's entire interest in the enterprise involved in racketeering is seized.[128] However, this response seems 'greatly excessive',[129] as it affects assets which are not the proceeds of crime.

Next, it is possible to order 'civil' forfeiture under the U.S. Acts either by way of a court action initiated by a private individual[130] or, in the case of drugs assets, by official seizure.[131] However, private individuals cannot be expected to take responsibility for anti-terrorism measures, whilst summary seizure appears 'fundamentally objectionable'[132] without proof of probable cause in a formal hearing. Nevertheless, a court action *in rem* might be acceptable when the suspected owner or holder cannot be prosecuted because he has absconded or died. Such a procedure exists in Australia and Canada and has been used in the Republic of Ireland.[133] By contrast, the forfeiture scheme in sections 25 and 26 of the Criminal Justice (International Cooperation) Act 1990 is less supportable. These provisions allow the seizure and forfeiture of cash sums over a prescribed limit which is being physically imported or exported and may derive from, or relate to, drug trafficking. There is judicial oversight in the form of a hearing before magistrates (a sheriff in Scotland), but the proceedings are not dependent upon any charges, prosecution or conviction and the civil standard of proof applies. The model seems to have been the powers to seize and detain goods under section 139 of the Customs and Excise Management Act 1979. However, the analogy between contraband and cash (in the context of either drugs or terrorist activities) is unfair. Cash is not akin to drugs, firearms or obscene materials, since its possession is not *per se* an offence nor is it necessarily evidence of an offence.

Finally, the impact of U.S. forfeiture legislation on lawyers' fees has caused much disquiet. For instance, if all assets are subject to pretrial restraint, lawyers may not be prepared to act for such clients in the bare hope that they will later be paid. Further, the possible forfeiture of assets from a client for whom a lawyer has agreed to act may cause conflicts of interests in the taking of instructions and plea-bargaining. If a client's assets are actually forfeited, a lawyer who has been paid may be called upon to give evidence about his funding. These considerations have produced conflicting court decisions and academic views on the constitutionality and desirability of the forfeiture of attorneys' fees.[134] However, the matter has now been settled in *U.S.* v. *Monsanto* and *Caplin and Drysdale* v. *U.S.*,[135] wherein the U.S. Supreme Court decided that the unambiguous statutory language afforded no mandatory exemption of lawyers' fees. This result was constitutional since tainted funds were not in law the defendant's to spend and could only be taken away on probable cause. Further, if the right to counsel were given special treatment, why not other constitutional rights (such as travel) which might involve expenditure? Any danger of oppression arising from forfeiture could be dealt with case by case, and the alleged ethical dilemmas for lawyers were by no means unique to forfeiture.

By contrast, lawyers have fared rather better under corresponding U.K. legislation,[136] as the confiscation codes expressly exempt reasonable legal expenses.[137] However, the position may be less certain under the Prevention of Terrorism Act in that there is a danger not just of the dissipation of assets but also of collusion, so that even the fair remuneration of a 'terrorist' lawyer is unacceptable since his fee remains 'terrorist funds'. The Government's expressed view is that there are 'terrorist' lawyers in Northern Ireland, and so it resisted an amendment to exclude from section 11 the payment of lawyers,[138] leaving them to stake their claims under section 13(6). In the light of this legislative history and the reasons rehearsed in the U.S. cases, there is a strong interpretive argument against any privilege for lawyers. However, the later Home Office Circular[139] and court rules[140] which implement Schedule 4 both assume that lawyers' fees may be exempted from restraint orders. On the whole, this solution seems preferable since, particularly in cases with political overtones, 'it is unseemly and unjust for the Government to beggar those it prosecutes in order to disable their defence at trial'.[141] In practice, legal aid funding, the relative reluctance of the D.P.P. for Northern Ireland to vilify defence solicitors and the careful taxation of costs[142] should obviate most problems.

4 Financial assistance: assessment

(a) Offences: contributions
(i) *Nature and extent of use* The statistics for the offence in Great Britain to the end of 1990 are set out in Table 3. In Northern Ireland, there were a modest twenty-eight charges (all under section 9(2)) before the 1989 Act, but a remarkable upsurge (sixteen charges under s. 9(2), twenty-six under s. 10) thereafter out of a total of 182 since 1974. One

Table 3 The operation of Part III offence in Great Britain

Offence	Charges	Not proceeded with	Guilty	Sentences (all imprisonment)		
				Under 1 year	1–5 years	Over 5 years
s. 9(1)	61	12	37	4	28	5
s. 9(2)	4	–	3	–	3	–
s. 9(1) & (2)	1	–	1	–	–	1
Total*	66	12	41	4	31	6

* Out of 216 charges relating to offences under the Act since November 1974.
Source: Home Office.

reason for the limited impact before 1989 may be that prosecutions could more readily be brought under section 28 of the Emergency Provisions Act, since most significant groups are prohibited in Northern Ireland.[143] Nowadays, prosecution policy seems to have switched to the Prevention of Terrorism Act, presumably to attract forfeiture.

Most prosecutions in Britain have centred on the cases of Loyalist fund-gathering in Scotland, as described in chapter 5. Other categories of offenders concern minor participants in major terrorist groups, collectors in public places and, in Northern Ireland, participants in protection rackets.

(*ii*) *Necessity* The Chief Constable of the R.U.C. has pointed out that:[144]

Money is a crucial factor in the continuance of terrorism. . . .

It must therefore be accepted that the criminal law should forbid gifts to terrorism. However, if they are already prohibited by 'normal' offences, sections 9 and 10 would breach the limiting principles set out in chapter 1. This issue will now be considered as an important step towards assessing this special offence.

The first point to be made in the sections' defence is that it might be difficult under regular law to prove that a contributor or fund-gatherer had the *mens rea* to be an accomplice to the crimes committed by the terrorist recipients.[145] In *Johnson* v. *Youden*, Goddard L.C.J. stated that:[146]

Before a person can be convicted of aiding and abetting the commission of an offence, he must at least know the essential matters which constitute that offence.

The precise circumstances of the particular crime need not be known, but it was held in *R.* v. *Bainbridge*[147] that there must be 'knowledge that a crime of the type in question was intended'.

On these tests, many of those aiding terrorism can be charged as accomplices.[148] However, there would be severe problems in securing a conviction in relation to the payment of money in response to such equivocal solicitations as 'to support the boys'. In such a case, as well as financing shootings and bombings, the money may alternatively be spent in connection with public order offences (such as unlawful drilling), administrative expenses (which are unlawful only if the organisation is proscribed) or the legitimate welfare needs of families of convicted terrorists.

Similar difficulties arose in the *Director of Public Prosecutions for Northern Ireland* v. *Maxwell*.[149] The defendant, a member of the U.V.F., guided a following car to a public house and then drove home. Meanwhile, unknown to him, the occupants of the other car planted a bomb. The defendant was charged as a principal in the second degree with various explosives offences. He confessed only that he knew he was on a 'job', by which he meant some kind of military activity.[150] Since this could encompass a wide range of offences, it was not possible to say that he contemplated any 'type' of crime so as to satisfy the *Bainbridge* test.[151] However, that test was supplemented with a new formula; a person is also an accomplice if:[152]

he contemplates the commission of one (or more) of a number of crimes by the principal and he intentionally lends his assistance in order that such crime will be committed.

Since the accused did contemplate a range of specific activities, perhaps not all of the same 'type' and not all unlawful, but including the explosives offences which had occurred, he could be convicted.[153]

Following Maxwell's case, a person who supplies terrorists with a specific item, such as a gun, will become an accomplice to the crimes committed with it. A gun can only perform a particular function, therefore, a range of specific crimes would be contemplated. By contrast, gifts of money or the loan of a car do not closely delimit the possible nefarious activities. Provided the money or property was not solicited for express criminal purposes, the vague nature of the transaction will render it difficult to prove that any set litany of crimes was contemplated. Consequently, by dealing with such situations, sections 9 and 10 are a significant extension of the criminal law.

A related advantage of sections 9 and 10 is that they dispense with the requirement of showing that an accomplice's involvement is linked to an offence which has been committed. This will be difficult to demonstrate when the contribution is financial, since it will probably be mixed with other funds and will not thereafter be referable to any particular results. However, the tracing of money through a terrorist organisation is not necessary under sections 9 and 10, so the police can make an early arrest without allowing the enterprise to reach its dangerous fruition. For example, in *R. v. Higgins and others*,[154] three defendants were convicted just for making approaches to purchase arms for the I.R.A.

Finally, it is also claimed that sections 9 and 10 overcome 'jurisdictional difficulties connected with a conspiracy',[155] since there is generally no liability for conspiracies in the U.K. to commit offences abroad. By contrast, sections 9 and 10 may take effect even if the terrorism assisted occurs abroad.[156] However, it is not an offence under Part III to provide assistance in the Republic of Ireland or U.S.A., both of which are important sources of finance for the I.R.A.[157] A solution might be the assumption of extra-territorial jurisdiction under section 10; this is not recommended for section 9 as it would lead to excessive intrusions into foreign politics. Whether such an extension would be effective is, of course, almost entirely dependent upon extradition arrangements.[158]

In conclusion, sections 9 and 10 cannot be declared superfluous, and the Shackleton, Jellicoe and Colville Reports supported them as a useful adjunct to proscription.[159] However, whether the offence should be retained in its present form or at all can only be determined finally after an examination of its drawbacks.

(iii) Drawbacks The first criticism of sections 9 and 10 is that they entail a greater derogation from regular law than is necessary. Instead of a special offence dependent on the unsatisfactory term 'terrorism', sections 9 and 10 could be replaced by relatively minor amendments to the ordinary criminal law. In particular, as well as prohibiting the control, management, organisation or training of a quasi-military group, section 2 of the Public Order Act 1936 could also penalise contributions to such associations in much the same way as sections 9 and 10 do at present.

A second defect is that sections 9 and 10, unlike section 18, contain no defence of reasonable excuse. Duress is an available defence but may not be sufficient. For example, a Belfast shopkeeper who is asked by a man wearing dark glasses and a black beret to make a contribution 'to fight the Brits' may not immediately or expressly be threatened so as to be under duress,[160] but he could be said to have a reasonable excuse for making a donation. Membership of groups such as the U.D.A. equally rules out a plea of duress.[161] The families or insurers of kidnap victims may also be placed in an invidious position.[162] The developing doctrine of duress of circumstances[163] may help, but a separate statutory defence seems advisable.

(iv) Conclusion An offence outlawing contributions to terrorism is justifiable in principle, but the present formulation of sections 9 and 10 is unsatisfactory in detail. At the same time, though the institution of an offence along the lines of sections 9 and 10 may be acceptable, its wide-

spread use is not. Persons involved in fund-raising are likely to be on the fringes of terrorism, so their removal will inflict limited damage on the terrorists but may sever one of the few leads which could identify important organisers and activists and may lead to the resentment of a community subject equally to paramilitary coercion and State sanctions. The fact that few charges have been brought under sections 9 and 10 reveals both a commendable degree of calculation on the part of the police and the correspondingly limited but important utility of the offence.

(b) Other offences, disclosure and forfeiture

(i) *Nature and extent of use* As the remaining provisions of Part III have only recently become operative, there are few statistical returns.[164] However, there is every expectation that the measures will work as effectively as those in the confiscation codes (subject to some doubts about cooperation from building societies and foreign banks).[165] The Government smoothed the path for the Prevention of Terrorism Act with extensive consultations with financial institutions and advisers.[166] They have responded to the similar drug-trafficking legislation with advice to their members to make regular checks for unusual transactions, especially a sudden increase in cash movements, to keep records, and to verify identities and undertake discreet inquiries of new customers especially those not appearing in person.[167] For their part, solicitors are advised to withdraw from dubious transactions so as to avoid disclosure; if they continue, they should impart any relevant information without taking instructions.[168] However, even the shrewdest banker or lawyer may find it difficult to discern that a transaction is part of a criminal enterprise and may find it harder still to detect that the wrongdoing is connected with terrorism rather than, say, drugs or robbery. Perhaps reflecting this, the point of contact for whistleblowers in Britain is the National Drugs Intelligence Unit.[169] Even when the professional adviser does become convinced of criminal or terrorist links, his position remains difficult:[170]

The role of the police informer does not fit well with the professional image which most [advisers] have of themselves.

(ii) *Comment* In principle, laundering offences and forfeiture are justifiable. They curtail resources which might finance terrorism. They curtail enterprises which could secure for groups like the I.R.A. a degree of entrenchment and support in the community. They prevent paramilitary operations, which may involve the running of businesses at a loss, from undermining the legitimate economy. Furthermore, if confiscation is needed for drug trafficking and serious frauds, it is surely required for offences which are threats to public safety and are particularly difficult to counter owing to the internal discipline of the participants. Thus, Part III of the Prevention of Terrorism Act opens a promising line of attack on terrorism. The I.R.A. is a major enterprise costing up to £4m. per annum,[171] most of which derives from within Northern Ireland.[172] Such large sums to some extent must pass through banks, accountants and solicitors, who form a delicate chain which is vulnerable to investigation and forfeiture. It may be predicted that there will be few prosecutions under these new measures, since the evidence is difficult to gather and the police may prefer to collect intelligence rather than to prosecute their sources. However, even a handful of convictions could have a major impact.

Whilst in principle justifiable, Part III has been criticised in detail, and it has indeed been argued that the Criminal Justice Act 1988 and 1990 Order could be adapted to apply instead.[173] As well as criticisms of the legislation, there are doubts in Northern Ireland about the enforcement agencies and as to whether sufficient action is taken to curtail funding at source. Amongst the enforcement agencies, the most important is probably the Anti-Racketeering Squad of the R.U.C.[174] but only minor staffing increases are envisaged as a result of the Act.[175] In addition, there is some inter-agency cooperation between police, Customs, Inland Revenue and others,[176] but the 'authorised investigators' now envisaged are not a proper substitute for the Serious Frauds Office. As for the curtailment of income at source, much action has already been taken,[177] but further measures may be necessary in the areas of European Community agricultural payments[178] and video piracy.[179]

5 Withholding information: provisions

(a) Offences
By section 18(1):[180]

A person is guilty of an offence if he has information which he knows or believes might be of material assistance –
(a) in preventing the commission by any other person of an act of terrorism connected with the affairs of Northern Ireland; or
(b) in securing the apprehension, prosecution or conviction of any other person for an offence involving the commission, preparation or instigation of such an act of terrorism, and fails without reasonable excuse to disclose that information as soon as reasonably practicable –
(i) in England and Wales, to a constable;
(ii) in Scotland, to a constable or the procurator fiscal; or
(iii) in Northern Ireland, to a constable or a member of Her Majesty's forces.

A person may commit this offence through total inactivity (by not answering police questions or by not volunteering information), through the partial suppression of information or by relating a false account when the true facts are known.

The information must be of a kind which is, or is believed to be, 'of material assistance'. This means that:[181]

> an ordinary citizen alive to his responsibilities would consider that it ought to be disclosed; . . . information based on rumour or idle gossip would not be of such a kind.

To prove this issue of fact, the police may have to describe their investigations up to that point, which obviously limits the attractiveness of section 18 until their inquiries are exhausted.

The 'act of terrorism' which is the subject of the material information may be planned or may already have happened. Following *McKee* v. *Chief Constable for Northern Ireland*,[182] it is not clear whether the information must concern 'active' terrorism. However, this seems a likely interpretation at least in Northern Ireland in regard to future terrorism, since section 18(1)(a) is similar in terms to the definition of 'terrorist' in section 66 of the Emergency Provisions Act, which was in issue in McKee's case.[183] Employment of the term 'terrorism' has been criticised in chapter 2, and the particular problems resulting under section 18 are as follows. One is that it makes the existence of a political motive a crucial element in the offence in contravention of the official policy of criminalisation.[184] Another difficulty is that the breadth of the definition may cause persons, unaware that their knowledge could be construed as being about terrorism, unwittingly to contravene the offence. Consequently, it would be preferable to refer to a list of terrorist-type offences, any one of which is planned or has occurred.[185] The 'act of terrorism' must relate to Northern Ireland. This is a welcome stance against the unnecessary diversion of the Act into the sphere of international terrorism, though the lack of consistency may cause some confusion.

The *mens rea*, 'knows or believes', means that it is not enough that the defendant strongly suspects the possession of material information or thinks it probable or that a reasonable person would have been put on inquiry.[186] Given this restrictive interpretation, it could be argued that a genuine suspicion should suffice. If section 18 is to facilitate the flow of information, it should be left to the police rather than its possessor to evaluate its importance. Provided the defendant does genuinely believe the information is relevant, an offence is committed even if it is neither material nor accurate.[187]

When there is a duty to disclose, the information must be imparted to one of the recipients named in section 18(1). Admissions via the confidential telephone in Northern Ireland would also exonerate the caller (since it is a way of informing the police), provided the message can later be identified.[188] It is not sufficient to contact other persons in authority, such

as magistrates or Members of Parliament,[189] unless perhaps they are requested and agree to pass on the information to an authorised recipient or
are known to be certain to do so automatically and promptly.

(b) Reasonable excuse

The defence of reasonable excuse in section 18(1) may apply to 'a well-
founded fear of personal injury falling outside the narrower bounds of the
defence of duress',[190] but it does not excuse one who simply does not wish
to 'get involved'. The operation of this defence gives rise to considerable
uncertainties in three contexts.

   The first is where there is a close personal relationship between the
person involved in terrorism and the person with knowledge of it, such as
a husband and wife. Equally problematical is the existence of a potentially
privileged relationship, such as between a lawyer and his terrorist client.
Some light may be shed on whether these links provide a 'reasonable
excuse' not to disclose by examining the analogous position under the
common law misdemeanour of misprision of felony. Until abolished in
1967, misprision comprised an offence to conceal, or to procure concealment
of, a felony known to have been committed.[191] In *Sykes* v. *Director of Public
Prosecutions*,[192] the defendant was convicted after he tried to supply stolen
firearms to the I.R.A. The House of Lords provided a number of *dicta* on
the two problems under scrutiny. Lord Denning's view was that a solicitor,
doctor or clergyman who received information in confidence would have
a defence but that close personal ties would not suffice.[193]

   The position adopted in Sykes' case should, it is submitted, be reproduced
under section 18.[194] On the one hand, a party to a normally privileged
relationship, such as a lawyer, should have a reasonable excuse for not
disclosing the confidences of his client. The Government conceded the
existence of some form of privilege in 1989 but sought to distinguish
between (unprivileged) information which may prevent terrorism and
(privileged) information which may assist the prosecution of terrorists.[195]
It is submitted that this contrast is unwarranted by the wording of section
18(1), though it is reflected in guidance from the Law Society that a
solicitor may reveal information which 'he believes necessary to prevent
the client from committing a criminal act that the solicitor believes
on reasonable grounds is likely to result in serious bodily harm'.[196] On the
other hand, the sanctity of personal ties is less defensible in the public
interest and so should be pierced. Though the latter result has caused some
anguish in Parliament, the uncompromising view of the sponsor of section
18[197] and of the Government was that it is right, even in such hard cases,
that:[198]

when dealing with foul and disgusting deeds, someone who knows that someone
else is likely to be threatened and imperilled has not only a moral duty to tell the
police, but a legal one as well.

However, in order to appease those expressing disquiet, the police are now advised by circular that:[199]

A relative of a terrorist who is not involved in terrorism himself should not be put under strain by being reminded in a routine manner of the provisions of section [18]. This use of section [18] can only be justified in extreme cases – where the withholding of information might lead to death, serious injury or the escape of a terrorist offender.

The Baker Report[200] criticised this guidance for being too restrictive, but it is desirable that restraint should be urged, and a more pressing defect is the absence of any advice concerning professional advisers.

The third situation which has caused misgivings is whether one's privilege against self-incrimination[201] provides a reasonable excuse for remaining silent. This issue has partly been settled by an amendment in 1984 to section 18, which provides that the information being suppressed must concern terrorist involvement by 'any other person'.[202] However, this wording does not directly resolve the problem; if a person's evidence implicates both himself and another, it must be disclosed even when the self-damning details cannot be severed. Therefore, it must still be determined whether the so-called 'right to silence' provides a defence of reasonable excuse in those circumstances.

One argument for recognising such a defence is that mere silence in response to incriminating questions did not amount to misprision of felony.[203] However, that offence might be distinguishable from section 18 for these purposes. The term 'terrorism' is meant to conjure a picture of extremely dangerous activity of a rather specialised kind. By contrast, misprision of felony covered a wide range of offences, so, if overridden, the privilege against self-incrimination would have been rendered almost worthless rather than simply qualified in one important respect, as might be said to be the position under section 18.

A second reason favouring the priority of the privilege is that relevant legislation which intends it to be supplanted by a statutory duty of disclosure commonly also grants immunity from prosecution.[204] Does the absence of this 'bargain principle'[205] from section 18 imply that the privilege is preserved? Yet some legislation has removed the right to silence without any compensating exemption. Various factors may overcome the strong judicial support for the privilege, including the importance of admissions to the working of the statute, the presence of alternative safeguards, the dangerousness of the activity and whether the statute envisages prosecutions.[206]

The application of the foregoing considerations to section 18 was undertaken in *H.M. Advocate* v. *Von*.[207] This prosecution arose out of fundraising activities on behalf of the U.V.F. in Scotland. During the first day of his interrogation, the suspect was reminded of the requirements of section 18. The following day, he stated that he:[208]

wished to make a statement and to tell of his own involvement but that he would not name anyone. At this stage police officers realising that he was about to make a statement implicating himself, advised him that what he said could be used in evidence.

The accused made an inculpatory statement but claimed at his trial that it should be excluded because he had not been informed that 'he could reasonably be excused from not disclosing information if the information would be self-incriminating'.[209] The presiding judge (Lord Ross) held that:[210]

> If . . . the accused had been given the usual full caution or had been informed that he was not obliged to give information which could incriminate himself and he had then made a statement, I would have thought that that statement would have been admissible as being a statement made in response to pressure or inducement or as a result of other unfair means. . . .
>
> So far as the evidence goes, the accused was left in total ignorance of the fact that he was not obliged to incriminate himself.

Accordingly, the statement was excluded. However, this judgment rested on the premise that Von did not have to make incriminating statements to avoid the commission of an offence under section 18. The reasons given for this assumption will now be examined.

One point was that a frequently used statutory duty to disclose, which does impliedly override the right to silence, was thought to be distinguishable. By section 172 of the Road Traffic Act 1988, a vehicle owner may be obliged to provide the police with the identity of any driver of it, even if this entails the disclosure of an offence.[211] Lord Ross opined that this was materially different from section 18 since the owner 'is not in normal circumstances even suspect . . .'.[212] However, questioning under section 172 may often lead to the owner being prosecuted for an offence either in that capacity or as the driver.[213] Consequently, a more satisfactory distinction is by reference to section 11 of the Road Traffic Offenders Act 1988 which is concerned with proof in court of statements made pursuant to section 172. This implies such statements are admissible, but there is no corresponding evidential clause in section 18.

The second argument adduced by Lord Ross was that:[214]

> if Parliament had intended to make statements of suspects admissible against them in the event of their being subsequently charged I would have expected Parliament to have made that clear.

However, examples already given, including section 172 itself, demonstrate that the privilege may be impliedly excluded when necessary to avoid frustrating the object of legislation. On that basis, obtaining information about a suspect's own crimes might be just as important as coercing from him knowledge about others' misdeeds.

On balance, the danger of self-incrimination was probably not envisaged by the architects of section 18 as a reasonable excuse. However, since reference to parliamentary debates is forbidden[215] and there is the strong precedent of Von's case, the courts are unlikely to curtail the normal right to silence just because the suspect's knowledge also implicates others.[216] The matter should in any event be settled by redrafting section 18 to make it clear that self-incrimination is not demanded in any circumstances.

A final concern about the relationship between section 18 and the privilege against self-incrimination is that, even to the extent that it is preserved, suspects may be unaware of their legal position. This problem does not pertain to Scotland since:[217]

the Von decision led to the adoption of guide-lines to the police which require them to inform a suspect specifically that the provisions of section [18] do not oblige him to incriminate himself.

The dangers of confusion have also been reduced by circulars issued to all police forces in 1983 which emphasise the Jellicoe Report's recommendation that section 18 should only be recited when the police believe a person possesses information 'which would if revealed prevent acts of terrorism or lead to the apprehension of terrorists offenders'.[218] Thus, the circulars discourage the duty to disclose being brandished against possessors of very low-level intelligence, but a more apposite reform would be to allow the citation of section 18 whenever it might elicit information but always subject to the special Scottish caution.[219]

6   Withholding information: comparisons

Information about terrorism is the focus of both sections 12 and 18 of the Prevention of Terrorism Act. However, there are two substantial differences between the two. First, in Hohfeldian terms, section 18 imposes a duty to disclose, whereas section 12 merely grants a privilege against the adverse consequences of a disclosure.[220] Next, section 18 demands the disclosure of information in connection with 'acts of terrorism', but section 12 may also relate to details concerning 'the resources' of a proscribed organisation.

As for past precedents, withholding of information from the police has frequently been penalised in bygone years.[221] For example, misprision of felony in English common law was the main inspiration behind section 18,[222] and statutory duties to disclose have been imposed specifically in connection with terrorism in Ireland during the past and present centuries.[223] However, following the abolition of misprision of felony in 1967, there is now no obvious rival to section 18 in Britain, though the field is less clear in Northern Ireland.

In English law,[224] misprision was partly replaced by sections 4 and 5 of the Criminal Law Act 1967, but neither prohibits the withholding of information *per se*. Under section 4, there must be some positive action impeding police investigations, and suppression is penalised by section 5 only if motivated by a bribe. Those on the fringes of terrorism would likewise evade conspiracy charges.[225] Conspiracy, as defined by section 1 of the Criminal Law Act 1977,[226] requires that 'a person agrees with any other person or persons that a course of conduct shall be pursued ...'. A Republican sympathiser may have foreknowledge of a terrorist attack and may desire it to occur, but a passive onlooker not sharing in the common design is not a conspirator. By contrast, section 18 catches a bystander, even if his knowledge has been attained unwittingly and even if he is appalled by the actions proposed or undertaken.

Section 5(1) of the Criminal Law Act (Northern Ireland) 1967 differs radically from its English counterpart:

where a person has committed an arrestable offence, it shall be the duty of every other person, who knows or believes –
(a) that the offence or some other arrestable offence has been committed; and
(b) that he has information which is likely to secure, or to be of material assistance in securing, the apprehension, prosecution or conviction of any person for that offence;
to give that information, within a reasonable time, to a constable and if, without reasonable excuse, he fails to do so he shall be guilty of an offence. ...'

Thus, non-disclosure is penalised whether or not it was induced by consideration, though, if money is accepted by way of genuine recompense, there may be a defence under subsection (2). Section 18 remains distinct in that the information must relate to 'terrorism' rather than an 'arrestable offence' and may concern future as well as past activities.[227] However, it is submitted that neither difference excuses the considerable duplication between the two offences. Statutory references to 'terrorism' have already been criticised, and the duty to reveal forthcoming terrorism seems hardly necessary in so far as preparations will almost certainly involve the commission of firearms, explosives, public order or conspiracy offences sufficient to trigger section 5(1).[228]

Apart from section 5(1), section 23 of the Emergency Provisions Act[229] in Northern Ireland empowers the security forces to stop persons to ascertain their identity, movements and knowledge concerning any recent terrorist incident. Section 23 does not make it an offence to fail to volunteer information without being asked. However, the combination of sections 5(1) and 23 surely provides adequate legal weaponry without resort to the Prevention of Terrorism Act.

In the Republic of Ireland, section 30(6) of the Offences against the State Act 1939 makes it an offence to refuse to give, or to give a false, name and address in response to a request by the police under section 30(5). It is also unlawful under section 52 for a person to fail to provide a full, or to give a false, account of his movements and actions during any specified period as well as of all information he possesses concerning terrorist offences. On the one hand, these provisions are narrower than section 18 in that they apply only to persons who have been arrested on suspicion of certain crimes under section 30 and have been expressly asked for information. On the other hand, they are wider in that they override the privilege against self-incrimination.[230]

Amongst other relevant provisions in the Republic not exclusively aimed at terrorists is section 15 of the Criminal Justice Act 1984[231] which penalises the suppression of information by someone found in the suspected unlawful possession of firearms. However, any response is inadmissible as evidence against the person (who need not be arrested) or his spouse. Sections 18 and 19 of the same Act allow adverse corroborative inferences to be drawn from a failure to answer certain police questions after an arrest. Section 18 concerns accounting for any suspicious object or mark (such as traces of explosives). Section 19 requires an explanation of an arrestee's presence at a particular place around the time the alleged offence was committed.

The Colville Report[232] expressed great interest in the Criminal Justice Act, which, together with other important factors, encouraged the passage of the Criminal Evidence (Northern Ireland) Order 1988.[233] It is not possible herein to detail the many controversial aspects of this Order;[234] only its relationship with the Prevention of Terrorism Act will be considered.

The Order contains four relevant measures. Firstly, Article 3 provides that if a person being questioned by the police about an offence or being charged with an offence fails to mention any fact which could reasonably have been mentioned at the time and was subsequently relied upon in his defence, the trial court may draw adverse inferences from the silence or may treat it as corroborating other evidence. Similarly, by Article 4, adverse inferences or corroboration may be drawn from silence during the trial itself. Articles 5 and 6 are the counterparts to the Criminal Justice Act. Article 5 relates to a refusal to account for objects, substances or marks, while Article 6 is concerned with a failure to explain one's presence at the scene of a crime. Each Article entails a special form of caution. For example, if minded to rely on Article 3, the constable should state that:[235]

You do not have to say anything unless you wish to do so but I must warn you that if you fail to mention any fact which you rely on in your defence in court, your failure to take this opportunity to mention it may be treated in court as supporting any relevant evidence against you. . . .

The interrelationship between the Order and section 18 of the Prevention of Terrorism Act is complex. When the suspect has committed an offence and remains silent, there is no infringement of section 18, but the Order (especially Article 3) may penalise silence. Thus, the statutory provisions do not overlap, but the police's incantation of a caution under the Order together with a recitation of section 18 may sow great confusion. Conversely, where the subject knows about another's wrongdoing but is not personally implicated, an offence may be committed under section 18. It follows that silence in response to questioning about that offence may also trigger Articles 3 and 4 of the Order.[236] Consequently, silence could be damning twice over; it forms the *actus reus* of section 18 and then leads to the adverse inference that the person has suppressed relevant information. Thus, section 18 can pull itself up by its own boot-straps with the aid of the Order.

7   Withholding information: assessment

(a) Extent and nature of use

In Great Britain, charges under section 18 to the end of 1990 have been infrequent, and the results suggest that it has been invoked mostly on weak evidence and against those on the fringes of terrorism. By contrast, the offence has figured more prominently in Northern Ireland. A possible cause of its greater popularity in that jurisdiction is simply that, terrorism being more widespread there than in Britain, more information is being withheld. Additional reasons may be that the R.U.C. is more conscious of the offence because of their experience with section 5(1) and is also more reliant upon it because certain parts of the community will not, or fears to, volunteer information.

Charges under section 18 seem to be relevant in four situations. The first is that, where the evidence of involvement in terrorism as an accomplice,

Table 4   The operation of s. 18 in the United Kingdom

Juris-diction	Charges	Not proceeded with	Await trial	Guilty	Sentences (all imprisonment)			
					Suspended	Under 1 year	1–5 years	Over 5 years
Great Britain	23	6	–	10	8	2	–	–
Northern Ireland	100	N/A	N/A	N/A	N/A[237]	N/A	N/A	N/A

Source: Home Office and Northern Ireland Office. *Note*: N/A = figures not available.

conspirator or member of a proscribed organisation is relatively weak, section 18 may be used as an additional, 'back-stop' count.[238]

Next, where the police have successfully detected active terrorists, those suspected of being less deeply implicated may be prosecuted under section 18. For example, Storey, Glenholmes, Campbell and Tuite were charged in December 1979 with trying to effect the escape of an I.R.A. convict from Brixton Prison. Other suspects, including the prisoner's wife, were prosecuted under section 18, though the charges were later withdrawn.[239] Similarly, three persons were prosecuted and acquitted and three others charged but never tried in connection with accommodation and transport allegedly supplied to the I.R.A. group responsible for the Brighton bombing.[240] However, some small fry were convicted in connection with a plot to kill a retired S.A.S. officer in Herefordshire[241] and the murder of two Army corporals at a West Belfast funeral.[242] Two persons, Mullen and Wadley, were prosecuted after an arms find at a Clapham flat in December 1988. Charges against the latter included withholding information, but he was acquitted on all counts.[243]

The third type of case is where a police investigation into a terrorist plot has largely failed, but evidence against some minor participants has been unearthed. This pattern was followed in the most important case in Britain involving section 18. In response to various I.R.A. attacks before Christmas 1978, police inquiries focused on Essex. However, when none of the prime suspects could be traced, the police arrested twenty-three people less deeply implicated; ten were eventually brought to trial, and seven were convicted under section 18.[244]

The fourth target, persons who have been coerced into aiding terrorists (especially by loaning their cars), arises exclusively in Northern Ireland.[245] The main objective is to motivate victims to contact the police automatically so that any planned outrage may be thwarted.

(b) Necessity

Justification of section 18 must in part depend, as it did for sections 9 and 10, on whether it can clearly be distinguished from preexisting, 'normal' crimes. Necessity in this sense has already been examined, and it was concluded that, whilst it has no close rival in British law, section 18 is largely unnecessary in Northern Ireland. Turning to the wider question of whether an offence of withholding information in any guise is acceptable, the main advantage is claimed to be that it will 'create an atmosphere in which it [is] respectable to provide . . . information'.[246] Given this objective, rates of prosecution and conviction are not decisive. The real value of the measure is to influence people to volunteer information; the prosecution of recalcitrant minor participants after violence has occurred is a second-best.

Reviewing all the available evidence, the Jellicoe Report concluded that:[247]

the section is of significant value to the police service, but that service could operate without it if required to do so. . . . however, the section should lapse only if the difficulties it causes or may cause in terms of abuse and of damage to civil liberties are genuinely serious and irremediable.

In view of this half-hearted support, the remainder of this chapter will catalogue the defects associated with the offence in order to decide whether they outweigh the supposed benefits.

(c) Drawbacks in principle

Lord Shackleton recommended the abolition of section 18 at least in Britain, since:[248]

There are genuine doubts about its implications in principle and about the way it might be used in the course of interviewing someone. . . . it has an unpleasant ring about it in terms of civil liberties.

His verdict was rightly attacked in Parliament as hardly 'persuasive rationally',[249] but more precise arguments for and against may be formulated.

The first justification for section 18 might be that offences involving withholding information are familiar to our legal system rather than a 'dangerous innovation'.[250] As well as misprision of felony and section 5(1) in Northern Ireland, other closely related provisions include section 6(2) of the Explosive Substances Act 1883, section 6(1) of the Official Secrets Act 1920[251] and the common law misdemeanour of misprision of treason.[252] As a result, there is authority for the view that, in exceptionally dangerous situations, society may compel its citizenry to provide succour. The contrary view of Viscount Colville – that there is nothing 'special' in withholding information about terrorism and so there is no good reason for section 18 (at least outside Northern Ireland)[253] – is thus controverted. The *raison d'être* for section 18 (and much else besides in the Act) is surely that terrorism is an extraordinarily dangerous activity which may give rise to exceptional duties.

Section 18 conforms to established precedents, but those precedents might themselves be unsound because they conflict with the accepted policy of policing by consent.[254] Thus, section 18 has been decried for creating the sort of 'informer's society which exists in totalitarian states'.[255] A radical response might argue that our traditional distaste for 'social responsibility' is misplaced.[256] Yet section 18 might still be justifiable even if it is viewed as exceptional. Given that this special offence has attracted substantial attention and support in Parliament,[257] it may legitimately be concluded that:[258]

in the case of terrorism, which is almost by definition criminal activity aimed at society as a whole, it seems . . . reasonable that there should be more than a merely moral duty to assist the police.

Another theoretical objection to section 18 is that it should not form part of the criminal law as it does not penalise any action undertaken by the defendant or any dishonest intention on his part.[259] In reply, having decided that it is acceptable to impose a legal, as well as a moral, duty to help the police to combat terrorism, it follows that an omission to fulfil that duty may properly incur legal sanctions. This is consistent with the view that failure to impart evidence is wicked because of the especially dangerous nature of terrorism.

(d) Drawbacks in practice

Two important drawbacks arise from the practical application of section 18. The first is that there is conflicting evidence that it has achieved its central goal of increasing the flow of information to the police, and it seems improbable that it will ever do so. It is presumably not claimed that section 18 carries much clout with hardened terrorists, so it must be primarily aimed against those on the periphery of terrorism. Yet even such soft targets are likely either to be more intimidated by terrorists than by section 18 or to provide to the police 'false and misleading information, in order to obtain their release'.[260] The result seems to be that, as the police recognise, there is little advantage in prosecuting petty offenders; there is a great deal more to be gained by keeping them under surveillance and following the leads they provide. The same reaction seems to apply in practice to kidnap negotiations either by relatives of the victim or by professionals (especially Control Risks).[261] Allegations that the latter may breach section 18 seem unfounded, as the company maintains liaison with the police.[262]

The second practical drawback concerns the effect of section 18 on the media. A reporter in Northern Ireland may discover information about terrorism by interviewing a terrorist leader or by witnessing a paramilitary display. Arranging, attending or reporting such events may implicate the journalist in various offences,[263] but section 18 has become most threatening of all, and its effects are felt in three directions.

Firstly, section 18 contributes to a 'chilling' effect on the reporting of terrorism. Correspondents can expect close attention from the police and hostility from their own superiors which, in the case of broadcasting, 'is so great that there is little point ever in attempting anything in this field'.[264]

Secondly, section 18 provides a pretext for imposing special restraints upon reporters especially in Britain and in the electronic media.[265] Such censorship will be described further in chapter 12.

The third effect of section 18 is via the direct threat of prosecution. A number of skirmishes have occurred between the journalistic ethic to protect confidential sources and the demand of section 18 to disclose them.[266] For example, a B.B.C. (Northern Ireland) programme in March 1977 contained an interview with a member of the I.N.L.A. The management supplied the names of the camera crew to the police, but no prosecutions followed. In 1978, Alain Frilet, of *Liberation* magazine, was arrested for an offence under section 18 in connection with the possession of photographs of an I.R.A. display.[267] More ominous rumblings occurred in 1979. In September of that year, Pierre Salinger was arrested in Belfast together with his American Broadcasting Company colleagues and the Provisional Sinn Fein politicians he had been interviewing. The R.U.C., believing that an illegal military display was planned, confiscated the film of the meeting but brought no charges.[268] The B.B.C. also encountered legal difficulties.[269] In July 1979, the *Tonight* programme included an interview with an I.N.L.A. representative who claimed responsibility in Dublin on behalf of his group for the murder of Airey Neave, M.P. Then, in October 1979, a *Panorama* crew filmed an I.R.A. road-block in Carrickmore, Northern Ireland. This publicity stunt was not in fact transmitted, but, as in the previous example, the reporters failed to inform the security forces until long after the trail was cold. Both events incurred the wrath of the Attorney-General, who publicly wrote to the B.B.C. on 20 June 1980 as follows:[270]

Although I have reached a decision not to institute criminal proceedings in respect of these two incidents I should like to make it clear that I regard conduct of the nature which took place as constituting in principle offences under section [18]. . . . Any interview with a person purporting to represent a terrorist organisation is potentially a source of information of the nature referred to in section [18] of the Act arising not only from the actual contents of the interview but also from any negotiations leading up to and the actual arrangements for it. Consequently, anyone seeking to interview persons he believes to be terrorists cannot be doing otherwise than seeking information which is likely to fall within the terms of section [18] and he is therefore likely to be under a duty to disclose it as soon as reasonably practicable to the appropriate Authority under the Act unless there is reasonable excuse for not doing so.

I would . . . accept that the *Panorama* Team did have a reasonable excuse while still in the vicinity of the members of the P.I.R.A. they filmed at Carrickmore but not later. Of course anyone who actually witnesses a terrorist offence, as at Carrickmore, or comes by information which he believes falls within the terms of section [18] is also under a duty to disclose it.

In response, the B.B.C. Chairman rejected allegations that the B.B.C. had transmitted propaganda or that false statements had been given to the police. However, he was less pugnacious when it came to section 18:

we accept that the law must be obeyed in the difficult area of reporting terrorism in Northern Ireland, and that the journalist has an obligation to disclose to the police anything he may have discovered in the course of an interview with suspected or known terrorists that might be of 'material assistance'. . . . There remains, however, one matter which causes us concern. . . . [Your letter] could be read as meaning that the police should be informed, at every turn, of the letters, phone calls, or meetings with go-betweens which are, I have no doubt, necessary if a journalist is ever to acquire information from known or suspected terrorists. If this is really what the law says, then all reporting of who terrorists are and what they say, would, in practice, be halted abruptly.

The exchange was terminated by a final warning from the Attorney-General that he would in future take a stricter view of such activities.

There have been no reported cases of charges under section 18 against journalists since 1979, but the offence was heavily utilised in 1988 to threaten the seizure of film of the murders at the Milltown Cemetery and of two corporals at a Belfast funeral procession.[271] The materials were released after legal advice, which presumably warned of the dangers of prosecution under section 18. Media witnesses were also called at the ensuing trials. Police intervention in these ways entails a threat to the safety of film crews and the independence of reporters. At the same time, there is a legitimate interest in the investigation of murders. The problem with section 18 is that there is no independent assessment of these conflicting considerations. In that respect, the procedure under the Police and Criminal Evidence legislation,[272] which requires proof of necessity before a judge, is preferable.

The overall effect of section 18 on the media is that coverage of Irish terrorism abounds with difficulties, so the temptation must be to steer clear of the subject altogether or at least to keep reports as simple and as superficial as possible.[273] If these are the results, it should finally be considered whether they are desirable. Supporters of the offence claim that a journalist may possess important information about terrorism, and the dangers of turning him into an I.R.A. sympathiser by forcing him to disgorge it are remote.[274] However, there are disadvantages. Any form of censorship may be useful propaganda for the terrorists and is, in any event, unlikely to be wholly effective. More importantly, though broadcasters should avoid allowing terrorists 'to extort publicity',[275] the operation of section 18 (together with proscription) tends to treat events in Northern Ireland as 'guilty secrets'.[276] This in turn fosters the misleading impression that extreme Republicanism has neither appeal nor rationale, and such misapprehensions increase the danger that the electorate and Government will react inappropriately to it. Finally, the practical success of section 18 in terms of coercing oral evidence from journalists is questionable; if the offence has to be invoked, the most likely outcome is the incarceration of a martyred journalist. Physical evidence (film, notes) is less easily withheld but should be sought by normal search powers rather than section 18.

(e) Conclusions
On balance, there is value in having an offence of withholding information, provided it is recognised that much of its value is superficial and that it carries grave dangers. To date, restraint has been demonstrated by both the Government (through its circulars) and the police (as evidenced by the

dearth of prosecutions). However, to be truly acceptable section 18 should be further limited to information about specified serious offences and should deal more generously with suspects, lawyers and journalists.[277]

Notes

1 *Beckford* v *R.* [1987] 3 W.L.R. 611; *R.* v. *Thain* [1985] 11 N.I.J.B. 31
2 J.C. Smith and B. Hogan, *Criminal Law* (6th ed., 1988) p. 848.
3 H.C. Debs. Vol. 143 col. 213 6 December 1988, Mr. Hurd.
4 H.C. Debs. Vol. 110 cols. 264–5 10 February 1987.
5 Para. 14.1.7.
6 Protection is thus afforded to the U.K. arms industry: W. Finnie, 'Old wine in new bottles' 1990 *J.R.* 1 at p. 11. The Colville Report (para. 14.18.) wisely confined the extension to acts in the U.K.
7 Such offences include: homicides by British citizens (Offences against the Person Act 1861 s. 9); certain acts against persons covered by the Internationally Protected Persons Act 1978; acts scheduled to the Suppression of Terrorism Act 1978 committed in a designated state (this may particularly affect Sikh extremists if India ever becomes designated); offences of hijacking and endangering the safety of aircraft (Aviation Security Act 1982); taking hostages (Taking of Hostages Act 1982); certain acts under the Nuclear Material (Offences) Act 1983; certain acts of torture (Criminal Justice Act 1988 s. 134). In addition, it is an offence to possess in the U.K. firearms or explosives with intent to commit terrorism abroad: Firearms Act 1968 s.16 (see *R.* v. *El-Hakkaoni* [1975] 2 All E.R. 146); Explosive Substances Act 1883 s. 4 (see *R.* v. *Berry* [1985] A.C. 246).
8 See: Export of Goods Control Order 1987 S.I. No. 2070. Compare: W. Finnie, 'Fourth bite at the cherry' 1989 *S.L.T.* 329.
9 Compare: Drug Trafficking Offences Act 1986 s. 38; Criminal Justice Act 1988 s. 102.
10 H.C. Debs. Standing Comm. B col. 237 10 January 1989.
11 Compare: *Re British Basic Slag Ltd.'s Agreements* [1963] 2 All E.R. 807.
12 H.C. Debs. Standing Comm. B col. 201 20 December 1989, Mr. Hogg. Sinn Fein may again escape liability because of the absence of any provable 'arrangement': col. 198.
13 *Saunders* v. *Richmond upon Thames L.B.C.* [1978] I.C.R. 75.
14 D. Feldman, *Criminal Confiscation Orders* (1988) p. 19.
15 See: H.C. Debs. Standing Comm. B col. 203 20 December 1988.
16 Compare: *Auchin* v. *Coulthard* [1942] 2 K.B 228 at p. 234.
17 Knowledge gained from other contexts may not be discounted as under the Trustee Act 1925 s. 28.
18 Criminal Attempts Act 1981 s. 1; *R.* v. *Shivpuri* [1987] A.C. 1.
19 See: *R.* v. *Griffiths* (1975) 60 Cr. App. R. 14; *Johnson* v. *Whitehouse* [1984] R.T.R. 38; *Holtham* v. *M.P.C.* (1987) *Times* 28 November.
20 *Tournier* v. *National and Provincial Union Bank of England* [1924] 1 K.B. 461.
21 H.L. Debs Vol. 472 cols. 1167–8 24 March 1986, Lord Denning.
22 The situation of barristers may be relevant, as they have no contract with

the ultimate client: D. Feldman, 'Conveyancers and the proceeds of crime' (1989) *Conv.* 389 at p. 393. Another example concerns trustees of a charity.

23   'Express' means it should be stated in words or writing so as to avoid any dispute: H.C. Debs. Vol. 146 col. 51 30 January 1989, Mr. Hogg. The person would do well to obtain written confirmation: Feldman, *loc. cit.* at p. 396.

24   The defence does not extend to those who solicit or receive funds contrary to ss. 9(1)(a), 10(1)(a).

25   The concept is therefore stricter than the idea that the disclosure be 'voluntary': H.C. Debs. Standing Comm. B col. 209 20 December 1988.

26   Feldman, *op. cit.* p. 24.

27   H.C. Debs. Standing Comm. B cols. 210–11 20 December 1988.

28   S. 13(1).

29   Drug Trafficking Offences Act 1986 s. 24.

30   See: *H.M.A.* v. *Walker and Edgar* (1986) *Times* 14 March p. 2; *Reid* v. *H.M.A.* 1990 S.C.C.R. 83. See also *R.* v. *O'Reilly* (1990) 6 B.N.I.L. n. 71 (judge believed maximum was ten years).

31   Para. 14.2.7.

32   See: Chief Constable for the R.U.C., *Annual Report for 1987* (1988) p. xiii.

33   S. 13(2)–(6).

34   These indirect activities may breach ss. 9(2)(b), 10(1)(c) and 11(1).

35   See: *R.* v. *Smith* [1989] 2 All E.R. 948.

36   But third parties may retain rights of set-off and forfeiture before the order: *In re K.* [1990] 2 W.L.R. 1224; *In re R.* [1990] 2 W.L.R. 1232.

37   See R.S.C. Ord. 115 rr. 24–36 (England and Wales); R.S.C. Ord. 116 (Northern Ireland); Rules of the Court of Session r. 201S-Y (Scotland).

38   Sched. 4 para. 1(1). Para. 21(1) (Northern Ireland) is identical, but para. 11(1) (Scotland) unaccountably has no equivalent to (a), though the scope of (d) could make up for any deficiency.

39   Sched. 4 para. 1(2), 11(3) (Scotland), 21(2) (Northern Ireland). The Scottish variant arises because some forms of appeal are not subject to a time-limit: H.L. Debs. Vol. 504 col. 997 28 February 1989.

40   Sched. 4 paras. 1(4), (5), 11(5) (Scotland), 21(4), (5) (Northern Ireland).

41   Sched. 4 paras. 1(6), 11(6) (Scotland), 21(6) (Northern Ireland).

42   Sched. 4 paras. 2(2), 12(2) (Scotland), 23(2) (Northern Ireland). Any shortfall must be paid by the prosecution. The receiver is not liable for any loss except through negligence: paras. 2(1), 12(1), 22(1).

43   Sched. 4 paras. 1(3), 11(4) (Scotland), 21(3) (Northern Ireland), 31(1).

44   The common law freezing of assets remains possible but is not as attractive owing to its uncertainties and extent: Feldman, *op. cit.*, ch. 7.

45   Sched. 4 paras. 3, 13 (Scotland), 23 (Northern Ireland). The jurisdiction is exercised by a judge of Q.B.D. or Ch.D. in Chambers: Ord. 115 r. 25 (England and Wales); Ord. 116 r. 2 (N.I.). The Colville Annual Report for 1990, para. 7.12 expresses concern that Sched. 4 demands a prospect of criminal charges, unlike s. 14 arrests. In Scotland, the application is by petition to the Outer House: r. 201T.

46   Sched. 4 paras. 4(1), 14(1) (Scotland), 24(1) (Northern Ireland). No delay is allowed in giving notice: Feldman, *op. cit.* p. 77.

47 Ord. 115 r. 26, Ord. 116 r. 3 (N.I.). In Scotland, the petition itself must narrate the facts: r. 191(a).

48 Ord. 115 r. 26; Ord. 116 r. 3 (N.I).

49 See: Feldman, *op. cit.* pp. 72, 77; *In re The Drug Trafficking Offences Act 1986* (1987, LEXIS).

50 Sched. 4 paras. 3(1), 13(1) (Scotland), 23(1) (Northern Ireland).

51 Feldman, *op. cit.*, pp. 77, 78.

52 Sched. 4 paras. 3(6), 13(5) (Scotland), 23(6) (Northern Ireland).

53 Feldman, *op. cit.*, p. 56.

54 See: *Re H.* (1988) *Times* 1 April. Special protection may be given to land: Sched. 4 paras. 6, 16, 26. For Northern Ireland, see para. 25B (Emergency Provisions Act 1991 Sched. 7).

55 Sched. 4 paras. 5, 15 (Scotland), 25 (Northern Ireland).

56 Sched. 4 paras. 3(7), 13(6) (Scotland), 23(7) (Northern Ireland).

57 H.C. Debs. Standing Comm. B cols. 246–7 10 January 1989, Mr. Hogg.

58 Sched. 4 paras. 4(2), (3), 14(2), (3) (Scotland), 24(2), (3) (Northern Ireland). The application is by summons Ord. 115 r. 28, Ord. 116 r. 5 (N.I.) except in Scotland, where it is by motion (r. 201V).

59 Sched. 4 paras. 3(5), 13(4) (Scotland), 23(5) (Northern Ireland).

60 A two-month (renewable) period was rejected: H.C. Debs. Standing Comm. B cols. 217–23 22 December 1988. Orders granted *ex parte* should only have effect until the date set for the full hearing (Ord. 115 r. 27(2), Ord. 116 r. 4(2) (N.I.)); time-limits under the Prosecution of Offences Act 1985 s. 22 may also intervene.

61 Ord. 115 r. 27, Ord. 116 r. 4 (N.I.).

62 *In re The Drug Trafficking Offences Act 1986, loc. cit.*

63 Sched. 4 paras. 7, 17 (Scotland), 27 (Northern Ireland), criticised by Colville Annual Report for 1990, para. 7.9.

64 H.C. Debs. Standing Comm. B col. 232 22 December 1988, Mr. Hogg.

65 The application is by summons Ord. 115 r. 29, Ord. 116 (r. 7 N.I.) or by petition in Scotland (r. 201V).

66 The action is expressly saved in Scotland only: Sched. 4 para. 17(2).

67 H.C. Debs. Standing Comm. B col. 231 22 December 1988, Mr. Hogg.

68 Criminal Justice Act 1988 s. 133. The rights are also narrower than suggested by the Hodgson Committee Report, *The Proceeds of Crime and their Recovery* (1984) pp. 108–9.

69 Paras. 8–10, 18–20 (Scotland), 28–30 (Northern Ireland).

70 Corresponding legislation is to be encouraged by the E.C. Council draft Directive on Money Laundering (COM. (90) 106 Final-SYN 254, Council Common Position (14282/91)). British legislation appears to comply in most respects: H.L. Select Committee on the European Communities, *Money Laundering* (1990–91) H.L. 6. See also: Council of Europe Convention on Laundering, Search, Seizure and Confiscation of the Proceeds from Crime (E.T.S. 141, 1990).

71 The Court of Session acts in Scotland: para. 20. The application is made *ex parte* and must be supported by an affidavit and may be heard by a master of the Q.B.D.: Ord. 115 rr. 25(2), 30, 31; Ord. 116 r. 8, 10 (N.I.).

72 Notice of registration must be given to persons affected: Ord. 115 r. 33,

Ord. 116 r. 12 (N.I.). A person may then apply to set aside registration by summons and affidavit: r. 34, r. 13 (N.I.). The beneficiary of a registered order must notify the English court if the 'home' court varies or discharges the order: r. 34, r. 15 (N.I.).

73 Para. 31.

74 Any contracts of sale may be executed (para. 31(4)), and if the insolvency is annulled, the forfeiture revives (para. 31(6), (7)).

75 Para. 32.

76 Para. 33. He may even deduct his expenses: para. 34.

77 See: H.L. Debs. Vol. 504 col. 1002 28 February 1989.

78 See Shackleton Report para. 64.

79 See further P.T.B.L. (1st ed.) pp. 37, 94, Smith and Hogan, *op. cit.* p. 845.

80 See P.V.L.I. pp. 138–9. However, the formula of words follows that used in the Prevention of Terrorism Act 1984 and so avoids the 'gap' just described.

81 *Ibid.* p. 252.

82 *Ibid.* pp. 253, 273.

83 Dail Debs. Vol. 292 col. 379 7 September 1976.

84 See: Feldman, *op. cit.*, ch. 3; C. Graham and C. Walker, 'The continued assault on the vaults' [1989] Crim. L.R. 185.

85 There is no equivalent to s. 24(1)(b) (see Feldman, *op. cit.* pp. 21, 22). The absence of personal gain as a motive under the Prevention of Terrorism Act and the breadth of the word 'arrangement' may be the explanation.

86 H.L. Debs. Vol. 474 col. 1118 13 May 1986, Viscount Davidson.

87 The defence in s. 11(2) is drawn from the Drug Trafficking Offences Act 1986 s. 24(4).

88 See: D. Wheatley, 'Guilty . . . said the Red Queen?' (1989) 139 *N.L.J.* 499; Home Affairs Committee, *Drug Trafficking and Related Serious Crimes* (1989–90 H.C. 320) para. 82, Vol. II p. 104.

89 H.L. Debs. Vol. 504 col. 959 28 February 1989, Earl Ferrers.

90 18 U.S.C. s. 1956. See: A. Abramovsky, 'Money laundering and narcotics prosecutions' (1956) 54 *Fordham L. Rev.* 471. Compare: Canadian Criminal Code s. 462.31.

91 18 U.S.C. ss. 1961, 1962. See also: Continuing Criminal Enterprise Act (21 U.S.C. s. 848).

92 *U.S.* v. *Ivic* 700 F.2d 51 (1983); *U.S.* v. *Bagaric* 706 F.2d 616 (1982); *U.S.* v. *Ferguson* 758 F.2d 843 (1985); *N.E. Women's Center Inc.* v. *McMonagle* 624 F. Supp. 736 (1985).

93 See: M. Zander, *Confiscation and Forfeiture Law* (1989) pp. 36–42; G.E. Lynch, 'RICO: the crime of being a criminal' (1987) 87 *Col. L. Rev.* 661, 920; M. Goldsmith, 'RICO and enterprise criminality' (1988) 88 *Col. L. Rev.* 774.

94 H.L. Debs. Vol. 504 col. 41 13 February 1989, Earl Ferrers.

95 31 U.S.C. s. 5311; *California Bankers Association* v. *Shultz* 416 U.S. 21 (1974). See also in Australia: Cash Transaction Reports Act 1988 (No. 64 Cth.) s. 7.

96 Zander, *op. cit.*, p. 48; Abramovsky, *loc. cit.*; J. Popham and M. Probus, 'Structured transactions in money laundering' (1987–88) 15 *Am. J. Crim. L.* 83; J.K. Villa, 'Critical view of Banking Secrecy Act enforcement and money laundering

statute' (1988) 37 *Cath. U.L. Rev.* 489; J.N. Welling, 'Smurfs, money laundering and the Federal Criminal law' (1989) 41 *Fla. L. Rev.*; Home Affairs Committee, *loc. cit.* para. 86, Government Response (Cm. 1164, 1990) p. 9.

97 Proceeds of Crime Act 1987 (No. 87 Cth.) ss. 73–5.

98 Cash Transaction Reports Act 1988 s. 17; Canadian Criminal Code s. 462.47.

99 These were encouraged by the Hodgson Committee Report, *op. cit.*

100 S.I. No. 2588.

101 See: R.S.C. Ord. 93, r. 5.

102 See P.V.L.I. pp. 250–1, 271–2.

103 Paras. 14.2.3–14.2.5.

104 In the event of conflict, the Prevention of Terrorism Act prevails: Sched. 8 paras. 7, 9, 10; Criminal Justice (Confiscation) (N.I.) Order 1990 Arts. 2, 3.

105 Drug Trafficking Offences Act 1986 ss. 8, 19, 24A–26A; Criminal Justice (Scotland) Act 1987 ss. 9, 26, 27–32; Criminal Justice Act 1988 ss. 77, 89, 94–7.

106 See the Scottish Law Commission, Discussion Paper No. 82, *Forfeiture and Confiscation* (1989).

107 S. 71.

108 Drug Trafficking Offences Act 1986 s. 6; Criminal Justice (Scotland) Act 1987 s. 7; Criminal Justice Act 1988 s. 75. Criminal Justice (Confiscation) (N.I.) Order 1990 Art. 10.

109 S. 2. See Hodgson Committee Report, *op. cit.* pp. 75, 82, 144.

110 S. 38. See: *R. v. Southwark Crown Court, ex p. C.C.E.* [1989] 3 W.L.R. 1054.

111 Drug Trafficking Offences Act 1986 ss. 15–17; Criminal Justice (Scotland) Act 1987 ss. 33–7; Criminal Justice Act 1988 ss. 84–6; Criminal Justice (Confiscation) (N.I.) Order 1990 Arts. 21, 22.

112 *Loc. cit.*, para. 5.12.

113 H.L. Debs. Vol. 504 col. 1002 28 February 1989, Earl Ferrers.

114 Drug Trafficking Offences Act 1986, s. 5; Criminal Justice (Scotland) Act 1987 s. 8(2); Criminal Justice Act 1988 s. 74; Criminal Justice (Confiscation) (N.I.) Order 1990 Art. 3.

115 Drug Trafficking Offences Act 1986 ss. 7–10; Criminal Justice Act 1988 ss. 76–9; Criminal Justice (Confiscation)(N.I.) Order 1990 Art. 14.

116 S. 3; Crown Court Rules r. 25A. See also: Criminal Justice (Scotland) Act 1987 s. 4; Criminal Justice Act 1988 s. 73; Criminal Justice (Confiscation) (N.I.) Order 1990 Art. 4.

117 See: H.C. Debs. Standing Comm. B col. 226 10 January 1989.

118 Colville Annual Report for 1990, para. 7.4.

119 *Ibid.* See also Colville Report on the E.P. Acts, para. 17.11.2.

120 H.C. Debs. Vol. 187 col. 295 6 March 1991, Mr. Brooke.

121 Compare Criminal Justice (International Cooperation) Act 1990 s. 15.

122 Compare: Criminal Justice (Serious Frauds) (N.I.) Order 1988, S.I. No. 1846.

123 H.L. Debs. Vol. 485 col. 356 26 February 1987.

124 In the meantime, forfeiture under the Prevention of Terrorism Act takes priority: Emergency Provisions Act s. 50(2).

125   H.C. Debs. Vol. 187 col. 311 6 March 1991, Mr. Brooke.

126   There is a vast amount of literature available. See especially S. Wisotsky, 'Crackdown' (1987) 38 *Hast. L. Rev.* 889; Zander, *op. cit.* Appendix; U.S. Dept. of Justice, *Topical Search: Asset Seizure and Forfeiture* (1990).

127   See: Proceeds of Crime Act 1987, Cash Transaction Reports Act 1988 (Australia); Criminal Code s. 462.3–462.5 (1988) (Canada); D. McLean, 'Seizing the proceeds of crime' (1989) 38 *I.C.L.Q.* 334; D. Feldman, 'Individual rights and legal values in proceeds of crime legislation' (1989) 18 *Anglo-Am. L.R.* 261.

128   See: 18 U.S.C. s. 1963; 21 U.S.C. s. 853.

129   Zander, *op. cit.* p. 43.

130   18 U.S.C s. 194. See: 'Civil RICO is a misnomer' (1987) 100 *Harv. L. Rev.* 1288; M. Goldsmith, 'Civil RICO reform' (1987) 71 *Minn. L. Rev.* 827.

131   21 U.S.C. s. 881. See: P.A. Winn, 'Seizure of private property in the war against drugs' (1988) 41 *Southwestern L.J.* 1111.

132   Zander, *op. cit.* p. 45.

133   Proceeds of Crime Act 1987 s. 17; Criminal Code s. 462.38; Offences against the State (Amendment) Act 1985. See also: Home Affairs Committee, *loc. cit.* para. 83.

134   See especially: L.F. Rackner, 'Forfeiture of attorneys' fees' (1987) 39 *Stan. L. Rev.* 663; K.F. Brinkey, 'Forfeiture of attorney's fees' (1986) 72 *Ca. L. Rev.* 493, 'Tainted assets and the right to counsel' (1988) 66 *Washington Univ. L.Q.* 47; L.F. Rackner, 'Against forfeiture of attorneys' fees under RICO' (1986) 61 *N.Y.U.L. Rev.* 124.

135   (1989) 109 S. Ct. 2657, 2646.

136   See also: Canadian Criminal Code s. 462.34.

137   Criminal Justice (Scotland) Act 1987 s. 9(5); Criminal Justice Act 1988 s. 77(2); Criminal Justice (Confiscation) (N.I.) Order 1990 Art 13(2). The Drug Trafficking Offences Act 1986 is silent, but see: Ord. 115 r. 4; *In re Peters* [1988] Q.B. 871.

138   H.L. Debs. Vol. 504 col. 1365 28 February 1989.

139   H.O. Circular, para 3.29.

140   Ord. 15 r. 27(1).

141   *U.S. v. Monsanto, loc. cit., per* Blackman J.

142   See: *In re P.* (1990) *Times* 11 April.

143   Up to the end of 1990, there were ninety-one charges of contributions under s. 28(1)(b) following detention under the Prevention of Terrorism Act alone.

144   Quoted in the Jellicoe Report, para. 213.

145   See Accessories and Abettors Act 1861 s. 8 as amended; Magistrates' Courts Act 1980 s. 4. The same applies to incitement and conspiracy.

146   [1950] 1 K.B. 544 at p. 546.

147   [1960] 1 Q.B. 129 at p. 134. See also: *R. v. Churchill* [1962] 2 A.C. 224; *R. v. Patel* [1970] Crim. L.R. 277. Compare: Criminal Attempts Act 1987 s. 9.

148   See: *R. v. McClafferty* [1981] 3 N.I. 1; *People (D.P.P.) v. Madden* [1977] I.R. 336.

149   [1978] 3 All E.R. 1140; R. Buxton, 'The extent of criminal complicity' (1979) 42 *M.L.R.* 315. See also: *R. v. Gibson and Lewis* [1986] 17 N.I.J.B. 1; *R. v. Hamilton* [1989] 6 N.I.J.B. 1; *R. v. Law* [1989] 10 N.I.J.B. 72

150   [1978] 3 All E.R. 1140 at pp. 1153, 1157.

F

151 *Ibid.* pp. 1149, 1150.

152 *Ibid.* p. 1145.

153 *Ibid.* p. 1158. See also: *R.* v. *Calderwood and Moore* [1983] N.I. 361; *Chan Wing-Sin* v. *R.* [1984] 3 W.L.R. 677; *R.* v. *Jubb and Rigby* [1984] Crim. L.R. 616.

154 (1977) *Times* 22 February p. 2, 7 April p. 1.

155 Colville Report, para. 14.1.5.

156 See: Smith and Hogan, *op. cit.* pp. 268, 269; n. 7 *supra*.

157 See: J. Adams, *The Financing of Terror* (1986) ch. 6; A. Guelke, *Northern Ireland: The International Perspective* (1988) ch. 7; J. Holland, *The American Connection* (1989). A conspiracy abroad to commit offences in U.K. is actionable: *Liangsiriprasert* v. *U.S. Govt.* [1990] 2 All E.R. 866; *R.* v. *Sansom* [1990] 2 W.L.R. 366.

158 Offences under Pt. III are extraditable: Sched. 8 paras. 1, 4.

159 Paras. 131, 233, 239; 14.1.6.

160 See: *R.* v. *Graham* [1982] 1 W.L.R. 294; *R.* v. *Calderwood and Moore*, *loc. cit.*

161 *R.* v. *Payne* (1990) 6 B.N.I.L. n. 72.

162 See: D. Bonner, 'Combating terrorism in the 1990s' (1989) *P.L.* 440 at p. 460.

163 See: *R.* v. *Conway* [1988] 3 W.L.R. 1238; *R.* v. *Martin* [1989] 1 All E.R. 652.

164 Three were charged in Northern Ireland under s. 11 to end of 1990. The Colville Report for 1990, para. 7.12, states that s. 12 is working satisfactorily in Britain but less so in Northern Ireland. No forfeiture orders have been made.

165 See: Graham and Walker, *loc. cit.* p. 192; Home Affairs Committee, *loc. cit.* paras. 67, 70, 72.

166 H.C. Debs. Standing Comm. B col. 15 13 December 1988, Mr. Hogg.

167 See: British Bankers' Association and the Building Societies Association, *Guidance Notes – Money Laundering* (1990). See also: Institute of Chartered Accountants, *The Auditor's Responsibility for Detecting and Reporting Fraud and Other Illegal Acts* (1988).

168 See: (1987) 84 *L.S. Gaz.* 3557; (1988) 85 *L.S. Gaz.* No. 3 p. 8; (1989) 86 *L.S. Gaz.* No. 24 p. 11. Earlier advice to obtain the client's consent to any disclosure is preposterous in view of the Drug Trafficking Offences Act 1986 s. 31.

169 H.O. Circular, para. 3.15.

170 D. Feldman, 'Conveyancers and the proceeds of crime' (1989) *Conv.* 389.

171 H.C. Debs. Vol. 143 col. 212 6 December 1988, Mr. Hurd.

172 H.C. Debs. Standing Comm. B col. 241 10 January 1989, Mr. Hogg. This admission may have inhibited earlier counter-measures. H.C. Debs. Vol. 143 cols. 240–1 6 December 1988, Mr. Mallon.

173 See: Colville Report on the E.P. Acts, para. 17.11.1.

174 See: *Chief Constable's Annual Report for 1987* (1988) p. 10.

175 See notes to the Bill.

176 See: J. Adams, R. Morgan and A. Bainbridge, *Ambush* (1988) p. 37.

177 See P.V.L.I. pp. 161–2; M. Dillon, *The Dirty War* (1990) chs. 16, 17.

178 See H.L. Select Committee on the European Communities, *Fraud against the Community* (1988–89 H.L. 27).

179 *Chief Constable's Annual Report for 1988* (1989) p. 12.

180 The maximum penalty is five years' imprisonment, a fine or both (on indictment) or six months' imprisonment, a fine up to £2,000 or both (summary conviction): s. 11(2). See s. 11(3) for the possible venues of any proceedings.

181 Smith and Hogan, *op. cit.* p. 849. Personal benefit from the concealment is probably not required; compare: *R.* v. *Aberg* [1948] 2 K.B. 143; *Sykes* v. *D.P.P.* [1962] A.C. 528 at p. 546; *Moore* v. *Secretary of State for N.I.* (1976) 8 N.I.J.B. The information may be recorded in permanent form or may simply be stored in a person's memory. Compare: K. Lidstone, 'PACE (N.I.) Order 1989' (1989) 40 *N.I.L.Q.* 333 at p. 343.

182 (1983) 11 N.I.J.B. (C.A.); [1984] 1 W.L.R. 1358.

183 By contrast, subsection (1)(b) uses the phrase 'commission, preparation or instigation of acts of terrorism' and so can relate to 'passive' ventures.

184 Jellicoe Report, para. 226.

185 Compare: H.C. Debs. Standing Comm. A col. 145 16 December 1975, Mr. Cunningham; Baker Report, para. 253.

186 The phrase derives from the Criminal Law Act 1967 s. 5(1) and the Theft Act 1968 s. 22. See: M. Wasik and M.P. Thompson, '"Turning a blind eye", as constituting mens rea' (1981) 32 *N.I.L.Q.* 328; *R.* v. *Grainger* [1984] Crim. L.R. 493; *R.* v. *Moys* (1984) 79 Cr. App. R. 72.

187 Smith and Hogan, *op. cit.* pp. 849–50.

188 H.C. Debs. Vol. 908 col. 164 22 March 1976, Dr. Summerskill; H.C. Debs. Vol. 449 col. 375 8 March 1984, Lord Elton.

189 H.L. Debs. Vol. 368 cols. 320–1 16 February 1976, Baroness Elles.

190 Smith and Hogan, *op. cit.* p. 798. See also: J.E. Stannard, N.I. Supplement to Smith and Hogan (1984) p. 153. Duress of circumstances may be more relevant: D.W. Elliott, 'Necessity, duress and self-defence' [1989] Crim. L.R. 611.

191 See: C.K. Allen, 'Misprision' (1962) 78 *L.Q.R.* 40; P. Glazebrook, 'Misprision of felony' (1964) 8 *Am. J. Legal History* 189, 283; Criminal Law Revision Committee Seventh Report, *Felonies and Misdemeanours* (Cmnd. 2659, 1965) para. 37.

192 [1962] A.C. 528. See: Allen, *loc. cit.*; P. Glazebrook 'How long, then, is the arm of the law to be?' (1962) 25 *M.L.R.* 301.

193 [1962] A.C. 528 at p. 564. See also: at p. 569 *per* Lord Goddard; *R.* v. *Casserly* (1938) *Times* 28 May; C.L.R.C., *loc. cit.* para. 39; *Blankenship* v. *U.S.* 328 F. 2d 19 (1964) *U.S.* v. *Pittman* 527 F. 2d 444 (1975), cert. den. 424 U.S. 923 (1976); *U.S.* v. *Graham* 487 F. Supp. 1317 (1980).

194 Compare: Smith and Hogan, *op. cit.*, p. 850.

195 H.L. Debs. Vol. 504 cols. 980–1 28 February 1989.

196 *The Guide to the Professional Conduct of Solicitors* (1990) para. 12.04. Accountants do not believe they have any privilege: Institute of Chartered Accountants, *Guidance for Members in Practice* (1988) s. 1.306, para. 10.

197 See: H.C. Debs. Vol. 882 col. 929 28 November 1974, Mr. Cunningham.

198 H.C. Debs. Standing Comm. D col. 243 24 November 1983, Mr. Waddington.

199 H.O. Circular No. 90/1983 para. 9. See also: H.O. Circular No. 27/1989 para. 7.4

200 Para. 252.

201   Criminal Evidence Act 1898 s. 1.
202   See: Jellicoe Report, para. 233.
203   *R.* v. *King* [1965] 1 W.L.R. 706. See also: C.L.R.C., *loc. cit.* para. 42; *U.S.*
v. *Farrar* 38 F. 2d 515 (1930); *Neal* v. *U.S.* 102 F. 2s 643 (1939); *Lancey* v. *U.S.*
356 F. 2d 407 (1966), cert. den. 385 U.S. 992; *U.S.* v. *King* 402 F 2d 694 (1968);
U.S. v. *Daddano* 432 F 2d 1119 (1970), cert. den. 402 U.S. 905; *U.S.* v. *Johnson*
546 F. 2d 1225 (1977); *U.S.* v. *Sheard* 566 F. 2d 1 (1977); *U.S.* v. *Hodges* 566
F. 2d 674 (1977); *U.S.* v. *Graham* 487 F. Supp. 1317 (1980); *U.S.* v. *Davila* 698
F. 2d 915 (1983); *U.S.* v. *Baez* 732 F 2d. 780 (1984). Self-incrimination is also a
reasonable excuse under the Criminal Law Act (N.I.) 1967: *R.* v. *Donnelly and
others* [1986] N.I. 54.
204   See, for example: Explosive Substances Act 1883 s. 6(2); Theft Act 1968
s. 31(1); Supreme Court Act 1981 s. 72.
205   J.D. Heydon, 'Obtaining evidence versus protecting the accused: two
conflicts' [1971] Crim. L.R. 13 at p. 13.
206   See: J.D. Heydon, 'Statutory restrictions on the privilege against self-
incrimination' (1971) 87 *L.Q.R.* 214.
207   1979 S.L.T. (Notes) 62.
208   *Ibid.* at p. 63.
209   *Ibid.*
210   *Ibid.* at p. 64.
211   See: *Foster* v. *Farrell* 1963 S.L.T. 182 (interpreting the Road Traffic Act
1960 s. 232). Compare: Vehicles (Excise) Act 1971 ss. 27, 32; Road Traffic
Regulation Act 1984 ss. 112, 113.
212   *Loc. cit.* at p. 63.
213   See: *Foster* v. *Farrell, loc. cit.*
214   *Loc. cit.,* at p. 64.
215   See: *Davies* v. *Johnson* [1979] A.C. 264.
216   Compare: Smith and Hogan, *op. cit.* p. 850; K.D. Ewing and W. Finnie,
Civil Liberties in Scotland (2nd ed., 1988) p. 131.
217   Jellicoe Report, para. 233. This caution is unaffected by later reenactments:
letters from the Chief Constables of Dumfries and Galloway and Strathclyde. The
Colville Report (para. 15.1.2) claims that s. 18 is not used in Scotland because of
doubts about the admissibility of statements. This reaction seems unnecessarily
cautious in the light of Lord Ross's views (n. 210 *supra*).
218   H.O. Circular No. 90/1983 para. 9.
219   The official circulars (including those in Scotland) nowhere advise a
special caution, nor does the Northern Ireland Office's *Guide to the Emergency
Powers* (1990).
220   For the possible adverse consequences under s. 18, see: Y. Cripps, *The Legal
Implications of Disclosure in the Public Interest* (1986) chs. 11, 12.
221   S. 18 incidentally penalises the relating of false information when the truth
is known. This activity is forbidden by many other offences; see: Law Commission,
Report No. 96: *Offences Relating to Interference with the Course of Justice* (1979–
80 H.C. 213) Pt. III; Criminal Law Act 1977 s. 51; Criminal Law (Amendment)
(N.I.) Order 1977 S.I. 1249 Art. 3.
222   But an offence against s. 18 can be committed by mere silence; compare:

R. v. *King, loc. cit.*; H.C. Debs. Vol. 882 cols. 925–6 28 November 1974, Mr. S. Silkin; H.C. Debs. Vol. 964 col. 1562 21 March 1979, Mr. Cunningham.

223 See, for example: Peace Preservation (Ireland) Act 1870 s. 13; Restoration of Order in Ireland Regulation 49 (S.R. & O. 1920 No. 1530); Civil Authorities (Special Powers) Act (N.I.) 1922 s. 2(3).

224 Giving false information in Scotland may be charged as an attempt to pervert the course of justice or wasting police time, but it is not generally a crime to withhold information. See: G.H. Gordon, *Criminal Law* (2nd ed., 1978) paras. 1.33–1.39; 48.38–48.47.

225 See: H.C. Debs. Vol. 901 cols. 931–2 26 November 1975, Mr. Cunningham; Colville Report, para. 15.1.2.

226 See also: *Crofter Hand-Woven Harris Tweed Co.* v. *Veitch* 1942 S.C. (H.L.) 1; Criminal Attempts and Conspiracy (N.I.) Order 1983 S.I. 1120 Art. 9.

227 See: Jellicoe Report, para. 224; Baker Report, paras. 246, 247; Stannard, *op. cit.* p. 172.

228 The Baker Report (para. 253) accepts this criticism but proposes the repeal of s. 5(1) in regard to terrorist-type offences and the replacement of s. 18 with an equivalent to be inserted into the Emergency Provisions Act.

229 See P.V.L.I. pp. 58–60.

230 See *ibid.* pp. 256–7.

231 See: S.A.C.H.R., *14th Report* (1988–89 H.C. 394) Annex A.

232 Paras. 15.1.5, 15.1.6.

233 S.I. No. 1987.

234 See: J.D. Jackson, 'Recent developments in criminal evidence' (1989) 49 *N.I.L.Q.* 105; A. Ashworth and P. Creighton, 'The right of silence in Northern Ireland' in J. Hayes and P. O'Higgins, *Lessons from Northern Ireland* (1990).

235 N.I.O., *Guide to the Emergency Powers* (1990) Pt. IV para. 50.

236 Arts. 5 and 6 require participation.

237 Up to 1 November 1982, there had been sixty-two charges, twenty-two convictions and sixteen cases pending. Charges under the Criminal Law Act (N.I.) s. 5 following arrest under the Prevention of Terrorism Act totalled 261 to end of 1990.

238 See: C. Scorer, *The Prevention of Terrorism Acts 1974 and 1976* (1976) p. 36; *R.* v. *Cubbon and Watt* (1987) *Times* 19 December p. 21, Colville Annual Report for 1987 para. 8.1.

239 *Times* 20 December 1979 p. 2, 4 January 1980 p. 2, 4 March 1981 p. 3, 17 March 1981 p. 2, 18 March 1981 p. 2.

240 *Times* 13 September 1985 p. 2, 16 October 1986 p. 5.

241 *R.* v. *Lynch* (1986) *Times* 7 February p. 3.

242 *R.* v. *Coogan* (1988) *Times* 1 April p. 1.

243 *Times* 7 January 1990 p. 1.

244 See: *R.* v. *Nea* (1980) *Guardian* 17 September p. 3; *Essex Chronicle* (1980) 17 September, 22 September, 8 December, 15 December. All received suspended sentences for failing to pass on information about a stolen driving licence and car later used by the I.R.A. and (in one case) about the whereabouts of Gerard Tuite (the most wanted suspect).

245 See: Jellicoe Report, para. 221; Baker Report, para. 252; C. Scorer, S.

Spencer and P. Hewitt, *The New Prevention of Terrorism Act* (1985) p. 58 (case of MacFarland).

246 H.C. Debs, Vol. 882 cols. 928–9 28 November 1974, Mr. Cunningham.

247 Para. 222.

248 Paras. 132, 133.

249 H.C. Debs. Vol. 969 col. 1562 21 March 1979, Mr. Cunningham.

250 Jellicoe Report, para. 223.

251 See: *Lewis* v. *Cattle* [1938] 2 K.B. 454; Official Secrets Act 1939.

252 The last charges were in R. v. *Thistlewood* (1820) 33 St. Tr. 681.

253 Paras. 15.1.3, 15.1.4.

254 See: *Rice* v. *Connolly* [1966] 2 Q.B. 414 at p. 419 *per* Parker L.C.J.; *The Brixton Disorders 10–12 April 1981: Report of an Inquiry by the Rt. Hon. the Lord Scarman O.B.E.* (Cmnd. 8427, 1981) paras. 4.55–4.60; Royal Commission on Criminal Procedure, *The Law and Procedure* (Cmnd. 8092–1, 1981) paras. 15–16.

255 H.C. Debs. Vol. 904 col. 475 28 January 1976, Mr. Mikardo.

256 A. Ashworth, 'The scope of criminal liability for omissions' (1989) 105 *L.Q.R.* 424. See also: Fifth Working Party of the Irish Council of Churches/Roman Catholic Joint Group on Social Questions, *Violence in Ireland* (1976) p. 80.

257 Compare: C.L.R.C., *loc. cit.* para. 42; Law Commission Report No. 96, *loc. cit.* para. 3.38.

258 Jellicoe Report, para. 101.

259 Compare: H. Gross, *A Theory of Criminal Justice* (1979) pp. 61–5; H.C. Home Affairs Select Committee, *Race Relations and the 'Sus' Law* (1979–80 H.C. 559) paras. 22, 23.

260 Scorer, *op. cit.* p. 37.

261 See: J. Adams, *The Financing of Terror* (1986) ch. 8.

262 The Attorney General found no evidence of an offence during the Jennifer Guinness kidnapping: *Times* 17 April 1986 p. 1.

263 Consider: Prevention of Terrorism Act 1984 s. 2; Criminal Law Act (N.I.) 1967 s. 5(1); Emergency Provisions Act 1991 ss. 29, 32, 33.

264 C. Dunkley, 'A deafening silence' in The Campaign for Free Speech on Ireland (ed.), *The British Media and Ireland: Truth the First Casualty* (1978) p. 8.

265 Newspapers do not generally impose comparable preconditions. The author thanks those editors who replied to his survey in 1985 on this matter. See also: M. Kelly, 'Power, control and media coverage of the Northern Ireland conflict' in P. Clancy, S. Drudy, K. Lynch and L. O'Dowd (eds.), *Ireland: A Sociological Profile* (1980).

266 Disclosure may also be demanded by way of search powers (see ch. 8) and contempt of court. See: Contempt of Court Act 1981 s. 10; R. v. *Bernard Falk* (1971, reported in R. Cathcart, *The Most Contrary Region* (1984) pp. 216–17); *In re Kevin O'Kelly* (1974) 108 *I.L.T.R.* 97.

267 R. Faligot, *Britain's Military Strategy in Ireland* (1983) p. 168.

268 *Guardian* 5 September 1979 pp. 1, 24.

269 See: R. Clutterbuck, *The Media and Political Violence* (2nd ed., 1983) ch. 11.

270   *Times* 2 August 1980 p. 2. The police seized *Panorama*'s film: L. Curtis, *Ireland, The Propaganda War* (1984) pp. 169–70.

271   See: K.D. Ewing and C.A. Gearty, *Freedom under Thatcher* (1990) pp. 241, 242.

272   See ch. 8.

273   The B.B.C. ignored communal conflict in Northern Ireland before 1965: *Report of the Committee on the Future of Broadcasting* (Cmnd. 6783, 1977) paras. 17.11, 17.12 (the 'Annan Report').

274   See H.C. Debs. Standing Comm. D col. 265 29 November 1983, Mr. Waddington.

275   Annan Report, para. 17.12.

276   Curtis, *op. cit.* p. 275.

277   If official patience becomes strained, then consideration should be given to a modified offence (confined to information about future dangers to life or held by direct witnesses to terrorist acts): J. Wanik, 'Forcing the bystander to get involved' (1985) 94 *Yale L.J.* 1787.

Chapter 8

Special powers of arrest and search

1 Arrest: provisions

By section 14(1) of the Prevention of Terrorism Act 1989:

a constable may arrest without warrant a person whom he has reasonable grounds for suspecting to be –
(a) a person guilty of an offence under section 2, 8, 9, 10 or 11 . . .;
(b) a person who is or has been concerned in the commission, preparation or instigation of an act of terrorism to which this section applies;
(c) a person subject to an exclusion order.

(a) Section 14(1)(a)
Pursuant to a recommendation in the Jellicoe Report,[1] suspicion of an offence under section 18 is no longer a ground for arrest, but this confinement is largely vitiated by the fact that sections 2, 8, 9, 10, 11 and 18 all attract the regular powers of arrest without warrant described hereafter. Consequently, the true purpose of section 14(1)(a) is not to grant needless arrest powers but to make available extra periods of detention and without an *inter partes*, judicial hearing.[2]

(b) Section 14(1)(b)
(*i*) *Meaning of terrorism* As discussed in chapter 2, both 'active' and 'passive' involvement in terrorism are probably relevant to section 14(1)(b). In either case, the power is not dependent upon reasonable suspicion of a specific crime.[3] Consequently, section 14(1)(b) represents an innovation in two ways. First, since 'terrorism' is not *per se* an offence, a wider range of activities become arrestable than under normal powers. Of course, terrorist plots and attacks usually do entail serious offences, and this convergence has prompted the European Court of Human Rights to accept terrorism as within the Convention's notion of an offence.[4] However, some of the preparatory stages of terrorism may fall outside any offence but may

nonetheless be arrestable under section 14(1)(b). This first feature is reinforced by the second, namely that terrorism can cover a multitude of activities, and no specific wrong need be isolated. These points may be illustrated by *R. v. Cullen, McCann and Shanahan* – the 'Winchester Three'.[5] Arrests were made under sections 14(1)(b) after Cullen and Shanahan were discovered in woods overlooking the home of the Secretary of State for Northern Ireland (Tom King). Arguably, they could have been arrested for conspiracy to murder, but the evidence was thin (no weapons were ever found) and equivocal. Certainly, a Home Office Minister viewed section 14(1)(b) as playing a crucial role in those circumstances.[6] Thus, where a suspect is acting alone (so that there can be no conspiracy) or where the activities of a group have not advanced further than preparations (such as spying on intended victims or the possession of death lists or guerrilla training manuals), section 14(1)(b) may be of unique value in allowing a preemptive strike. Yet most arrestees will be reasonably suspected of arrestable offences, especially conspiracy or incitement to murder, conspiracy to cause explosions or the possession of firearms with intent to endanger life, all of which arise well before any attack is mounted, all of which confer extra-territorial jurisdiction, and all of which (at least outside Scotland) attract fulsome police powers.[7] Preliminary acts falling outside the scope of such wide-ranging offences will be too equivocal to attach policing sanctions with any degree of certainty. Consequently, it may be inferred that it is the special consequences of arrest under section 14(1)(b) which are again of prime importance.

(ii)   Relevant types of terrorism   By section 14(2), the types of terrorism (which may occur outside the U.K.)[8] relevant to section 14(1)(b) are the following:

(a)   acts of terrorism connected with the affairs of Northern Ireland; and
(b)   acts of terrorism of any other description except acts connected solely with the affairs of the United Kingdom other than Northern Ireland.

The target in (a) accords with the origins of the Act. The second quarry, international terrorists, represents an innovation advocated by the Jellicoe Report,[9] which has been fiercely criticised for several reasons.

First, it is denied that there is 'ample justification'[10] for the extension. Though there have been about two dozen non-Irish terrorist murders since 1977 (aside from those at Lockerbie, which were effectively perpetrated elsewhere), the Jellicoe Report failed to acknowledge the notable and frequent police successes in tracing those responsible'[11] or to explain how the 'normal' legal weaponry was inadequate.

Secondly, section 14(1)(b) is badly drafted. Not only does it exceed the recommendations in the Jellicoe Report (which proposed deploying the

Act only against international terrorism inflicted in the United Kingdom),[12] but also it confers a wide and politically sensitive discretion on the police which might be used to curtail the activities of groups like the African National Congress and the Palestine Liberation Organisation.[13] To allay such disquiet,[14] the Government has resorted to the palliative of unenforceable circulars to the police, which advise that:[15]

In the case of acts of international terrorism committed or to be committed outside the United Kingdom, the powers should be used only when it appears that there is some prospect of a charge before United Kingdom courts or of the person concerned being deported.

The first ground does effectively restrict arrests; a prospect of criminal charges arises only if the international terrorism is committed in this country or if the police suspect one from a relatively short list of offences creating extra-territorial jurisdiction.[16] By contrast, the circulars fail to delimit police action as a prelude to deportation for the public good under section 3(5)(b) of the Immigration Act 1971, as this power is not conditional upon proof of any criminal or undesirable activity committed within the United Kingdom. A more acceptable solution (assuming special measures are needed at all) would have been to confine section 14 to acts of terrorism committed anywhere but intended to influence policy or opinion in this country[17] or perhaps in any State which has signed the Council of Europe's Convention on the Suppression of Terrorism.[18]

A third objection concerns the apparent inconsistency of extending the Act to international terrorism while excluding non-Irish, domestic terrorism.[19] The Jellicoe Report primarily wished to exempt Scottish and Welsh terrorists because:[20]

Nothing in the past history or likely future activity of terrorist groups indigenous to Great Britain persuades me that the use of these powers against them is necessary or would be of real value.

Statistically, international terrorism has indeed been more deadly and destructive, though domestic non-Irish terrorism is more prolific. However, part of the explanation for the divergence is surely that the police can more easily monitor native groups and so prevent their schemes reaching fruition rather than because they represent a trifling public danger.

The fourth argument against the application of section 14(1)(b) to foreign terrorism is that its impact is blunted by diplomatic immunities and privileges.[21] Under Articles 29 and 31 of the Vienna Convention on Diplomatic Relations of 1961[22] (as implemented by the Diplomatic Privileges Act 1964), diplomats are not liable to arrest or criminal prosecution, even if they contravene their duty under Article 41 to respect the laws of the receiving State. Furthermore, Article 22 forbids entry into mission premises to make an arrest or to gather evidence.[23] The legislative history of the Convention strongly suggests that these exemptions even benefit diplomats engaged in, and diplomatic premises used for, terrorism.[24] Police intervention is probably justifiable only under general international law principles, such as self-defence or as a reprisal for a breach of Article 41, provided there is a continuing threat.[25] Consequently, no invasion of diplomatic premises followed the shootings from the Libyan People's Bureau in April 1984 until diplomatic relations had been severed,[26] and the departing diplomats were not arrested. A more robust approach was adopted when those involved in the kidnapping of Dikko were apprehended in July 1984. Though the crate in which he was imprisoned came from the Nigerian High Commission, seventeen arrests were made under section 14(1)(b), and one of those charged was denied diplomatic immunity.[27] However, later cases in 1988 involving shootings by Cuban and Vietnamese diplomats resulted only in expulsions.[28]

In conclusion, diplomatic law may severely curtail the use of section 14(1)(b) against foreign terrorists, thereby casting further doubt on the value of its extension in 1984. Thus, diplomats advocating or engaging in political violence may be declared *persona non grata* but will not be arrested.

(c) Section 14(1)(c)
The third arrest power under section 14 concerns persons reasonably suspected to be subject to an exclusion order. To prevent harassment, this provision was clarified in 1984 by the insertion of section 14(3), which requires the police also to suspect that the person's presence in Britain or Northern Ireland is in breach of an order under sections 5 or 6.[29]

Since individuals contravening exclusion orders contrary to section 8 can be detained under section 14(1)(a), subsection (c) is really aimed against anyone who has not been served with an order, commonly because the person was outside the relevant territory when it was issued. Such an individual is not liable to removal and so cannot be arrested under section 14(1)(a) for contravention of section 8. Once an exclusion order has been served, detention will continue under Schedule 2.[30]

(d) Common features
(i) *Meaning of arrest* The courts have indicated that arrests under special anti-terrorist powers are accomplished in the usual ways, either by force or by words or conduct which make it clear that force will be used in the event of resistance; the defendant need not be aware of the restraint.[31]

(ii) *Reasonable suspicion* A constable must have 'reasonable grounds for suspecting' under section 14(1),[32] in other words, evidence such as would influence a reasonable person. Reasonable suspicion may be based on information received or direct observations but can never be grounded solely in 'stereotyped images'[33] or previous convictions.[34] A common and rather troubling question is whether the reasonable suspicion of an arresting officer can be inculcated by way of a briefing from a superior officer. A positive answer may be given in principle, provided the credibility of the superior and information imparted is sufficiently established and provided also the recipient genuinely and subjectively believes the allegations. Thus, in *Hanna* v. *Chief Constable, R.U.C.*[35] and *Stratford* v. *Chief Constable, R.U.C.*,[36] a constable had reasonable suspicion under section 14 based on the instructions of his superior. The same point has also been established in relation to arrests under other special powers[37] but creates some danger that a valid arrest may be ordered maliciously by a superior whose motives are unknown to the inferior carrying out the arrest. One safeguard would be to supply the arrester with the factual background to the superior's suspicions in a prior briefing,[38] but no such requirement is specified in guidance about the Act.

The objective standard of proof required by reasonable suspicion may be tested judicially. An example of review via a civil claim for false imprisonment is *Connolly* v. *Metropolitan Police Commissioner*.[39] In 1977, the plaintiff and some friends visited the Old Bailey to view the trial of two alleged I.R.A. bombers. The police were screening all arrivals, so Connolly, fearing delay because of his Irish name, turned back. The police noticed his departure and asked his friends about his identity. They refused to answer and were arrested. Connolly went to the police station to extricate them, whereupon he was himself arrested and detained for seven hours. His complaint was based on two grounds: that the police had no reasonable suspicion and that he was never informed why he was arrested. The police replied that he was arrested under section 14(1)(a) because they suspected an offence under section 18 (the concealment of his name) and that he had been notified of that reason. The jury found for Connolly on the second, but not the first, complaint, though only £1 in damages was awarded and there was no order as to costs. Cases from Northern Ireland include *Hanna* v. *Chief Constable, R.U.C.*,[40] in which the plaintiff was arrested for involvement in terrorism after reporting that his vehicle had been hijacked. Though he was released without charge, it was accepted that there had been ample evidence both to arrest and detain him. However, in *Petticrew* v. *Chief Constable, R.U.C.*[41] and *Davey* v. *Chief Constable, R.U.C.*,[42] false imprisonments arose when the detentions were extended after the final interviews had ended in order that an unrequested medical examination could be held or administrative purposes completed.

The alternative remedy of habeas corpus has likewise rarely succeeded,[43] as illustrated by the case of Jacqueline O'Mally.[44] On the 12 December,

1979, twenty-four persons, including O'Mally, were arrested in an operation described by the police as a 'preemptive strike'. On the 14 December, O'Mally was granted leave to apply for a writ of habeas corpus, but the hearing was adjourned twice until the 19 December, which marked the expiration of the detention period allowed by section 14. In fact, the issue was then resolved, as O'Mally was charged and later pleaded guilty to involvement in a conspiracy to effect the escape from Brixton Prison of an I.R.A. prisoner.[45] Nevertheless, it is disturbing that the legality of the arrest remained untested until seven days had elapsed, by which time the police had had ample opportunity to secure evidence by interrogation. In *Re Copeland's Application*,[46] the High Court in Northern Ireland warned against litigation as a disruptive tactic and demanded that even *ex parte* applications be accompanied by affidavit.

(*iii*) *Purposes of arrest* It was accepted by Lord Chief Justice Lowry in *R.* v. *Officer in charge of Police Office, Castlereagh, ex parte Lynch* that:[47]

no specific crime need be suspected in order to ground a proper arrest under section [14](1)(b) ... No charge may follow at all; thus an arrest is not necessarily ... the first step in a criminal proceeding against a suspected person on a charge which was intended to be judicially investigated.... Rather it is usually the first step in the investigation of the suspected person's involvement in terrorism.

Consequently, arrests under section 14(1)(b) facilitate interviews to gather intelligence as well as the traditional police concern, interrogations to produce admissible evidence. Although this dual purpose is one of the central attractions of section 14, it has prompted two complications.

Firstly, the proactive, intelligence-gathering purpose has predominated, so a relatively low charging rate (described later) has inevitably resulted. Some commentators have thereby been led to query 'whether most arrests are based on reasonable suspicion at all or whether the arrest powers continue to be used mainly for intelligence-gathering rather than apprehending those involved in criminal activity'.[48] However, the dichotomy is false; the criteria and purposes of valid arrests are distinct issues, and reasonable suspicion can and should be established under section 14 even if the purpose is intelligence-gathering.

The second difficulty is that arrests for intelligence-gathering are contrary to the permitted purposes of detentions under Article 5(1) of the European Convention. Thus, with the case of *Brogan* v. *U.K.*[49] looming, Government Ministers have substantially modified their pronouncements about section 14 and no longer let slip that detentions may not be designed to find admissible evidence[50] nor to investigate specific offences.[51] Instead, it was emphasised during the renewal debates in 1989 that the only legitimate purpose of an arrest is to bring charges before a court and that extended detentions will not be allowed for other reasons.[52] However, the wording of section 14(1)(b) was not altered in 1989, and there are recent indications that a wider interpretation prevails. For example, the Northern Ireland Office's *Guide to the Emergency Powers*[53] reminds police of the necessity to caution before questioning only when the detainee is suspected of an offence and when questions are put for the purpose of obtaining evidence to be put in court. The inference may be correctly drawn that not all persons are detained in connection with offences nor questioned about them. By contrast, Home Office advice[54] emphasises that arrests must be for the purpose of bringing charges and forbids arrests 'simply to gather intelligence' and not based on reasonable suspicion of involvement in terrorism. However, this statement confusingly implies that an intelligence-gathering exercise cannot be prompted by reasonable suspicion of terrorism. Other sources have more forthrightly defended intelligence-gathering as legitimate. For example, the head of the Metropolitan Police's Anti-Terrorist Squad wrote in 1987 that the Prevention of Terrorism Act 'permits the detention of suspected terrorists in order to obtain intelligence and/or evidence'.[55] Finally, amendments were subtly made to the legislation in 1989 so that detention for intelligence-gathering could persist. Thus, the original draft of Schedule 3 (described later) had allowed detentions to be authorised on police review to investigate offences relating to terrorism; the reference to criminal offences was later deleted so that detention could be permitted for wider purposes.[56]

(iv)   Reasons for arrest   Another consequence of arrests under section 14 is that, according to section 28 of the Police and Criminal Evidence Act 1984 (Article 30 of the equivalent Northern Ireland Order), an arrested person must be informed of the arrest and the ground for it.

The latter requirement causes problems under section 14(1)(b), since such information may disclose police methods or informers or may bolster the anti-interrogation training of suspects.[57] Thus, in *ex parte Lynch*, a constable arrested Lynch under section 14(1)(b) and told him that:[58]

I was arresting him under section [14] of the Prevention of Terrorism (Temporary Provision) Act 1976 as I suspected him of being involved in terrorist activities. . . .

Lynch alleged that this recital was inadequate (he was actually suspected of membership of the I.R.A. and the murder of a policeman) and applied for habeas corpus. Lord Chief Justice Lowry was wary of committing himself to the view that any reasons had to be provided under section 14(1)(b) because of its intelligence purpose and distance from offences, as just described.[59] However, assuming this point in the applicant's favour, the Court was satisfied that the constable had reasonably conveyed the nature of his suspicion, although it could be argued that the court confused grounds with authority.[60]

Very similar issues arose in *Re McElduff*[61] under the Civil Authorities (Special Powers) Acts (Northern Ireland) 1922–43.[62] The High Court decided that the giving of reasons was a 'fundamental right'[63] of the arrestee but that, owing to the vague and wide nature of the powers involved and to the sensitive information motivating its use, an arrestor merely had to specify the particular power being invoked together with:[64]

in the case of [an arrest for] a crime or offence the general nature of the crime or offence ... and in the case of [an arrest for] suspicion, whether it was a suspicion directed to a past act, a present or a future intention, or even a combination of two or all three in the conjunctive.

By comparison, the second requirement was not properly observed in Lynch's case as there was no intimation of the two offences suspected; as for the first requirement, Lord Lowry indicated that no specific offence or act need ever be mentioned.[65] In both respects *Re McElduff* is to be preferred,[66] but official guidance from the Northern Ireland Office merely asserts that a police officer is not required 'to state his reasonable suspicion'.[67]

Finally, the reasons must normally be imparted on arrest but may be delayed under section 28/Article 30 on grounds of impracticability. The arrester's difficulties in conveying the message may be caused by the arrestee or third parties and may be actual or potential.[68] Article 5.2 of the European Convention allows a few hours' delay with the effect that reasons may be deduced from a later interrogation.[69]

(*v*) *Use of force on arrest* The amount of force used to effect an arrest under section 14 is governed by section 3(1) of the Criminal Law Act 1967,[70] which requires it to be 'reasonable in the circumstances'. Whilst in principle fair,[71] the present legal regime suffers from many defects.[72] Since most are not confined to terrorism situations and arise in Northern Ireland rather than Britain, only an outline can be offered here.

One problem is that the present formulation is vague and uninformative especially in regard to the most dramatic employment of force, namely the firing of lethal weapons. This application of section 3 has spawned numerous cases in Northern Ireland, which have either provided little elucidation or widened the opportunities for the use of force, so that the Ministry of Defence has felt it worthwhile to issue more detailed advice to soldiers by means of the 'Yellow Card'.[73] In consequence, firmer legal guidance should be provided as to the use of force in connection with arrests under section 14.[74] Next, the relationship between section 3 and other defences, especially self-defence[75] and superior orders,[76] should be clarified. The legal consequences of killings are also unsatisfactory. Investigations by way of inquests raise expectations which cannot realistically be satisfied; a wider judicial inquiry is warranted.[77] Further, even when the force applied appears excessive, a manslaughter charge may more fairly reflect the difficulties of the soldier.[78] Finally, the range of equipment employed should be reviewed.[79]

(*vi*) *Incidental detention powers* It is common for arrest and search operations in Northern Ireland to entail the incidental detention of all occupants of a household. This practice was approved by the House of Lords in *Murray* v. *Ministry of Defence*,[80] at least in connection with army searches, as a 'reasonable precaution' to stop distractions, warnings to others or resistance. It is arguable that corresponding detention powers, however dubiously based, could equally be implied into section 14.

(*vii*) *Detention following arrest* The most important incident of arrests under section 14 is the special period of detention which applies as follows:[81]

(4)   Subject to subsection (5) below, a person arrested under this section shall not be detained in right of the arrest for more than forty-eight hours after his arrest.
(5)   The Secretary of State may, in any particular case, extend the period of forty-eight hours by a period or periods specified by him but any such further period or periods shall not exceed five days in all. . . .

The procedure for obtaining an extension is that a police force in England and Wales submits a written report and request signed by a senior officer to the National Joint Unit at New Scotland Yard. Applications will usually specify personal details, any past criminal record, the reasons for the arrest and an explanation of the need for, and desired length of, the extension. The request is then processed through the Unit and Home Office up to the Secretary of State, who now always takes the decision personally 'unless circumstances make it impossible'.[82] Nevertheless, the Secretary of State may lawfully act through civil servants.[83] Applications in Northern Ireland and Scotland are processed exclusively within those jurisdictions. To encourage the police to limit detentions, successive extensions may be granted (up to the five-day maximum)[84] and, since 1983, follow-up reports to the Secretary of State must be produced.[85] By section 14(5), a detainee shall be given as soon as practicable notice of an application and its timing. This notification procedure, introduced in 1989, does not extend to allowing the detainee to make representations before the application nor to consult a lawyer (rights granted in connection with the comparatively unimportant reviews under Schedule 3, described later). Furthermore, only detainees in Northern Ireland need be informed that an application has been approved and the length of extra time granted.[86]

Two substantial criticisms may be levelled against extended detentions. The first is that the system is open to abuse since the detainee is not allowed any hearing (as just described) nor is the power vested in an independent judicial officer. Further, no criteria are specified for the grant of an application, though the following are in practice viewed as relevant:[87]

1   Checking of fingerprints
2   Forensic tests
3   Checking the detainee's replies against intelligence
4   New lines of enquiry
5   Interrogation to identify accomplices
6   Correlating information obtained from one or more other detained person in the same case
7   Awaiting a decision by the DPP
8   Finding and consulting other witnesses
9   Identification parade
10 Checking an alibi
11 Translating documents
12 Obtaining an interpreter and then carrying out the necessary interview with his assistance
13 Communications with foreign police forces sometimes across timezones and language difficulties
14 Evaluation of documents once translated and further investigated

One wonders why this list cannot be distilled into the Act, especially as police reviews under Schedule 3 are subject to set criteria. Another point is that interrogation *per se* is not mentioned, and the Colville Report downplayed its importance in view of anti-interrogation training.[88] Though reliance upon forensic evidence may be increasing, it remains clear that prolonged questioning to wear down suspects remains commonplace.[89] The list is also deficient in that extensions are not conditional upon ordinary detention powers being inadequate.[90] By contrast, detention beyond thirty-six hours is possible under section 43(4)/Article 44(4) of the Police and Criminal Evidence legislation only if approved by magistrates after an *inter partes* hearing in private on the basis that:

(a) his detention without charge is necessary to secure or preserve evidence relating to an offence for which he is under arrest or to obtain such evidence by questioning him;
(b) the offence for which he is under arrest is a serious arrestable offence; and
(c) the investigation is being conducted diligently and expeditiously.

Even if it is conceded that prolonged detention is defensible, the necessity for the powers in section 14 may still be doubted, since persons (including murderers and international fraudsters) suspected of serious arrestable offences outside Scotland can be detained for up to ninety-six hours under the Police and Criminal Evidence legislation. However, the degree of redundancy of section 14 in Scotland is more debatable, since suspects must be charged on arrest[91] and must then appear in court not later than the following day.[92] Powers of detention for questioning for up to six hours appear in sections 1 and 2 of the Criminal Justice (Scotland) Act 1980, but these hardly rival section 14.[93]

Some of these criticisms were canvassed in *Brogan and others* v. *U.K.*[94] The four applicants had been arrested in Northern Ireland under the Act and had been detained without charge for periods ranging from four days six hours to six days sixteen and a half hours. Their complaints before the European Court of Human Rights included, under Article 5(3), that they had not been 'brought promptly before a judge' after arrest. In response, the European Court of Human Rights emphasised the inflexibility of the word 'promptly' and concluded that even the shortest detention period suffered by the applicants had been excessive.[95] This judgment may be questioned on two grounds. The first is that precedent suggests that periods well in excess of four days have been previously acceptable.[96] Secondly, given that four days represent the 'normal' detention power in most of the U.K., insufficient weight was accorded to the difficulties of terrorism[97] unless, of course, that normal power itself breaches Article 5.3.[98] The Court left entirely vague what would be an acceptable detention period, but a later complaint involving a detention shorter than four days has been declared inadmissible by the Commission.[99]

The U.K. Government was faced with two possible choices in its response to the judgment: accommodation by amendment to section 14 or derogation under Article 15 of the Convention. The former strategy seemed to be preferred, and discussions towards that end ensued.[100] The option of derogation was immediately adopted as an interim solution[101] but eventually became permanent. The precise terms of the notice (given on 23 December 1988) are important.[102] The Government wished to protect the seven-day detention powers (and not only those under section 14) because:

There have been in the United Kingdom in recent years campaigns of organised terrorism associated with the affairs of Northern Ireland. . . .

It will be observed that detentions in connection with foreign terrorism do not appear to gain protection from Article 15. Accordingly, the Home Office has advised police forces that applications for detention beyond four days 'will only be considered appropriate in the most exceptional circumstances'.[103] This remarkable compromise means that the Government is prepared to countenance an occasional breach of the Convention.

The resort to Article 15 may be attacked on various grounds and is now being challenged in *Brannigan and McBride* v. *U.K.*[104] and *McGlinchy, Quinn and Barrow* v. *U.K.*[105] One is that there is no public emergency threatening the nation as a whole, though the Court has accepted that action can be taken in response to localised problems.[106] Another concerns the restrospective nature of the notice of derogation issued in 1988, though undue reliance upon Article 15 might follow if member States could not react after the event.[107] The most serious criticism is that the notice is excessive in that it extends to Britain, that it allows seven days rather than, say, five and that it avoids entirely the scrutiny of judges even though the Court was prepared to accept 'appropriate procedural precautions'.[108]

Another response would have been to reduce the detention period substantially. For example, the Colville Report was remarkably sanguine (perhaps in the light of statistical evidence) about a cut to five days.[109] Alternatively, or in addition, there is the option of judicial review, but this was rejected by the Home Secretary as it would be a 'radical departure from the principles which govern judicial proceedings in this country and could severely affect public trust and confidence in the judiciary'.[110] Thus, the conditions of review (private hearings without disclosure of evidence) are deemed to render the issue non-justiciable and to create the danger that judges will be viewed as stooges of the executive. In response, it should be noted that judges readily preside over *ex parte, in camera* hearings in other pre-trial contexts (such as applications for search warrants or interim injunctions) and have been employed in the review of warrants issued under the Interception of Communications Act 1985 and the Security Service Act 1989. In addition, there may be more public confidence in their judgments than those taken by a politician because of their independence and legal competence. Furthermore, the loss of parliamentary accountability through the Minister would hardly be noticed; nor would a few designated judges present greater security difficulties, unavailability or inconsistency than does a succession of over-worked, under-trained and transient politicians.

Though the Brogan case produced no concessions, a system of police reviews of detentions was introduced in 1989 into Schedule 3, mainly under the influence of the Colville Report[111] and the Police and Criminal Evidence legislation.[112] The review officer must not be involved in the investigation, must hold a superior rank (an inspector for the first twenty-four hours, thereafter a superintendent) and may require security clearance.[113] The first review occurs as soon as possible after detention commences; subsequent reviews continue at twelve-hourly intervals, until the suspect is released or until an application for extension is made.[114] Reviews may be postponed if circumstances, such as prejudice to the investigation or the unavailability of a reviewer, make them impracticable.[115] Before a review, a suspect shall be given the opportunity to make representations, unless that person is asleep or otherwise unfit; a solicitor may make representations on the person's behalf, but only if available at the time.[116] Ironically, there is no specific right to consult a lawyer before the review, but the detainee shall be reminded of his possible rights before (except in Northern Ireland) and afterwards.[117] The review officer takes the decision on three separate grounds. By Schedule 3 paragraph 3(3), continued detention shall be authorised if the reviewer is satisfied it is necessary to obtain (by questioning or otherwise) or preserve evidence about offences under sections 2, 8, 9, 10 or 11 of the Act or about the detainee's involvement in terrorism or subjection to an exclusion order. It must also be shown that the investigation is being conducted diligently and expeditiously. By Schedule 3 paragraph 3(4) continued detention may be authorised pending consideration of whether the detainee is subject to an exclusion order, whether in the Secretary of State's view he should be subject to an exclusion or deportation order or whether proceedings should be instituted by the prosecuting authorities. In addition (by paragraph 3(5)) detention may be continued pending a police decision to apply for exclusion or deportation, but the reviewer must then be satisfied that the detention is necessary and that the consideration is being undertaken diligently and expeditiously. The main difference between paragraphs 3(3) and the others is that the reviewer's discretion is more limited in the former; provided a *bona fide* police investigation is pending, he cannot interfere. There is more latitude once the evidence has been secured. Written records are to be made of the review process, if possible, in the presence of the detainee, who shall be told of the 'grounds' for authorisation.[118]

This system compares unfavourably with that under the Police and Criminal Evidence legislation. In particular, reviews are less frequent (twelve-hourly rather than nine-hourly), suggesting that the Government preferred a scheme which permits the greatest degree of police discretion and pressure. In addition, reviews terminate on an application for extension to the Secretary of State, thereby placing undue reliance upon the thoroughness of his scrutiny and wrongly implying that there is no need for continued vigilance thereafter. It is unacceptable that the persons detained pending exclusion or held under normal police powers are better off than persons suspected of serious terrorist offences, the most vulnerable category of detainees. Furthermore, police custody officers cannot fulfil the independent judicial review demanded by Brogan, and the 'greatest concern' has been expressed about their work in Northern Ireland.[119]

(*viii*) *Treatment during detention* The custodial regime in England and Wales is expressly tied by Schedule 8 paragraph 6(8) to the Police and Criminal Evidence Act 1984 and its Code of Practice for the Detention, Treatment and Questioning of Persons by the Police.[120] Similar rules operate in Scotland via police force orders,[121] while a *Guide to the Emergency Powers* applies in Northern Ireland until replaced by a Code of Practice under section 61 of the Emergency Provisions Act 1991.[122]

In some respects, detainees under the Prevention of Terrorism Act receive unusually favourable treatment. For example, it was recognised by both the Shackleton and Jellicoe Reports[123] that extra concessions as to diet, bedding and exercise are advisable because of the prolonged duration of arrests under the Act, and these points are emphasised (though no standards are specified) in the Police and Criminal Evidence Code and Northern Ireland Office *Guide*.[124] Extra protective measures have also been instituted in Northern Ireland following the Bennett Report in 1979.[125] In response to allegations of improper and unlawful treatment of terrorist suspects,[126] the Report prescribed the following administrative safeguards: greater supervision by senior uniformed officers, meticulous documentation, limits on interviews, viewing lenses and closed-circuit television, greater medical supervision, an unconditional right of access to a lawyer after each forty-eight hours of detention and a code of conduct for interviewing officers enforced by police discipline rules. These proposals have largely been implemented.[127] The Jellicoe Report accepted that the Bennett system works well and hoped that the Police and Criminal Evidence legislation would implement corresponding arrangements elsewhere.[128] Though this prediction has proved largely accurate, there remain some important deficiencies, especially the absence of viewing lenses, closed-circuit television and routine medical checks.[129]

In contrast to the foregoing favourable treatment, there are various respects in which fewer rights are accorded than normal: cautions, tape-recording and access to outsiders.

As for cautions, paragraph 10.1 of the Code specifies that:

A person whom there are grounds to suspect of an offence must be cautioned before any questions about it (or further question if it is his answers to previous questions that provide grounds for suspicion) are put to him for the purpose of obtaining evidence which may be given to a court in a prosecution. He therefore need not be cautioned if questions are put for other purposes, for example, to establish his identity, his ownership or responsibility for any vehicle or the need to search him in the exercise of powers of stop and search.

Since this measure links cautions with arrests and subsequent questioning in connection with specific offences, warnings may not be obligatory following all arrests under section 14(1)(b) or (c), as discussed previously.[130]

The techniques of interrogation allowed in Northern Ireland differ markedly from elsewhere, since oppression, inducements or threats are not necessarily grounds for inadmissibility.[131] By contrast, questions about specific offences must cease as soon as there is sufficient evidence to charge, whereas questioning may continue under the Police and Criminal Evidence legislation until there is evidence for a prosecution to succeed.[132] In practice, continued interrogation of terrorists may be easily justified as mere intelligence-gathering.[133] Furthermore, detentions are sometimes prolonged in Northern Ireland to allow questioning about other matters. This eventuality is assisted by Article 3 of the Criminal Justice (Northern Ireland) Order 1991, allowing remands into police custody.[134]

Another way in which terrorist suspects receive comparatively unfavourable treatment is that interviews are not tape-recorded in contrast to section 60/Article 60 of the Police and Criminal Evidence legislation, nor even, in Northern Ireland, is the written record of an interview read over to, and signed by, the suspect. The Northern Ireland Office claims as an excuse that allegations about mistreatment will shift to corridors[135] – surely a reason for cameras in corridors rather than a black-out. The Home Office cites two obstacles. One is 'the need to protect sources of intelligence and police operational methods'.[136] The other is the danger of reprisals against the suspect from colleagues when they hear the disclosures made on tape.[137] Aside from the unconvincing nature of these arguments (the same problems should arise from accurate written records), a combination of pressure from official reviews[138] and the salutary experience of the Guildford Four case (described in chapter 11) provoked a concession in March 1990, by which tape-recording of 'summaries of interviews' and the comments of the suspect thereon has been introduced as a two-year experiment by the Metropolitan and Merseyside Police.[139] Even if adopted permanently and nationally, this model of retrospective taping would neither combat 'verballing' and the fabrication of confessions nor would it at all check wrongful conduct during an interview.[140] A better compromise would be to record (preferably by video)[141] contemporaneously but (as in the experiment) to permit access to the tape only by suspects who are being subpoenaed or prosecuted. Recordings not made available would still provide a safeguard against physical or verbal abuse,[142] while disclosure in the two situations mentioned is without risk, since any statements will eventually be made public anyway.

Next, the rights of detainees to outside help are unusually constrained. Normally, section 56 (Article 57 in Northern Ireland) of the Police and Criminal Evidence legislation allows intimation of the fact and location of arrest to be sent to a friend or relative, and section 58/Article 59 grants the right to consult privately with a solicitor.[143] Both rights may be withheld for up to thirty-six hours when the person is detained for a serious arrestable offence[144] and a police superintendent reasonably believes that exercise of the right will lead to interference with evidence, physical harm to others, the alerting of suspects still at large or the hindrance of the recovery of property unlawfully obtained.

These rights are further diminished for persons held under section 14. First, delay is permitted for a maximum of forty-eight, rather than thirty-six, hours[145] and, in England and Wales on the additional grounds that notification:[146]

will lead to interference with the gathering of information about the commission, preparation or instigation of acts of terrorism; or . . . by alerting any person, will make it more difficult

(i)   to prevent an act of terrorism; or

(ii) to secure the apprehension, prosecution or conviction of any person in connection with the commission, preparation or instigation of an act of terrorism.

Furthermore, a commander or assistant chief constable may direct (on the same criteria as for delay) that legal consultations, when granted, take place in the sight and hearing of a police inspector unconnected with the case.[147]

The corresponding rules in Northern Ireland are even stricter, but those in Scotland are more favourable to the suspect. Under sections 44 and 45 of the Northern Ireland (Emergency Provisions) Act 1991 access is only granted after forty-eight hours at forty-eight-hourly intervals rather than whenever reasonable.[148] However, access to solicitors may also be affected by the Criminal Evidence (Northern Ireland) Order 1988, as described previously, which may require the availability of legal advice before the courts can rely on silence as evidence.[149] By contrast, section 35 of the Law Reform (Miscellaneous Provisions) (Scotland) Act 1985 allows the denial of access only 'in the interests of the investigation or prevention of crime, or of the apprehension, prosecution or conviction of offenders'. This wording (which is based on, and amends, section 3(1) of the Criminal Justice (Scotland) Act 1980) makes no reference to 'terrorism' but does not require the offence to be serious.[150]

In practice as well as law, access to outsiders varies according to jurisdiction. It seems that refusal of legal intervention for forty-eight hours is commonest in Northern Ireland,[151] as is the denial of privacy and of the presence of a lawyer during an interview.[152] Refusal to notify family members is rarely a problem in Northern Ireland, where arrests are often at home,[153] but may arise in Britain.[154] These features are reflected in Table 5, which also reveals an unusually high (52 per cent in 1987–88)[155] rate of requests for solicitors in Northern Ireland.

These access provisions may be criticised as follows. Firstly, the legislative scheme is over-complex. The rules should be consolidated within the Prevention of Terrorism Act and should adopt a common standard. Secondly, extra legal aid should be available to the victims of section 14.[156] Next, the denial of legal advice is unfair to suspects and conduces to unfounded suspicions that lawyers are in cahoots with their paramilitary clients.[157] If restraints really are necessary, could there at least be access to lawyers from an approved list within forty-eight hours? In any event, a delay of forty-eight hours is excessive,[158] and the proviso which permits overhearing transforms access into either a trap or a hollow ritual.[159] The treatment of lawyers in England and Wales contrasts curiously with the

Table 5 The operation of ss. 44, 45 of the Emergency Provisions Act 1991

Year	Operation of s. 44 E.P. Act		Operations of s. 45 E.P. Act	
	Requests	Immediately granted	Requests	Immediately granted
1987	72	66	476	212
1988	310	292	1165	467
1989	283	283	1152	380
1990	299	274	1360	654
Total	964	915 (95%)	4153	1713 (41%)

Source: Northern Ireland Office.

rights of foreigners (including Irish citizens) to communicate and consult with consular officials,[160] rights which may undermine the interrogation of Middle Eastern suspects whose governments are also implicated.

Finally, the sanctions for breaches of the protective rules in the case of terrorists may be even more illusory and uncertain than normal. In particular, confessions can be admitted in Northern Ireland according to a special low threshold (detailed in chapter 13), the Northern Ireland *Guide* cannot, until replaced by a statutory code, be enforced directly by police disciplinary proceedings,[161] nor does it facilitate proof of breaches by allowing access to the custody record. Suggestions for reform might include: a clearer and directly enforceable code of practice;[162] the separate monitoring of complaints arising from section 14 detentions;[163] better police training;[164] and a greater readiness on the part of the courts to use torts and habeas corpus as remedies against abuse.[165] Lay visitors may provide not only a safeguard against abuse but also confidence in the police, and experiments have begun in Northern Ireland.[166] A system of inspections has also been established by the European Convention for the Prevention of Torture and Inhuman or Degrading Treatment or Punishment,[167] while, pursuant to a corresponding U.N. Convention,[168] section 134 of the Criminal Justice Act 1988 provides that a public official commits torture if he 'intentionally inflicts severe pain or suffering on another in the performance or purported performance of his official duties'. Such activity was, of course, unlawful well before 1988, but section 134 has value as a policy statement and by establishing universal jurisdiction.

Improvements in the protection of terrorist suspects may to some extent neutralise the impact of detention and interrogation. Yet evidence obtained under oppressive conditions against suspects uniquely vulnerable to police maltreatment is of uncertain value. In any event, unconscionable methods may be counter-productive as a strategy against terrorists, who may seek to make capital out of their treatment even if they have been convincingly convicted.

2   Arrest: comparisons

(a)   *Normal powers*

Almost all terrorist arrests in England, Wales and Northern Ireland under section 14(1)(a) or (b) could alternatively be executed under section 24/ Article 26 of the Police and Criminal Evidence legislation.[169] Indeed, the police are advised by circular (except in Northern Ireland) that section 14 'should not be used where a lesser power under the general law would achieve the same ends'.[170] By contrast, there is no regular substitute for arrests under section 14(1)(c), but this measure is rarely used. The principal advantages of section 14 are said to be its preemptive nature and its extensive detention power, the values of which have been considered.[171]

The operation of section 14 may more readily be justified in Scotland, where normal arrest provisions are fragmentary and periods of detention for questioning are very limited.[172] However, in so far as special powers to arrest and detain may be unavoidable, they should be designed by reference to 'scheduled offences' rather than the undesirably vague term 'terrorism'.

(b)   *Special powers*

Very similar powers to those in section 14 existed under section 4(1)of the Prevention of Violence (Temporary Provisions) Act 1939, but more recent precedents may be found in Northern Ireland.[173]

Under section 11 of the Northern Ireland (Emergency Provisions) Act 1978, a constable could arrest without warrant and detain for seventy-two hours anyone whom he suspects of being a 'terrorist'. Section 11 was abolished as an arrest power in 1987.[174] Thus, section 14 has been preferred mainly because, firstly, it demands reasonable suspicion for arrests and thereby may satisfy Article 5(1) of the European Convention[175] and, secondly, its detention period is both more carefully scrutinised and more extensive.[176]

A further police power to arrest without warrant on suspicion of any 'scheduled offence' is granted by section 17 of the Emergency Provisions Act. The principal differences between sections 17 and 14 are that the former does not attract extraordinary detention periods (and, therefore, has been invoked very sparingly) and that the range of activities covered is much narrower.[177]

Remaining detention powers in Northern Ireland have no counterparts in the Prevention of Terrorism Act. These include section 18 of the

Emergency Provisions Act, which allows soldiers to make arrests without warrant for any offence and to hold persons for up to four hours. In view of their lack of training and accountability, soldiers should not, if possible, be given tasks which bring them into confrontation with civilians. Thus, section 14 of the Prevention of Terrorism Act, which is confined to constables, is to be preferred. Next, section 23 of the Emergency Provisions Act allows soldiers and constables to stop and question persons to ascertain their identity and movements or what they know about recent terrorist incidents. In principle, any power to detain for questioning is to be deprecated since:[178]

there is a risk that it might be misapplied and the results of that could be damaging to police relations with the public. . . . the reluctant or obstreperous witness . . . is, in any event, unlikely to be particularly reliable if he is acting under compulsion.

Nonetheless, detention for questioning can be valuable if confined to situations where it is most likely to produce information. There are perhaps three such contexts: in the vicinity of a terrorist incident; in areas which are likely terrorist targets, such as a shopping centre; and adjacent to the Irish border. It is doubtful whether such powers are required in Britain in the absence of evidence to suggest the public is not prepared to help police investigations into terrorism.

The main special power directed against terrorists in the Republic is section 30(1) of the Offences against the State Act 1939:[179]

A member of the Garda Siochana . . . may without warrant stop, search, interrogate, and arrest any person, or do any one or more of those things in respect of any person, whom he suspects of having committed or being about to commit or being or having been concerned in the commission of an offence under any section or sub-section of this Act or an offence which is for the time being a scheduled offence . . . or whom he suspects of carrying a document relating to . . . any such offence as aforesaid or whom he suspects of being in possession of information relating to . . . any such offence as aforesaid.

A suspect may be detained for only twenty-four hours, with a further twenty-four hours available at the discretion of a chief superintendent. Section 30 differs from section 14 in that it relates to 'scheduled offences' not 'terrorism'; this is a preferable approach provided in practice the offences listed really do relate to terrorism, which is far from true in the Republic. Partly as a consequence of this first distinction, section 30 must not be used for intelligence-gathering.[180] Section 2 of the Emergency Powers Act 1976 contains powers almost identical to those in section 30 but is closer to section 14 of the Prevention of Terrorism Act in that the suspicion for an arrest must be reasonable and detention may subsist for forty-eight hours extendable by a further five days if a chief superintendent agrees.[181] This Act ceased to operate in 1977 but may be revived by order.

Finally, section 2 of the Offences against the State (Amendment) Act 1972[182] grants powers similar to section 23 of the Emergency Provisions Act, though limited to questioning following terrorist incidents, one of the more promising applications of such a power, as indicated earlier.

(c) Successive arrests[183]

In *ex parte Lynch*,[184] Lord Chief Justice Lowry could 'find nothing in section 11 of the 1978 Act or section [14] of the [1991] Act to place a fetter on the right to arrest first under one Act and then under the other . . .' or even 'twice in quick succession under the same provision . . .'. Support for these views was supposedly found in section 14(7) of the Prevention of Terrorism Act, which states that:

The provisions of this section are without prejudice to any power of arrest exercisable apart from this section.

It was inferred that Parliament intended section 14 to be used in combination with existing arrest powers. Unfortunately, this conclusion misinterprets section 14(7) which, though never fully explained during enactment, is intended to permit the police to continue to arrest persons reasonably suspected of terrorist crimes under 'normal' arrest powers instead of under section 14.[185] Furthermore, subsection (7) cannot possibly justify successive arrests exclusively under section 14, since it refers only to 'powers of arrest exercisable apart from this section'.

In conclusion, assertions that serial arrests can lawfully be undertaken involving section 14 should be rejected as threatening individual liberty and should be reversed by statute, save perhaps in three situations.[186] The first is when the first arrest was by a soldier under section 18 of the Emergency Provisions Act, since it was always envisaged that rearrest by the police could follow this short spell of detention.[187] The second is when the later arrest is carried out to charge the person immediately with an offence; this sequence does not negate the statutory limitations on interrogation in custody. The third is where the subsequent arrest is based on substantially fresh evidence.[188]

3 Arrest: assessment

(a) Nature and extent of use

(i) *Great Britain* If it is presumed that all arrests other than at ports and airports are carried out under section 14, the figures in Table 6 result. Four features attract attention. First, only in 1974, 1984 to 1986, 1989 and 1990 were most detentions carried out under section 14. The earlier peak probably reflects a high level of police operations against Irish suspects resident in Britain. Once they had been dealt with by way of

Table 6 The operation of special detention powers in Great Britain

Year	Detentions (ss. 14 & 16)			Arrests under s. 14			Extension beyond 48 hours under s. 14			Removals after arrest			Criminal charge after detention (ss. 14, 16)		
	N.I.	International	Total	N.I.	International	Total	N.I.	International	Total	Exclusion	Deportations	Total	N.I.	International	Total
1974	59	N/A	59	49	N/A	49	46	N/A	46	11	N/A	11	8	N/A	8
1975	1067	N/A	1067	437	N/A	437	137	N/A	137	21	N/A	21	63	N/A	63
1976	1066	N/A	1066	254	N/A	254	59	N/A	59	8	N/A	8	57	N/A	57
1977	853	N/A	853	192	N/A	192	29	N/A	29	5	N/A	5	47	N/A	47
1978	622	N/A	622	113	N/A	113	23	N/A	23	9	N/A	9	19	N/A	19
1979	857	N/A	857	284	N/A	284	135	N/A	135	6	N/A	6	108	N/A	108
1980	537	N/A	537	96	N/A	96	40	N/A	40	3	N/A	3	42	N/A	42
1981	274	N/A	274	111	N/A	111	39	N/A	39	2	N/A	2	39	N/A	39
1982	220	N/A	220	60	N/A	60	20	N/A	20	2	N/A	2	22	N/A	22
1983	191	N/A	191	59	N/A	59	24	N/A	24	2	N/A	2	31	N/A	31
1984	159	44	203	75	39	114	9	17	26	1	13	14	23	8	31
1985	193	73	266	122	70	192	49	40	89	2	18	20	38	15	53
1986	147	55	202	73	43	116	34	19	53	7	9	16	31	5	36
1987	184	41	225	50	31	81	13	18	31	15	9	24	17	8	25
1988	170	16	186	60	10	70	13	2	15	16	0	16	18	3	21
1989	163	18	181	85	14	99	14	5	19	9	2	11	19	3	22
1990	169	24	193	116	20	136	21	6	26	14	2	16	25	3	28
Total	6931	271	7202	2236	227	2463	705	107	811	133	53	186	607	45	652

Source: Home Office. Note: N/A = figures not applicable.

Table 7   Duration of special detentions in Great Britain

Length of detention	Persons detained under s. 14 and charged 1979–82	Persons detained (ss. 14, 16) and not charged or excluded	
		1974–84	*1984–89*
Up to 24 hours	N/A	857	200
24–36 hours	N/A	421	265
36–48 hours	N/A	292	176
Total under 48 hours	50 (33%)	1570 (84%)	641 (84%)
48–72 hours	N/A	117	32
72–96 hours	N/A	61	43
Total under 96 hours	N/A	1748 (94%)	716 (94%)
4–5 days		34	22
5–6 days		29	7
6 and 7 days		57	18
Total	150	1868	763

Source: Home Office. *Note*: N/A = figures not available.

interrogation, exclusion or even prosecution, police attention switched primarily to those arriving in Britain from Ireland. The peak in 1984 to 1986 results from a similar processing of foreign terrorists, who represented 36 per cent of the total during that period. Next, these figures also illustrate a general decline in police activity under the Act in line with a lower level of terrorist activity after 1976 until an upsurge in 1989 and 1990. Thirdly, most arrests are probably under section 14(1)(b); only 227 charges related to offences under the Act itself and most of those concern breaches of port controls following detention under section 16. Finally, foreign terrorism has become a significant ground for arrests, but there has been a marked decline recently, which may strengthen the arguments for repeal.

The statistics for extended detentions reveal that the proportion has settled down to about a third of those arrested. Table 7 reveals the precise time spent in detention. About 84 per cent of suspects not charged or excluded are processed within forty-eight hours and 94 per cent within ninety-eight hours. However, 66 per cent of those charged are interrogated for more than 48 hours. Consequently, while early checks are important, a lengthy period of custody has paid dividends.

Table 8   Length of extensions of special detention in Great Britain

Year	N.I. terrorism – days allowed per application					International terrorism – days allowed per application				
	1	2	3	4	5	1	2	3	4	5
1986	3	14	12	3	11	–	8	15	1	3
1987	6	19	12	1	2	2	8	10	–	3
1988	5	12	6	–	3	1	1	–	–	–
1989	7	25	7	–	–	–	6	–	–	–
1990	10	13	2	–	9	–	6	–	–	–
Total	31	83	39	4	25	3	29	25	1	6

Source: Home Office.

Two further points should be noted concerning extensions. First, extensions since the passage of the 1984 Act are often far less than five days (see Table 8). Rather less encouraging is the remarkable fact that no application has ever been rejected by the Home Office. Such perfection may to some extent reflect police expertise in forwarding only meritorious applications,[189] but probably owes much to the inadequacy of a non-judicial review system.

Perhaps the most important statistics are those relating to charges following arrest under section 14. Assuming from the figures given for 1979 to 1982 that 71 per cent (150 out of 211) of criminal charges relate to detainees under section 14, the overall charge rate for section 14 from 1974 to 1989 is 19 per cent, with exclusions or removals in a further 7 per cent of cases. A success rate of 26 per cent is very low[190] and emphasises the intelligence-gathering purposes of many arrests.

(ii) Northern Ireland   As Table 9 shows, the returns for Northern Ireland are strikingly different. The dearth of arrests before 1976 is probably explicable by the facts that the Prevention of Terrorism Acts were primarily viewed as protecting Britain and that powers under the Emergency Provisions Act were already in operation. However, the attractions of section 14 were evidently noted by the R.U.C. during 1975, and it began to be invoked 'primarily for cases in which detention for a longer period is likely to be thought necessary'.[191] In the following decade, its use became predominant, and it wholly supplanted section 11 in 1987, since when it has become the most important 'special' provision of all. As in Britain, most arrests are under section 14(1)(b); only eighty-two persons

Table 9   The operation of s. 14 in Northern Ireland

Year	Persons detained under s. 14	Extensions beyond 48 hours	Persons excluded	Persons charged (except under the Act)
1974	–	–	–	–
1975	8	5	1	2
1976	246	202	1	130
1977	162	123	–	81
1978	155	144	2	72
1979	162	126	4	51
1980	222	186	3	103
1981	495	401	11	153
1982	828	639	2	325
1983	1174	727	4	464
1984	980	533	2	271
1985	938	557	–	230
1986	1309	484	–	353
1987	1459	451	1	342
1988	1717	542	1	365
1989	1583	530	1	385
1990	1549	460	1	376
Total	12987	6110	34	3703

Source: Northern Ireland Office.

have been charged with an offence under the Act following an arrest under section 14. All arrests relate to Northern Ireland rather than foreign terrorism.[192]

Detentions are extended in 47 per cent of cases – substantially higher than the British figure, but one which was affected by the erstwhile operation of section 11 of the Emergency Provisions Act in less serious cases. Thus the rate was just 30 per cent in 1990. Samples of the length of detention of persons not subsequently charged or excluded, which also reflect this changing pattern of use, are set out in Table 10. In addition, out of 3,785 persons charged following arrest under section 14 up to the end of 1990 (including 82 charged with offences under the Act), 2,449 (65 per cent) were held for an extended period. Thus, charges were brought in 40 per cent of all cases involving extended detention but only in 20 per cent of arrests terminating within forty-eight hours. However, most statements are in reality obtained within twenty-four hours of arrest, thereby casting further doubt on whether seven days should be available.[193]

As in Britain, astoundingly few applications for extension fail: thirty

Table 10   The duration of special detentions in Northern Ireland

Length of detention under s. 14	Persons detained but not charged or excluded	
	1983	1986
Up to 24 hours	98	230
24–36 hours	102	232
36–48 hours	145	183
Total under 48 hours	345 (49%)	645 (68%)
48–72 hours	45	18
72–96 hours	61	104
Total under 96 hours	451 (64%)	767 (81%)
4–5 days	77	128
5–6 days	77	15
6 and 7 days	95	41
Total	700	951

Source: Northern Ireland Office (figures later revised).

have been withdrawn and six refused, though many more are filtered out by the police themselves.[194] On a brighter note, only in twenty instances up to 31 March 1984 was an extension granted for less than five days; since then, shorter periods have become commonplace (see Table 11).

Up to the end of 1988 and including persons charged under the Act itself, the charging rate under section 14 was 29 per cent (persons excluded add under 1 per cent). This relatively rosy finding is misleading, since account must also be taken of the rate of charges under section 11 of the Emergency Provisions Act, which was correspondingly abysmal.[195] Accordingly the charging rate under section 14 (excluding offences in the Act itself) has fallen from 46 per cent for the period between 1974 and 1980 to 36 per cent for 1981 to 1984, to 25 per cent for 1985 to 1990, while the proportion of extensions in the same periods (some indication of strong and serious cases) are 82 per cent, 68 per cent and 35 per cent. These trends could also reflect greater resistance to interviews because of training or intimidation[196] but may equally indicate that there is now a greater readiness to enlist section 14 on flimsier grounds, as already occurs in Britain.

Finally, whilst the operation of the Act in Britain has given rise to few formal complaints against the police from detainees,[197] complaints in Northern Ireland are far more frequent (though rarely substantiated) – see Table 12.

Table 11 Length of extensions of special detention in Northern Ireland

Year	Days allowed per application				
	1	2	3	4	5
1986	8	114	297	–	64
1987	15	175	233	–	27
1988	21	225	270	2	23
1989	47	267	214	–	12
1990	22	258	189	–	–
Total	113	1039	1203	2	126

Source: Northern Ireland Office.

(b) *Advantages and drawbacks*
A leading purpose of arrests under section 14 is to interrogate suspects so as to uncover admissible evidence sufficient to put before a court.[198] Section 14 facilitates questioning, for example, by allowing apprehension without reasonable suspicion of a specific offence, thereby encouraging arrest and leaving open the lines of investigation to be taken.[199] In addition, the extraordinary detention period may be invaluable against hardened terrorists – especially, for reasons given earlier, in Scotland.

Even if a statement obtained during detention under section 14 is inadmissible or is simply not damning enough to warrant criminal charges, the exercise may still be worthwhile. Indeed, it may be misleading to claim that the 'prime objective'[200] of questioning is to enable proceedings to be instituted. The rate of charging betokens a dominant police interest in gathering background information through questioning a detainee about his political views, friends and colleagues.[201] Lord Shackleton was prepared to sanction such a practice on a wide scale:[202]

the police are bound to follow up any information or suspicion about involvement in terrorism. . . . The Prevention of Terrorism is not simply a question of arresting people who can promptly be charged with offences. . . .

The Jellicoe Report more cautiously argued that intelligence-gathering should be confined to persons suspected of personal involvement in terrorism.[203] Nevertheless, it also accepted that 'good intelligence saves lives', and section 14 should be used to obtain it.[204]

Intelligence-gathering powers may be essential when 'large sections of the community are either afraid or unwilling to cooperate . . . making it impossible for the [police] to gather the information it needs through normal police channels'.[205] However, one of the main disadvantages of

G

Table 12 Complaints from detainees under special arrest powers in Northern Ireland

Year	1976	1977	1978	1979	1980	1981	1982	1983 (to Nov.)	1984	1985	1986	1987	1988	1989
Total complaints (to 1986) or allegations (thereafter)	347	667	411	265	119	130	207	64	820	232	251	364	244	381
Complaints of assault	220	443	266	168	65	72	113	27	N/A	N/A	N/A	227	160	246

Table 12 continued

Allegations by detainees under the Prevention of Terrorism and Emergency Provisions Acts	Year			
	1986	1987	1988	1989
Assault at police station	101	156	131	246
Assault before arrival	11	5	7	11
Forced standing	20	18	9	33
Statement falsified	7	13	7	3
Verbal abuse	12	8	11	28
Threats	14	17	15	29
Refusal of access to doctor or solicitor	18	3	3	6
Other	25	23	18	25
Total	208	243	201	381
Results of investigations (cases)				
Incapable of investigation	129	182	169	238
Not substantiated	–	66	44	76
Substantiated	1	2	3	–
Withdrawn	–	36	–	5
Total	130	286	216	319

Source: Police Complaints Board and Independent Commission for Police Complaints. Note: N/A = figures not available.

section 14 relates to its application in this way in that it can readily be perceived as 'racial harassment of Irish people and victimisation of supporters of Republicanism'.[206] The effect is as likely to impede the voluntary flow of information from Irish communities as it is likely to increase it from those detained.

Related dubious applications of section 14 have also arisen, all of which have similar counter-productive effects.

Firstly, some of those arrested appear to have been selected primarily because of involvement in, or even knowledge about,[207] Republican politics rather than suspected terrorism. For example, members of Sinn Fein and the Irish Civil Rights Association have been frequent targets for questioning in custody.[208] To counteract this tendency, the police are warned to take special precautions to ensure that persons do not appear to be arrested for their political activities.[209]

A second problem is that section 14 has sometimes been transformed into a form of forty-eight-hour internment.[210] For example, shortly before the death from hunger-strike of Bobby Sands, M.P., in April 1981, thirty Republicans were arrested in Northern Ireland and held for a number of days, thereby disrupting their protest plans.[211]

Another example of improper use is that section 14 may be invoked to detain suspects in connection with crimes unrelated to terrorism, such as theft and robbery.[212] This problem seems most acute in Northern Ireland, where it has been estimated that approximately 40 per cent of cases in the special 'Diplock' courts are classifiable as 'ordinary' crimes.[213]

The fourth type of overuse concerns police 'sweeps', wherein everyone connected with a person against whom there is firm evidence may be arrested. For example, two large police operations in Southampton in December 1974 and November 1975 netted seventy-six and forty-six persons respectively, but only four were convicted and another was excluded.[214] Exercises of this kind also occurred before Christmas in 1979, 1981 and 1983.

(c) Conclusions
The Jellicoe Report concluded that:[215]

there can be no clear proof that the arrest powers in the Prevention of Terrorism Act are, or are not, an essential weapon in the fight against terrorism.

Nevertheless, the Report recommended their continuance 'while a substantial threat from terrorism remains . . .'.[216] Yet such equivocal support is insufficient in view of the limiting principles in chapter 2, which set any presumption against special powers. Thus, while section 14 has proved the most important and helpful provision in the Prevention of Terrorism Act, it is unacceptable as presently designed and executed. Section 14 has allowed excessive intelligence-gathering and oppressive interrogations and detentions, which have caused great damage on balance to the criminal justice system. In so far as special powers are currently necessary (which is probably true only in Northern Ireland),[217] a preferable design will be outlined in chapter 13.

4 Powers of search: provisions

(a) Terrorist investigations

Aside from an attack on terrorist finances, the other major development in the Prevention of Terrorism Act of 1989 concerns special search powers. The two matters are linked, since the principal need for new search powers in Viscount Colville's mind was as an aid to investigations into terrorist funds.[218] However, the wording of the Act transcends that purpose, and other likely targets of the new powers include political organisations, commercial ventures which have allegedly received subventions from the I.R.A.,[219] business advisers, bankers and journalists.

Accordingly, section 17(1) provides for powers to obtain information for the purpose of 'terrorist investigations' into:

(a) ... (i) the commission, preparation or instigation of acts of terrorism to which section 14 ... applies; or
(ii) any other act which appears to have been done in furtherance of or in connection with such acts of terrorism, including any act which appears to constitute an offence under section 2, 9, 10 or 11 [of this Act] or sections 27 or 28 of the [Emergency Provisions Act]; or
(iii) without prejudice to sub-paragraph (ii) above, the resources of a proscribed organisation within the meaning of this Act or [the Emergency Provisions Act]; and
(b) investigations into whether there are grounds justifying the making of a [proscription] order under section 1(2)(a) [of this Act] or [under the Emergency Provisions Act].

The effective pursuit of such investigations is protected by a broad offence under section 17(2) (with up to five years' imprisonment) which may be committed whenever a person:

(a) makes any disclosure which is likely to prejudice the investigation; or
(b) falsifies, conceals or destroys or otherwise disposes of, or causes or permits the falsification, concealment, destruction or disposal of, material which is likely to be relevant to the investigation.

As for the *mens rea*, it is sufficient that a person knows or has reasonable cause to suspect that an investigation is in progress; no subjective intent as to the consequences of disclosure is necessary. The scope of the offence is uncertain in that there is no definition as to when an investigation ends, though the effective start for the purposes of section 17(2) is when a search warrant or production order under the Act has been applied for or made.

It is not an offence under the Act to tip off suspects about the use of other powers (but this may amount to an obstruction of the police in the execution of their duty).[220] The 'materials' referred to under section 17(2)(b) will usually be written records or data but could include weapons or explosives if they are the object of the investigation.[221]

In contrast to the offence of withholding information contrary to section 18, section 17(2) requires a positive act of obstruction, such as tipping off or burning papers, rather than mere inaction. Thus, concerns about self-incrimination do not arise. However, another contrast is that the relevant information is about investigations and not terrorism, and this difference may put at risk solicitors or accountants, whose records are themselves investigated because of suspicions about a client or who simply hear rumours about pending police activity. If a solicitor wishes in either eventuality to take instructions and thereby divulge the existence of the investigation, he may be able to avoid liability by reliance upon section 17(3), by which it is a defence to section 17(2)(a) to prove:

(a) that he did not know and had not reasonable cause to suspect that the disclosure was likely to prejudice the investigation; or
(b) that he had lawful authority or reasonable excuse for making the disclosure.

It must be shown under section 17(3)(a) (the onus lies on the defendant) that there was no knowledge or reasonable suspicion as to the existence of an investigation or that the disclosure would be damaging; the latter is especially hard to prove given that only the police know the scope of any investigation.[222] 'Lawful authority' may arise under section 17(3)(b) if there is express permission from the police or prosecution to disclosure, perhaps after a decision not to proceed.[223] 'Reasonable excuse' may arise from threats not amounting to duress[224] or possibly from the demands of the solicitor/client relationship. In relation to a similar defence under section 31 of the Drug Trafficking Offences Act 1986, it was suggested *obiter* by Lord Griffiths in *R. v. Central Criminal Court, ex parte Francis and Francis*[225] that the defence could excuse a solicitor who in good faith takes instructions for the purpose of possible legal proceedings. However, the propriety of the disclosure will be a matter of proof in each case, since the Government rejected the suggestion that there should be a blanket exemption for communications between solicitors and clients. In the Minister's opinion, the good faith of all solicitors in Northern Ireland cannot be trusted, since some are 'unduly sympathetic to the cause of the I.R.A. . . .'.[226] The Government also propounded the rather hostile views that solicitors should not contact their clients about orders against the clients[227] and that solicitors themselves the subject of investigation because of their clients should not obtain instructions as to whether they should contest the police's action.[228] To an extent unwarranted by *ex parte Francis and Francis*, the

English Law Society has succumbed to these warnings by advising that 'it would be prudent for a solicitor not to disclose to his client that an order or warrant has been applied for, made or issued unless the solicitor has ascertained that the investigating authorities have no serious objection'.[229] Faced with a 'terrorist investigation', it is submitted that the solicitor should first quiz the police as to the nature of their inquiries and then assess what disclosures would be prejudicial. Secondly, the police should be encouraged to take away materials under warrant in sealed bags so that no prejudice is suffered before privileges can be asserted in court. Thirdly, the client should be contacted for instructions; in their absence, no costs may be recoverable for any action taken.[230] Total inaction is not a breach of contract in the light of the Law Society's advice and the decision in *Barclays Bank* v. *Taylor*[231] (on a similar situation under the Police and Criminal Evidence Act 1984) but is hardly helpful to the client or the business reputation of the solicitor.

Another defence to section 17(2)(b) is contained in subsection (4), by which the defendant must prove 'he had no intention of concealing' the relevant material from the investigators. Thus, an accountant who weeds out dead files, having forgotten or failed to understand (whether reasonably or not) their significance to the police, will be excused.

The small print of the new search machinery, in Schedule 7, is clearly based on sections 8 to 14 (Articles 10 to 16 in Northern Ireland) and Schedule 1 of the Police and Criminal Evidence legislation. Thus, applications for search warrants are normally issued under paragraph 2 of Schedule 7 by a justice of the peace:

(1) ... if satisfied that a terrorist investigation is being carried out and that there are reasonable grounds for believing –

(a) that there is material ... which is likely to be of substantial value ... to the investigation;

(b) that the material does not consist of or include items subject to legal privilege, excluded material or special procedure material; and

(c) that any of the conditions in subparagraph (2) below are fulfilled. [i.e.]

(2)(a) ... that it is not practicable to communicate with any person entitled to grant entry to the premises;

(b) that it is ... not practicable to communicate with any person entitled to grant access to the material;

(c) that entry to the premises will not be granted unless a warrant is produced;

(d) that the purpose of a search may be frustrated or seriously prejudicial unless a constable arriving at the premises can secure immediate entry to them.

On the authority of a warrant, a constable may enter, search and seize under paragraph 2(3) material (unless legally privileged) if he reasonably believes it is of substantial value to the investigation and that its immediate removal is necessary. It will be noted that this and other powers under

Schedule 7 may be used at an early stage in the investigation; no specific or serious offence need be alleged nor need (unlike in the Police and Criminal Evidence legislation) any wrongdoer (whether the occupier or otherwise) be identified.[232] The appointment of justices as the issuing authorities is commonplace but should be criticised because of their tendency to 'rubber-stamp police requests'.[233] Circuit judges would be preferable.[234] The search power is also excessive in that the police may search not only the premises but also any person found there, without requiring reasonable suspicion in each case.[235]

When the police seek 'special procedure' or 'excluded' material (as defined in sections 11–14/Articles 13–16 of the Police and Criminal Evidence legislation), they must apply to a circuit judge (county court judge in Northern Ireland) for an order either that it be produced for removal or that access be allowed. Such orders may be issued under paragraph 3, provided it does not consist of legally privileged material and provided:[236]

(5) ... (a) that a terrorist investigation is being carried out and that there are reasonable grounds for believing that the material is likely to be of substantial value ... to the investigation ... and

(b) that there are reasonable grounds for believing that it is in the public interest having regard –

(i) to the benefit likely to accrue to the investigation if the material is obtained; and

(ii) to the circumstances under which the person in possession of the material holds it, that the material should be produced or that access to it should be given.

Orders may relate to material (such as transaction records) which come into existence within twenty-eight days and may be varied or discharged (under paragraph 4) on further application to a Crown Court.

A search warrant may exceptionally[237] be issued instead of a production order by a judge under paragraph 5, provided an order has not been obeyed, or no one with authority to grant access can be contacted or application by way of an order might seriously prejudice the investigation. Persons found on the premises may be searched and materials seized on the same grounds as in paragraph 2 above.

The various investigative powers are subject to several forms of restraint. Controls in the Act itself include the requirements that any force used be reasonable (section 20(2)), that any personal searches be conducted by an officer of the same sex (Schedule 7 paragraph 10(2)) and the express application of sections 21 and 22 of the Police and Criminal Evidence Act concerning access to and retention of seized materials (Schedule 7 paragraph 10(1)).[238] Sections 15 and 16 of that Act (Articles 17 and 18 in Northern Ireland), which concern applications for and the execution of warrants, are also relevant. Next, the Police and Criminal Evidence Act

Code B[239] (in England and Wales only) imposes the requirements, *inter alia*, that applications under Schedule 7 be made on the authority of a superintendent and executed in the presence and under the charge of an inspector.

Although Schedule 7 broadly reflects the Police and Criminal Evidence legislation, it contains some significant variants as to jurisdiction, procedures and powers.

One major jurisdictional difference is that Schedule 7 applies in Scotland, where there are no plans otherwise to reproduce the Police and Criminal Evidence legislation. In Scotland, applications for production orders, search warrants and explanation orders are all to be made (under paragraphs 12, 14 and 15) by a procurator fiscal to a sheriff.[240] Given this unified procedure, no distinction need be drawn between special procedure materials and others, though items subject to legal privilege do receive some protection (by paragraph 17).[241] Regrettably, there is no express equivalent to the restraints concerning excluded materials under the Police and Criminal Evidence legislation. A second jurisdictional difference is that the criteria for the issuance of warrants or orders are laxer under Schedule 7. The materials need only appear 'likely to be of substantial value' but may not necessarily be 'relevant evidence' (as in the Police and Criminal Evidence legislation). Furthermore, applications to judges for production orders need not demonstrate that other methods of obtaining the materials have been tried unsuccessfully or are doomed to failure. A third distinction is that the powers of circuit judges under Schedule 7 extend to excluded materials,[242] which are recoverable under the Police and Criminal Evidence legislation only if some independent power allows it (which is rare).

The main procedural differences include, as already noted, the absence of higher authorisations outside England and Wales. In addition, applications for production orders under paragraph 3 are not necessarily on notice or heard *inter partes*. However, such orders will specify some delay before compliance so that objectors may apply for variation or discharge.

A number of powers under Schedule 7 are not mirrored in the Police and Criminal Evidence legislation. Firstly, by paragraph 6 (paragraph 15 in Scotland), a judge can order on application by the police (or authorised investigator under section 57 of Northern Ireland (Emergency Provisions) Act 1991, as described in Chapter 7) any person to provide an explanation of produced or seized material. Legally privileged or self-incriminatory information need not be divulged,[243] but legal privilege is defined as not including the name and address of a client. Secondly, by paragraph 3(2), if special procedure or excluded material which is the subject of an order turns out not to be in the possession of the person named in the order, that person is under a duty to state to the best of his knowledge and belief the location of the material. Thirdly, by paragraph 3(3), orders may relate to materials expected to come into existence within twenty-eight days. Fourthly, authorised investigators are granted powers to access police materials. Finally, Schedule 7 allows two unique procedures. By paragraph 7(1) (paragraph 16 in Scotland), if a police superintendent reasonably believes 'that the case is one of great emergency and . . . in the interests of the State immediate action is necessary',[244] he may issue orders equivalent to search warrants or explanation orders.[245] Of even greater concern is the power granted by paragraph 8 to the Secretary of State for Northern Ireland[246] to issue orders corresponding to those in paragraphs 2, 3, 5 and 6 in connection with inquiries into offences under Part III, provided:

(a)   he is satisfied as to the matters specified in [paragraphs 2, 3 or 5]; and
(b)   it appears to him that the disclosure of information that would be necessary for an application under those provisions would be likely to prejudice the capability of members of the Royal Ulster Constabulary in relation to the investigation of offences under Part III of this Act or otherwise prejudice the safety of, or of persons in, Northern Ireland.

This breathtaking breach of constitutional decencies should be rejected as a threat to liberty and privacy.[247] The only likely explanations for paragraph 8 (none was officially offered in Parliament or the Colville Report)[248] would seem to be either that the police do not trust the judiciary to keep their mouths shut or to grant dubious requests or that court papers are insecure.[249] By contrast, the Secretary of State is sound on all counts. The final power which used to be peculiar to Schedule 7 was that access was granted to Land Registry records on application (paragraph 9). This procedure has been extended to criminal investigations in general by the Land Registration Act 1988, but there remains a separate power to assist 'terrorist investigators'.[250] Other governmental records are obtainable either by informal arrangement or through the judicial procedures in Schedule 7 (and paragraph 4(6) (13(5) in Scotland) envisages such applications).[251]

(b)   Searches supplementary to section 14 arrests
In order to facilitate arrests, a new search power was included in section 15(1) of the 1989 Act:[252]

If a justice of the peace is satisfied that there are reasonable grounds for suspecting that a person whom a constable believes to be liable to arrest under section 14(1)(b) above is to be found on any premises he may grant a search warrant authorising any constable to enter those premises for the purpose of searching for and arresting that person.

The same power is invested in sheriffs or justices in Scotland (section 15(2)). However, the corresponding power in section 16 of the Emergency Provisions Act 1991 (as substituted by section 6 of the 1987 Act) allows entry and search without warrant on reasonable suspicion. Given that the special power is only vital when it is not possible to enter premises under the Police and Criminal Evidence legislation (section 17/Article 19) in connection with arrestable offences, it is submitted that the Northern Ireland version should be amended in line with section 15(1) so as to obviate the dangers of overuse.[253] It would also be preferable for a judge to decide such important issues.[254]

By section 15(3):

In any circumstances in which a constable has power under section 14 above to arrest a person, he may also, for the purpose of ascertaining whether he has in his possession any document or other article which may constitute evidence that he is a person liable to arrest, stop that person, and search him.

The principal drawback with such stop and search measures, especially ones unrelated to any specific offence, is their susceptibility to abuse.[255] Consequently, the Police and Criminal Evidence Act[256] attempts to prohibit 'fishing expeditions' by demanding the giving of reasons in advance of any search, the keeping of detailed records (to be available also to the suspect) and the compilation of statistics, and by indicating the necessary level of suspicion, which, by the wording of section 15(3), remains linked to the standard for arrests.[257]

Another power of warrantless search is granted by section 15(4):[258]

Where a constable has arrested a person [under section 14] for any reason other than the commission of a criminal offence, he, or any other constable, may search him for the purpose of ascertaining whether he has in his possession any document or other article which may constitute evidence that he is a person liable to arrest.

Searches of persons and premises following arrest for a specific offence (including those mentioned in section 14(1)(a)) are permitted by the Police and Criminal Evidence legislation[259] and so are expressly excepted from section 15(4).[260] 'Intimate' and 'strip' searches are restricted just as for non-terrorist detainees (except in Scotland).[261] A 'search' under section 15(4) for evidence in the suspect's possession should be distinguished from the taking of a bodily sample which has no separate existence until extracted.[262] Regrettably, the two were confused at common law by the Northern Ireland Court of Appeal in *R. v. Mulvenna*,[263] and this mistake could encourage brutality towards a suspect.

Next, when a person has been detained under section 14, section 15(9) provides that:

any constable or prison officer, or any other person authorised by the Secretary of State, may take all such steps as may be reasonably necessary for photographing, measuring or otherwise identifying him.

Section 15(9) significantly deviates from the normal fingerprinting procedures[264] under section 61/Article 61 of the Police and Criminal Evidence legislation.[265] For example, assuming a person refuses to be fingerprinted by consent, a police superintendent must authorise their taking by force under section 61/Article 61 which he may do when the individual has been charged with a recordable offence or informed that he will be reported for it, is reasonably suspected of involvement in it, has not already undergone fingerprinting and the prints will tend to confirm or disprove his guilt. By contrast, fingerprinting under section 15(9) may be enforced under section 15(10) on the authority of a superintendent:

if he is satisfied that it is necessary to do so in order to assist in determining –
(a)   whether that person is or has been concerned in the commission, preparation or instigation of acts of terrorism to which section 14 applies; or
(b)   whether he is subject to the exclusion order . . .;
or if the officer has reasonable grounds for suspecting that person's involvement in an offence under any of the provisions mentioned in [section 14(1)(a)] and for believing that his fingerprints will tend to confirm or disprove his involvement.

Section 15(10) was introduced into the Act in 1989 but extends only to England and Wales. Section 46 of the Emergency Provisions Act 1991 contains corresponding measures for that jurisdiction, but fingerprinting remains unaffected in Scotland. Furthermore, the first leg of section 15(10) is far laxer than the Police and Criminal Evidence Act equivalent (which resembles the second leg). Consequently, fingerprinting will continue to be applied routinely:[266]

All those arrested under the [Prevention of Terrorism Act] have had their fingerprints taken, and the vast majority have also been photographed and undergone forensic tests.

Another difference is that the fingerprint, samples or data records relating to fingerprints of a suspect not prosecuted for, or acquitted of, an offence must be destroyed according to section 64/Article 64 of the Police and Criminal Evidence legislation. There is no corresponding duty under section 15(9), provided the detention was lawful.[267] Consequently, fingerprints (and samples and photographs) of detainees under the Prevention of Terrorism Act are being retained so long as the legislation subsists.[268] Such records are stored centrally, presumably by the Metropolitan Police's Special Branch,[269] but they are utilised solely for counter-terrorism purposes and are filed separately from criminal records.[270] The retention of records may be justifiable in view of the vital importance of intelligence-gathering, so it may be more fruitful to strengthen controls over the use of such data rather than to demand its destruction.[271] A third deviation is that section 15(9), allows fingerprinting for 'identifying' the detainee rather than for evidence-gathering as under the Police and Criminal evidence legislation.[272] Consequently, section 15(9) should not be invoked when a suspect is already known to the police. This restriction has given rise to some concern[273] but does not seem to be observed in reality. The same point applies to the taking of bodily samples under section 15(9),[274] though the R.U.C. are encouraged to resort instead to powers under the Police and Criminal Evidence Order (originally in Schedule 14 of the Criminal Justice Act 1988). Thus, by Article 87(5), arrestees under section 14(1)(b) are deemed to be detained for a serious arrestable offence and so are subject to Articles 62 and 63. Furthermore, in order to facilitate the use of D.N.A. profiling, Article 53 defines as 'non-intimate', and therefore obtainable without consent, samples of saliva and mouth tissue. It is said that these powers are needed because of 'the more determined and systematic attempts made by criminals in Northern Ireland, compared with those by criminals in the mainland, to withhold and conceal evidence of forensic value to the police'.[275] In response, it has been argued[276] that the powers are a dangerous incitement to ill-treatment and have not been shown to be uniquely necessary since the passage of the Police and Criminal Evidence legislation, which contains adequate measures. If special powers are to be invoked, they should all be contained in the Prevention of Terrorism Act, and they should be subject to judicial authorisation.

(c) Incidental powers

As mentioned in regard to arrest, incidental powers to detain and search the occupants of target premises have been implied in relation to Army search powers under section 18 of the Emergency Provisions Act 1991.[277] The Prevention of Terrorism Act, section 21, furthers this initiative by attaching incidental powers now within section 19 of the Emergency Provisions Act. The position in relation to other substantive powers (including those in the Prevention of Terrorism Act) remains less certain,[278] but it has been argued elsewhere that these incidental attributes are unwarranted, dangerous and may breach Article 5(1) of the European Convention.[279]

5 Powers of search: comparisons

Precedents for special police search provisions may readily be traced. For example, the Prevention of Violence (Temporary Provisions) Act 1939 contained systems of judicial and police search warrants but not stop and search powers. [280] However, the recent additions in Schedule 7, which supplanted much more modest provisions in earlier versions,[281] were foreshadowed by a combination of the Police and Criminal Evidence legislation,[282] the Drug Trafficking Offences Act 1986,[283] the Criminal Justice (Scotland) Act 1987 and the English Criminal Justice Acts of 1987[284] and 1988.[285] In addition to these police powers, section 3 of the Security Service Act 1989 enables in startlingly loose terms the Secretary of State to issue warrants to agents which authorise interferences with property rights.

In the Republic of Ireland,[286] search warrants may be issued judicially under section 29 of the Offences against the State Act 1939 in respect of 'scheduled' and other terrorist-type offences. Stop and search powers in respect of scheduled offences are contained in section 30, and vehicle check-points may be operated under sections 8 and 15 of the Criminal Law Act 1976.[287] Persons arrested under section 30 of the Offences against the State Act or section 2 of the Emergency Powers Act 1976 may also be searched, photographed and fingerprinted, and section 7 of the Criminal Law Act allows the taking of swabs and hair samples to detect recent contact with explosives or firearms.

More fulsome powers are found in the Northern Ireland (Emergency Provisions) Act 1991.[288] Section 19 allows searches in connection with munitions and communications equipment, and section 21 deals with searches for kidnapped persons. Entry into a dwelling-house may be effected on reasonable suspicion and under the authority (not necessarily in writing) of a chief inspector or Army officer. Access to other premises may be obtained without observing either condition, and this equally applies to the additional power to stop and search vehicles or pedestrians for munitions or transmitters under section 19(6). On the foot of the foregoing powers, section 22 allows the police and soldiers to examine without prior reason and to seize documents which may contain information helpful to terrorists.

6 Powers of search: assessment

(a) Nature and extent of use

There were forty-five orders under Schedule 7 between 1 September 1989 and 6 March 1990, a surprisingly high number but one which corresponds to that under the Police and Criminal Evidence legislation.[289] Searches under police authority are rare,[290] but the alarming Secretary of State's power has been used 'on a substantial scale'.[291] The impact of these orders is not yet clear, and they may in part represent a switch away from evidence-gathering under sections 14 or 18 of the Act. Reliance upon Schedule 7 is at least to be preferred to those avenues and should prove fruitful. No statistics are available as to the powers to stop and search or to search on arrest, but they are probably heavily employed.[292]

Two forms of investigation give rise to particular concerns. One is the increasing emphasis upon forensic testing especially as applied to traces of explosives and bodily materials.[293] Terrorists are equally conscious of the evidential trail left behind and often take precautions, such as the burning of outer clothing and elaborate washing procedures. Reliance upon forensic testing is to be supported in principle, provided the testing is conducted according to proper standards and does not create dangers of bodily harm.

In the light of the Guildford and Maguire cases (discussed in chapter 11) and the unsupervised powers described earlier, reform is clearly needed. The other area of concern, especially in Northern Ireland, relates to home searches and the dangers of excessive damage and consequent aggravation to community relations. These dangers have been addressed by the Northern Ireland Office *Guide*, which requires the police or Army team itself to be frisked before and after the search and full written records be kept.[294] These procedures were described in *Murray* v. *Ministry of Defence* as 'an excellent blend of efficiency and thoroughness of search on the one hand and tact and consideration for the property and feelings of the household during it on the other'.[295] However, the *Guide* is unenforceable, and no similar rules apply in Britain.

(b) Deficiencies

One gap in the Prevention of Terrorism Act may be that, while section 15(3) permits the stopping of persons on reasonable suspicion, intervention may be justifiable as a matter of routine. This would be of greatest benefit in areas where there is a reasonable suspicion that terroristic incidents have taken place or will do so, such as in city centres and border areas in Northern Ireland. This first shortcoming may be partly alleviated by section 4/Article 6 of the Police and Criminal Evidence legislation, which allows road-checks when a serious arrestable offence has been, or is likely to be, committed in a given locality.[296] However, section 4 does not permit the stopping of pedestrians, so there remains a case for special stop and search powers, though not to the extent of those in section 23 of the Emergency Provisions Act 1991.

The comparative material from Northern Ireland further implies that powers to enter and search premises without judicial warrant or reasonable suspicion are of assistance. However, because of public resentment concerning their use, and doubts about their legality under the European Convention,[297] the powers in section 15(1) and Schedule 7 of the Prevention of Terrorism Act should suffice.

A third possible deficiency is that section 15(9) does not envisage bodily examinations for the purpose of evidence-gathering. However, any problem would be better solved by reliance upon the English version of the Police and Criminal Evidence legislation, which might be replicated in Scotland.

The fourth direction in which powers are apparently lacking is in regard to searching by electronic and technical devices, for example by telephone-tapping or by planting bugs or hidden cameras. Despite the Act's silence, it has been officially admitted that telephone-tapping is an extremely important method of combating terrorism,[298] though such evidence is rarely produced in courts.[299] Technological surveillance is in principle acceptable, but it is also vital that it should be properly authorised and monitored.[300] Unfortunately, the Interception of Communications Act 1985[301] provides feeble controls. For example, despite the absence of any definition of terrorism in the Act, the Commissioner (Lloyd L.J.) complacently believes that:[302]

> terrorism is easy enough to recognise. A man knows whether he is a terrorist or not, even if he thinks of himself as a freedom fighter.

In short, the Act inadequately regulates those methods of search within its ambit and ignores altogether certain relevant forms of surveillance, such as electronic bugs and spy cameras,[303] a loophole which the police can readily exploit.

Another problem concerns the unregulated access to governmental records. Access to Land Registry records is scrutinised to some extent,[304] but it is probable that other official information is imparted on informal request. Access to all personal records should be permitted but subject to formal approach to a judge.[305]

One final problem, which affects search powers both in the Prevention of Terrorism Act and elsewhere, is the impact of diplomatic privileges and immunities. Article 22 of the Vienna Convention of 1961 prohibits searches of missions, and Article 27 demands absolute freedom from interference for diplomatic communications. Personal searches are similarly forbidden by Article 29. These comprehensive restrictions, as implemented by the Diplomatic Privileges Act 1964, hampered police investigations following the shootings from the Libyan People's Bureau in 1984. The police declined to search the diplomats' baggage, even though it was believed to contain a murder weapon, and the mission was searched only after diplomatic relations had been severed. Although this restraint was mainly motivated by the political consideration of the threat of retaliation,[306] any search would also have been illegal,[307] subject to three exceptions. One is that a continuing, immediate threat of violence probably permits entry in self-defence, to protect life or as a reprisal.[308] Next, reservations in the treaty establishing diplomatic relations sometimes allow the receiving State to search with consent or, if refused, to return diplomatic bags.[309] Thirdly, electronic surveillance of bags, for example by X-rays, is permissible and will be employed 'on specific occasions when the grounds for suspicion are sufficiently strong'.[310] By contrast diplomatic immunities proved less troublesome during the Dikko affair. The crate containing the victim was sent from the Nigerian Commission but was not treated as a diplomatic bag within Article 27. It did not bear the appropriate visible external marks of its character, and, even if it had, a search would still have been justified to protect life.[311]

As was concluded in regard to arrests, diplomatic law fetters police inquiries into foreign terrorism. However, any solution must lie in a combination of the more astute invocation of sanctions prescribed by the Vienna Convention and greater international cooperation against diplomatic abuses.[312]

(c) Superfluity

Having probed the Prevention of Terrorism Act for gaps, a fair assessment should also consider whether the relevant paragraphs unnecessarily duplicate 'normal' search powers.

In the case of searches under warrant, a variety of provisions aside from those in the Act could be available. The most suitable alternatives are sections 8 and 9/Articles 10 and 11 of the Police and Criminal Evidence legislation, which authorise search warrants and production orders in connection with serious arrestable offences.[313] There are also more specific statutory powers of relevance,[314] some of which allow the police to act on their own authority.[315] Scottish common law also entitles the police to search premises without warrant in emergencies and on a wider basis than paragraph 4(4).[316] From the foregoing survey, it must be deduced that section 15(1) and Schedule 7 are largely dispensable, save that they allow the police to obtain excluded material under Schedule 1 of the Police and Criminal Evidence legislation and to act outside of arrest or emergency situations in Scotland.

As for the powers of search without warrant, adequate regular powers cover most of the field.[317] Consequently, the vague provisions in section 15(3) and (4) are unnecessary and undesirable, though some alternative special powers, especially to conduct routine searches, may be helpful. Furthermore, the case for the retention of section 15(9) is weak, given the already over-generous provisions in the Police and Criminal Evidence legislation.

(d) Conclusions

The uncovering of physical evidence is indispensable in the prevention of planned terrorism and the investigation of attacks already perpetrated. However, in view of the large degree of overlap just described, existing search measures should be radically overhauled, as outlined in chapter 13, in order to reduce their serious threat to personal liberty.

Notes

1 Jellicoe Report, para. 232. Compare: Baker Report, para. 252.
2 See: H.O. Circular, para. 4.2; S.H.H.D. Circular, para. 4.2; H.C. Debs. Standing Comm. B. col. 321 10 January 1989.
3 The S.A.C.H.R. *9th Report* (1983–84 H.C. No. 262 para. 7) proposes it should be.

4   See: *Ireland* v. *U.K.*, Appl. No. 5310/71, Judgment of Court Ser. A No. 25 para. 196; *Brogan* v. *U.K.* Appl. Nos. 11209, 11234, 11266/84, 11386/85, Judgment of Court Ser. A. No. 145-B para. 50; W. Finnie, 'The Prevention of Terrorism Act and the European Court of Human Rights' (1989) 52 *M.L.R.* 703 at p. 706.

5   *Times* 29 October 1988 p. 1, (1990) *Times* 1 May.

6   H.C. Debs. Vol. 168 col. 839 6 March 1990 Mr. Patten. But see ch. 11.

7   See: Police and Criminal Evidence Act 1984 s. 24 and (Northern Ireland) Order 1989 S.I. No. 1341 Art. 26. Compare Colville Report, paras. 4.1.7–4.1.11.

8   *Ibid.*, para. 4.1.1.

9   Paras. 13, 23, 75–8.

10   The Philips Annual Report for 1984, para. 46.

11   See: ch. 3. The Home Secretary claimed that s. 14 was invaluable in a bomb plot involving an Abu Nidhal cell in 1986, since the Immigration Act 1971 allows detention only for removal not for questioning and by immigration officials rather than the police (H.C. Debs. Vol. 110 cols. 264–5 10 February 1987, Mr. Hurd). Little more was achieved by s. 14, as only one person was convicted and the rest were deported. Furthermore, questioning about terrorism is relevant to immigration purposes and may form part of an examination after entry (see: *Puttick* v. *Secretary of State for the Home Dept.* [1984] Imm. A.R. 118; *Baljinder Singh* v. *Hammond* [1987] 1 W.L.R. 283).

12   Para. 76.

13   The police also encountered difficulties in regard to S.W.A.P.O.: H.C. Debs. Vol. 92 col. 422 19 February 1986, Mr. Kaufman.

14   Some guidance might be unearthed in the Final Act of the Diplomatic Conference on the Reaffirmation and Development of International Humanitarian Law Applicable in Armed Conflicts, with Protocol I, Protocol II and Resolutions adopted at the Fourth Session (Cmnd. 6927, 1977).

15   H.O. Circular, para. 4.6. Compare: Jellicoe Report, para. 77. The critical comments of the N.C.C.L. (see C. Scorer, S. Spencer and P. Hewitt, *The New Prevention of Terrorism Act* (1985) p. 55) are based on a misprint.

16   See especially: Offences against the Person Act 1861 s. 9; Explosive Substances Act 1883 ss. 2, 3 (as amended); Tokyo Convention Act 1967 s. 1; Suppression of Terrorism Act 1978 s. 4; International Protected Persons Act 1978 s. 1; Aviation Security Act 1982 Pt. I; Taking of Hostages Act 1982 s. 1; Nuclear Material (Offences) Act 1983 ss. 1, 2.

17   See: H.C. Debs. Vol. 52 col. 981 25 January 1984, Mr. Powell. This formula would allow action against those who attack British diplomats or military installations abroad.

18   Cmnd. 7031, 1977.

19   Before 1984, this limit was supposedly achieved by circular: H.O. Circular No. 40/1976; S.H.H.D. Circular No. 11/1976 (see now H.O. Circular 27/1989, para. 4.5). However, s. 14 was used against Scottish nationalists twenty-six times between 1980 and 1984 (Colville Report, para. 7.92) and possibly against English hunt saboteurs (H.C. Debs. Vol. 92 col. 422 19 February 1986, Mr. Kaufman). The distinction between domestic and international terrorism may be fine when the assailants or targets (or even both) are U.K. residents. In practice, Sikh terrorism is usually treated as international (see ch. 3). Animal liberation groups could also

be viewed as having international ideals (D. Bonner, 'Combating terrorism in the 1990's' (1989) *P.L.* 440 at p. 446 n. 53) but are not commonly arrested under s. 14.

20   Para. 77. The Colville Report (paras. 7.1.4, 7.1.5) agrees with this conclusion but suggested a power to amend the ambit by statutory instrument.

21   See: E. Denza, *Diplomatic Law* (1976).

22   Cmnd. 1368. See also: International Organisations Act 1968.

23   Significantly less protection is afforded by the Vienna Convention on Consular Relations of 1963 (Cmnd. 2113, as implemented by the Consular Relations Act 1968), but this rarely applies to principal consulates by virtue of Art. 70. See: F. Brenchley, *Diplomatic Immunities and State-Sponsored Terrorism* (1984) p. 9; *Diplomatic Immunities and Privileges* (Cmnd. 9497, 1985) para. 18.

24   See: E.L. Kerley, 'Some aspects of the Vienna Conference on diplomatic intercourse and immunities' (1962) 56 *J.I.L.* 88.

25   See: Denza, *op. cit.* p. 268; First Report from the Foreign Affairs Committee, *The Abuse of Diplomatic Immunities and Privileges* (1984–85 H.C. 127) para. 95.

26   See: First Report from the Foreign Affairs Committee, *loc. cit.* ch. III; *Diplomatic Immunities and Privileges*, *loc. cit.* paras. 82, 83.

27   *R.* v. *Barak and others* (1985) *Times* 13 February p. 3. *R.* v. *Lambeth JJ., ex p. Yusufu* (1985) *Times* 20 February. See also: *Times* 28 August 1984 p. 3; First Report from the Foreign Affairs Committee, *loc. cit.* ch. IV; *Diplomatic Immunities and Privileges, loc. cit.* para. 84.

28   *Times* 13 September 1988 p. 1, 14 September p. 1.

29   Persons excluded under s. 7 are not arrestable under s. 14(1)(c).

30   Ch. 5. Compare: P. Hall, 'The Prevention of Terrorism Acts' in A. Jennings (ed.), *Justice under Fire* (2nd ed., 1990) p. 174.

31   *Murray* v. *Ministry of Defence* [1988] 1 W.L.R. 692; Walker, 'Army special powers on parade' (1989) 40 *N.I.L.Q.* 1.

32   Compare: Police and Criminal Evidence Act 1984 s. 24(4)(a), (5)(c), (7)(a).

33   N.I.O., *Guide* p. 7. Hearsay evidence may be relied upon: *Mabana* v. *Commissioner of Police, Kwandebeli* 1988 (4) S.A. 446 (T.P.D.).

34   *Fox, Campbell and Hartley* v. *U.K.* Appl. Nos. 12244, 12245, 12383/86, Judgment of Ct. Ser. A Vol. 182 para. 35; W. Finnie, 'Anti-terrorist legislation and the E.C.H.R.' (1991) 34 *M.L.R.* 288.

35   [1986] N.I. 103. See also: *Moore* v. *Chief Constable, R.U.C.* [1988] N.I. 456. Compare: J.D. Jackson, 'Northern Ireland (Emergency Provisions) Act 1987' (1988) 39 *N.I.L.Q.* 235 at pp. 244–5.

36   [1988] N.I. 361. See also *Clinton* v. *Chief Constable* (1991) 3 B.N.I.L. n. 93.

37   See: *McKee* v. *Chief Constable for Northern Ireland* [1984] 1 W.L.R. 1358, Walker, 'Emergency arrest powers' (1985) 36 *N.I.L.Q.* 145; *Murray* v. *Ministry of Defence, loc. cit.*

38   As an alternative, the superior may be sued: *Roy* v. *Prior* [1971] A.C. 471; *Clark and Lindsell on Torts* (16th ed., 1989) para. 19.09.

39   *Times* 24 April 1980 p. 4, 25 April p. 25, 1 May p. 4.

40   *Loc. cit.*

41 [1988] N.I. 192 (£300 damages).

42 [1988] 8 N.I.J.B. 1 (£600).

43 The burden and standard of proof is similar in both actions: *Hanna* v. *Chief Constable, R.U.C., loc. cit.* at p. 82. S. 15(6) is no bar to action but authorises detentions for intelligence-gathering, allows detentions in places other than prisons or police stations and settles doubts as to the detention regime: R.J. Sharpe, *The Law of Habeas Corpus* (2nd ed., 1989) p. 99; *R.* v. *S.S.H.D., ex p. Cheblak* [1991] 2 All E. R. 319.

44 *Times* 13 December 1979 p. 1, 15 December p. 2, 18 December p. 4, 19 December p. 4, 20 December p. 2, 4 January 1980 p. 2.

45 *Times* 4 March 1981 p. 3, 6 March p. 4, 12 March p. 2, 18 March p. 2.

46 (1990) 9 B.N.I.L. n. 67.

47 [1980] N.I. 126 at p. 131. Compare: *Murray* v. *M.O.D., (loc. cit.)* which may be distinguished since the Emergency Provisions Act 1991 s. 18 always requires an offence to be suspected. It is lawful to use an arrest to pressurise a suspect: *Hanna* v. *Chief Constable, loc.cit.*

48 S. Livingstone, 'A week is a long time in detention' (1989) 40 *N.I.L.Q.* at 288 at p. 289. Compare Colville Report, paras. 5.2.2, 5.2.5.

49 *Loc. cit.* On the facts, the court upheld the purposes of the arrests whilst recognising that others may be unacceptable: para. 53.

50 H.C. Debs. Vol. 47 col. 56 24 October 1983, Mr. Brittan.

51 H.C. Debs. 1st Scottish Standing Committee col. 867 26 March 1985, Mr. Fraser.

52 H.C. Debs. Standing Comm. B col. 292 10 January 1989, Vol. 146 col. 67 30 January 1989, Mr. Hurd.

53 (1990) Pt. IV para. 49. Compare: R.U.C. Directive SB 16/13 (1976) (in P. Taylor, *Beating the Terrorist?* (1980) App. 2); *Report of David Calcutt Q.C. on his Inquiry into the Interrogations carried out by service police in Cyprus in February and March 1984* (Cmnd. 9281, 1986) para. 5.9; Landau Report, para. 2.17

54 H.O. Circular, paras. 4.5, 4.12.

55 S. Crawshaw, 'Combating terrorism' in R.H. Ward and H.E. Smith (eds.), *International Terrorism* (1987) p. 20.

56 H.L. Debs. Vol. 504 col. 998 28 February 1989, Earl Ferrers.

57 T.P. Coogan, *The I.R.A.* (revised ed., 1987) ch. 34; *Brogan* v. *U.K.*, Report of the Commission Ser. B. Vol. 135 para. 61.

58 *Loc. cit.* at p. 128. A bare reference to s. 14 was inadequate in *Van Hout* v. *Chief Constable, N.I.* (1984) 21 June (Q.B.D.).

59 The same arguments do not apply to s. 14(1)(a) or (c): *ex p. Lynch, ibid.* at pp. 130–1; *Forbes* v. *H.M. Advocate* 1990 S.C.C.R. 69.

60 Compare: *The People (A.G.)* v. *McDermott* (1974), reported in J.M. Kelly, *The Irish Constitution* (2nd ed., 1984) p. 520; *D.P.P.* v. *Connolly and Moran* (1985) 3 I.L.T. 83; *Nkondo and Gumede and others* v. *Minister of Law and Order and another* 1986 (2) S.A. 756 (A); *R.* v. *S.S.H.D., ex p. Cheblak, loc. cit.* A complaint under Art. 5.2 was withdrawn in *Brogan* v. *U.K., loc. cit.*

61 [1972] N.I. 1. See also: *Murray* v. *M.O.D.* [1985] 12 N.I.J.B. 1 at pp. 25–6.

62   See: S.R. & O. (N.I.) 1956 No. 191.

63   *Loc. cit.* p. 14.

64   *Ibid.* p. 15.

65   *Loc. cit.* p. 137. Compare: W. Finnie, 'Rights of persons detained under the anti-terrorist legislation' (1982) 45 *M.L.R.* 215 at pp. 218–19; D.P.J. Walsh, *The Use and Abuse of Emergency Legislation in Northern Ireland* (1983) p. 27; Baker Report, para. 287.

66   See: W. Finnie, 'The Prevention of Terrorism Act and the European Convention on Human Rights' (1989) 52 *M.L.R.* 703 at p. 707.

67   *Guide to the Emergency Powers* (1990) p. 7.

68   *Murray* v. *M.O.D.*, *loc. cit.* Compare: Walker, 'Special Army powers on parade, *loc. cit.* at pp. 9–10.

69   *Fox, Campbell and Hartley* v. *U.K.*, *loc. cit.* para. 42. See: Finnie, 'Anti-terrorist legislation and the E.C.H.R.', *loc. cit.* at pp. 292–3.

70   See also: Criminal Law Act (N.I.) 1967 s. 3(1).

71   See: *Stewart* v. *U.K.*, Application No. 10044/82; *Farrell* v. *U.K.* Appl. No. 9013/80.

72   See: P.V.L.I., pp. vii, 64–9; Amnesty International, *Killings by Security Forces and Supergrass Trials* (1988); C.A.J. Pamphlet No. 15, *Plastic Bullets and the Law* (1990); R. Murray, The S.A.S. in Ireland (1990).

73   Amnesty International, *op. cit.* p. 10; N.I.O. *Guide*, Pt. I para. 11. For British-based forces, see: H.O. Circular 47/1983, *Guidelines for the Police on the Issue and Use of Firearms*; P.A.J. Waddington, *Arming an Unarmed Police* (1988); Defence Committee, *The Physical Security of Military Installations in the U.K.* (1983–84 H.C. 397 and reply (Cmnd. 9422, 1985).

74   For example, see H.C. Debs. Vol. 187 cols. 377–8 6 March 1991.

75   See: B. Robertson, 'Deadly force and risk control in the UK' (1988) *P.L.* 13; Law Commission No. 177, *A Criminal Code for England and Wales* (1988–89 H.C. 299) cl. 44.

76   See: I. Brownlee, 'Superior Orders' [1989] Crim. L.R. 396.

77   See especially: H. Kitchin, *The Gibraltar Report* (1989); Amnesty International, *Investigating Lethal Shootings* (1989); *McKerr* v. *Armagh Coroner* [1990] 1 W.L.R. 649; A. Jennings, 'The death of an inquest' (1990) 140 *N.L.J.* 633; Murray, *op. cit.*; Fatal Accidents and Sudden Deaths Inquiry (Scotland) Act 1976.

78   See P.V.L.I., *loc. cit.*; H.L. Select Committee on Murder and Life Imprisonment (1988–89 H.L. 78) paras. 75–9; Colville Annual Reports on the E.P. Acts for 1988, para. 8.5.6, for 1989, para. 2; Law Com. No. 177, *loc. cit.* cl. 59.

79   See C.A.J., *Plastic Bullets and the Law*.

80   *Loc. cit.* at p. 700. See: Walker, 'Army special powers on parade' *loc. cit.* pp. 11–15.

81   The arrest must first be lawful: H.L. Debs. Vol. 449 col. 397 8 March 1984, Lord Elton. By s. 15(6), a person may be detained in such place as the Secretary of State has directed (port detention facilities, police stations, places of safety for persons under seventeen): H.O. Circular, Annex B.

82   H.C. Debs. Vol. 47 col. 59 24 October 1983, Mr. Brittan. See: Jellicoe Report, paras. 40–4, 73; H.O. Circular, para. 4.10.

83   *H.M. Advocate* v. *Copeland* 1987 S.C.C.R. 232; *H.M. Advocate* v. *Robertson*

(1988) 3 C.L. n. 638; *R.* v. *Harper* (1990) 8 B.N.I.L. n. 16. The Government ignored delegation in *Brogan and others* v. *U.K.*, *loc. cit.* para. 56.

84   See: Jellicoe Report, para. 71.

85   See: *ibid.* para. 72; H.C. Debs. Vol. 47 col. 59 24 October 1983, Mr. Brittan.

86   N.I.O., *Guide*, Pt. I para. 15.

87   H.O. Circular, para. 4.11. Compare: Shackleton Report, paras. 59, 60, 72; Jellicoe Report, paras. 59, 60; Philips Annual Report for 1984, paras. 19, 45; Colville Report, para. 5.1.6. See also: *Brady* v. *Chief Constable* (1991) 4 B.N.I.L. n. 142.

88   Para. 5.1.4. See also: H.L. Debs. Vol. 504 col. 12 13 February 1989, Earl Ferrers.

89   See: *R.* v. *Howell* (1987) 5 N.I.J.B. 10, *R.* v. *Mullen* [1988] 10 N.I.J.B. 36.

90   Though not specified, it is claimed that this issue is relevant: H.C. Debs. Standing Comm. D col. 268 29 November 1983, Mr. Brittan.

91   See: *Chalmers* v. *Lord Advocate* 1954 S.L.T. 177.

92   See: Criminal Procedure (Scotland) Act 1975 ss. 321(3), 295(1); Police (Scotland) Act 1967 s. 17(1).

93   See: Shackleton Report, para. 108; Jellicoe Report, para. 64; T. St. J.N. Bates, 'The Shackleton Report on terrorism' (1979) *S.L.T.* 205 at p. 206.

94   *Loc. cit.*

95   *Ibid.*, paras. 59, 61, 62.

96   See: *De Jong and others* v. *Neths.* Appl. Nos. 8805, 8806/79, 9242/81, 8 E.H.R.R.; *McGoff* v. *Sweden* Appl. No. 9017/80, 8 E.H.R.R. 246; *Ruga* v. *Italy*, Appl. No. 10990/84, 10 E.H.R.R. 532; *Koster* v. *Neths.* Appl. No. 12843/87; R. Treschsel, 'The right to liberty and security of the person' (1980) 1 *H.R.L.J.* 88.

97   Reliance upon this special weighting has been criticised but may be preferable to resort to Art. 15; compare: Livingstone, *op. cit.*

98   But see: *Skoogstrom* v. *Sweden* Appl. Nos. 12867/87, 14073/88.

99   *X* v. *U.K.*, Appl. No. 14671/89. Compare the opinion of the Commission in *Brogan*, Vol. 135 B para. 107.

100   H.C. Debs. Standing Comm. B col. 17 13 December 1988.

101   H.C. Debs. Standing Comm. B col. 254 10 January 1989.

102   DH (89) 1 (Def.) 10–14.

103   Letter to Chief Officers, 28 March 1989.

104   Appl. Nos. 14553, 14554/89.

105   Appl. Nos. 15096–8/89.

106   See: D. Bonner, 'Combating terrorism in the 1990s' (1989) *P.L.* 440 at pp. 448–50; S.R. Chowdhury, *Rule of Law in a State of Emergency* (1989) p. 25.

107   Compare: Livingstone, *loc. cit.*, pp. 300–1; Chowdhury, *op. cit.* pp. 26, 41.

108   *Loc. cit.* para. 61.

109   Paras. 4.14, 5.1.2. See also: S.A.C.H.R., *14th Report* (1988–89 H.C. 394) Annex E p. 107.

110   H.C. Debs. Vol. 160 col. 210 w.a. 14 November 1989, Mr. Waddington. See also: Jellicoe Report, para. 70; Colville Report, ch. 12; Livingstone, *loc. cit.* pp. 297, 298.

111 Paras. 5.3.2, 5.3.4.

112 S. 40/Art. 41.

113 Sched. 3 paras. 4, 9; H.O. Circular, Annex G para. 4 (as inserted by H.O. Circular No. 60/1989).

114 Sched. 3 para. 3.

115 Sched. 3 para. 5. These reasons relate solely to police capabilities not to the condition of the detainee.

116 Sched. 3 para. 6. The police are advised to bring forward reviews to avoid rest periods: H.O. Circular, Annex G para. 7; Police and Criminal Evidence Code C para. 15A.

117 Code C para. 15.3; Sched. 3 para. 7.

118 Sched. 4 para. 8. Only the formal statutory words need be cited: Home Office Circular, Annex G, para. 16. These records comprise part of the custody record: para. 18.

119 Colville Annual Report for 1990, para. 5.7.

120 See: Colville Report, para. 5.3.6; H.O. Circular No. 114/1979; Police and Criminal Evidence Code C, para. 1.11.

121 See: *ibid.* para. 5.1.3, S.H.H.D. Circular nos. 11/1979 para. 8, 3/1989 Annex A para. 24.

122 Pt. IV. In addition, the Police and Criminal Evidence (N.I.) Order 1989 itself is applied (Art. 2(3)) except where expressly modified (see Arts. 32(15), 49(3)).

123 Paras. 81, 144. Compare: *Nestor and others* v. *Minister of Police and others* 1984 (4) S.A. 230 (S.W.A.).

124 See: Code C para. 8B; N.I.O., *Guide* Pt. IV para. 36; H.O. Circular No. 114/1979, paras. 5–7; S.H.H.D. Circular No. 11/1979 paras. 5–7.

125 Comparisons are made in H. Rudolph, *Security, Terrorism and Torture* (1984) ch. 2; D. Foster, *Detention and Torture in South Africa* (1987) ch. 7. See also: O'Briain Report, Rabie Report, Landau Report; Criminal Justice Act 1984 (Ir.) ss. 5, 7, 27.

126 See: *Report of an Amnesty International Mission to N.I. 1977* (1978); Taylor, *op. cit.*

127 See: Jellicoe Report, paras. 82–94; N.I.O., *Guide*, Pt. IV. Checks by the detainee's own doctor remain a 'bone of contention' in Northern Ireland (Colville Annual Report for 1987, para. 5.6.1, 5.6.7), but there is freer access elsewhere (Code C para. 9.4, compare N.I.O., *Guide* Pt. IV para. 4.6).

128 Paras. 102–5. The alleged success of the system is considered in P.V.L.I. pp. 116–19. As the legislation does not cover Scotland, compliance is more variable: Colville Annual Report for 1987 (1988), para. 5.11.

129 Compare: Code C, para. 9; Rabie Report, para. 10.85. The Bennett protections need only be extended to about four British police stations, since the Metropolitan, Liverpool, Glasgow and Galloway police areas process the bulk of detainees.

130 See also: Bennett Report, paras. 85, 101; Jellicoe Report, para. 100; *R.* v. *Clarke* [1973] N.I. 45.

131 See P.V.L.I. pp. 109–19.

132 Compare: N.I.O. *Guide* Pt. IV para. 58; Code C paras. 11.4, 16.1.

133 See: Colville Annual Report on the Emergency Provisions Acts for 1988 (1989), para. 3.2.2.

134 See: Colville Report on the Emergency Provisions Acts, para. 7.3.1, Colville Annual Report for 1990, para. 1.13; S.I. No. 1711.

135 H.C. Debs. Vol. 180 col. 33 8 November 1990.

136 H.C. Debs. Vol. 168 col. 821 6 March 1990, Mr. Waddington.

137 H.C. Debs. Vol. 181 col. 102 19 November 1990, Mr. Cope. The interviewing officers may also be at risk, so written records refer only to warrant numbers: Code C paras. 2.2, 2.6, 11.6, 12.6. Compare: N.I.O., *Guide* Pt. IV para. 6.

138 See: Bennett Report, paras. 199–201; Jellicoe Report, para. 107; Baker Report, paras. 308–19; Colville Report on the E.P. Acts, paras. 4.5–4.8; S.A.C.H.R., *14th Report* (1988–89 H.C. 394) ch. 6, para. 55. See also: O'Briain Report, para. 67; Landau Report, ch. 2.

139 H.C. Debs. Vol. 168 col. 273 w.a. 1 March 1990. The detainee has no veto over recording which applies in all s. 14 cases; contemporaneous note-taking continues in tandem (Home Office, *Notes for Guidance*, 1990).

140 The same applies to fuller custody records. Compare: Colville Annual Report for 1990, paras. 6.4, 6.7.

141 S.A.C.H.R., *15th Report* (1989–90 H.C. 459) Annex F para. 27.

142 See: Walsh, *op. cit.* pp. 67–8, 75.

143 Solicitors must be properly qualified: *Vella* v. *U.K.* Appl. No. 11465/85.

144 Ss. 2, 8, 9, 10 and 11 fall within this definition: Sched. 8 para. 6(7). In Scotland, the right to a solicitor is absolute (Criminal Procedure (Scotland) Act 1975 ss. 19, 305), but notification to others may be delayed (Criminal Justice (Scotland) Act 1980 s. 3).

145 Ss. 56(11); 58(13)(a) (from the time of arrest rather than arrival at the police station). See: Jellicoe Report, para. 108; J. Sim and P.A. Thomas, 'The Prevention of Terrorism Act' (1983) 10 *J. of L. & S.* 71 at pp. 75–6; H.O. Circular Nos. 114/1979, para. 9, S.H.H.D. Circular No. 11/1979 para. 9. Writing materials and access to the telephone may be refused on the same grounds: Police and Criminal Evidence Code C para. 5.6. There are no corresponding rights in Northern Ireland.

146 Ss. 56(11); 58(13)(c). See: Jellicoe Report, para. 112. The circumstances of Northern Ireland make it more likely that solicitors will be threatened or act as dupes: *R.* v. *Harper* (1990) 8 B.N.I.L. n. 16.

147 S. 58(15)–(18). See Jellicoe Report, para. 111. The decision should be discussed at a case conference including the custody officer: H.O. Circular No. 51/1987, para. 3. The Colville Report (para. 6.1.5) alarmingly relates that some forces operate 'a presumption against such contact', which is surely unlawful. Suspects are given a leaflet about their rights on arrival (para. 6.1.2) and will be reminded on reviews of detention (Sched. 3 para. 7) but not in Northern Ireland when the grounds for delay cease (compare Code C Annex B para. 9).

148 See: P.V.L.I., p. 117. The N.I.O. *Guide* does not grant more than one attempt to make contact.

149 See: Colville Annual Report on the E.P. Acts for 1988, para. 8.2.2; H.C. Debs. Standing Comm. B. col. 266 29 January 1991.

150 See: Jellicoe Report, para. 112.

151 See: Shackleton Report, paras. 92, 148; Jellicoe Report, paras. 94, 112; Walsh, *op. cit.* pp. 66–7. This unfavorable treatment may be encouraged by special rules as to admissibility but probably owes more to R.U.C. suspicions about the deviousness of terrorists and the collaboration of certain lawyers.

152 There may be a breach of the European Convention, Art. 6(3)(b) in some circumstances: *Krocher and Moller* v. *Switzerland* Appl. No. 8463/78, D.R. 26 p. 24; *Can* v. *Austria* Appl. No. 9300/81; *Di Stefano* v. *U.K.* Appl. No. 12391/86; *X* v. *U.K.* Appl. No. 12323/86; *S* v. *Switzerland*, Appl. Nos. 12629/87, 13965/88.

153 See: Colville Annual Report for 1986, para. 3.2.1.

154 *Ibid.* paras. 3.2.5, 3.2.6.

155 Compare: *Report of the Working Group on the Right of Silence* (1989) Appendix C.

156 See: Jellicoe Report, para. 93; Baker Report, para. 322.

157 Pat Finucane, solicitor, was murdered in 1989: R. O'Connor, 'Lawyers and "the troubles"' (1989) 133 *Sol. Jo.* 238; G. Bindman, 'Lawyers under pressure in Northern Ireland' (1989) 9 *Socialist Lawyer* 12; M. Dillon, *The Dirty War* (1990) p. 461

158 No delay is allowed in the Republic: *The People (D.P.P.)* v. *Healy* [1990] 10 I.L.R.M. 313. A delay of forty-five hours in contacting the wife of a detainee was found to be in breach of Art. 8 of the European Convention in *McVeigh, O'Neill and Evans* v. *U.K.* (Appl. Nos. 8022, 8025, 8027/77, Report of Commission D.R. 25 p. 15 paras. 237–40). The Committee of Ministers (Res. DH (82) 1, D.R. 25 p. 15 at p. 57) accepted that the introduction of the Criminal Law Act 1977 s. 62 (see now: Police and Criminal Evidence Act s. 56) was sufficient remedy.

159 Compare: Bennett Report, para. 278; *Mokoena* v. *Commissioner of Prisons and another* 1985 (1) S.A. 368 (W.L.D.).

160 See: Code C para. 7; Colville Report, paras. 6.2.1, 6.2.2; Colville Annual Report for 1990, para. 4.2. *Di Stafano* v. *U.K.*, *loc. cit.* Amendment may be difficult because of treaty arrangements (especially the Vienna Convention on Consular Relations 1963 (Cmnd. 2113) Art. 36.1), but corresponding rights in Northern Ireland do not extend to Irish citizens.

161 See: S.A.C.H.R., *15th Report*, *loc. cit.* ch. 4 para. 40; Colville Annual Report on the E.P. Acts for 1988, para. 8.3.3.

162 Apart from detainees under s. 14 (covered by the Emergency Provisions Act 1991 s. 61), the Guide is to remain: H.C. Debs. Vol. 193 col. 510 20 January 1991.

163 Such statistics were published between 1985 and 1987 (H.O. Circular No. 84/1985; Colville Annual Report for 1987 para. 6.2) and are still kept: H.O. Circular, paras. 9.2, 9.3.

164 See: Amnesty International, *Torture in the Eighties* (1984) ch. 6.

165 See: *In re Gillen's Application* [1988] N.I. 40; case of Eamonn Collins (1987) *Guardian* 19 March p. 7; *Moore* v. *Chief Constable, R.U.C.* [1988] N.I. 456.

166 See: Walker, 'Police and community in Northern Ireland' (1990) 40 *N.I.L.Q.* 105; Internal Security Act 1982 (South Africa) s. 44. Lay visitors do not enter interrogation centres in Northern Ireland, so an independent commissioner is contemplated: H.C. Debs. Vol. 193 cols. 508–9 20 January 1991.

167   Cm. 339, 1988. See: S.A.C.H.R., *14th Report, loc. cit.* ch. 12. B. Robertson, 'The European Convention on Torture' (1990) 154 J.P. 159. T. O'Malley, 'A ray of hope for prisoners' (1990) 8 *I.L.T.* 216.

168   Cmnd. 9593, 1985. See: J. Donnelly, 'The emerging international regime against torture' (1986) 33 *Neths. Int. L.R.* I; N.S. Rodley, *The Treatment of Prisoners under International Law* (1987) ch. 4; J.H Burgers and H. Danelius, *The U.N. Convention Against Torture* (1988).

169   S. 14 is preserved: s. 26/Article 28(2), Sched. 2. Foreign terrorists might also be detained for examination under the Immigration Act 1971 Sched. 2 para. 2(3).

170   H.O. Circular No. 90/1983, S.H.H.D. Circular No. 12/1983 para. 4. The circulars follow the Jellicoe Report (para. 68). For R.U.C. policy see: Bennett Report, para. 70; Walsh, *op. cit.* p. 32. The courts will not demand that lesser alternatives be considered: *Ngqumba* v. *State President* 1988 (4) S.A. 224 (A.A.).

171   See also: S.A.C.H.R., *14th Report, loc. cit.*, Annex G para. 2.3.

172   See: K.D. Ewing and W. Finnie, *Civil Liberties in Scotland: Cases and Materials* (2nd ed., 1988) pp. 60–99.

173   See P.V.L.I. pp. 46–63.

174   Northern Ireland (Emergency Provisions) Act 1987 s. 6 (now 1991 Act s. 16).

175   See: *Fox, Campbell and Hartley* v. *U.K., loc. cit.* In practice, reasonable suspicion was latterly requested under s. 11: Baker Report, para. 283.

176   See: Jellicoe Report, paras. 57, 63, 65; Baker Report, paras. 273–9, 283, 299, 301–4, 306–7, 346; S.A.C.H.R., *10th Report* (1984–85 H.C. 175) App. B para. 21.

177   S. 17 is retained for the reasons given in the Colville Annual Report on the E.P. Acts for 1989, paras. 4.1–4.8.

178   Royal Commission on Criminal Procedure, *Report* (Cmnd. 8092, 1981) para. 3.90.

179   See P.V.L.I. pp. 192–209.

180   *The People (D.P.P.)* v. *Shaw* [1982] I.R. 1.

181   An amendment transferring authorisations to the Minister for Justice was defeated: Dail Debs. Vol. 292 col. 861 9 September 1976, Mr. Cooney.

182   Certain witnesses may be arrested under the 1939 and 1976 Acts: *The State (Hoey)* v. *Garvey* [1978] I.R. 1 at p. 13 *per* Finlay J.

183   For a fuller discussion, see: Walker, 'Arrest and rearrest' (1984) 35 *N.I.L.Q.* 1; Baker Report, para. 294; Sharpe, *op. cit.* ch. 9.

184   *Loc. cit* at p. 133, followed in *R.* v. *McGrath* [1980] N.I. 91.

185   See: H.C. Debs. Standing Comm. A col. 102 11 December 1975, Dr. Summerskill.

186   The practice has been complacently described as 'disquieting [but not] oppression': Colville Annual Report for 1987, para. 3.6.

187   Diplock Report, paras. 48, 50.

188   Compare: Police and Criminal Evidence Act 1984 ss. 41(9), 42(11), 43(19); Criminal Justice Act 1984 s. 10.

189   See: Shackleton Report, para. 80; Jellicoe Report, para. 68; Baker Report, para. 271.

190 The rate under the Police and Criminal Evidence Act 1984 is 56 per cent: D. Brown, Detention at the Police Station under PACE (H.O.R.S. No. 104, 1989) Chap. 6.

191 Bennett Report, p. 24 n. 6.

192 Colville Annual Report for 1986, para. 2.2.2.

193 See: K. Boyle, T. Hadden and P. Hillyard, *Ten Years on in Northern Ireland* (1980) p. 45; Walsh, *op. cit.* pp. 61–4, 68, 74; Jellicoe Report, para. 59. In any event, the significant point is ninety-six hours (as in the Police and Criminal Evidence legislation) rather than forty-eight hours. Compare P. Wilkinson, *Terrorism and the Liberal State* (2nd ed., 1986) p. 171.

194 10 per cent according to the Colville Annual Report for 1986, para. 2.4.1.

195 D.P.J. Walsh (*op. cit.*, p. 33) suggests about 10 per cent.

196 Baker Report, para. 282; S.A.C.H.R., *12th Report* (1986–87 H.C. 151) ch. 7 para. 3; *Report of the Working Group on the Right to Silence* (1989) para. 56.

197 Thirteen complaints between 1986 and 1989: Colville Annual Reports.

198 For the rules as to admissibility, see: (in Scotland) *Chalmers* v. *Lord Advocate* 1954 S.L.T. 177, *Hartley* v. *Lord Advocate* 1979 S.L.T. 26, Jellicoe Report, para. 64; (in England and Wales) Police and Criminal Evidence Act 1984 ss. 76, 78; (in Northern Ireland) Northern Ireland (Emergency Provisions) Act 1991 s. 11, Police and Criminal Evidence (N.I.) Order 1989 Arts. 74, 76.

199 See: *R.* v. *Houghton and Franchiosy* (1978) 68 Cr. App. R. 197 at p. 205; Walsh, *op. cit.* pp. 22–3

200 H.O. Circular, para. 2.4.5.

201 See: Walsh, *op. cit.* pp. 69–70; R. Faligot, *Britain's Military Strategy in Ireland* (1983) ch. 5; P. Hillyard, 'Political and social dimensions of emergency law in Northern Ireland' in A. Jennings (ed.), *Justice under Fire* (2nd ed., 1990) pp. 195, 197.

202 Paras. 84, 135. Compare: Rabie Report, paras. 10.64–10.69, 10.78.

203 Para. 232.

204 Para. 67. See also: K.G. Robertson, 'Intelligence, terrorism and civil liberties' in P. Wilkinson and A.M. Stewart (eds.), *Contemporary Research on Terrorism* (1987).

205 Walsh, 'Arrest and interrogation' in Jennings (ed.), *op. cit.* p. 37.

206 P. Hall, 'The Prevention of Terrorism Act' in Jennings (ed.), *op. cit.* p. 173.

207 See the cases of Paddy Prendervill (Hibernia journalist), Margaret Fletcher (Labour Party), Nick Mullen (Troops Out Movement), reported in Scorer, Spencer and Hewitt, *op. cit.*, pp. 37, 42.

208 See: case of Bridgit Nicholas (reported in C. Scorer, *The Prevention of Terrorism Acts 1974 and 1976* (1976) pp. 27–8); case of Margaret O'Brien (reported in B. Rose-Smith, 'Police powers and the terrorism legislation' in P. Hain (ed.), *Policing the Police* Vol. 1 (1979) pp. 131–2.

209 H.O. Circular, para. 4.12.

210 Few records are made up to that time: Colville Report, para. 5.2.2, 5.3.1.

211 See: *Times* 27 April 1981 p. 1, 28 April p. 1, 30 April p. 1. Similar allegations were made on the visit of the Indian Prime Minister in 1985, but charges were brought: Colville Annual Report for 1986, para. 2.4.7.

212   See: cases of Paul O'Sullivan and Roland Joffe (reported in Scorer, *op. cit.* pp. 28–30); *R. v. Howell and others* [1987] 5 N.I.J.B. 10.

213   Walsh, *op. cit.* p. 60. See, for example: *R. v. McBrien and Harman* [1984] N.I. 280.

214   See: *R. v. McCartney* (1975) *Times* 8 May p. 2; *R. v. Baker, Bennett and McCaffery, Times* 11 November 1975 p. 2, 15 November p. 3, 18 November p. 1, 25 November pp. 2, 3, 5, 3 January 1976 p. 2.

215   Para. 55.

216   Para. 79. See also: Colville Report, paras. 4.1.11, 5.1.7.

217   Baker Report, para. 257.

218   Para. 4.1.2, ch. 14.

219   See: H.L. Debs. Vol. 504 col. 14 13 February 1989, Earl Ferrers; P. Bishop and E. Mallie, *The Provisional I.R.A.* (1987) ch. 20.

220   H.C. Debs. Standing Comm. B col. 484 14 January 1989.

221   *Ibid.* col. 486.

222   D. Feldman, 'Conveyancers and the proceeds of crime' (1989) Conv. 389 at p. 398.

223   Criminal Law Revision Committee, *Felonies and Misdemeanours* (Cmnd. 2659) para. 28.

224   H.C. Debs. Standing Comm. B col. 480 17 January 1989.

225   [1988] 3 W.L.R. 989 at p. 1008. The same argument is unlikely to avail relatives, and they are also denied any express privilege: H.C. Debs. Standing Comm. B col. 473 17 January 1989.

226   H.C. Debs. Standing Comm. B col. 508 17 January 1989, Mr. Hogg. This remark allegedly encouraged the murder of Pat Finucane: *Times,* 14 February 1989 p. 1.

227   H.C. Debs. Standing Comm. B col. 512 17 January 1989, Mr. Hogg.

228   H.L. Debs. Vol. 504 col. 978 28 February 1989, Earl Ferrers.

229   *The Guide to the Professional Conduct of Solicitors* (1990) para. 12.07.7. Compare: Feldman, *loc. cit*; E. Hiley, 'Production orders under the Police and Criminal Evidence Act' (1987) 84 *L.S. Gaz.* 3008.

230   *Allen* v. *Bone* (1841) 49 E.R. 429.

231   [1989] 1 W.L.R. 1066. Compare: *Groom* v. *Crocker* [1939] 1 K.B. 194 at p. 222.

232   H.C. Debs. Standing Comm. B col. 472 17 January 1989; H.O. Circular, para. 6.11.

233   Royal Commission on Criminal Procedure, *loc. cit.* para. 3.37. See also: K.W. Lidstone, 'Magistrates, the police and search warrants' [1984] Crim. L.R. 449.

234   Compare: Incitement to Disaffection Act 1934 s. 2(2); Public Order Act 1936 s. 2(5).

235   Compare: Misuse of Drugs Act 1971 s. 23(3).

236   Access to legal material which the police claim is not privileged should be by way of para. 3: *R. v. Guildhall Mag. Ct. ex p. Primlaks* (1989) 89 Cr. App. R. 215; H.O. Circular, para. 6.13. For the meaning of 'public interest', see: *R. v. Bristol Crown Court, ex p. Bristol Press and Picture Agency* (1987) 85 Cr. App. R. 190; *R. v. Central Criminal Court, ex p. Carr* (1987) *Independent* 5 March.

237   See: *R. v. Maidstone Crown Court, ex p. Waitt* (1988) *Times* 4 January.

There is no recourse to contempt procedures unlike in the Police and Criminal Evidence legislation, since the warrant power here is wider. Reasons must be offered on an application: Police and Criminal Evidence Code B para. 2.7 (but not in Northern Ireland).

238   In Northern Ireland, Articles 23 and 24 are directly applicable as they make no reference to offences.

239   Paras. 2.4, 5.13. But the executing officers need not be specified (R. Stone, *Entry, Search and Seizure* (1985) para. 4.2.1), and officers need only be specified by warrant number: paras. 5.5, 5.8, 7.2.

240   Sheriffs are invited to identify the executing officers: para. 14(5).

241   Compare: Criminal Justice (Scotland) Act 1987 s. 40.

242   As suggested P.T.B.L. (1st ed.) pp. 145, 201–2.

243   The maximum penalty for false information is two years' imprisonment.

244   For the definition of 'necessary', see: *In re an Inquiry under the Company Securities (Insider Dealing) Act 1985* [1988] 2 W.L.R. 33 at p. 65. The phrase 'interests of the State' is inappropriately borrowed from the Official Secrets Act 1911 s. 9(2).

245   The exercise of such powers should be reported to the Home Secretary (H.O. Circular, para. 6.29) but not to the courts.

246   It is promised in practice (but not in para. 8) that orders will be considered personally: H.L. Debs. Vol. 504 col. 15 13 February 1989, Earl Ferrers.

247   There is no set procedure by which the subject of an order can apply for variation or revocation.

248   See Colville Report, para. 14.2.7. Government briefing notes referred to the need to protect intelligence sources, but it should be remembered that applications under Sched. 7 can be *ex parte*: B. Dickson, 'The Prevention of Terrorism (Temporary Provisions) Act 1989' (1989) 40 *N.I.L.Q.* 250 at p. 263.

249 On the latter, see: Colville Annual Report for 1990, para. 7.15.

250   See Land Registration (Open Register) Rules 1990 S.I. No. 1362.

251   It is desirable that these restrictions be observed even when information is freely available from State agencies; compare: Final Report of the Select Committee to Study Governmental Operations with respect to intelligence activities (U.S. Senate 94th Cong. 2d. Sess. Report No. 94-755, 1976) Book II pp. 313, 315, 319 (hereafter cited as the 'Church Committee'); Hope Report, para. 158 (see now: Australian Security Intelligence Organisation Act 1979 s. 25); McDonald Commission, Pt. III ch. 5 para. 96, ch. 6 para. 44, Pt. V ch. 4 para. 177, Pt. X ch. 4 para. 32, Annex I para. 6. Informal access to records held by private institutions should also be curtailed as in the Right to Financial Privacy Act 1978 (12 U.S.C. s. 3401). See: Report by the Review Committee, *Banking Services* (Cm. 622, 1989) and *Reply* (Cm. 1026, 1990).

252   Reasonable force may be used: s. 20(2). The Police and Criminal Evidence legislation ss. 15, 16/Arts. 17, 18 is applicable: H.O. Circular, para. 4.13.

253   See: H.C. Debs. Standing Comm. B col. 373 12 January 1989. Section 11 should be consolidated into the Prevention of Terrorism Act: Colville Report on the E.P. Acts, para. 2.5.

254   *Ibid.*, col. 368, Mr. Archer.

255   See: L.H. Leigh, 'Comment' (1975) *P.L.* 1 at p. 6; Royal Commission on Criminal Procedure, *loc. cit.* paras. 3.23–3.28; The Brixton Disorders 10–12 April

1981; *Report of an Inquiry by the Rt. Hon. The Lord Scarman* (Cmnd. 8427, 1981) para. 4.67; Hall, *op. cit.* p. 180.

256   Ss. 2, 3, 5; Code of Practice for the Exercise by Police Officers of Statutory Powers of Stop and Search (Annex A). Officers need not identify themselves by name: paras. 2.4, 2.5. The N.I.O. *Guide* (Pt. III Section G) is substantially similar except in regard to record-keeping. The search must be by an officer of the same sex: s. 15(5).

257   Compare: Police and Criminal Evidence Code A para. 1.6.

258   See also s. 15(5).

259   Ss. 32, 54, 55/Arts. 34, 55, 56; Prevention of Terrorism Act Sched. 8 para. 6(3). At common law, see: *Petticrew* v. *Chief Constable, R.U.C.* [1988] 3 N.I.J.B. 86.

260   Compare: *R.* v. *Mulvenna* [1987] 9 N.I.J.B. 52 at p. 79. Common law powers are superseded by the Police and Criminal Evidence legislation.

261   Police and Criminal Evidence legislation ss. 54, 55/Arts. 55, 56; N.I.O., *Guide* Annex D. Note also the Prevention of Terrorism Act. Sched. 9.

262   S.A.C.H.R., *15th Report, loc. cit.* Annex E, p. 152.

263   *Loc. cit.* It may be conceded that nail-scrapings could provide 'articles'.

264   Such provisions may be used cumulatively with s. 15(9): *In re Power* [1983] 14 N.I.J.B. The precedent for s. 15(9) is the Immigration Act 1971 Sched. 2 para. 18(2).

265   S. 15(9) is preserved by ss. 61(9), 64(7)/Arts. 61(9), 64(8). See also: Code of Practice (D) for the Identification of Persons Suspected of Crime. Similar points may be made about photographing suspects; see: Code of Practice, para. 4. For Scotland see: *Adair* v. *McGarry* 1933 J.C. 72.

266   *Scorer, op. cit.* p. 34.

267   An order for destruction was obtained in *Connolly* v. *M.P.C. loc. cit.* Compare: *Carlisle* v. *Chief Constable, R.U.C.* [1988] N.I. 307; *In re Gillen's Application* (1990) 4 B.N.I.L. n. 1. There is no duty to destroy records of samples in the 'normal' law, but assurances have been given that they will be destroyed in Northern Ireland: H.L. Debs. Vol. 499. col. 1659 22 July 1989, Lord Lyall; S.A.C.H.R., *15th Report, loc. cit.* ch. 4 para. 35. The N.I.O. *Guide* is silent.

268   H.C. Debs. Vol. 980 col. 436 4 March 1980, Mr. Whitelaw.

269   H.C. Debs. Vol. 1000 col. 235 w.a. 9 March 1981.

270   This practice does not contravene Art. 8 of the European Convention: *McVeigh, O'Neill and Evans* v. *U.K. loc. cit.* D.R. 25 p. 14, paras. 48, 49, 224–32.

271   See: C. Walker and I. Cram, 'DNA profiling and police powers' [1990] Crim. L.R. 479 at p. 490.

272   See: Baker Report, para. 295. The use of force is one of the 'steps as may be reasonably necessary'. The Scottish common law powers may also be used for evidence-gathering.

273   See: Baker Report, para. 297; Colville Annual Report on E.P. Acts for 1988, para. 6.2.1; Colville Report on the E.P. Acts, para. 16.7. Colville viewed s. 15(10) as advantageous to the police by extending fingerprinting to investigative as well as identification purposes, even though s. 15(10) refers back to s. 15(9).

274   Compare: Police and Criminal Evidence Act 1984 ss. 62, 63; Ewing and

Finnie, *op. cit.* pp. 102–16; Scottish Law Commission No. 120, *Report on Evidence* (1988–89 H.C. 572).

275 H.C. Debs. Vol. 135 col. 653 16 June 1988, Mr. Starky.

276 S.A.C.H.R., *15th Report, loc. cit.* ch. 4 paras. 12–19; M.A. Gelowitz, 'Yet he opened not his mouth' [1989] Crim. L.R. 198; Walker and Cram, *loc. cit.*

277 *Murray* v. *M.O.D., loc. cit.*

278 The N.I.O., *Guide* Pt. III Section C assumes such powers in regard to Sched. 7 investigations. The powers in s. 19/Art. 21 of the Police and Criminal Evidence legislation also remain available: Sched. 7 para. 10(1).

279 S.A.C.H.R., *14th Report, loc. cit.* Annex F p. 112; Walker, 'Army special powers on parade' *loc. cit.*; Dickson, *loc. cit.* at p. 264.

280 Ss. 4(3), (4).

281 P.T.B.L. (1st ed.) pp. 139–40.

282 Sched. 1.

283 Ss. 27, 28, 30, 31.

284 S. 2.

285 Pt. VI.

286 See P.V.L.I., pp. 213–15.

287 S. 15 lapsed in 1977 along with the Emergency Powers Act 1976.

288 See P.V.L.I., pp. 60–3. The Baker Report (para. 380) calls for the consolidation of the overlapping search provisions in Northern Ireland, especially s. 15(3), (4).

289 H.C. Debs. Vol. 168 col. 820; K.W. Lidstone, 'PACE (N.I.) Order 1989' (1989) 40 *N.I.L.Q.* 333 at pp. 342, 344.

290 Seven times between 1978–87 in Britain, never in Northern Ireland: H.C. Debs. Standing Comm. B cols. 533, 546, 17 January 1989. No use is recorded since 1989: Colville Annual Report for 1990, para. 7.14.

291 Colville Annual Report for 1990, para. 7.15.

292 Lidstone, *loc. cit.* p. 355.

293 See: *R.* v. *Mulvenna, loc. cit.*; *R.* v. *Lanigan and Kerr* [1987] 6 N.I.J.B. 24; *R.* v. *Gilmartin* [1987] 9 N.I.J.B. 26; *R.* v. *Colhoun* [1989] 12 N.I.J.B. 16; cases of Magee and others, McNamee, Sindicic, and Quinn, discussed in chapter 11; cases of Timkin and Basra in H.C. Debs. Vol. 127 col. 930 16 February 1988.

294 Pt. III Section C.

295 *Loc. cit.* at p. 88 *per* Kelly L.J.

296 The Road Traffic Act 1972 s. 159 was previously applied in this way: H.C. Debs. Standing Comm. A cols. 97–8, 102–3 11 December 1975.

297 Relevant parts of the Emergency Provisions Act probably contravene Art. 8 of the European Convention: Greek cases, Appl. Nos. 3321, 3322, 3323, 3344/67, 12 Y.B.E.C. Pt. II Report of the Commission para. 345, Decision of the Committee of Ministers para. 10.

298 See: *Interception of Communications in G.B.* (Cmnd. 7873, 1980) para. 23; *Interception of Communications in the U.K.* (Cmnd. 9438, 1985) para. 4; *Reports of the Commissioner for 1986* (Cm. 108, 1987) para. 53 and *1989* (Cm. 1063, 1990) para. 7.

299 It was disclosed in the cases of Lee and others (1987) *Times* 5 February p. 3, 6 February pp. 1, 3, and William Murphy (1989) *Times* 22 August p. 5.

300   See: Royal Commission on Criminal Procedure, *The Law and Procedure* (Cmnd. 8092–1) App. 10, 11; Walker, 'Police surveillance by technical devices' (1980) *P.L.* 184; P.J. Duffy, 'Secret surveillance' (1982) *P.L.* 381; H.C. Debs. Vol. 70 col. 158 w.a. 19 December 1984; *Malone* v. *U.K.* Appl. No. 8691, Judgment of Ct. Ser. A No. 82. Covert surveillance may be assisted by exemptions from certain road traffic regulations; see: McDonald Commission Pt. III ch. 8, Pt. V ch. 4 para. 57; Pt. X ch. 5 para. 34.

301   Compare: Omnibus Crime Control and Safe Streets Act 1968 Title III (18 U.S.C. ss. 2510–20).

302   *Report for 1989, loc. cit.* para. 7.

303   See: J.B. Wolf, *Anti-terrorist Initiatives* (1989) p. 60; Dillon. *op. cit.* ch. 15.

304   Compare: Drug Trafficking Offences Act 1986 s. 30.

305   See n. 251 *supra.*

306   *First Report from the Foreign Affairs Committee, loc. cit.* para. 101.

307   *Ibid.* para. 97; *Diplomatic Immunities and Privilege, loc. cit.* paras. 82, 83; Kerley, *loc. cit.*

308   *Diplomatic Immunities and Privileges, loc. cit.* para. 48.

309   See: *First Report from the Foreign Affairs Committee, loc. cit.* paras. 98, 99, Minutes of Evidence p. 4; Denza, *op. cit.* p. 128.

310   *Diplomatic Immunities and Privileges, loc. cit.* para. 53. See also: Denza, *op. cit.* p. 127; *First Report from the Foreign Affairs Committee, loc. cit.* paras. 29, 77, 102.

311   See: *First Report from the Foreign Affairs Committee, loc. cit.* para. 109; *Diplomatic Immunities and Privileges, loc. cit.* paras. 49, 84, 111.

312   See: *First Report from the Foreign Affairs Committee, loc. cit.*, para. 109 76th Session of the Council of Europe Committee of Ministers (1985).

313   Covert searches under warrant are excessively forbidden by s. 16(7); compare: Church Committee, Book II p. 328; McDonald Commission, Pt. III ch. 2, Pt. V ch. 4 paras. 2, 137, Pt. X ch. 5 para. 7.

314   See: Offences against the Person Act 1861 s. 65 (as amended); Explosives Act 1875 s. 75 (as amended); Official Secrets Act 1911 s. 9(1) (as amended); Firearms (N.I.) Order 1981 S.I. No. 155 Art. 45(1). In Scotland, arrest and search warrants may authorise the searchings of premises in connection with a wide range of offences; see: Ewing and Finnie, *op. cit.* pp. 61–2, 108–16.

315   See: Explosives Act 1875 s. 73; Official Secrets Act 1911 s. 9(2); Firearms Act 1968 s. 47; Firearms (N.I.) Order 1981 Art. 45(2).

316   See: *H.M. Advocate* v. *McGuigan* 1936 S.L.T. 161; *Laverie* v. *Murray* 1964 S.L.T. (Notes) 3; *McHugh* v. *H.M. Advocate* 1978 J.C. 12; *Walsh* v. *McPhail* 1978 S.L.T. (Notes) 29. Compare: Shackleton Report, para. 109; T.St.J.N. Bates, 'The Shackleton Report on Terrorism' 1979 *S.L.T.* 205 at p. 208.

317   See: Firearms Act 1968 s. 47; Firearms (N.I.) Order 1981 Art. 46; Police and Criminal Evidence Act 1984 ss. 1, 18, 32, 54, 55. One remaining gap in the regular law is the absence of stop and search powers for explosives (except when in the form of offensive weapons: *R.* v. *Main and Gawthorpe* (1982) 4 Cr. App. R. (S) 42).

Chapter 9

Port controls

1 Provisions

(a) Examinations: conditions

The examination of sea or air travellers (including transit passengers) to or from Great Britain or Northern Ireland is envisaged by section 16 of the Prevention of Terrorism Act and is detailed in paragraph 2(1) of Schedule 5,[1] by which:

Any person who has arrived in, or is seeking to leave, Great Britain or Northern Ireland by ship or aircraft may be examined by an examining officer for the purpose of determining –
(a) whether that person appears to be a person who is or has been concerned in the transmission, preparation or instigation of acts of terrorism to which this paragraph applies; or
(b) whether any such person is subject to an exclusion order; or
(c) whether there are grounds for suspecting that any such person has committed an offence under section 8 of this Act.

The power to examine, as distinct from arrests under section 14, is exercisable without reasonable or indeed any suspicion, which severely curtails judicial review. For example, on an application for habeas corpus in *Re Boyle, O'Hara and McAllister*,[2] Lord Donaldson stated that a court could only enquire as to whether an enforcement officer 'is acting *bona fide* and whether . . . his conduct is *prima facie* such as no reasonable person could have taken'. Similarly, in *McVeigh, O'Neill and Evans* v. *United Kingdom*,[3] the applicants contended that judicial intervention was permissible only:[4]

if the persons responsible admitted that they had no good cause for the action or had acted for improper purposes. Alternatively, the onus was on the detainees to establish lack of good faith or improper purposes.

The initial implementation of examinations is wholly unfettered by the Police and Criminal Evidence Act Codes or the Northern Ireland Office *Guide*, though the Government has insisted that:[5]

in practice an examining officer would not wish to detain a passenger unless his suspicions ... had been aroused. ...

The unconditional power to examine continues for twelve hours. Thereafter, an enforcement officer may issue under paragraph 2(4) a written 'notice to submit to further examination' provided he reasonably suspects that the person is involved in terrorism, the same ground as for arrests under section 14(1)(b). This restriction (which was first imposed by the 1984 Act)[6] properly reflects the distinction between establishing the identities of travellers under port powers and investigating their activities on arrest, though the period of unfettered examination remains excessive.

The three grounds for an examination under Schedule 5 paragraph 2(1) are almost identical to those in section 14(1), including the coverage of international terrorism[7] and the danger of successive detentions on the same grounds.[8] The main difference is that the sole criminal offence which can be investigated under Schedule 5 is section 8, presumably because identification is the only evidence required from a traveller relevant to a breach of an exclusion order. Unfortunately, this strict limit is fudged by the alternative power to examine in connection with involvement in terrorism, which may arise out of the contravention of sections 2, 9, 10 or 11 and may not be settled purely by reference to identity.

As examinations are not dependent upon any suspicion and are usually operated on the basis of security information, enforcement officers probably do not have to supply a factual catalogue of reasons to those formally detained. Thus, in the McVeigh case, the applicants received a recital of the relevant parts of the Prevention of Terrorism Act but not any factual grounds.[9]

The corresponding control of travellers across the Irish land border may occur in three situations.[10] Firstly, persons arriving by train may be examined at the first scheduled stop in Northern Ireland.[11] Secondly, persons found within one mile of the border may be examined to ascertain whether they are in the course of traversing it. Thirdly, officers may examine anyone entering or leaving Northern Ireland by land for the same purpose; this applies to approved road-crossings, even where the check-point is located more than one mile from the border.

A further land border, the Channel Tunnel, will shortly open. Accordingly, the Channel Tunnel (Fire Services, Immigration and Prevention of Terrorism) Order 1990[12] applies the power to conduct examinations under Schedule 5 paragraph 2(1).

Port examinations of travellers from the Irish Republic were upheld by the European Commission of Human Rights in the McVeigh case as amounting to 'the lawful arrest or detention of a person' in order to secure the fulfilment of any obligation prescribed by law' within Article 5(1)(b) of the Convention.[13] The same view was adopted in regard to passengers between Britain and Northern Ireland in *Harkin, X, Lyttle, Gillen and McCann* v. *U.K.*,[14] since Article 5(1)(b) can apply to the regulation of passage over a clear geographical boundary within a state. Intelligence-gathering purposes[15] and the absence of reasonable suspicion do not vitiate these findings.

(b) Examinations: mechanics

'Examining officers' may be police constables, immigration officers (and customs officials employed as such) or, in Northern Ireland, soldiers.[16] In practice, Special Branch constables undertake examinations at ports with substantial traffic with Ireland and provide liaison and advice for all British port units through a National Ports Office at Heathrow.[17] Customs and immigration officers are supposed to operate the Act elsewhere.[18]

The task of monitoring the millions of travellers affected by the Act is designed to be eased in three ways. One is that the points of entry and departure by sea and air between Britain and both parts of Ireland are restricted to 'designated' ports in the United Kingdom.[19] Before commercial sea carriers wish to call at an undesignated port, an examining officer must grant approval,[20] which will be forthcoming unless the police wish to check the arrival but are unable to do so because of 'manpower difficulties'.[21] Ships not carrying passengers for reward may be examined but need not call at designated ports.[22] This loophole responds to the difficulty of closely monitoring the thousands of small boats in the U.K. All that is expected of police forces is that they will coordinate with the coastal authorities and produce a reference manual for officers.[23] Private aircraft have been subjected to the full control scheme since 1976, though requests for special dispensation are viewed 'sympathetically'.[24]

Once landed at a designated port, passengers are herded through 'control areas', which may be specified by order under Schedule 5 paragraph 9. In fact, no control area has ever been designated by law, since the Government has successfully secured the agreement of the port authorities.[25] However, this informal approach has contributed to 'woefully inadequate' facilities,[26] which neither minimise delays for travellers nor maximise privacy for detainees. The problem has persisted, despite a report by H.M. Inspector of Constabulary Brownlow, which led in 1987 to the establishment of a Standing Committee and the appointment of a National Coordinator of Ports Policing.[27] The obstacles in the way of improvements include lack of space and, in view of the temporary nature of the Act, commitment. Accordingly, paragraph 9 contains a new power to specify facilities within control areas, and a Home Office Circular has specified the minimum conditions to be secured (a control room with a telephone, a secure telephone, video and fax, a place for wanted notices, and a separate interview room screened from the public).[28] Nevertheless, the Government still hopes to avoid formal enforcement[29] and has not indicated any willingness to commit public finances.[30] Thus, port controls fare badly in comparison with aviation security.[31]

The processing of travellers is further aided by securing the cooperation of the captains of ships and aircraft. By Schedule 5 paragraph 10, captains carrying passengers for reward must ensure that their passengers and crew embark or disembark in accordance with arrangements approved by examining officers. Commercial passenger carriers and all aircraft captains must also, unless excused by an officer, provide on arrival lists of the names and nationalities of passengers and similar details as to crew.[32] The captains of ships not carrying passengers for reward must furnish such details within twelve hours of arrival and must also specify the inland destination (if any) of persons on board. The latter requirement was first enacted in 1989 and compensates to some extent for the lack of 'carding' (described shortly). A reciprocal duty is placed upon passengers to furnish the necessary details in all cases.

Having ensured that most Irish, and some foreign,[33] travellers can be monitored, the Prevention of Terrorism Act aids examining officers to sift out terrorists by various devices. For example, sea or air passengers may be required under Schedule 5 paragraph 5 to complete a 'landing' or 'embarkation' card. Corresponding 'entry' and 'departure' cards apply on the Irish border except for examinations within one mile, where they would often be impractical and might be used as a form of harassment by Army and police patrols. All cards, which should follow official designs,[34] ask for the identity and nationality of travellers and the purpose of their visits. 'Carding' is at the discretion of examining officers rather than automatic but subject to exemption as for the completion of passenger and crew lists. The explanation for this difference is that the police will probably wish to record all movements as a matter of course but will conduct carding only when a particular individual arouses special interest. Travellers from the Republic who have been 'carded' under Schedule 2 of the Immigration Act 1971 are excused from repeating the process under the Prevention of Terrorism Act, which also cannot apply to journeys to or from beyond the British Isles. These limitations may place too much reliance upon immigration officers, whose concerns are directed otherwise. Another special group concerns Members of the European Parliament, who claim exemption from carding based on the Protocol on the Privileges and Immunities of the European Communities.[35] In practice, the Home Office has accepted production of the European Communities Laissez Passez as a sufficient alternative.[36]

Searches for physical evidence which may be relevant to any of the grounds in paragraph 2 are permitted under paragraph 4 of ships, aircraft, vehicles and travellers and their baggage.[37] The breadth of these powers is remarkable. There is no need for reasonable suspicion, nor is the Police and Criminal Evidence Code A on stop and search powers applicable, though the police are advised to observe it 'so far as practicable'[38] and Schedule 5 paragraph 4(5) demands that personal searches be conducted by a person of the same sex. Strip searches are also limited by circulars which advise the police first to detain the suspect in a police station so that the normal rules (under section 54/Article 55 and Annex A of Code C of the Police and Criminal Evidence legislation) will apply.[39] There is no equivalent guidance in Scotland, save in regard to strip searches.[40] The Northern Ireland Office *Guide* does cover searches under paragraph 4 but concerns itself only with unnecessary delays to ships or aircraft and ignores the treatment of the suspect.[41]

Evidence may further be obtained from passengers, who may be obliged under Schedule 5 paragraph 3 to furnish 'all such information in [their] possession as [an examining officer] may require for the purpose of his functions'. An officer may also demand the production of a valid passport or other identity papers or 'documents of any relevant description specified' (such as a driving licence or perhaps a cheque book).[42] The Act does not require travellers to carry identity papers, but their possession is advisable.[43] Paragraph 3 curtails the rights of a suspect in several respects. For example, 'information in his possession' extends to self-incriminatory knowledge and evidence which must be produced in response to questioning by examining officers, though there may be (subject to section 18) no positive duty of candour.[44] Furthermore, there is no protection for special procedure, excluded or legally privileged materials, though protection for the latter may be implied by the courts.[45]

Schedule 5 next curtails personal freedom in order to facilitate examinations. In fact, an examination may proceed without any formal detention if the traveller is cooperative.[46] However, examinations without detention must terminate after twenty-four hours (by paragraph 2(4)). Formal detention powers are available thereafter or whenever a traveller refuses to remain by consent. Officers may then detain and, if need be, formally arrest suspects under paragraph 6 for up to forty-eight hours from when the examination began pending the conclusion of the examination, consideration of whether to exclude and consideration of whether to issue criminal proceedings.[47] Any examination (whether by consent or detention) may only exceed twelve hours if an officer has reasonable grounds for suspecting (as in section 14(1)(b)) involvement in terrorism. The Secretary of State may extend the detention for up to five days, as under section 14.[48] Detention of Irish suspects during this exceptional period is either acceptable under Article 5(1)(b) of the European Convention or may be covered by the derogation under Article 15.[49]

Travellers can be detained on board a ship or aircraft or as directed by the Secretary of State.[50] Since port facilities are meagre, suspects are invariably transferred to police stations between one and twelve hours after the first official contact.[51] Thereafter, arrangements for detainees are similar to those under section 14, at least for those, according to Schedule 8 paragraph 6(8), who have been 'arrested . . . by an examining officer who is a constable' and have been taken to a police station.[52] Unfortunately, this wording leaves outside the protection of the Police and Criminal Evidence Act 1984 persons being examined without any detention, persons who have been detained under Schedule 5 but not formally arrested, persons who have been detained or arrested elsewhere than at a police station and persons examined by officials other than constables. In practice, police forces are encouraged to keep custody records on all persons 'detained' in police custody.[53]

The treatment of suspects held under port controls differs from section 14 arrestees in the following respects. First, cautioning is often inappropriate, because there may be no suspicion (and even no offence) on which the detention is grounded. Next, suspects at ports are to be handed one hour after the commencement of the examination (rather than forthwith under section 14) a written notice of their rights to contact a lawyer and notify a relatives.[54] This notice serves the purpose not only of informing persons of their rights but also of emphasising that an examination is in progress. The rights may be denied on the grounds as described for section 14, and a refusal to notify family members for forty-five hours breached Article 8 of the European Convention in the McVeigh case.[55] This Commission decision has been followed by closer statutory regulation, which better ensures that any denial will be 'necessary' for the purposes of Article 8(2). Rights of access and notification may not be denied to persons being examined without detention. Such individuals are treated as cooperating voluntarily and so may contact outsiders at any time.[56] The final contrast is that, though by section 16(2) examinations must be reviewed under Schedule 3 paragraphs 2 and 3,[57] the timing and grounds of reviews sometimes differ from those under section 14. For persons not formally detained, the first (and only review) will occur not later than twelve hours after the beginning of the examination and the reviewer must ensure only that inquiries are being conducted 'diligently and expeditiously'. The review process should also in practice consider whether there are reasonable grounds for suspecting involvement in terrorism under Schedule 5 paragraph 2(4).[58] If a person has been detained under Schedule 5 paragraph 6, reviews take place as under section 14.

Paragraph 7 of Schedule 5 contains equivalent measures to section 15. Thus, it allows warrants to be issued to search for persons liable to arrest under paragraph 6,[59] and suspects may also be photographed, measured or identified, including by the taking of fingerprints. Fingerprinting is now subject to similar restraints as under section 14 in England and Wales[60] but regrettably not elsewhere.

By way of reinforcement of this substantial catalogue of controls under Schedule 5, the Northern Ireland Secretary is empowered by section 16(4) to issue by order further measures in respect of travellers by land across the border. This novel, unrestrained power is a hedge against unforeseen security breaches[61] and might be invoked, for example, to demand the production of specified identity documents or to specify permitted crossing points so that any breach will be an offence under the Act. The power in section 16(4) is undesirable as it reduces Parliamentary scrutiny and is largely unnecessary in view of the comprehensive nature of Schedule 5.

Finally, a person who knowingly contravenes or fails to comply with a port examination infringes paragraph 11 of Schedule 5. The penalties are a fine not exceeding level 4 under section 37 of the Criminal Justice Act 1982, imprisonment up to three months or both.

2 Comparisons

(a) Special port controls

Special restrictions on movement have rarely featured in anti-terrorist legislation in Ireland. The closest parallels[62] are two regulations made under the Civil Authorities (Special Powers) Acts (Northern Ireland) 1922–43 during the 1956 to 1962 'Border' campaign of the I.R.A.[63] These provided firstly that a person entering Northern Ireland except from Britain could be required by a policeman to show that his purpose was not detrimental to peace and order and, secondly, that no one was to disembark from ships at any specified port in Northern Ireland without official permission.

The main reasons for the relative absence of port controls in Irish legislation are that terrorism in those jurisdictions is indigenous and that surveillance of border traffic[64] is already conducted under customs measures and section 23 of the Northern Ireland (Emergency Provisions) Act 1991. These factors equally mean that 'the port powers are of less significance . . .' in Northern Ireland.[65]

(b) Normal port controls: United Kingdom and elsewhere

The port controls are applied by section 20(3) notwithstanding rights of entry under the Immigration Act 1971. Thus, the two codes operate in tandem,[66] which prompts the question, how far can terrorist movements be controlled under regular law?

To recap the ground already covered in chapter 6 in relation to exclusion orders, the 'Common Travel Area'[67] means that citizens of the Republic are free to enter without control or leave. Consequently, the Prevention of Terrorism Act regularised and extended *ad hoc* Special Branch operations which had been undertaken before November 1974, whenever

I.R.A. bombing missions had taken place or were anticipated.[68] Admittedly, the problem could alternatively have been solved by removing the Republic from the Common Travel Area. However, such a wholesale revision would have created substantial manpower problems as well as political discord.

Non-Irish foreigners entering the United Kingdom are normally subject to inspections under the Immigration Act[69] which are similar to the port controls but are often more stringently applied. However, these restrictions are as shall be described later relaxed by European Community law for citizens of member States, and controls over all foreigners arriving via the Republic[70] are not in practice applied. Consequently, the port controls were extended in 1984 to international terrorism partly to fill these gaps.[71] However, no evidence was presented that alien terrorists had ever entered Britain via Ireland, and it is now officially admitted that the amendment of section 16 was mainly to achieve consistency with section 14. Therefore, examining officers are advised to give priority to Irish traffic.[72]

Next, the Customs and Excise Management Act 1979 provides some additional travel controls.[73] However, as the Act exists to prevent the unlawful importation or exportation of dutiable or prohibited items, its deliberate application against terrorist personnel would be an abuse of power.

Finally, the stringent security measures developed at airports against hijacking and other forms of attack entail close surveillance of passengers. These measures, which are being extended to seaports, will be described in chapter 12.

(c) Normal port controls: Great Britain and Northern Ireland
Travel between Britain and Northern Ireland is unfettered by Immigration or customs restrictions. Consequently, such port controls as existed before November 1974 were unofficial though occasionally very significant. For example, the Price sisters and others were intercepted at Heathrow after a special alert.[74] Consequently, section 16 has systemised and provided legal authority for earlier police practices. Nor would the powers to stop and search under section 1/Article 3 of the Police and Criminal Evidence legislation or to detain under sections 1 and 2 of the Criminal Justice (Scotland) Act 1980 offer adequate substitutes. They do not permit the channelling of traffic, though their insistence upon reasonable suspicion before exercise would be a viable improvement.[75]

3 Assessment

(a) Extent of use
For reasons already cited, the port controls have little impact in Northern Ireland and have generated a 'negligible' number of detentions.[76] It is not

possible to seal the border without serious social dislocation and conflict.[77] As for Britain, the following points can be drawn from Table 13.[78] The first feature is that the preponderance of detentions occurs under section 16 rather than section 14 and that the totals declined markedly after 1980 but are now static. Both trends have been explained in chapter 8 and reaffirm that the prime targets are Irish, rather than foreign, terrorists. The second feature is that a minute proportion of the approximately four million people[79] passing through six of the major designated ports each year are detained for more than one hour. Table 13 in fact under-represents the impact of port controls in at least two ways. Detentions under one hour are not recorded, nor are examinations which do not lead to detentions. The limited statistics in Tables 14 and 15 may help to complete the picture.

The 'searches' in Table 15 are highly misleading and frequently mis-understood.[80] Such 'searches' are checks concerning terrorist suspects against police Special Branch records. The returns are not confined to inquiries from examining officers, nor need they relate to persons being examined or detained. However, the level of searches does suggest a far higher degree of scrutiny at ports than is evidenced by examinations and detentions alone.

Since 1979, 15 per cent of detentions were extended,[81] a lower rate than under section 14 and one which evidences the lax criteria for the original invocation of port detention powers. However, the two sections are very similar in terms of the rarity of rejections of applications (just sixteen to the end of 1990) and the tendency to extend detentions for less than five days.

Statistics as to the length of detentions not terminated by criminal charges or exclusion have been produced in the foregoing chapter. Table 16 relates that period to the charging rate under section 16 and also indicates how it compares to section 14.

Deducing from the samples in Table 16 that roughly a quarter of all criminal charges relate to travellers, the success rate for detentions over one hour since 1974 is about 3 per cent (10 per cent if exclusion and deportation orders are included). The lax criteria of section 16 account both for this extremely low proportion and for the relatively frequent resort to exclusion. The brevity of the custody of most of those charged suggest they were suspected of trivial, non-terrorist offences. This hypothesis may be supported by comparing the types of charges arising out of sections 14 and 16 in Britain to those secured purely by section 14 in Northern Ireland (see Table 17).

Assuming that the final three categories of offences in Table 17 are mostly unrelated to terrorism, 25 per cent of offences in Britain, but only 9 per cent in Northern Ireland can be deemed incidental. This does not prove that examining officers set out deliberately to catch petty offenders

Table 13 The operation of detentions pursuant to port controls in Great Britain

Year	Persons detained in total (ss. 14, 16)			Persons detained beyond 1 hour at port/airport			Persons detained beyond 48 hours at port/airport			Exclusion order issued at port/airport	Persons deported or removed in total (ss. 14, 16)	Total excluded or deported	Persons subjected to criminal charges in total (ss. 14, 16)		
	N.I.	International	Total	N.I.	International	Total	N.I.	International	Total				N.I.	International	Total
1974	59	N/A	N/A	10	N/A	N/A		N/A	N/A	1	N/A	N/A	8	N/A	N/A
1975	1067	N/A	N/A	630	N/A	N/A		N/A	N/A	25	N/A	N/A	63	N/A	N/A
1976	1066	N/A	N/A	812	N/A	N/A	1*	N/A	N/A	15	N/A	N/A	57	N/A	N/A
1977	853	N/A	N/A	661	N/A	N/A		N/A	N/A	12	N/A	N/A	47	N/A	N/A
1978	622	N/A	N/A	509	N/A	N/A		N/A	N/A	40	N/A	N/A	19	N/A	N/A
1979	857	N/A	N/A	573	N/A	N/A	105	N/A	N/A	42	N/A	N/A	108	N/A	N/A
1980	537	N/A	N/A	441	N/A	N/A	86	N/A	N/A	42	N/A	N/A	42	N/A	N/A
1981	274	N/A	N/A	163	N/A	N/A	17	N/A	N/A	8	N/A	N/A	39	N/A	N/A
1982	220	N/A	N/A	160	N/A	N/A	17	N/A	N/A	9	N/A	N/A	22	N/A	N/A
1983	191	N/A	N/A	132	N/A	N/A	21	N/A	N/A	11	N/A	N/A	31	N/A	N/A
1984	159	44	203	84	5	89	13	2	15	1	13	14	23	8	31
1985	193	73	266	71	3	74	5		5	1	18	19	38	15	53
1986	147	55	202	74	12	86	3	1	4	1	9	10	31	5	36
1987	184	41	225	134	10	144	19	1	20	10	9	19	17	8	25
1988	170	16	186	110	6	116	10		10	9		9	18	3	21
1989	163	18	181	78	4	82	16	1	17	7	2	9	19	3	22
1990	169	24	193	53	4	57	8	–	8	4	2	6	25	3	28
Total	6931	271	7202	4695	44	4739	321	5	326	238	53	291	607	45	652

Source: Home Office. Notes: N/A = figures not applicable. * Detention lasted 10 days.

Table 14 Examinations without detention in Great Britain

Duration (hours)	1984			1985			1986			1987			1988			1989			1990		
	N.I.	Int.	Total	N.I.	Int.	Total	N.I.	Int.	Total	N.I.	Int.	Total	N.I.	Int.	Total	N.I.	Int.	Total	N.I.	Int.	Total
1–2	8	7	15	6	3	9	17	3	20	30	2	32	65	8	73	53	–	53	91	5	96
2–4	12	4	16	26	8	34	12	6	18	22	–	22	46	1	47	76	10	86	125	10	135
4–12	11	1	12	6	11	17	11	11	22	16	5	21	15	6	21	55	8	63	31	9	40
12–24	–	–	–	–	–	–	–	–	–	–	–	–	–	–	–	2	–	2	2	–	2
Total	31	12	43	38	22	60	40	20	60	68	7	75	126	15	141	186	18	204	249	24	273
Charged with offence	–	–	–	–	–	–	2	1	3 (5%)	2	4	6 (8%)	4	–	4 (3%)	5	–	5 (2%)	8	5	13 (5%)

Source: Home Office.

Table 15   Port detentions under 12 hours and searches of records in Great Britain

Year	Detentions			Searches of records
	Up to 1 hr.	1–12 hrs.	Total	
1979	N/A	N/A	878	41936
1980	N/A	N/A	557	48090
1981	N/A	N/A	181	50687
1982	N/A	N/A	213	44696
1983	N/A	N/A	187	44906
1984	109	76	185	47779
1985	74	60	134	55328
1986	86	60	146	59481
1987	144	75	219	81060
1988	116	141	257	77472
1989	N/A	202	N/A	101766
1990	N/A	271	N/A	83753

Source: H.M.C.I.C. Reports and Home Office. *Note*: N/A = figures not available.

Table 16   Outcomes of port detentions in Great Britain

Year	Persons subjected to criminal charges in total (ss. 14,16)	Persons charged at port/airport	Persons charged following an extension under s. 16	Exclusion orders against persons at port/airport
1979	108	13	–	42
1980	42	16	3	42
1981	39	14	1	8
1982	22	8	–	9
Total	211	51	4	101

Source: Jellicoe Report.

– indeed, circulars warn against such a misuse of power.[82] Nonetheless, the detection of terrorists by port controls is an inexact science, so it is unremarkable that other criminals are incidentally detected.[83]

Finally, 117 persons have been charged with breaching the port controls; 113 were convicted, resulting in 9 discharges, 79 fines and 25 sentences of imprisonment.[84] These modest results imply that charges are brought to

Table 17   Charges following detentions under ss. 14, 16

Offences to end of 1990	*Great Britain: persons charged*	*Northern Ireland: criminal charges*
Offences relating to Prevention of Terrorisn or Emergency Provisions Acts	230	1112
Homicides	35	430
Other offences against the person	19	761
Explosives offences	151	971
Firearms offences	55	1343
Hijacking	–	284
Robbery	8	596
Burglary	25	72
Other offences against property	91	333
Miscellaneous	52	168
Total	662	6070

Sources: Home Office and Northern Ireland Office.

encourage compliance with the system rather than to imprison terrorists.[85] By contrast, suspected terrorists are unlikely to be detained for this minor offence. For example, Robert Campbell was noted by the police (probably because of his conviction for armed robbery in Northern Ireland) on arrival at Liverpool, where he had aroused further suspicion by attempting to evade controls. The police allowed him to proceed under observation, and he was later convicted with his fellow conspirators for attempting to free an I.R.A. organiser from Brixton Prison.[86] The port controls may also have aided the conviction of Paul Kavanagh, Thomas Quigley and Natalino Vella. Vella was trailed by the police on arrival from Dublin first to Kavanagh and then to arms caches in Northamptonshire and Nottingham.[87] Surveillances at ports finally secured the detection of McLaughlin and McCotter, who were observed landing near Holyhead from a trawler and then followed to a store of weapons.[88]

(b)   Advantages and drawbacks
Mobility is a necessary feature of Irish and foreign terrorism in Britain which port controls can exploit in two ways. The Jellicoe Report considered that their purpose is 'primarily deterrent and protective',[89] the theory being that terrorists will be discouraged by having to undergo scrutiny. However, this first justification is unconvincing. In so far as terrorism is prevented in Britain, the unacceptable consequence will probably be its

displacement to Northern Ireland. A more cogent argument for the monitoring of movements is that it provides 'choke points' at which the security forces can gather intelligence.[90] Consequently, travellers subjected to the closest attention are participants in Irish politics[91] and those who have been arrested or prosecuted in Northern Ireland.[92] Routine surveillance of such targets mainly distils low-level information but may occasionally unearth a vital lead, as in the cases cited above.

Whatever the dominant purpose of section 16, the Jellicoe Report[93] expressed concern about the lack of uniformity in its implementation, which ranges from laxity, especially at locations where immigration officers are in the ascendant, to, in one police area, blanket carding and subsequent visits upon, and interrogation of, Irishmen remaining in the area.[94] As a result of such criticism, circulars now remind immigration officers of their duties,[95] and a Home Office Working Group on Port Units reviewed in 1984 levels of staffing, training, equipment, accommodation and carding. One notable conclusion of the Group was its rejection of the Jellicoe Report's proposal that carding should be universal.[96] The Group's view won the approval of subsequent reviews[97] and of the Home Office[98] and deserves support for the following reasons. One is that there is no magic in these cards. The information supplied might be false, so the cards only become significant in conjunction with other investigations, which are practicable only in selected cases.[99] Secondly, it would be operationally misguided to attempt blanket carding. To require the police to treat everyone as equally suspect denies the value of their experience and training and would leave them even less time to concentrate on leading suspects. Perhaps a more worthwhile reform would be to link port controls to a system of identity cards issued to all inhabitants of Northern Ireland. Demands for their production need not be more indiscriminate than carding,[100] but they would impede the supply of false information in an examination.

Despite the administrative efforts at uniformity in carding the Colville Report still discovered wide variations, including universal application at most provincial airports.[101] The official response was a Senior Port Officers' Conference in 1987 and the appointment of a National Coordinator of Ports Policing (a Metropolitan Police commander) who reports to a Standing Committee chaired by H.M. Chief Inspector of Constabulary.[102] The Metropolitan Police Special Branch National Ports Office also offers training under its National Ports Scheme.[103]

The principal criticism of port controls is their cost in terms of the general targeting of Irish people without due cause, inconvenience and distress caused to innocent travellers[104] and the dangers arising from the unregulated storage of information.[105] A major contributory cause is that, even after the 1984 reforms, examinations overlap unnecessarily with arrest and search powers, a confusion which also increases the danger that section

16 might be diverted into catching 'normal' criminals. It should be accepted that 'the aim of examinations should be to establish identity',[106] and all ancillary powers should be expressly predicated upon that purpose. By contrast, inquiries are currently permitted under the guise of port controls into an individual's involvement in terrorism even when identity is firmly established. In situations where suspicion arises from information relating to identity or where that identity strengthens existing incriminating evidence, the subject should be arrested under section 14 or searched under section 15, during which the status of the subject is far clearer and better regulated than under section 16. A limited version of section 16 might then be justifiable,[107] since:[108]

while there remains a significant threat from terrorism related to Northern Ireland ... minor inconvenience to innocent people is an acceptable price to pay for an increase in the safety of all.

(c) Future developments

Port controls are under threat from developing transport and economic links encouraged by the Single European Act and the Channel Tunnel.[109] Consequently, the focus upon ports with an Irish connection will become pointless and may already have done so, since 'an Irish terrorist is now as likely to arrive from Amsterdam, Paris or Hamburg ...'.[110] There are two possible responses. One is to scrap the port controls and to divert police attention elsewhere. This option is favoured by the European Commission, which calls for vigilance at Community external, but not internal, borders.[111] However, the Commission's desire is regarded by British police as a 'nightmare'.[112] Heightened checks at the Community's ring-fence could combat neither terrorism which originates within Europe nor foreign threats which do not afflict all member States. Furthermore, the Commission's policy demands more of police and judicial mutual cooperation than might reasonably be expected[113] and could lead irresistibly to 'compensation' by way of extra policing controls, such as identity cards, residence registration, powers to stop and question and even transnational observation and pursuit.[114] The scrapping of controls within the Common Travel Area highlights both of these problems, with friction over extradition and a host of special powers. Conversely, sea or air crossings to Britain represent, albeit as an accident of geography, an obstacle which can be readily raised against terrorists. Therefore, the favoured option of the British authorities is to maintain port controls. Consequently, it is necessary to consider how the powers might be redesigned to take account of the new Community milieu and how far existing or future measures are compatible with Community law.

As for reformulation, the Colville Report considered that the port controls should be 'universal, standard and permanent'.[115] Two consequences would seem to follow. The first is that designation should end, so that the police would be encouraged to attend at any port, as and when they felt it fruitful.[116] Comprehensive application might also reduce the appearance of discrimination against Irish travellers.[117] A second consequence (not considered by Colville) is that the implementation of port controls on a wider basis will inevitably require more police personnel.[118] An increase should also flow from reduced customs and immigration scrutiny pursuant to the Single European Act.

The application of redesigned port controls to the Channel Tunnel will be complicated in view of the volume and speed of traffic and the fact that points of embarkation and disembarkation will be diffuse. The details are yet to be finalised,[119] but the U.K. Government is committed to maintaining checks under the Act on all passengers.[120]

The operation of port controls in the face of Community developments may prove even more problematical, since not only will traffic increase but also communication restraints must be reduced. Border controls affecting Community citizens[121] should be applied without discrimination,[122] and breaches *per se* should not be treated as warranting deportation (or perhaps exclusion).[123] A more fundamental challenge under existing law was mounted in *Re Belgian Passport Controls*.[124] Adult aliens in Belgium must possess residence documents at all times, and the police may demand production of them at borders or elsewhere. The Commission argued that, in so far as applied at borders, the checks contravened Article 3 of Directives 68/360 and 73/148:

1. Member states shall grant . . . the right to enter their territory merely on production of a valid identity card or passport.
2. No entry visa or equivalent requirement may be demanded.

The Court of Justice declared that controls at entry may breach Community law if applied 'in a systematic, arbitrary or unnecessarily restrictive manner'.[125] Although the Belgian measures did not fit that description, the Prevention of Terrorism Act may be more at risk. Not only is it systematic and, as against any individual traveller, arbitrary, but it is more blatantly a border check without equivalent powers against internal residents. Port controls do not allow for the refusal of entry but might be said to make movement 'unnecessarily restrictive' by delaying entry or making it more complex. The Act might be slightly more defensible if, as suggested earlier, it amounted to no more than a police spot check to investigate the identities of suspicious individuals.[126]

Further impetus towards the lifting of travel barriers will be provided by the Single European Act, Article 13 of which demands the establishment of 'an area without internal frontiers', though subject to the General Declaration that 'Nothing . . . shall affect the right of Member States to

take such measures as they consider necessary ... to combat terrorism. ....'
Assuming that traffic covered by the port controls will be defined as 'internal',[127] the combating of terrorism may persist, at least on the modified basis suggested in response to the Belgian case. In this way, the demands of the Single Market could be accommodated without unduly damaging Britain's anti-terrorism shield. The main drawback is that 'cold stops' (without any reason) would have to end, but these are less likely to net terrorists than, say drug couriers in possession of damning evidence.[128] The official response has been less pliable[129]:

The Government remains committed to maintaining the system of police checks for counter-terrorism purposes which are operated under the powers in Schedule 5 to the Act, and this is wholly in keeping with the Single European Act and the Treaty of Rome.

Their view has been supported by experts in Parliament and elsewhere.[130] Consequently, despite its deficiencies under Community law, the status quo may prevail for some time, especially as the Commission may not wish to dispute such a sensitive matter.

(d) Conclusions

Freedom of movement has been increasingly restricted by United Kingdom law during this century. In terms of this trend, port controls represent an important new step, since they relate to internal travel, a form of repression much criticised in other countries. Nevertheless, though unacceptable in their present form, port controls contribute significantly to the prevention and control of Irish terrorism in Britain. In the view of the Metropolitan Police:[131]

the presence of Special Branch officers at ports deters Irish terrorists from attempting to launch attacks against the British mainland. The I.R.A. is known to have gone to extreme lengths to get its operatives and equipment into Great Britain without having to pass through what it clearly acknowledges to be the stringent and effective controls at our ports.

With such backing, the port controls are likely to form a lingering residue of the Prevention of Terrorism Acts.[132]

Notes

1 Most of Schedule 5 was relocated from the Prevention of Terrorism (Supplemental Temporary Provisions) Orders 1984 S.I. 417 (N.I.), 418 (G.B.) on the recommendation of the Colville Report, para. 8.6.2.
2 (1980), reported in the Jellicoe Report, para. 119. Two of the applicants were later excluded: *Guardian* 1 November 1980 p. 3. Compare: *Anderson* v. *Reid* (1902) 86 L.T. 713 (K.B.).

3   Appl. Nos. 8022, 8025, 8027/77; D.R. 18 p. 66 (admissibility), D.R. 25 p. 15 (final report) (hereafter cited as the 'McVeigh case'). See: C. Warbrick, 'The Prevention of Terrorism (Temporary Provisions) Act 1976 and the European Convention on Human Rights: the McVeigh case' (1983) 32 *I.C.L.Q.* 757.

4   Decision as to admissibility, p. 13.

5   *Ibid.* p. 16 See also: D.R. 25 p. 15 paras. 41, 94, 166, 213–18.

6   See: Jellicoe Report, paras. 141, 142.

7   See: *ibid.*, para. 144; Sched. 5 para. 2(2).

8   There should be an express prohibition, as in the Police and Criminal Evidence legislation, and not simply reliance upon reviews of detention. Compare: H.C. Debs. Standing Comm. B col. 413 12 January 1989, Mr. Hogg.

9   D.R. 25 p. 15 para. 53. See also: Decision on admissibility pp. 10, 12, 14. Examining officers (unlike interrogating officers under s. 14) should identify themselves: H.O. Circular 90/1983 para. 6; Jellicoe Report, para. 151. The formalities delineated in *Re McElduff* [1972] N.I. 1 should be observed.

10   See: Sched. 5 para. 2(3).

11   No purpose is specified for the examination: W. Finnie, 'Old wine in new bottles?' 1990 *J.R.* 1 at p. 18.

12   S.I. No. 2227. The order is made under the Channel Tunnel Act 1987.

13   *Loc. cit.*

14   Appl. Nos. 11539, 11641, 11650, 11651, 11652/85, 9 E.H.R.R. 381.

15   The Colville Annual Report for 1986 (para. 7.3) distinguishes intelligence-gathering under ss. 14 and 16, suggesting that the former is unlawful but the latter is lawful.

16   Sched. 5 para. 1. No formal instructions under para. 1(4) have appeared: H.O. Circular, para. 5.7.

17   See: Fourth Report from the Home Affairs Committee, *Special Branch* (1984–85 H.C. 71 – iv.) p. 77.

18   See: Jellicoe Report, paras. 136, 137, H.O. Circular, para. 5.8; Home Affairs Committee, *Practical Police Cooperation in the European Communities* (1989–90 H.C. 363) Vol. II Memo. from Home Office paras. 31, 32. Conversely, the police cannot act as immigration officers, which limits the scope for manpower savings: Colville Report, paras. 9.4.1, 9.4.2.

19   S. 16 (3), Sched. 6; 1990 S.I. No. 1579. Designation depends on traffic levels: H.C. Debs. Standing Comm. B col. 470 12 January 1989. 'Approved' crossings on the Northern Ireland land border may be limited by the Customs and Excise Management Act 1979 s. 26.

20   Sched. 5 para. 8. This power is widely used: Colville Report, para. 9.16.

21   H.O. Circular, para. 5.32.

22   See: Shackleton Report, para. 100; Jellicoe Report, para. 153; Colville Report, para. 9.3.1.

23   See: H.O. Circular, No. 24/1988 para. 4. The Colville Annual Report for 1989, paras. 7.8, 7.9 expressed concern about these meagre controls.

24   H.O. Circular, para. 5.32.

25   H.C. Debs. Standing Comm. B cols. 445, 452 12 January 1989.

26   Colville Report, para. 10.1.5. See also Jellicoe Report, para. 131.

27 Colville Report, paras. 10.1.3; H.O. Circular No. 70/1987; H.M. Chief Inspector of Constabulary, *Report for 1988* (1988–89 H.C. 449) para. 8.3.4.

28 H.O. Circular No. 24/1988, para. 5. Compare Colville Report, para. 10.1.8.

29 H.O. Circular, para. 5.35.

30 Compare: Colville Report, para. 10.1.9.

31 *Ibid.*, para. 10.2.6., and ch. 13.

32 Officers may check the accuracy of the lists by searching: para. 4(1).

33 No new port was designated in 1984, and no east coast sea-port is listed. However, immigration controls do apply instead: Colville Annual Report for 1986, para. 3.5.2.

34 H.O. Circular, para. 5.16, Annex E. There was no direction as to form (and so no legal obligation to complete) until 1977: Shackleton Report, para. 95.

35 Art. 8.

36 H.O. Circular, para. 5.20, Annex E. See also H.O. Circular, 84/1985 para. 9.

37 Examining officers may delegate their powers to, for example, customs officers, mechanics or doctors (see: H.O. Circular, para. 5.15), who may use reasonable force: para. 4(7)–(9).

38 N. 1C.

39 Para. 5.12. The Police and Criminal Evidence legislation ss. 2, 5. Arts. 4, 7 will apply to searches at ports. Transfer is obligatory before intimate searches: s. 55/Art. 56.

40 S.H.H.D. Circular, para. 5.12.

41 Pt. III para. 44.

42 The Shackleton Report (para. 93) implies that other documents specified must concern identity, but the splitting of the different categories of documents between para. 3(2)(a) and (b) weighs against the *eiusdem generis* rule.

43 H.O. Circular, para. 5.10.

44 Compare: *R. v. S.S.H.D., ex p. Khera and Khawaja* [1984] A.C. 24; *Choudhry v. M.P.C.* (1984, Q.B.D.). If a Gaelic name is given, the traveller may be asked whether s/he has ever travelled under any other version: H.O. Circular, para. 5.11.

45 H.C. Debs. Standing Comm. B col. 435 12 January 1989, Mr. Hogg. See: *R. v. Heston-Francois* [1984] 2 W.L.R. 309.

46 Colville Report, para. 8.2.5. Reasonable force may not be used: s. 20(2).

47 The latter is new and relevant when non-terrorist charges are possible. Immigration officers would detain pending deportation: H.C. Debs. Vol. 146 col. 52 30 January 1989.

48 Until 1979, officers could detain under their own authority for seven days or, if the Secretary of State directed, for a period not exceeding five days from the day on which the examination was concluded; see: Shackleton Report, paras. 153, 154; 1979 S.I. Nos. 168, 169.

49 The Government denies that there is any breach: H.C. Debs. Standing Comm. B cols. 413, 415 12 January 1989, Mr. Hogg. Compare: W. Finnie, 'The Prevention of Terrorism Act and the European Convention on Human Rights' (1989) 52 M.L.R. 703 at p. 710; 'Old wine in new bottles?', *loc. cit.* pp. 19–20.

50 Sched. 5 para. 7(4); H.O. Circular, para. 5.2.6.

232 *The prevention of terrorism in British law*

51   Colville Report, para. 8.2.8. See also Sched. 5 para. 7(7).

52   Police and Criminal Evidence Code C, para. 1.11.

53   H.O. Circular, Annex G paras. 23, 24; N.I.O. *Guide*, Pt. IV para. 1.

54   H.O. Circular, para. 5.4, Annex C. See Jellicoe Report, paras. 142, 143. The Notice confusingly refers to the now repealed Supplementary Orders.

55   Jellicoe Report, para. 240.

56   See: Colville Report, para. 8.3.4. The police review officer must intervene even if the person is being examined by other agencies: H.O. Circular, Annex G para. 2.

57   H.O. Circular, Annex G para. 21.

58   Ibid.

59   See N.I.O., *Guide* Pt. III paras. 19–22. No incidental detention power is claimed.

60   The power to fingerprint in England and Wales is narrower under Sched. 5 than under s. 14 in that the only specified offence is s. 8. The requirement of authorisation is not an effective check: Colville Annual Report for 1989, para 1.5.

61   H.C. Debs. Standing Comm. B cols. 392, 395 12 January 1989.

62   See also: Defence of the Realm Regulation 14E (1916 S.R. & O. 561); Defence (General) Regulation 18 (1939 S.R. & O 927); Civil Authorities (Special Powers) Regulation 1B (1940 S.R. & O. (N.I.) 61).

63   Reg. 20 (1956 S.R. & O. (N.I.) 199; reg. 37 (1957 S.R. & O. 16).

64   For the difficulties, see: J.K. Cilliers, *Counter-Insurgency in Rhodesia* (1985) ch. 4.

65   Shackleton Report, para. 106.

66   The 1971 Act was the model: Colville Report, para. 8.1.1.

67   Immigration Act 1971 ss. 1(3), 9(4).

68   See: *R.* v. *Price and others* (1973) *Times* 1 November pp. 1, 2, 18; *R.* v. *Byrne and others* (1976) 62 Cr. App. R. 159. The Special Branch has operated watches at ports since before 1914; R. Allason, *The Branch* (1983) pp. 37, 71, 121, 150.

69   S. 3, Sched. 2, Immigration (Landing and Embarkation Cards) Order 1975 S.I. 65.

70   See: Immigration (Control of Entry through Republic of Ireland) Orders 1972 S.I. No. 1610, 1979 S.I. No. 730, 1980 S.I. No. 1859, 1982 S.I. No. 1028.

71   Jellicoe Report, para. 144. Port examinations are still not equatable with immigration controls, since examining officers cannot deny entry: H.O. Circular, para. 5.7. Foreigners may, therefore, be detained successively under s. 16 and the Immigration Act 1971 Sched. 2 para. 16; see the Philips Annual Report for 1984, para. 45. This combination of powers is even more threatening than under s. 14 since there are no express limits under para. 16 (but see: *R.* v. *Governor of Durham Prison, ex p. Singh* [1984] 1 All E.R. 983).

72   H.O. Circular, para. 5.8. Compare the fears expressed in the Colville Report, para. 8.1.6.

73   See ss. 19, 21, 26, 27, 163, 164.

74   See: ch. 11.

75   See: Philips Annual Report for 1985, para. 26.

76   Jellicoe Report, para. 51; Colville Annual Report for 1986, para. 2.2.1.

77   Home Affairs Committee, *loc. cit.* paras. 22, 26.

78   It is assumed that all detentions at ports/airports are under s. 16. A 'detention' occurs whenever anyone is prevented from leaving the examination area: H.O. Circular, para. 5.23. Statistical practices before 1984 were variable: Jellicoe Report, paras. 120, 145.

79   Shackleton Report, para. 98. See also: Jellicoe Report, para. 129.

80   For example, C. Scorer, S. Spencer and P. Hewitt, *The New Prevention of Terrorism Act* (1985) p. 36; P. Hall, 'The Prevention of Terrorism Acts' in A. Jennings (ed.), *Justice under Fire* (2nd ed., 1990) p. 176. Following criticism in the Colville Report (para. 16.1.3), the figures ceased to be published.

81   For before 1979, see: n. 46 *supra*; Shackleton Report, para. 98.

82   See: H.O. Circular 90/1983, para. 5; Jellicoe Report, para. 151.

83   The compilation of terrorist profiles or stereotypes might assist; see: Jellicoe Report, para. 134; *U.S.* v. *Lopez* 328 F. Supp. 1077 (1971). The idea is rejected by the Colville Report, para. 8.2.3.

84   There was one offence in Northern Ireland to the end of 1990.

85   See, for example: *R.* v. *McCormack and Bishop* (1985) *Times* 2 January p. 2 (£50 fine each).

86   *Times* 20 December 1979 p. 2, 4 March 1981 p. 3, 17 March p. 3, 18 March p. 3.

87   *Times* 14 February 1985 p. 3, 15 February p. 3, 7 March p. 3, 8 March p. 3.

88   *Times* 8 June 1988 p. 3, 14 June p. 3, 18 June p. 3, 21 June pp. 1, 4.

89   Para. 116. The Government agrees: H.C. Debs. Vol. 38 col. 635 7 March 1983, Mr. Waddington.

90   Home Affairs Committee, *loc. cit.* paras. 22, 23.

91   For example: cases of Margareta D'Arcy (H-Block Prisoners), Dervla Murphy (writer) and Eamonn McCann (journalist) (see: Scorer, Spencer and Hewitt, *op. cit.* pp. 38, 39); case of Pat Arrowsmith (see: B. Rose-Smith, 'Police powers and terrorism legislation' in P. Hain (ed.), *Policing the Police* Vol. 1 (1979) pp. 137–8); case of McVeigh (Clann na'h Eireann), *loc. cit.*; case of Sheena Clarke (Labour Committee on Ireland) (see: *Guardian* 6 May 1985 p. 20); case of Alex Maskey (Sinn Fein councillor) in *Times* 2 December 1987 p. 24.

92   For example: case of Philip Flynn (see: *Times* 31 December 1977 p. 2); case of Albert McCann (see: P. Taylor, *Beating the Terrorists?* (1980) pp. 191–2).

93   Paras. 131–3, 138, 146–52, 154.

94   See: Philips Annual Report for 1984, para. 37.

95   See: H.O. Circular, para. 5.8.

96   Para. 148.

97   Philips Annual Report for 1984, para. 36; Colville Report, para. 9.24; S.A.C.H.R., *11th Report* (1985–86 H.C. 394) para. 64.

98   H.O. Circular, para. 5.18.

99   It is not implied that carding is useless. It allows the police to engage a suspect, and to consider what is written down and the writer's demeanour. Compare: S.A.C.H.R., *13th Report* (1987–88 H.C. 298) App. D. para. 28.

100   Compare: Shackleton Report, para. 152.

101   Para. 9.2.3.

102   H.M. Chie.´ Inspector of Constabulary, *Annual Report for 1987* (1987–88 H.C. 521) para. 8.20, *Annual Report for 1988* (1988–89 H.C. 449) para. 8.35.

103   Colville Annual Report for 1989, para. 2.

104   See: *McVeigh, Evans and O'Neill* v. *U.K.*, *loc. cit.*; cases of Arbuckle, Barren, Lofgray, O'Brien and Forgione (Scorer, Spencer and Hewitt, *op. cit.* p. 40).

105   The cards are eventually destroyed, but some information is stored as criminal intelligence by different police forces: Colville Report, para. 9.2.10. It is regrettable both that there is such inefficient use made of the information and that there is no independent oversight of it. However, computerisation is being developed: Home Affairs Committee, *Criminal Records* (1989–90 H.C. 285) and *Government Reply* (Cm. 1163, 1990).

106   H.C. Debs. Standing Comm. D col. 344 6 December 1983, Mr. Soley.

107   On the precedent of the Emergency Provisions Act 1991 s. 18, there should be a detention power lasting four hours on reasonable suspicion and with the ability to question and search for physical evidence as to identity; thereafter, the powers in ss. 14, 15 must be used. Compare: Colville Report, paras. 8.2.6, 8.3.3, 8.3.4; S.A.C.H.R., *14th Report*, *loc. cit.*, Annex F p. 114; D. Bonner, 'Combating terrorism in the 1990's' (1989) *P.L.* 440 at p. 445. A four-hour period should allow initial inquiries and the transfer into police custody where relevant (which is rarely necessary: H.C. Debs. Standing Comm. B cols. 400, 412 12 January 1989).

108   Jellicoe Report, para. 140; A. Dummett and A. Nichol, *Subjects, Citizens, Aliens and Others* (1990) p. 165. Compare: S.A.C.H.R., *13th Report*, *loc. cit.* App. D para. 20.

109   See European Communities (Amendment) Act 1986; Channel Tunnel Act 1987.

110   Colville Report, para. 9.1.4.

111   See: Commission communication on the abolition of controls of persons at intra-Community borders (10412/88, COM (88) 640 Final). See also *Report on problems relating to combating terrorism* (European Parliament, Committee on Legal Affairs and Citizens Rights, A2-155/89) para. 13. The ('Schengen') Agreement on the Gradual Abolition of Checks at Common Borders (1985) is presented as a blueprint: House of Lords Select Committee on the European Communities, *1992, Border Control of People* (1988–89 H.L. 90) para. 3, App. 3.

112   Colville Report, para. 8.1.4.

113   Difficulties have arisen even within the Schengen Agreement: F. Geysels, 'Europe from the inside' (1990) 6 *Policing* 338.

114   Home Affairs Committee, *loc. cit.* para. 41.

115   Para. 8.1.2. See also Aviation and Maritime Security Act 1990 (ch. 12).

116   Para. 9.1.4–9.1.7.

117   Para. 9.2.9.

118   There are 780 officers (plus 110 reserves) employed on the National Ports Scheme (which covers all major ports and not just those designated): H.M. Chief Inspector of Constabulary, *Report for 1989* (1989–90 H.C. 524) para. 8.24.

119   See: Treaty between the U.K. and France concerning the construction and operation by private concessionaires of a Channel Fixed Link (Cmnd. 9745, 1986) Arts. 4, 5, 6, 8; P. Hermitage, 'Light on the start of the Tunnel' (1989) 5 *Policing*

121. Control areas can be designated (1990 S.I. No. 2227), but their location is not yet settled.

120   Government Reply to the Home Affairs Committee, *Report on Passport Control* (Cm. 313, 1988) p. 3.

121   See *R.* v. *Saunders* [1979] 3 W.L.R. 359.

122   *Rutili* v. *Minister of the Interior* [1976] 1 C.M.L.R. 140; *State* v. *Watson and Belmann* [1976] 2 C.M.L.R. 552.

123   *State* v. *Royer* [1976] 2 C.M.L.R. 619; *R.* v. *Pieck* [1980] 3 C.M.L.R. 220.

124   [1990] 2 C.M.L.R. 492. See also: *Commission* v. *Netherlands* (1991).

125   *Ibid.* at p. 499.

126   See: H.L. Select Committee on the European Communities, *loc. cit.* paras. 27, 91.

127   See *ibid.* paras. 14–23.

128   See *ibid.* Minutes of Evidence, p. 33.

129   H.C. Debs. Vol. 168 col. 820 6 March 1990, Mr. Waddington.

130   H.L. Select Committee, *loc. cit.* para. 92; K.G. Robertson, *1992: The Security Implications* (1989) pp. 33, 34.

131   H.L. Select Committee, *loc. cit.* Minutes of Evidence, p. 171.

132   Shackleton Report, para. 155; Jellicoe Report, paras. 140, 152.

Chapter 10

Miscellaneous matters

1 Statutory orders

Statutory orders may be issued in various contexts under the Prevention of Terrorism Act. Those relating to proscription, port controls and the renewal of the Act have already been noted. Orders under section 28(3), which extend the Act to the Channel Islands and the Isle of Man, will be described hereafter.

The procedures for making orders are not uniform. Those pursuant to section 28(3) and those designating ports under section 16(3) can simply be issued through the Privy Council without notifying Parliament. Instruments augmenting port examinations in Northern Ireland are subject to annulment by resolution of either House,[1] but the closest scrutiny is reserved for delegated legislation concerning proscription and the continuance of the Act. This must normally be approved in draft by affirmative resolution of each House[2] but may be activated without approval when:[3]

it is declared in the order that it appears to the Secretary of State that by reason of urgency it is necessary to make the order without a draft having been so approved.

However, such orders must subsequently be laid before Parliament and shall cease to have effect unless approved within forty days of their making.[4] This emergency procedure might be appropriate when a new terrorist group emerges[5] or when a lapsed provision is revived.

As has been described previously,[6] parliamentary scrutiny of the Act has been feeble. All orders should be subjected to the affirmative procedure.

2 Local variations

The Act was applied in the Channel Islands and the Isle of Man (subject to adaptations) by Orders in Council, and those issued under the 1984 Act[7] are extended by section 25(6) until replaced by fresh Orders under section

28(3) or by Islands' legislation. The plan was to utilise the latter in view of the facts that the 1989 Act has permanent status and contains important new measures affecting offshore financial operations. Pursuant to this aim, Islands' legislation has reached different stages of preparedness. No Bill has yet been tabled in Jersey, though one is planned.[8] In Guernsey, the Prevention of Terrorism (Bailiwick of Guernsey) Law 1990 has been passed in terms virtually identical to the U.K. version.[9]

Replacement legislation in the Isle of Man takes the form of the Prevention of Terrorism Act 1990.[10] This Act departs from the U.K. model in several important respects. The first is that detention under the special arrest powers may be extended after forty-eight hours only for a further three days (section 12(4)). The Brogan case[11] prompted this amendment,[12] and the Attorney-General asserted that it brought the legislation 'much closer' to the judgment.[13] This claim is doubtful, as a five-day period without judicial authorisation was also condemned by the Court. However, another change, that reviews of detention under Schedule 3 must be reported to the High Bailiff (a judicial officer) who may countermand the police's decision,[14] may save the legislation. The idea was again to comply with Brogan, but the reform still allows detention well beyond three days without judicial authorisation since Schedule 3 reviews cease once an application is made for an extension. Thus, it would have been more appropriate to require judicial oversight on the forty-eight hour review. A third difference in the Isle of Man Act is that arrests of suspects must be made under warrant unless 'the circumstances make it impracticable to apply for such a warrant' (section 12(7)). Such circumstances will often prevail, but the subsection is a welcome attempt to impose restraint. The fourth change is that interviews with detainees are to be taped, and a code of practice is to be issued (section 13(9)). Further protection for detainees is granted by section 13(8), by which records of samples and prints are to be destroyed if a suspect is not prosecuted or is cleared. Another feature of the Isle of Man legislation is that there is no added protection for special procedure or excluded materials under Schedule 7, and the power to issue warrants under section 3 of the Security Service Act 1989 is specifically adopted. Finally, the Act remains permanently in force without annual renewal, subject only to repeal by Order (section 21). It was dubiously claimed in debates that this feature flowed from the Colville Report.[15]

The Home Office, which vetted these local modifications prior to Assent,[16] would no doubt warn against any extrapolation from arrangements for a small jurisdiction which is a backwater in terms of terrorist threats, as evidenced by the statistics in Table 18. Nevertheless, this argument is less persuasive in regard to the employment of judges in detention decisions, since the main plank of the Government's opposition in the U.K. Parliament was that such issues are in principle non-justiciable.

Table 18   Operation of the Act in the islands

Statutory provision	Jurisdiction	Total to 1 November 1982
Exclusion orders	Isle of Man	3
	Guernsey	3
	Jersey	6
Arrests	Isle of Man	38
	Guernsey	15
	Jersey	4
Examinations	Isle of Man	89
	Guernsey	10
	Jersey	30

Source: Jellicoe Report.

3   The role of the Attorney General

(a)   Provisions

By section 19, proceedings shall not be instituted in England and Wales or Northern Ireland for offences under the Act except by, or with the consent of, the relevant Attorney General.[17] Only prosecutions under Schedule 2 paragraphs 6 and 7 and Schedule 5 paragraph 11 (for failure to cooperate with exclusion arrangements and port controls) are unrestricted, presumably because lesser penalties pertain.

The procedures for intimating assent have been considered under section 7(1) of the Explosive Substances Act 1883,[18] which contains identical requirements. The consent must be in writing, but the Attorney General need not have considered the charges in detail and may consent in wide terms,[19] subject to two exceptions. First, express reference must appear to any added counts of conspiracy to commit an offence under the Act.[20] Second, consent from the Attorney General for Northern Ireland must be factually precise.[21] It would appear that the practice in neither jurisdiction is satisfactory. On the one hand, a general consent diminishes the value of the safeguard. On the other hand, minute precision is an unnecessary technicality. Consent which indicates the nature of activity alleged and the relevant offences would be a preferable compromise.

(b)   Practice

In order to explain the purpose of this 'important safeguard'[22] a comparison will be made with the corresponding role of the Attorney General under the Official Secrets Acts.[23] Five justifications were listed in the Home

Office's Memorandum to the Departmental Commission on section 2 of the Official Secrets Act 1911.[24] Consent might be necessary to secure consistency in prosecuting practice and to prevent vexatious or embarrassing private prosecutions, for example of a Government official who has held discussions with terrorists.[25] Next, the requirement enables account to be taken of mitigating factors, such as the unwillingness of a recipient of information about terrorism.[26] Central control may also provide a shield against prosecutions which threaten political activities, and it finally ensures that political considerations are given due weight.

In summary, there are sound reasons for restraining prosecutions under the Prevention of Terrorism Act, but whether the Attorney General adequately fulfils that function is another matter. In principle, it is difficult to accept that he exerts an independent control,[27] and in practice also it would appear that consent is almost a formality. For example, five cases were submitted to the Attorney General of England and Wales in 1977, but his fiat was refused just once.[28] Accordingly, the filter of consent might be more effective and independent if transferred to the Directors of Public Prosecutions.

4 Further provisions for Northern Ireland

The confusing overlap between the Prevention of Terrorism (Temporary Provisions) Act 1989, the Northern Ireland (Emergency Provisions) Acts and regular Northern Ireland law is compounded by Part VI of the Prevention of Terrorism (Temporary Provisions) Act 1989, which dabbled in both areas and, by section 27(11), had its duration determined by section 33 of the Emergency Provisions Act 1978. This confusion has now been eliminated by the Northern Ireland (Emergency Provisions) Act 1991, sections 14, 15, 19 and 59 of which incorporate Part VI.

Apart from section 21 of the Prevention of Terrorism (Temporary Provisions) Act 1989, which, as described in chapter 8, amended special search powers, the sentencing of terrorists in Northern Ireland was the concern of Part VI. Section 22 provided that remission in respect of a sentence of imprisonment of five years or more for a 'scheduled offence', as defined by Schedule 1 of the Northern Ireland (Emergency Provisions) Act 1991, shall be reduced from 50 per cent (a level introduced in 1976 as compensation for the phasing-out of special-category status and the absence of any substantial pre-release parole programme)[29] to 33 per cent. This reduction was prompted by the Home Secretary's policy after 1983 not to grant parole to violent offenders sentenced to more than five years' imprisonment, which created the disparity that Irish terrorists sentenced in Britain for crimes of violence now serve 66 per cent of their sentences.[30] By way of comment, treating like cases alike is always a valid principle for a

Table 19   Reconviction rates in Northern Ireland, 1984 (%)

First offence	No further offence	Second offence (if any)	
		Terrorist	Non-terrorist
Non-terrorist	40	25	35
Terrorist	60	20	20

system of penal justice, but it is ironic that the policy in Britain should have been expanded shortly after being rightly condemned by the Carlisle Report as 'flawed in principle and harmful in practice'.[31] The objections in principle arise because the policy implies that a sentence of, say, seven years for a violent offence is more serious than a sentence of seven years for fraud, whereas the sentencer should already have taken full account of the differing nature of the offences. Practical difficulties arise mainly because of the policy's negative impact on the maintenance of prison discipline and the incentives for rehabilitation. These effects may be particularly damaging in Northern Ireland prisons, where paramilitary groups exert a strong counter-influence.[32]

A further penological reform was effected by section 23. If a person has been sentenced to imprisonment for more than a year, has been discharged by way of a remission, but has been convicted on indictment of a scheduled offence during the period of remission, then the unexpired sentence up to the date on which it would have expired but for his discharge must be added consecutively to any new term of imprisonment for the second offence and must be served in full. These extra sanctions were said to be justified by alarming reconviction rates (see Table 19).[33] Four comments may be offered. First, terrorist reoffending does not appear high in comparison with non-terrorists, British figures[34] or in absolute terms. This result seems intuitively correct. Terrorists who have been detected and convicted must represent security risks to the paramilitary organisations and may also be more deterred than ordinary criminals by the prospect of reconviction, since they face heavier deterrent sentences. Second, there appears to be a remarkable absence of discrimination between terrorist and non-terrorist reoffending, which may in part be explained by the scheduling of armed robbery, much of which is committed by non-terrorists.[35] The high level of terrorist reoffending by non-terrorists may also reflect the pervasive influence of paramilitary groups in Northern Ireland prisons. This facet of reoffending also explains why the Government was insistent that the first offence relevant to section 22 should not be confined to terrorist-type offences. Thirdly, conditional release was favoured for all offenders by the Carlisle Report.[36] Consequently, section 23 may be more acceptable in principle than section 22, but it should be realised that such a possibility already exists under the Treatment of Offenders (Northern Ireland) Order 1976,[37] and it might have been more profitable to have considered the current working and possible reform of that measure. Fourthly, until legislation allowing conditional release in Britain is passed,[38] section 23 establishes a new disparity, just at the same time as section 22 has removed another. Of course, it may be significant that the new disparity encourages imprisonment, whereas the old one favoured liberty.

The final measure in Part VI (section 24) allowed account to be taken of security, as well as safety, grounds in the licensing of explosives factories and magazines in Northern Ireland. Thus, a perfectly safe new operator may be denied permission simply because of the extra potential strain on police resources.

Notes

1 S. 16(6). This procedure is adopted because such orders do not add to primary legislation: H.C. Debs. Standing Comm. D col. 359 8 December 1983, Mr. Waddington.

2 S. 1(3)(a). See also: Statutory Instruments Act 1946 ss. 6, 7.

3 S. 1(3)(b).

4 S. 1(4),(5). See also: Laying of Documents before Parliament (Interpretation) Act 1948. Compare: Emergency Powers Act 1920.

5 See S.I. 1979 No. 745.

6 See ch. 4.

7 S.I. 1984 Nos. 860, 1165, 1166.

8 Law Drafting Programme (12 June 1990).

9 See ch. XXV; 1990 S.I. No. 2296. Local variations include extensions of arrests by H.M. Procureur (the Attorney General), no criteria for the taking of identifying samples and prints, no equivalents to Sched. 4 paras. 31–5 and Sched. 7 para. 8, and no extra protection for special procedure and excluded materials. The Colville Annual Report for 1989 (para. 4.4) doubtfully argues that reference to H.M. Procureur may secure compliance with the European Convention.

10 See 1990 S.I. No. 2151.

11 *Brogan* v. *U.K.* Application Nos. 11209, 11234, 11266/84, 11386/85, Judgment of Court Ser. A No. 145-B.

12 House of Keys K. 1108 13 March 1990.

13 Legislative Council C 318 1 May 1990.

14 Para. 4. Note also that persons asleep should be awakened to make representations: para. 6.

15 House of Keys K. 922 27 February 1990.

16 There is extensive consultation during drafting (Royal Commission on the Constitution, *Report* (Cmnd. 5460, 1973) para. 1434), and Assent is not 'a mere

formality' (Joint Evidence of Home Office and Tynwald to the Royal Commission on the Constitution (1970) para. 6).

17   In Scotland, the Lord Advocate undertakes or oversees almost all such prosecutions.

18   As amended by the Administration of Justice Act 1982 s. 63.

19   *R.* v. *Cain and Schollick* (1975) 61 Cr. App. R. 186.

20   *R.* v. *Pearce* (1981) 72 Cr. App. R. 295. See also: *R.* v. *McLaughlin* (1982) 76 Cr. App. R. 42.

21   *R.* v. *Taylor* [1960] N.I. 136; *R.* v. *Downey* [1971] N.I. 224.

22   H.C. Debs. Standing Comm. B col. 80 15 December 1988, Mr. Hogg.

23   See: Official Secrets Acts 1911 s. 8, 1989 s. 9.

24   (Cmnd. 5104, 1972) App. VII. Compare: Rabie Report, paras. 8.4.3.4, 8.4.3.5, 9.3.6.2.

25   Compare: Southern Rhodesia (Immunity for Persons Attending Meetings and Consultations) Orders S.I. 1979 Nos. 820, 1374.

26   Jellicoe Report, para. 230.

27   Compare: J. Ll. J. Edwards, *The Attorney General, Politics and the Public Interest* (1984); Baker Report, para. 253.

28   Royal Commission on Criminal Procedure, *The Law and Procedure* (Cmnd. 8092–1, 1981) App. 24

29   See: H.C. Debs. Vol. 881, col. 238 4 November 1975, Mr. Rees; Prison (Amendment) Rules (N.I.) 1976 S.R. No. 53. Parole only arises in Northern Ireland as part of pre-release arrangements. See: Northern Ireland Office, *Report on the Work of the Prison Service 1987–88* (1988–89 H.C. 42) para. 12.3.

30   See *In re Findlay* [1985] A.C. 318; Report of the Review Committee, *The Parole System in England and Wales* (Cm. 532, 1988) para. 33 (the 'Carlisle Report'). The Northern Ireland Secretary of State at first resisted the application of the Home Secretary's policy: H.C. Debs. Vol. 47 col. 441 (w.a.) 3 November 1983, Mr. Prior. The disparity only applied between violent offenders in the respective jurisdictions, and it could now be argued that non-violent scheduled offenders in Northern Ireland are treated unfairly by comparison both with their counterparts in Britain (who are relatively few) and with non-violent non-scheduled offenders in Northern Ireland.

31   *Ibid.*, para. 190. The Report calls for eligibility for parole for all sentences over four years at 50 per cent of the term and release in any event at 66 per cent.

32   The prisons in Northern Ireland offer freedom from paramilitary influence only 'as far as possible': Northern Ireland Office, *Report on the Work of the Prison Service, loc. cit.* para. 2.1.

33   H.C. Debs. Standing Committee B col. 605 17 January 1989, Ms. Mowlem. The sample size was several hundred, but no precise details were given (*ibid.*, col. 615). Compare: Baker Report, para. 455.

34   See: Carlisle Report, *loc. cit.* para. 277, 281. It would be fair to point out that the figures from Northern Ireland probably under-record reoffending, especially terrorist reoffending, to a greater degree than those from Britain because of greater difficulties of detection and prosecution: H.C. Debs. Standing Committee B col. 617 19 January 1989, Mr. Stewart.

35   See D.P.J. Walsh, *The Use and Abuse of Emergency Legislation in Northern*

Ireland (1983). It is possible that a scheduled offence which has been certified by the Attorney General as suitable for trial by jury remains a scheduled offence and so relevant to s. 23. The Government rejects this interpretation: H.C. Debs. Standing Committee B cols. 624 and 627 17 January 1989, Mr. Stewart. By comparison, it should be noted that the Northern Ireland (Emergency Provisions) Act 1991 s. 11 (special rules as to the admissibility of confessions) continues to apply when a scheduled offence is certified out and is only excluded when a scheduled offence is tried summarily by the express effect of subsection (4).

36   *Loc. cit.* paras. 277, 281.
37   S.I. No. 226, Article 3. See: *R.* v. *Ferguson* (1988) 9 B.N.I.L. n. 42.
38   See: *Criminal Justice and Protecting the Public* (Cm. 965, 1990) ch. 6.

Chapter 11

The overall effects of the Prevention of Terrorism Acts

1 Methods of testing

Having studied the Prevention of Terrorism Acts piecemeal, their overall effects will now be evaluated. The Shackleton, Jellicoe and Colville Reports all contended that there was a continuing need for such special laws,[1] but, while noting these weighty statements of support, two more objective lines of assessment will be taken. Firstly, one might seek positive proof that terrorism has been prevented or controlled by the Acts. Secondly, there is a negative test – whether any of the reputed achievements of the legislation could have been attained through the application of 'regular' law, which is more acceptable in principle. In pursuit of both studies, attention will be confined to Irish Republican terrorism. As stated in chapter 3, international terrorism in the United Kingdom neither warrants special legislation nor is greatly affected by it, whilst the relatively few cases involving Loyalists have been described in chapter 5.

2 Positive considerations

(a) Prevention in Britain

Prevention is especially difficult to gauge, since it involves the proof of an omission.[2] Nevertheless, a crude method of determining whether the Prevention of Terrorism Acts have lived up to their title would be to search for any increase or decrease in terrorist activities since November 1974.[3]

A quick survey reveals that enactment had no immediate discernible effect. Thus, the I.R.A.'s campaign continued during the remainder of 1974, through 1975 and into 1976, broken only by two lulls when 'ceasefires' were arranged over Christmas 1974 and for a few months after February 1975. The attacks were concentrated mainly in London, and twelve people (including Ross McWhirter)[4] were killed and over 300 were injured.

For reasons to be explained, mid-1976 seems to have marked a significant watershed, for a pattern then emerged of an isolated attack or a
concentrated burst of them, followed by substantial periods of quiescence.
Amongst the notable incidents were the I.R.A. operations around Christmas
1978, including the shooting of a policeman and explosions at Greenwich
gas-works.[5] Christmas campaigns were also undertaken in 1980 and 1983,
the latter including a car-bomb at Harrods which killed six people and
injured ninety-three.[6] In March 1979, the I.N.L.A. made its first foray into
Britain, when Airey Neave, M.P., was killed by a car bomb in the precincts
of Parliament.[7] Another attempted assassination occurred in May 1981,
when there was an explosion at an oil refinery in Shetland during a visit
by the Queen.[8] In October and November 1981, attacks were perpetrated
on soldiers at Chelsea Barracks, Sir Steuart Pringle (then Commandant
General of the Royal Marines), a restaurant in Oxford Street and Sir
Michael Havers (the Attorney General), resulting in three deaths and dozens
of injuries.[9] In July 1982, explosions directed against Army bandsmen and
cavalry in London killed eleven and injured about thirty.[10]

Attacks on civilian targets, including the Harrods bombing and a bomb
at Victoria Station in which one person was killed in 1991,[11] have continued
intermittently. However, I.R.A. attention has increasingly turned to military
or political victims, with more incidents in 1990 than in any year since
1975. Most prominent amongst political targets was the bomb at the
Grand Hotel, Brighton in October 1984, which almost claimed the lives of
several Cabinet Ministers attending the Conservative Party Conference.
Five people were killed (including one M.P.) and thirty-two injured.[12]
Munitions found near Scarborough in March 1989 were also linked to
a forthcoming Conservative gathering,[13] and a spate of letter-bombs was
sent to politicians and civil servants in April 1987.[14] Recent political targets
have included Lord McAlpine, Ian Gow, M.P., who was murdered, Sir
Peter Terry (ex-Governor of Gibraltar) and a mortar attack on Downing
Street.[15] Soldiers and military installations have more frequently been at
risk. There was an explosion in August 1988 at the Inglis Barracks, London
(resulting in one death and nine injuries),[16] and several other Army sites
have been under fire: Tern Hill, Shropshire in February 1989 (one injured),[17]
the Royal Marines' School of Music, Deal in September 1989 (eleven dead
and twenty-two injured),[18] Colchester Barracks in November 1989 (two
injured),[19] the Army Directorate of Education, Eltham in May 1990 (seven
injured) and a shooting in June 1990 at a railway station in Lichfield in
which one soldier was killed.[20] There were also attacks on Army recruitment
centres, and one soldier was killed at offices in Wembley in May 1990.
Aside from the I.R.A., the I.N.L.A. was responsible for an attempted
bombing of Chelsea barracks in 1985.[21]

In the light of this chronicle of Republican terrorism in Britain, it seems fair to conclude that political violence has generally been less frequent but more carefully targeted since 1974. Yet these trends do not coincide with the passage of the Prevention of Terrorism Acts nor with any development in their enforcement. Therefore, other factors must be taken into account.

One such cause may be an increasing public awareness of the threat from terrorism. For example, almost all letter-bombs have been intercepted. Discoveries by the public have also included a gunman in a car at Clapham (which led to arms in a nearby flat) in December 1988,[22] a cache of explosives at Tottenham and on Hampstead Heath[23] and a weapons dump on the Dyffed coast in 1989.[24] Police expertise has correspondingly grown and is reflected structurally. Thus, a Metropolitan Police Bomb Squad was established in 1971 and was reorganised in 1976 as the Anti-Terrorist Squad, which works alongside the long-standing Irish Squad in the Metropolitan Police's Special Branch.[25]

Terrorism may next have been inhibited by the prosecution of those responsible. No doubt, replacements may be recruited, trained and installed in Britain, but there is in the meantime disruption and a loss of effectiveness. Apart from during the early days of its campaign, the I.R.A. has tended to rely upon volunteers from Ireland who do not live in the Irish community in Britain and either depart after a short stay or change their addresses frequently. To determine whether the Prevention of Terrorism Acts have been of assistance in tracking such elusive targets, detailed consideration will be given to some of the relevant prosecutions since November 1974.

One important caveat must first be entered. Some convictions have been fiercely disputed,[26] and some (the 'Birmingham Six', 'Guildford Four' and 'Maguire Seven', described later) have been totally discredited. Whether other defendants are in reality innocent remains a matter of speculation. However, the fact that some verdicts have been set aside should give pause for thought concerning the wisdom of special policing powers within the Prevention of Terrorism Act, the operation of which may have contributed to miscarriages of justice. More generally, the chances of wrongful conviction are heightened in prosecutions involving alleged Irish terrorists, even without the impact of the Act. In these cases, the due process model of criminal justice, which emphasises the primacy of the individual and the acquittal of the innocent, may be compromised by communal or state interests which seek to condemn the values represented by the defendant and to extol those of the State.[27] Accordingly, the acquittal of terrorist defendants costs the State dearly in terms of its prestige and the missed opportunity to denounce its opponents, and these costs increase on appeal or referral back.

Subject to these apprehensions, two of the earliest police successes occurred in Southampton, but in neither case were the Acts of importance. In the first, Ronald Joseph McCartney was convicted of attempted murder and other offences for shooting at a policeman, having been identified from his actions at the time.[28] In the second, Baker, Bennett and McCaffery were found guilty of explosives offences after a tip-off from neighbours about suspicious baggage.[29] In both instances, the Acts were used to carry out arrests on a wide scale but to little avail. They were also largely irrelevant in the capture of an I.R.A. unit operating in Liverpool, Manchester and Birmingham and comprised of Dowd, Kinsella, Nordone, Norney and Gibson. The group was betrayed by 'the antics of the young volunteers', who produced a firearm after being refused a bottle of wine in a restaurant.[30] Another invaluable police success not attributable to the Acts concerned possibly the most productive I.R.A. unit ever assembled, consisting of Butler, Doherty, Duggan and O'Connell. After their attacks on West End restaurants in late 1975, the police mounted blanket coverage of the area and, when the next assault was mounted, were able to trace the assailants via their car registration number. The four were arrested following a siege at a flat in Balcombe Street.[31] Their replacements, Donnelly, Hackett and Hayes, were in turn caught when Hackett severely injured himself in an explosion.[32] An alleged associate of the Balcombe Street gang, William Quinn, who was convicted of the murder of Police Constable Tibble in 1975, was also traced through routine vigilance.[33] Tibble and a colleague, Blackledge, had stopped Quinn in the street. Quinn ran off and shot dead the pursuing Tibble. A gun and bomb-making equipment were discovered at Quinn's flat, and his fingerprints were also traced at premises used by the Balcombe Street gang (where the murder weapon was located). Quinn was identified by Blackledge at a trial in Dublin shortly afterwards and was eventually extradited from the U.S.A.[34] On the other side of the coin, detection has occasionally been aided by the Prevention of Terrorism Acts. For example, as described in chapter 9, one important lead to the team headed by Gerard Tuite was provided by Robert Campbell, who aroused the attention of examining officers at Liverpool.[35] The port controls may also have helped to secure the conviction in 1985 of Kavanagh, Quigley and Vella, responsible for explosions in 1981.[36] The police trailed Vella from Dublin and were led to arms dumps in Nottinghamshire and Northamptonshire. Another cache, in Berkshire, was discovered by chance, and the fingerprints of Kavanagh and Quigley were obtained from it. Evidence from these finds also secured the conviction in 1987 of Gilbert McNamee, who was charged with conspiracy with Kavanagh and others to cause explosions between 1982 and 1984.[37] His prints matched some taken after arrest for that purpose under the Act.

Perhaps the most important prosecution of the 1980s concerned those responsible for the Brighton bombing.[38] Evidence was amassed from two main sources. First, the fingerprints of Patrick Magee were detected on a registration card at the Grand Hotel. These prints matched others taken from him as a juvenile offender in England and, more significantly, on an unexploded bomb at the Reubens Hotel, London in June 1985. Secondly, information was also provided by an informer, Raymond O'Connor, who had told the police of plans to bomb an Army base in Blackpool in 1983. Magee and his colleagues were eventually traced through Donal Craig, an I.R.A. messenger. Craig was observed meeting Magee in Carlisle and then travelling to Glasgow, whereupon arrests were made under the Act and incriminating evidence was found. Altogether, thirteen persons were charged with some degree of involvement. Magee was convicted of murder and explosives offences, six others (Craig, McDonnell, Sherry, Anderson, McShane and McKerney) were convicted of conspiracy to cause explosions. Others charged with withholding information were all acquitted. The impact of the Act was mixed. The checking of ports may have aided the police, but their surveillance was only effective in conjunction with background intelligence and forensic information, which had to be gathered by the usual painstaking methods. Similarly, arrests under the Act could easily have been accomplished under normal powers.

Later cases have tended to confirm the marginal role of the Prevention of Terrorism Act. For example, Peter Jordan and William Grimes were convicted in 1986 of conspiracy to attack a retired soldier and, in Grimes' case, of the possession of a detonator. Peter Lynch was convicted of withholding information.[39] Again, the port controls may have assisted, as Grimes was tracked from Dublin to Liverpool, though why the police had focused on him was not revealed. Port controls played a more prominent role in the convictions of McLaughlin and McCotter for conspiring to cause explosions. The two had been trailed after a surreptitious landing in Holyhead to arms in Chester.[40] By contrast, public rather than police vigilance secured two further prosecutions. The first concerned Patrick McLaughlin, who was convicted of conspiring to bomb the Chelsea Barracks on behalf of the I.N.L.A. in 1985.[41] The person who had planted the bomb had panicked after being spotted by passers-by, and McLaughlin's fingerprints (amongst others) were found on a bag in which the bomb was kept. Similarly, the discovery of weapons at a flat in Clapham in 1988 came about through a member of the public disturbing a gunman sitting in a car outside. Nicholas Mullen was found guilty of supplying accommodation, explosives and transport.[42] Similarly, Liam O'Dhuibhir and Damien McComb were convicted of conspiring to cause explosions after the Dyffed arms cache had been put under surveillance.[43]

Claims that the Act has been vital in securing convictions might be examined in two cases. One is described by Viscount Colville and involved a dozen or so suspects arrested and detained in Scotland over a period of a week, ten of whom were charged with aiding the U.V.F.[44] It has been conceded in chapter 8 that normal arrest provisions in Scotland are very restrictive and may justify extra powers, though the same arguments do not apply in England. The second case was the prosecution of Cullen, McCann and Shanahan – 'the Winchester Three' – for conspiring to murder the then Secretary of State, Tom King, at his home in Wiltshire.[45] The arrest powers under the Act were said to be vital because they allowed the police to intervene at an early stage before a real danger to life had arisen and also before a firm suspicion of any concrete offence had been established. It should be emphasised that the convictions were overturned on appeal because of prejudicial statements by King and Lord Denning.[46] Even assuming the conviction had not been overturned, it might be questioned whether the Act was as indispensable as claimed. Being discovered in hiding in the property of a wealthy person (such as King) could found suspicions of burglary or theft (both arrestable offences). The fact that the intruders wore camouflage jackets and had Irish accents could lead to (perhaps weak) suspicions in the circumstances of conspiracy to murder or cause explosions (both arrestable offences). Thereafter, was there really any need for five days of fruitless interrogation under the Prevention of Terrorism Act rather than four days under the Police and Criminal Evidence Act?

This survey of terrorist prosecutions since November 1974 confirms that the criminal justice system has taken its toll.[47] Yet most of the successes were attributable to chance, routine police work and terrorist incompetence. The special powers and port controls have been a contributory element in some cases but have rarely been the decisive factor.

Exclusion under Part II of the Act is of course equally supposed to remove terrorist threats. However, there is scant evidence in the foregoing cases that any of the various bands mentioned were disrupted by the removal of members of their team. It follows that police interest in exclusion has declined and the sounder method of evidence-gathering with a view to prosecution has been preferred.

The final factor which may have abated terrorism in Britain since 1974 may be a refinement in I.R.A. tactics. It was evident by the middle of the last decade that even the most menacing campaign of violence would not produce the downfall of a British Government because of its Irish policy. Thus, as there seems no immediate prospect of fundamental political gains from widespread terrorism in Britain, the scale of operations outside Ireland has probably been deliberately reduced. In common with prosecutions, the Prevention of Terrorism Acts may have had some influence on this strategic adaptation, for, by December 1978, the I.R.A. admitted (and the Metropolitan Police Special Branch have likewise claimed) that it was experiencing 'logistical problems' in Britain.[48] However, these have not prevented a substantial campaign in 1989 and 1990, so surely more decisive in encouraging a change of tactics were political rather than military calculations.

In conclusion, the Prevention of Terrorism Acts (mainly in the form of their special policing powers) have achieved some preventive influence over terrorism in Britain. However, it is probably mistaken to believe that legislation has been the main inhibitor.

(b) Prevention in Northern Ireland

It is impossible to describe in the space available the 31,346 shootings, well over 8,000 explosions, 2,871 deaths and 31,300 injuries attributable to terrorism or its suppression in Northern Ireland between 1971 and 1990.[49] However, in outline, the highest number of incidents was in 1972, and there followed a steady decline until about 1977, since when the annual totals have been fairly static and represent mainly attacks by Republicans on the security forces. These observations do not suggest that the Prevention of Terrorism Acts have significantly restrained violence either in 1974, when first passed, or in 1976 when section 14 was fully activated. Consequently, explanations must be sought elsewhere for the decline described.

Some of the alternative influences have probably been the same as for Britain, especially an increase in police expertise (and numerical strength)[50] and an evolution of terrorist tactics towards a greater emphasis on State-related targets. Other considerations may be indigenous to Northern Ireland. In particular, account must be taken of the impact of the Northern Ireland (Emergency Provisions) Acts 1973–91. By comparison, only the arrest power in the Prevention of Terrorism Acts plays an important role, while exclusion and the port controls are hardly utilised at all. In any event, a more crucial determinant of the number of persons charged has been the switch at the end of 1975 from a military security to a criminalisation policy.[51]

(c) Control in Britain

Another basis on which to judge the Prevention of Terrorism Acts is to consider whether they would have helped to deal effectively with terrorism which has taken place. This entails consideration both of convictions under the Acts and of convictions under other offences but with the assistance of the Acts.

The latter point has already been examined, and it was concluded that most terrorists have been apprehended since 1974 largely without the crutch of special provisions. However, it was also inferred that the special policing powers were occasionally helpful. On the other hand, proscription and exclusion probably make police work more difficult, the former by encouraging secrecy, the latter by removing suspects from known haunts and contacts.

The numbers and outcomes in terms of sentences of prosecutions for offences under the Prevention of Terrorism Acts signify that they are not an important element in the control of terrorism. Membership is a dead-letter, and withholding information is an infrequent charge.

(d)   Control in Northern Ireland

By far the most important element of the Act used to control terrorism in Northern Ireland is section 14. However, evidence as to its modest influence has already been adduced. As for prosecutions under the Act, withholding information has been employed against a significant number of defendants, but two considerations undermine its value. Firstly, most charges could alternatively have been formulated under section 5(1) of the Criminal Law Act (Northern Ireland) 1967. Secondly, the offence is usually invoked against persons on the edge, or even victims, of terrorism.

(e)   Prevention and control in Continental Europe

Two questions arise in connection with the upsurge in incidents in Western Europe since 1986: has the Prevention of Terrorism Act in any way thwarted the attacks; and has the impact of the Act at home prompted terrorism abroad?

As for the first question, the successes of the security forces may be attributable to three factors. Most important is good intelligence. An example concerns the attempted bombing at Gibraltar in 1988 by McCann, Savage and Farrell, who had been successfully tracked to Spain and recognised in Gibraltar. The background information was far from perfect, as it was mistakenly believed that a bomb had been planted and could be detonated by remote control. These errors were accepted by the coroner's jury as genuine and reasonable, and so the killings of the three by S.A.S. soldiers were categorised as justifiable.[52] Intelligence sources were probably also responsible for the detention of a Loyalist group which attempted to obtain weapons from the South African embassy in Paris; three members were convicted, and three diplomats each were expelled by France and Britain.[53] The crew of the *Eksund*, delivering arms from Libya to the I.R.A., were also carefully monitored and intercepted off France.[54] Suspected terrorists in Western Europe have also been apprehended through border checks and port controls, for example by the French police at Le Havre,[55] by the German police at the Dutch border[56] and by the Irish police at Rosslare.[57] A third response has been to improve physical security at British military facilities and to increase the state of alert.[58] In summary, there is again evidence that border controls are significant, and those in the Prevention of Terrorism Act may have assisted. However, other factors are also important, such as chance, which played a large part in the arrest of some suspects (later acquitted) for shooting two Australians in Roermond in 1990.[59]

Finally, do I.R.A. activities outside the British Isles bear testimony to tight security in Britain engendered by the Prevention of Terrorism Act? It would seem that Western Europe may offer safer travel routes, but this gain should be balanced against the greater difficulties of supply, fitting into the local community and finding suitable targets. Accordingly, political calculations, such as the demonstration of adaptability and the creation of tension in the British Army, may be more important factors. In so far as the Act has persuaded the I.R.A. to shift its attention, the effect is, of course, displacement rather than prevention and so hardly amounts to an unadulterated success.

3 Negative considerations

The second method of appraising the Prevention of Terrorism Acts is to determine whether any goal the Act has achieved or will achieve could be secured by the regular law.

(a) Prevention

Can it firstly be maintained that the regular law adequately prevents terrorism? This is an important question, since Governments have frequently claimed that the terrible beauty of the Prevention of Terrorism Acts is that they are not concerned with the detention and conviction of ordinary criminals but with pre-empting the extraordinarily dangerous activity of terrorism.[60] The response to this assertion must be that it is rather optimistic in regard to the efficacy of the Acts and rather pessimistic in regard to that of the regular law.

As for the former, the capacity of the Prevention of Terrorism Acts has been found to be undistinguished. As for the latter, it must be conceded that the threat of punishment may not deeply impress highly motivated terrorists. It is also possible that terrorist groups do not greet the conviction of a few members with unbridled dismay, since imprisonment provides fresh opportunities for protest and disruption. However, the high probability of detection and conviction of talented personnel on a large scale is presumably to be avoided, so, to the extent it can be shown likely by the operation of the regular law, it must have some inhibiting effect. The cases discussed earlier demonstrate that many terrorists operating in Britain have been imprisoned and that this has been achieved largely by the use of regular methods and offences. Only in Northern Ireland can it convincingly be claimed that the normal laws are overwhelmed by terrorism and that the Prevention of Terrorism and Emergency Provisions Acts are a necessary riposte.[61]

(b) Control

Similar verdicts may be reached on the ability of the regular law to deal with terrorism already inflicted. Special measures may have been an un-

avoidable supplement in Northern Ireland, but there are many examples
of terrorists in Britain being captured before November 1974. While this
implies that the Prevention of Terrorism Act is far from vital, it does not
prove that it is completely irrelevant. Its true value might be better measured
by a closer scrutiny of some of the important prosecutions in Britain
before November 1974.

The first important conviction[62] concerned the Aldershot car-bombing in
1972.[63] The car involved was traced to Francis Kissane, whilst Michael
Duignan was arrested in a London street because he was carrying a
suspicious holdall, later found to contain a gun. Statements by them led
to Noel Jenkinson, a search of whose garage produced two bombs, on the
basis of which he was convicted of murder. Kissane and Duignan were
found guilty of relatively minor preparatory offences.

Another early coup was the capture of Dolours Price and others, who
had planted car-bombs in London in March 1973.[64] Detection was mainly
attributable to assiduous police work. Special Branch officers, already on
the alert at Heathrow Airport because of fears of a response to the Border
Poll in Northern Ireland, detained the group after they aroused suspicion
by giving false identities and by possessing consecutive ticket numbers.
During the subsequent interviews, some members confessed and implicated
the others. The conclusion to be drawn is that special port controls and
powers of interrogation could have been helpful in this case, and, though
some legal measures were relevant before November 1974, the Prevention
of Terrorism Act has the advantage of granting more definite, formal and
wider provisions. The same points applied in the case of Judith Ward, who
was convicted in 1974 for handling a bomb planted on an Army coach in
which twelve passengers were killed.[65] Ward was also convicted of bombings
at Euston station and the Latimer Defence College, Buckinghamshire. Her
arrest at Liverpool en route to Northern Ireland was prompted because
she was staring at a policeman, and she made a confession during her
interrogation. The Prevention of Terrorism Act could have provided a
sounder footing for the police's action, but this case gives rise to concern
because of the unstable character of Ward and the dubious quality of
forensic evidence in view of which an appeal is pending.

Around the same time, there were a number of prosecutions involving
I.R.A. volunteers who had been living in England for some years. One
such case[66] involved a squad in Coventry, including Father Fell, Stagg,
Lynch and Rush.[67] All were convicted of conspiring to cause criminal
damage. Fell and Stagg were additionally found guilty under section 2 of
the Public Order Act 1936 and Lynch of possessing articles with intent to
destroy property. It is noticeable that not all of the members could be
charged with managing the group contrary to section 2, whereas they
would now be charged with belonging to a proscribed organisation.

However, the extra count would have made little difference, since it would have had to be founded upon the same preparations, for which Lynch was sentenced to ten years' imprisonment (the same as Stagg) and Rush to seven years'.

One of the earliest prosecutions of full-time I.R.A. units in Britain whose schemes had reached fruition concerned two gangs (with some cross-membership) in Manchester and Birmingham.[68] The police breakthrough came when, during a lecture on bomb-making at a house in Manchester, one of the students 'made the mistake of smoking . . .'.[69] An explosion followed, and the instructor, Byrne, had to be taken to hospital, where traces of explosives were found. Two associates were arrested at the ferry terminal at Holyhead (again confirming the value of port checks), others were found in Birmingham.

Two alleged London I.R.A. teams were also apprehended by routine police investigations.[70] First, McFadden, Cunningham and six others, who perpetrated several attacks in early 1974, were stumbled upon when they squatted in a house in Maidenhead and the estate agents called the police. To their surprise, the officers found bomb-making equipment and were able to arrest those involved.[71]

The second alleged group, Hill, Conlon, Armstrong and Richardson – 'the Guildford Four' – were convicted of causing explosions at public houses in Guildford and Woolwich in October and November 1974. They were initially detected when, while visiting Belfast, statements said to be made by Hill came to the attention of the security forces.[72] Once one member had been identified, information against the remainder came through his interrogation after the first ever arrest under section 14. An appeal against conviction failed in 1977, although Dowd and some members of the Balcombe Street gang had by then convincingly claimed responsibility.[73] Hill's confessions also prompted the arrest of Anne Maguire, his aunt, who had allegedly provided instruction in bomb-making. Six relatives and friends were also eventually convicted of explosives offences, principally on the basis of forensic tests, and the Court of Appeal confirmed the verdicts in 1977.[74] The Guildford and Maguire cases continued to create disquiet,[75] and the Home Secretary referred the former back to the Court of Appeal in 1989. The disturbing outcome was the discovery that the Surrey detectives had in 1974 fabricated incriminating statements and suppressed possible exculpatory evidence, so the convictions were quashed.[76] Both the Guildford and Maguire cases are currently being studied by a Commission headed by Lord Justice May[77] and the Court of Appeal has also quashed the Maguire convictions as unsupportable.[78] The subsequent revelations in both cases have wide-ranging implications for the criminal justice system and especially the way it handles alleged miscarriages of justice. These issues go well beyond the scope of this study.[79] As far as the

Prevention of Terrorism Act is concerned, the two cases certainly give pause for thought concerning the desirability of a prolonged period of isolated detention and also clearly demonstrate an urgent need for fuller recording of any interview.

Finally, I.R.A. activities in the Midlands were also counteracted before the advent of the Prevention of Terrorism Acts. In particular,[80] those thought to be responsible for the Birmingham pub bombings were apprehended when five people were intercepted at Heysham en route for Belfast and were convicted along with four others subsequently arrested in Birmingham.[81] However, the evidence against the 'Birmingham Six', who had been convicted of murder, was disputed. Thus, their confessions were allegedly beaten out of them, forensic tests were said to be unreliable and remaining evidence all highly circumstantial. Having been refused leave to appeal in 1976,[82] the Six resorted to the civil courts, but their actions for damages for assault against the police and prison authorities were eventually blocked as an abuse of process.[83] New evidence[84] was then presented on a referral back to the Court of Appeal in 1988, but the convictions were upheld.[85] However, further revelations about police fabrication of statements and the uncertain quality of the forensic evidence prompted another referral to the Court of Appeal which, in March 1991, resulted in the quashing of six convictions.[86] A Royal Commission has been established to investigate the disturbing implications for the criminal justice process.

From this lengthy list of prosecutions, the control of terrorism in Britain was in full swing well before the Prevention of Terrorism Acts were invented and could have continued without their help. However, some of the cases suggest that extensive powers of arrest and interrogation and port controls have paid dividends. In these respects, the Acts may be helpful by expressly conferring such powers in clear terms, though over-generosity in drafting has had its price. By contrast, remaining parts of the Acts, including proscription, exclusion and special offences, appear to be of negligible application.

4 Conclusions

(a) A final assessment

The prevention and control of terrorism did not commence with the Prevention of Terrorism Acts or significantly alter in nature thereafter. In Britain, the regular law had already secured much success and has continued to do so. It is, therefore, hardly surprising that the Metropolitan Police Commissioner of the day has since revealed that the Act 'was not sought by the police . . .'.[87] Similarly, special measures had been operating in Northern Ireland for decades, and the Prevention of Terrorism Acts added little. Nevertheless, two positive claims on behalf of the Acts should be finally assessed.

The first is that they have helped to catch or convict terrorists. From the evidence presented in this chapter, the special policing powers have been helpful, though many of their advantages are now attainable under the Police and Criminal Evidence legislation.

The second claim is that the Acts (especially the port controls) have influenced terrorists to curtail their activities. There has indeed been a reduction in Irish terrorism in Britain, but any successes must be put in perspective. Account must be taken of displacement, for example to Continental Europe. In any event, it has been argued that political calculations as much as military strategy curtailed the I.R.A.'s campaign in England. Finally, the change has hardly been decisive; even official analysts believe that I.R.A. activities can continue for the foreseeable future.[88]

Supporters of the Acts also suggest a number of more symbolic benefits. One is that the Acts help, especially by proscription, to criminalise Irish Republicanism. However, the impact of prosecutions for homicides and explosives offences is surely greater, and, as described earlier, the emphasis upon this role of the criminal justice system may explain why damaging miscarriages of justice have arisen. In any event, perceptions have not been affected in Northern Ireland.[89] Another symbolic role is the distancing of Irish troubles from British public life, especially through exclusion. Again, other mechanisms, such as media censorship, are probably more important, and one wonders whether such a strategy is consistent with the long-term health of the union between Britain and Northern Ireland. The final symbolic role – 'so that the Government can be seen to be doing something'[90] – attended the birth of the Acts and does seem to remain characteristic.

Assertions that the Prevention of Terrorism Act is 'increasingly useful and necessary for the police' or 'the most powerful weapon in our counter-terrorism armoury'[91] are misplaced. The strengthening of normal police powers and the declining use of the Act's special provisions suggest a diminished importance to the point where redundancy might be declared. At least if the Acts are indeed largely peripheral in effect, this also means that the more strident criticisms of them are misplaced.[92] However, it is fair to note that the provisions which are furthest divorced from regular law, proscription and exclusion, appear the least important. Counter-terrorism measures do not necessarily prosper in proportion to their severity, and less eye-catching reforms, especially to police powers, are in reality more vital.

Aside from their contribution to miscarriages of justice, as described, how else have the Prevention of Terrorism Acts been pernicious? One charge against them is 'seepage'[93] in two ways. The first, the application of the Acts to 'ordinary' criminals, has been a common complaint in Northern Ireland.[94] A more insidious problem is that the Acts have formed models for 'normal' laws. Assuming that the Acts cannot now themselves be classified as 'normal', this danger has largely been averted to date, and the attitude of British lawyers and legislators has all too often been one of total ignorance or indifference rather than zealous imitation. It is true that the Police and Criminal Evidence legislation has tended to converge towards the Prevention of Terrorism Acts. However, it is submitted that this trend has been caused by the independent perception that policing by consent is no longer as feasible as it once was, especially as some ethnic minorities in Britain to some degree mirror the alienation experienced by Nationalists in Northern Ireland.[95] It follows that there was virtually no mention of special legislation in the Philips Royal Commission on Criminal Procedure.[96] A brief visit by some Commissioners was arranged to observe the workings of the police interrogation centres in the light of the Bennett Report.[97] However, in so far as the Bennett regime was adopted in England and Wales, one could argue that this seepage was beneficial rather than pernicious, since it secured greater safeguards for the accused than previously existed. Rather than seeking out legislative seepage, it is submitted that the experience of the Northern Ireland troubles has been far more influential in the fields of police training, tactics and weaponry, especially in response to public disorder.[98] Yet even this form of imitation should not be exaggerated, as it cannot realistically be said that British forces have adopted the R.U.C. as their role-model. Finally, while the Prevention of Terrorism Acts may not have seeped into common usage, other anti-terrorist laws have had a wider impact, including the power to take mouth swabs in Schedule 14 of the Criminal Justice Act 1988 (now in the Police and Criminal Evidence (Northern Ireland) Order 1989) and the modifications to the right to silence in the Criminal Evidence (Northern Ireland) Order 1988. Both measures were direct responses to horrific terrorist attacks on soldiers in Lisburn in June 1988 and Omagh in August 1988.[99] Yet neither is confined to terrorist cases, and a variety of other offenders is covered. Accordingly, in this third form of seepage, terrorism is being used as the spur to legislative action, but the legislative reaction is general in its terms. Even worse, these two examples of seepage in Northern Ireland threaten to contaminate British law.[100]

(b) Counter-terrorism reconsidered

One might forgive Parliament for its haste in 1974, which resulted in the birth of an Act useful to the protection of life only in patches and dangerous to liberty in others. One might feel less magnanimous that later versions lamentably failed to venture much beyond the confines of the established code. This raises the issue of what would have been the correct legislative course to have taken. Chapter 13 will attempt a response, once a description has been provided of anti-terrorist measures outside the Acts.

Notes

1   Shackleton Report, para. 160; Jellicoe Report, para. 1; Colville Report, para. 1.1.2.

2   See: Shackleton Report, para. 116; Colville Report, para. 3.1.2.

3   For a history of the earlier period, see chs. 3 and 4.

4   See: *Times* 28 November 1975 p. 1.

5   See: *Times* 21 November 1978 p. 1; *Daily Telegraph* 18 January 1979 p. 1.

6   See: *Times* 14 December 1983 p. 2.

7   See: *Daily Telegraph* 31 March 1979 pp. 1, 36; M. Dillon, *The Dirty War* (1990), ch. 11

8   See: *Times* 12 May 1982 p. 3.

9   See: *Times* 12 October 1981 pp. 1, 2; *Sunday Times* 18 October 1981 p. 1; *Times* 27 October 1981 p. 1; *Sunday Times* 15 November 1981 p. 1.

10   See: *Times* 21 July 1982 pp. 1, 26.

11   See: *Times* 19 February 1991 pp. 1, 3.

12   See: *Times* 13 October 1984 p. 1, 14 November p. 1; Report by John Hoddinott (H.C. Debs. Vol. 71 cols. 864–66 22 January 1985).

13   See: *Times* 8 March 1989 p. 1.

14   See: *Times* 16 April 1987 p. 1; 18 April p. 1; 21 April p. 2.

15   See: *Times* 14 June 1990 pp. 1, 3; 31 July 1990 p. 1; 20 September 1990 p. 1, 8 February 1991 pp. 1, 2.

16   See: *Times* 2 August 1988 p. 1.

17   See: *Times* 21 February 1989 pp. 1, 24.

18   See: *Times* 23 September 1989 pp. 1, 2; 20 October p. 6.

19   See: *Times* 20 November 1989 pp. 1, 24.

20   See: *Times* 2 June 1990 p. 1.

21   See: *Times* 13 November 1985 p. 1.

22   See: *Times* 22 December 1988 p. 1.

23   See: *Times* 12 October 1989 p. 2.

24   See: *Times* 23 October 1989 pp. 1, 3.

25   See: R. Allason, *The Branch* (1983) p. 166.

26   B. Woffinden, *Miscarriages of Justice* (2nd ed., 1989). See also: *R.* v. *Latimer* [1988] 11 N.I.J.B. 11.

27   See: H. Packer, *The Limits of the Criminal Sanction* (1969); M. King, *The Framework of Criminal Justice* (1981).

28   See: *Times* 8 May 1976 p. 3.

29   See: *Times* 27 November 1976 p. 3.

30   See: *Times* 12 May 1976 pp. 1, 4. Dowd admitted involvement with I.R.A. groups in London. See: P. Bishop and E. Mallie, *The Provisional I.R.A.* (1987) pp. 202, 203.

31   See: *Times* 10 February 1977 pp. 1, 2; 11 February p. 1.

32   See: *Times* 23 April 1976 pp. 1, 3; 4 July 1977 p. 4.

33   *R.* v. *Quinn* (1990) *Times* 31 March.

34   *Quinn* v. *Robinson* 783 F. 2d 766 (1986).

35   Tuite escaped but was later convicted in the Republic: *Times* 17 December 1980 p. 1, 6 March 1982 p. 2, 8 March 1982 p. 2, 4 May 1983 pp. 1, 3. Another

associate, John Gabriel McComb, was also convicted (*R.* v. *Lambeth Met. Stipendiary Magistrate, ex p. McComb* [1983] 1 Q.B. 551; *Times* 27 May 1983 p. 3).

36 See: T.P. Coogan, *The I.R.A.* (3rd ed., 1987) pp. 647–9.

37 See: *Times* 28 October 1987 pp. 1, 3; *R.* v. *Ellis, Times* 31 October 1991 pp. 1, 3.

38 See: *Times* 11–22 June 1986 (main trial), *R.* v. *Anderson* [1988] 2 W.L.R. 1017 (appeal).

39 See: *Times* 5–7 February 1986.

40 See: *Times* 21 June 1988 pp. 1, 14.

41 See: *R.* v. *O'Loughlin and McLaughlin* [1988] 3 All E.R. 431; *Times* 26 November 1986 pp. 1, 20.

42 See: *Times* 1 May 1990 p. 3, 7 June 1990 p. 1. Appeal refused: *Guardian* 22 March 1991 p. 2.

43 See: *Times* 7 December 1990 pp. 1, 3.

44 Appendix C; *H.M. Advocate* v. *Copeland* 1987 S.C.C.R. 232. See ch. 5 n. 94.

45 See: *Times* 29 October 1988 p. 1; B. Woffinden, 'The case of the Winchester Three' (1990) 140 *N.L.J.* 164.

46 (1990) *Times* 1 May.

47 There was a clear-up rate of 68 per cent for the 130 terrorist incidents between 1973 and 1977: Allason, *op. cit.* p. 164.

48 *Times* 19 December 1978 p. 1; H.L. Select Committee on the European Communities, *1992* (1988–89 H.L. 90) Minutes of Evidence p. 171.

49 Source: Northern Ireland Office. See also P.V.L.I. ch. 7.

50 See: Walker, 'Police and community in Northern Ireland' (1990) 41 *N.I.L.Q.* 105.

51 See: K. Boyle, T. Hadden and P. Hillyard, *Law and State* (1975) pp. 41–3; Ministerial Committee on Law and Order (H.C. Debs. Vol. 914 cols. 880–5 2 July 1976, Mr. Rees); Baker Report, paras. 33, 34; P. Hillyard, 'The normalisation of special powers' in P. Scraton (ed.), *Law, Order and the Authoritarian State* (1987).

52 See: *Times* 7–10 March 1988 (shooting); 6 September–1 October 1988 (inquest); J. Adams, R. Morgan and A. Bambridge, *Ambush* (1988) chs. 8–11; H. Kitchen, *The Gibraltar Report* (1989); R. Murray, *The S.A.S. in Ireland* (1990).

53 Cases of *Little et al., Times* 25 April 1989 p. 1, 6 May p. 1, 29 October 1991 p. 2.

54 Cases of *Hopkins et al., Times* 7 March 1991 pp. 1, 2, 30 July p. 5.

55 Case of Robert Versteegh, *Times* 1 July 1988 p. 9.

56 See: *Times* 2 September 1988 p. 1.

57 See: *Times* 15 July 1989 p. 1. This interception sparked further arrests in France: *Times* 18 July 1989 pp. 1, 22.

58 Bombs have since been spotted: *Times* 20 June 1989 p. 2, 29 August p. 1, 5 May 1990 pp. 1, 2.

59 Cases of *Harte et al., Times* 3 April 1991 pp. 1, 3, 6 July p. 3.

60 See: H.C. Debs. Vol. 946 col. 594 15 March 1978, Mr. Rees.

61 See: Diplock Report, ch. 3; Gardiner Report, ch. 1; Baker Report, paras. 28–32.

62 See also: Allason, *op. cit.* p. 154 (case of Petticrew and others, *Times* 13 June 1972, p. 4).

63 See: *Times* 15 November 1972 pp. 1, 2.

64 See: *Times* 1 November 1973 pp. 1, 2, 18. Bishop and Mallie (*op. cit.* pp. 198–9) also allege a tip-off. Three defendants appealed against sentence: *Times* 2 August 1991 p. 3.

65 See: *Times* 5 November 1974 p. 4.

66 See also: R. v. *Colley* and others (1973) *Times* 23 October p. 2; R. v. *Mealey and others* (1973) *Times* 20 November 1973 p. 7, 7 December 1973 p. 5, 30 July 1974 p. 11; R. v. *O'Brien* (1974) 59 Cr. App. R. 222, G. Robertson, *Reluctant Judas* (1976).

67 See: *Times* 9 October 1973 p. 2, 2 November p. 11; [1975] Crim. L.R. 673.

68 R. v. *Byrne and others* (1976) 62 Cr. App. R. 159; R. v. *Coughlan and others* (1976) 63 Cr. App. R. 37.

69 *Loc. cit.* at p. 160 *per* Lawton L.J.

70 See also: R. v. *Joseph John Coughlan* (1977) 64 Cr. App. R. 11.

71 See: *Times* 7 January 1975 p. 2, 11 January p. 2, 19 March p. 4, (1976) 62 Cr. App. R. 187. Compare: R. v. *Gallagher* [1974] 1 W.L.R. 1204.

72 See: *Times* 17 September 1975 p. 1, 23 October pp. 1, 5.

73 See: *Times* 28 February 1977 p. 2.

74 See: *Times* 5 March 1976 p. 1. The appeal was not reported.

75 See: R. Kee, *Trial and Error* (1986); Lords Devlin and Scarman, 'Justice and the Guildford Four' (1988) *Times* 30 November p. 16; G. McKee and R. Franey, *Time Bombs* (1988).

76 R. v. *Richardson and others* (1989) *Times* 20 October. Hill awaits a separate appeal relating to a murder in Northern Ireland. See: G. Conlon, *Proved Innocent* (1990); P. Hill and R. Bennett, *Stolen Years* (1990).

77 See: Interim Report (1989–90 H.C. 556).

78 See: (1990) *Times* 28 June.

79 See: Home Affairs Committee, 'Miscarriages of justice' (1981–82 H.C. 421); Justice, *Miscarriages of Justice* (1989); A. Scrivener, 'The Guildford Four' (1989) *Counsel* November p. 15; B. Hilliard 'The time-bomb goes off' (1989) 97 *Police Rev.* 2174.

80 See also: R. v. *McLaughlin* (1975) *Times* 12 March p. 2.

81 R. v. *Hill and others* (1975) *Times* 16 August pp. 1, 2. Six were convicted of murder, three of lesser offences. It is also alleged that one of the defendants acted as an informant.

82 See: *Times* 31 March 1976 p. 9.

83 *Hunter* v. *Chief Constable of the West Midlands* [1981] 3 W.L.R. 906.

84 See: J. Yahuda, 'The Birmingham Bombers' (1988) 152 *J.P.* 230; R. Smith, 'Judging the courts' (1988) March *L.A.G.* 6; C. Mullin, *Error of Judgment* (2nd ed., 1990).

85 R. v. *Callaghan* [1988] 1 W.L.R. 1; (1988) *Times* 29 January p. 5; (1988) 88 Cr. App. R. 40. See D. Dunne, *The Birmingham Six* (2nd ed., 1989).

86 R. v. *McIlkenney* (1991) *Times* 1 April.

87 Sir R. Mark, *In the Office of Constable* (1976) p. 173. See also: H.C. Debs. Vol. 1 col. 361 18 March 1981, Mr. Lyon. But, by 1983, the Home Secretary reported that the police 'strongly favour renewal of the Act' (H.C. Debs. Vol. 38 col. 570 7 March 1983).

88 Glover Report, *loc. cit.* App. 4 para. 3.

89 See: P. Hillyard, 'Political and social dimensions of emergency law' in A. Jennings (ed.), *Justice under Fire* (2nd ed., 1990) p. 202.

90 B. Dickson, 'The Prevention of Terrorism Act 1989' (1989) 40 *N.I.L.Q.* 250 at p. 267.

91 P. Wilkinson, 'British policy on terrorism' in J. Lodge (ed.), *The Threat of Terrorism* (1988) p. 44; H.L. Select Committee on the European Communities, *loc. cit.* p. 172.

92 Compare: L.H. Leigh, *Police Powers in England and Wales* (1975) p. 20; K. Kelly, *The Longest War* (1982) p. 227.

93 For past examples, see: P. O'Higgins, 'English law and the Irish question' (1966) 1 *Ir. Jur.* 59.

94 Compare: D.P.J. Walsh, *The Use and Abuse of Emergency Legislation in Northern Ireland* (1983); P.V.L.I. pp. 195–8. The Home Office has no plans to extend the Act: Home Affairs Committee, *Practical Police Cooperation in the European Communities* (1989–90 H.C. 363) para. 129.

95 Compare: P. Hillyard, 'The normalisation of special powers' in P. Scraton (ed.), *Law, Order and the Authoritarian State* (1987) pp. 279, 304, 307; J. Hayes and P. O'Higgins (eds.), *Lessons from Northern Ireland* (1990) p. 100.

96 Cmnd. 8091, 1981.

97 *Report of the Committee of Inquiry into Police Interrogation Procedures in Northern Ireland* (Cmnd. 7497, 1979).

98 See: G. Northam, *Shooting in the Dark* (1988).

99 See: *Times* 17 June 1988 p. 1, 22 August p. 1.

100 See H.C. Debs. Vol. 135 col. 653 16 June 1988; *Report of the Working Group on the Right of Silence* (1989).

Chapter 12

Other relevant laws against terrorism

In the light of the assertion in the previous chapter that the legal restraint of terrorism neither commenced with, nor is confined to the Prevention of Terrorism Acts, other relevant laws will now be considered. Two warnings should be noted. Firstly, it is intended to describe only those measures which are expressly designed to combat terrorism; 'normal' powers and offences which can operate as alternatives to the Acts have been rehearsed in earlier chapters. Secondly, the following categorisation into domestic and foreign terrorism reflects the origins and main focus of each measure, but both sources of terrorism may be covered in all cases.

1 Domestic terrorism

(a) Explosives offences

Perhaps the most important legal response to domestic terrorism (originally by Fenians and anarchists) outside the Prevention of Terrorisms Acts is the Explosive Substances Act 1883.[1] The Act[2] is centred around four offences.

First, by section 2:[3]

A person who in the United Kingdom or (being a citizen of the United Kingdom and Colonies) in the Republic of Ireland unlawfully and maliciously causes by any explosive substance an explosion of a nature likely to endanger life or to cause serious injury to property shall, whether any injury to person or property has been actually caused or not, be guilty of an offence and on conviction on indictment shall be liable to imprisonment for life.

Participation at an earlier stage is caught by section 3(1):[4]

A person who in the United Kingdom or a dependency or (being a citizen of the United Kingdom and Colonies) elsewhere unlawfully and maliciously –
(a) does any act with intent to cause, or conspires to cause, by an explosive substance an explosion of a nature likely to endanger life, or to cause serious injury to property, whether in the United Kingdom or the Republic of Ireland, or

(b) makes or has in his possession or under his control an explosive substance with intent by means thereof to endanger life or cause serious injury to property, whether in the United Kingdom or the Republic of Ireland, or to enable any other person so to do,
shall whether any explosion does or does not take place, and whether any injury to person or property is actually caused or not, be guilty of an offence and on conviction on indictment shall be liable to imprisonment for life, and the explosive substance shall be forfeited.

This offence differs from section 2 in that no explosion need occur, nor need the threat to life or property be immediate,[5] thereby allowing timely intervention by the police.

Section 4(1) goes a step further:[6]

Any person who makes or knowingly has in his possession or under his control any explosive substance, under such circumstances as to give rise to a reasonable suspicion that he is not making it or does not have it in his possession or under his control for a lawful object, shall, unless he can show that he made it or had it in his possession or under his control for a lawful object, be guilty of [an offence]. . . .

'Explosive substances' include all their ingredients and any apparatus used for causing or aiding an explosion.[7] However, most possessors escape prosecution by virtue of their 'lawful object'[8] or by the Attorney General refusing consent to proceedings under section 7. Despite these restraints, section 4 remains unduly vague and should be rendered more precise by requiring proof of a reasonable suspicion of possession, not for any unlawful purposes, but only for purposes unlawful under sections 2 and 3.[9] This modified version would remain distinct from section 3(b) because it would not demand specific proof as to intent.

Finally, the extra-territorial effects of the Act[10] should comprehend activities committed anywhere relating to explosions perpetrated, planned or suspected in the United Kingdom or, perhaps, in any State which is a signatory to the European Convention on the Suppression of Terrorism.[11]

(b) Offences against the State

Offences such as treason and sedition have long been shaped by the threat of political violence and may feature three principal attractions compared to less venerable crimes. Firstly, they emphasise the seriousness of the conduct involved. Secondly, they have a wider sweep than more technical explosives or firearms offences. Thirdly, treason carries the death penalty, the merits of which will be considered in the next chapter.

Various headings of the Treason Act 1351[12] could apply to modern-day terrorists, such as compassing the death of specified members of the Royal Family[13] or adhering to the State's enemies in wartime.[14] However, the most apposite charge is where 'a man do levy war against our Lord the King in his realm'. A substantial campaign of terrorism can amount to 'an insurrection raised to reform some national grievance ... or for any ... purpose which usurps the Government in matters of a public and general nature'.[15] Moreover, while the levying of war traditionally required 'a forcible disturbance that is produced by a considerable number of persons',[16] trials in the late nineteenth century involving Fenian activities in England demonstrated that 'a mustering of forces or an irregular mass of men'[17] was no longer necessary and that a mere handful of rebels armed with modern munitions could levy war.[18] Consequently, overt acts of levying war can include causing explosions in public places or attacks on the security forces (as in some recent South African cases).[19] Even non-violent aid, such as supplying information and delivering messages to, or rousing support on behalf of, groups viewed as terroristic, was held to suffice in *S. v. Hogan*.[20]

Though the foregoing survey demonstrates the availability of high treason, many of the prosecutions in Ireland during the last century encountered difficulties. Not only were there considerable procedural complications,[21] but there were also doubts as to whether words alone could be treasonous.[22] Further, the mandatory death penalty was thought to deter guilty verdicts. Some of these problems were by-passed by section 3 of the Treason Felony Act 1848, which provides that:

If any person ... compass, imagine, invent, devise or intend to deprive or depose ... the Queen from the style honour, or royal name of the imperial crown of the United Kingdom ... or to levy war against her Majesty ... in her ... measures or counsels, or in order to put any force or constraint upon or in order to intimidate or overawe both Houses or either House of Parliament, or to move or stir any foreigner or stranger with force to invade the United Kingdom ... and such compassings, imaginations, inventions, devices, or intentions, or any of them, shall express, utter, or declare, by publishing any printing or writing ... by any overt act or deed, [s/he] ... shall be liable ... [to imprisonment for life or any shorter term]. ...

Both the first and second forms of treason felony have been interpreted widely. In *R. v. Dowling*,[23] it was decided that depriving the Queen of her title includes any attempt to substitute a new form of government or to dismember the United Kingdom, while the levying of war need only entail the use of force or intimidation against the State and not actual conflict. Consequently, proceedings have been brought successfully on a number of occasions in connection with terrorist activities. For example thirteen participants in an I.R.A. court-martial were convicted in Belfast in 1936,[24] and eight volunteers were imprisoned after an attack on Omagh Barracks in 1954.[25] More recently, Callinan, Quinn and Marcantonio, who had tried to recruit in Hyde Park volunteers for the 'Northern Ireland Minority

Defence Force' in 1972, were charged with treason felony, though this count was later dropped.[26]

One might next estimate the relevance of seditious offences, in other words, a publication conveying a seditious intention or a conspiracy to further by deed a seditious intention. A 'seditious intention' was defined in *R. v. Burns* by Cave J. as:[27]

an intention to bring into hatred or contempt, or to excite disaffection against the person of, Her Majesty, her heirs or successors, or the government and constitution of the United Kingdom, as by law established, or either House of Parliament, or the administration of justice, or to excite Her Majesty's subjects to attempt, otherwise than by lawful means, the alteration of any matter in Church or State by law established, or to raise discontent or disaffection amongst Her Majesty's subjects, or to promote feelings of ill-will or hostility between different classes of such subjects.

Though criticisms with a view to reformation or incitements to change by lawful means were in the same judgment held not to be seditious, such charges were not infrequently levelled against Irish politicians and publishers during the last century.[28] However, there have been only a couple of relevant examples since 1945. One arose in 1953, when Liam Kelly, leader of 'Saor Uladh', a paramilitary Nationalist organisation, was convicted in Northern Ireland of seditious libel.[29] Another was the case of Callinan and others, mentioned previously, in which two of the defendants were convicted of seditious libel. At the same time, although seditious offences appear applicable to terrorists,[30] their rarity in modern times results from various drawbacks, including the political associations of the offence and its uncertain nature. At least the latter impediment has been recently eased by the decision in *R. v. Bow St. Magistrates' Court, ex parte Choudhury*,[31] in which it was emphasised that the intention required extends to the incitement of violence and the disturbance of the constituted government.

Whatever the present relevance of treasonous and seditious offences, few would deny the need for reform as a prelude to any resurrection. Indeed, this course has been followed whenever the United Kingdom Government wished to utilise these crimes in wartime or colonial crises.[32] The Law Commission has likewise proposed the redrawing of treason and treason felony and favours the total abolition of seditious offences.[33] Most comparable jurisdictions have likewise either abolished or reformulated these crimes,[34] including the Republic of Ireland.[35]

Whether translated into contemporary idiom or not, it is doubtful whether revival would be worthwhile. Substitute charges, such as offences against the person and munitions offences, are adequate in scope and severity, create fewer dangers for 'robust political opposition'[36] and, though they do not carry the death penalty or imply the same unique condemnation, this may be to their advantage. As the Law Commission recognised:[37]

from the practical point of view it is normally found more expedient to charge ordinary criminal offences than to imply that importance is being attached to the activities by treating them as treasonable, or that there could be any political justification for the conduct, even in the mind of the offenders.

Thus, it is notable that the modernised versions in the Republic have rarely been invoked against terrorists and that the common law English offences were not laid even against the Brighton bombers. As the Attorney General explained:[38]

there are substantial problems in bringing a prosecution based on the language of a statute designed for the different circumstances of more than six centuries ago. The common law remedy of murder, coupled with legislation on explosives and firearms, has proved both appropriate and effective for all recent cases.

(c)   Other offences

Amongst other offences formulated partly against terrorists is the making of a bomb hoax. By section 51 of the Criminal Law Act 1977:[39]

(1)   A person who –
(a)   places any article in any place whatever; or
(b)   dispatches any article by post, rail or any other means whatever of sending things from one place to another,
with the intention (in either case) of inducing in some other person a belief that it is likely to explode or ignite and thereby cause personal injury or damage to property is guilty of an offence.
In this subsection 'article' includes substance.
(2)   A person who communicates any information which he knows or believes to be false to another person with the intention of inducing in him or any other person a false belief that a bomb or other thing liable to explode or ignite is present in any place or location whatever is guilty of an offence.

The *actus reus* is extremely broad, consequently 'the gist of the offences is the *mens rea*'.[40] The statutory provision supplants various less direct means of dealing with the problem (such as public nuisance, blackmail, wasting police time and threats to property),[41] though these alternatives (and breach of the peace) still prevail in Scotland.[42] The principal obstacle to the prosecution of hoaxers is the difficulty of detection.[43] Thus, most defendants to appear in court have been pranksters (often immature, drunk or both)[44] rather than sophisticated terrorists seeking to disrupt society,[45] though any bomb hoax runs the danger of masking a real bomb threat. Detection may eventually be helped by more sophisticated telephone exchange equipment which allows tracing; in the meantime, the penalties for the offence are to be increased.[46]

A related offence is food contamination contrary to section 38 of the Public Order Act 1986:[47]

(1) It is an offence for a person, with the intention –

(a) of causing public alarm or anxiety, or

(b) of causing injury to members of the public consuming or using the goods, or

(c) of causing economic loss to any person by reason of the goods being shunned by members of the public; or

(d) of causing economic loss to any person by reason of steps taken to avoid any such alarm or anxiety, injury or loss,

to contaminate or interfere with goods, or make it appear that goods have been contaminated or interfered with, or which appear to have been contaminated or interfered with, in a place where goods of that description are consumed, used, sold or otherwise supplied.'

It is also an offence to make threats or claims along these lines (section 38(2)) or to possess materials with a view to the commission of an offence (section 38(3)). Similar to bomb hoaxes, the intent of the perpetrator is all important. Thus, under subsection (1), the contamination need not actually be harmful, nor need the public in fact be alarmed; under subsection (2), a claim may be true, unless it amounts to a *bona fide* warning excused by subsection (5).

Section 38 responded to a small number of well-publicised incidents of consumer terrorism, a minority of which involved animal liberationists.[48] As in the case of bomb hoaxes, the preexisting law was felt to be inadequate, so it is odd that the offence applies in Northern Ireland but not Scotland, where offences such as breach of the peace, malicious mischief and extortion must suffice.[49] The difficulties of detection remain formidable, so a more effective counteraction has consisted of new packaging technology, stock records and consumer awareness.[50]

(d) Media controls

If the ultimate pointer to terroristic success in a democracy is the degree of public support which it attains, there is an inevitable interest in how the media portray both terrorists and the State. It is hardly surprising then that both have attempted to manipulate the media explicitly and indirectly. The perspective hereafter will concentrate on official interferences, though it will be considered whether any are justified by terrorist pressures.

(i) Indirect controls Government influence over the reporting and analysis of events has been pervasive and effective owing to the reliance of reporters upon official sources for their copy.[51] The result has been to mould the whole texture and context of information about violence in Ireland.[52] More specific instances of news management have also been detected,[53] especially amongst broadcasters. For example, both the B.B.C. and I.B.A. (succeeded now by the I.T.C.) adopted under pressure in 1971 the officially inspired policy that they should not maintain impartiality between the I.R.A. and

the security forces,[54] and ministerial displeasure in 1977 curtailed later reporting in *This Week* about the treatment of police detainees in Northern Ireland.[55] The spectre of governmental attack also inspired in 1971 stringent internal controls by way of a reference-up system. A typical situation by way of illustration is where a T.V. reporter wishes to interview a representative of the I.R.A. or Sinn Fein.[56]

As regards the B.B.C., the project must be submitted to the Editors of News and Current Affairs in Belfast and London, who must be convinced that the interview would be a 'unique and first opportunity'.[57] Approval by various superiors up to Assistant Director General is also required before an interview is recorded, following which there will be further discussion at top editorial level in Belfast and London to determine whether there is new material 'which the public needs to know'.[58] The result is that many programmes have been stopped, delayed or amended,[59] including at least three which contained interviews with terrorist representations. Most controversial was a B.B.C. *Real Lives* programme in 1985, 'At the Edge of the Union', in which Martin McGuiness (of Sinn Fein) participated. The interview was criticised by the Prime Minister as giving the 'oxygen of publicity' to terrorists,[60] and the Governors postponed its transmission because it lacked balance and the internal reference procedure had not been properly observed.[61]

Corresponding practices in the I.T.C. are governed by its Programme Code:[62]

Any plans for a programme item which explores and exposes the views of people who within Northern Ireland (or elsewhere within the British Isles) use or advocate violence or other criminal measures for the achievement of political ends must be referred to senior management before any arrangments for filming or videotaping are made. A producer should therefore not plan to record members of proscribed organisations, for example, members of the Provisional IRA or other paramilitary organisations, without the specific consent of the licensee's Chief Executive or most senior programme executive. . . .

In exceptional and unforeseen circumstances, it may be impossible for a reporting team to consult before recording such an item. Consultation with senior management is still essential to determine whether the item can still be transmitted.

Until the end of 1992 [broadcasters] are required to consult the I.T.C. on all proposals to record members of proscribed organisations before arrangements for filming or recording are made.

In the example given of a proposed interview with a terrorist, permission from the individual company and the I.T.C. will be granted or refused on the basis of 'all the political relevance' of the recording.[63] The outcome, as with the B.B.C., is that most footage of I.R.A. spokesmen has succumbed to these obstacles.[64]

Ominous evidence that the Government was becoming dissatisfied even with the tightest degree of self-control arose from its reaction to the broadcasting of 'Death on the Rock' about the Gibraltar shootings in 1988. The Foreign Secretary complained bitterly that the programme would prejudice the pending inquest and suffered from inaccuracies,[65] allegations rejected by the independent Windelsham-Rampton Report.[66]

(*ii*) *Explicit controls* Outright censorship has long been advocated[67] but has only gradually been imposed. Free expression about political violence in Northern Ireland has long been curtailed by the Incitement to Disaffection Act 1934,[68] restrictions on Irish demonstrations in Trafalgar Square[69] and the use of coercive powers to harass, or obtain information from, journalists.[70] More recently, restraint has been imposed by sections 2 and 18 of the Prevention of Terrorism Act, as already described. Once again, broadcasters have suffered the heaviest pressure.

External controls over the B.B.C. can be imposed under clause 13(4) of its Licence on written notice from the Home Secretary.[71] The issuance of such a notice was allegedly considered in 1972 in relation to a proposed discussion programme, *The Question of Ulster*, but, in the event, the Home Secretary contented himself with a public letter of criticism to the Chairman.[72] As regards commercial T.V., section 29(3) of the Broadcasting Act 1981 (now 1990 Act, section 10), remained equally dormant.[73] However, these powers were eventually exercised in November 1988 in response to some recent terrorist attacks and to alleged media misbehaviour (as in 'Death on the Rock').[74] The orders issued by the Home Secretary require the broadcasters to refrain from transmitting (by paragraph 1):[75]

any words spoken, whether in the course of an interview or discussion or otherwise, by a person who appears or is heard on the programme in which the matter is broadcast where
(a)   the person speaking the words represents or purports to represent a [specified organisation], or
(b)   the words support or solicit or invite support for such an organisation. . . .

The organisations specified in paragraph 2 are those proscribed under the Prevention of Terrorism Act and Northern Ireland (Emergency Provisions) Acts plus Sinn Fein, Republican Sinn Fein and the U.D.A. However, exemption is granted by paragraph 3 to words spoken:

(a)   in the course of proceedings in Parliament, or
(b)   by or in support of a candidate at a parliamentary European Parliamentary, or local elections pending that election.

The ban has been criticised on three levels: in detail, law and principle.

The inconsistencies and uncertainties in detail are evidenced by a number of clarifications which the Home Secretary has had to issue, though some highlighted rather than resolved the broadcasters' difficulties. For example,

it is now clear that the Government intends the ban to be applied retrospectively, even to figures of history, which caused Channel 4 to re-edit
The Troubles in 1989.[76] Again, the exemption for election broadcasts and
parliamentary debates does not extend to other events of public interest,
such as the proceedings of the European Parliament or local authorities.
Fictional representations are beyond the scope of the ban, but Irish 'rebel'
songs have been suppressed.[77] The meaning of 'represents' is especially
tricky. The speaker must be acting for the forbidden group rather than in
some other capacity. Thus, a Sinn Fein councillor may convey personal or
council views but not Sinn Fein policy, whether on terrorism or the repair
of local drains.[78] Similarly, a 'supporter' means one who supports the aims
and objectives of the group; opponents of the broadcasting ban are not per
se supporters, but the distinction may be hard to draw in practice.[79] Finally,
it is odd that the ban did not initially extend to satellite broadcasting, but
the Cable Authority did itself issue a similar directive.[80]

Some of these uncertainties might have been avoided if the ban had been
scrutinised before, rather than after, issuance. Indeed, a total absence of
parliamentary pre-notification or subsequent periodical review may be
counted as a further defect. In the light of all these problems, broadcasters
have coped with the ban by various stratagems. Most common has been
the voice-over; subtitles and preliminary warnings about the ban are not
often favoured, which may be further evidence of the broadcasters' timidity
in the face of governmental pressure.[81]

A legal assault on the ban has been mounted unsuccessfully in *R. v.
Secretary of State for the Home Department, ex parte Brind*.[82] Allegations
that the ban breached the European Convention were rejected as the
Convention was not applicable to the interpretation of delegated legislation
or executive action taken under lawful authority.[83] Complaints about the
disproportionality of the ban were equally ill-conceived, since no such
ground for challenge was recognised in English law or at least should be
applied in Brind's case. Irrationality was more appropriate but was not
sustainable. In the view of Lord Donaldson:[84]

Perhaps the most striking feature of the directives is how little they restrict the
supply of the 'oxygen of publicity' to the organisations specified in the directives.

Thus, the excessive or inconsistent nature of the ban was not so grave as
to render it ultra vires. Furthermore, the ban was found not to be illegal
because it conflicted with the broadcasters' duty to maintain due impartiality.
Apart from the difficulty of measuring its impact,[85] 'due' impartiality does
not require balance between 'the terrorist and the terrorised'.[86] The more
general argument that the ban illegally conflicted with the underlying legal
policy in favour of free expression was also rejected. That policy was itself
subject to exceptions which had been properly invoked in the public in-

terest. Finally, those powers were held to encompass a wide, blanket ban as well as narrower versions. A further legal challenge in Belfast, which had raised the additional complaint that the ban was discriminatory contrary to section 19 of the Northern Ireland Constitution Act 1973, was dismissed *in Re* McLaughlin's Application.[87]

Turning to the issue of principle, media controls have been imposed in other jurisdictions.[88] In particular, sections 11 to 14 of the Offences against the State Act 1939 in the Republic of Ireland can restrict newspapers,[89] and broadcasters are constrained by section 31 of the Broadcasting Act 1961 (as amended), which extends to Sinn Fein, the U.D.A. and any organisation proscribed in Northern Ireland.[90] This widespread censorship emanates from the fear that reporters are too easily seduced by the drama of terrorism and that publicity will encourage further violence by conferring on terrorists enhanced authority and notoriety. Other arguments are that the transmission of the views of terrorists causes fear, offence and intimidation.[91] The first argument is somewhat misplaced, since it implies that publicity is the ultimate, rather than intermediate, goal of terrorists, so it is not surprising that levels of Republican violence appear unaffected by the ban. In any event, the authority of terrorists is hardly enhanced by the hostile treatment they usually receive at the hands of reporters. As for the effects on the audience, research suggests that most people (at least in Britain) favour more rather than less coverage.[92] In any event a blanket ban cannot be justified by the alleged effects of particular forms of message. A final argument is that express censorship is more open and certain than informal pressures, thereby complying with the rule of law and encouraging reporters towards areas outside the restrictions.[93] However, the assumptions implied, that any explicit restrictions will be clear and that implicit controls will fade away, have certainly not been reflected in the 1988 ban.

The substantial disadvantages of censorship must next be considered. State interference is a source of propaganda for terrorists and may damage the credibility of media sources. There are also doubts whether wide-scale restrictions can be effective,[94] though the 1988 broadcasting ban has had the desired effect of reducing still further appearances and interviews by terrorist groups and Sinn Fein.[95] Intervention might also produce the long-term failings, as suggested flowed from sections 2 and 10 of the Prevention of Terrorism Act, of governmental self-delusion, public misconceptions and the suppression of well-informed discussion. Moreover, individual rights to free expression are curtailed by the 1988 ban without any obvious gains in terms of the rights (for example, to life) of others. There is the added danger that, having established censorship on dubious grounds (offence or mere political distaste) in one area, it will spread to others.[96]

Real dangers do sometimes arise from media coverage of terrorism. In particular, technical information as to weapons, tactics or potential targets could be divulged.[97] The timing and extent of media disclosures in siege and hostage situations could endanger victims.[98] Thus, respect for life in those contexts demands media self-restraint or, in default, legal regulation.[99] To this end, voluntary arrangements have been adopted in the U.K. These include the I.T.C's *Guidelines*,[100] which forbids the transmission of 'any information . . . that could endanger lives or prejudice the success of attempts to deal with [a] hijack [or] kidnapping' and warn against 'attempts to exploit television'. The Home Office correspondingly advises the police to seek media cooperation in kidnaps or hostage situations 'if it can be justified as necessary to protect the lives of innocent people'.[101] Rather less acceptable is the informal agreement that the B.B.C. will inform the Metropolitan Police of intended programmes in 'delicate' cases.[102]

In conclusion, as was accepted by the *Report of the Study Group on Censorship*[103] and by the Government in reply,[104] it should primarily be left to the security forces to control the initial output of information rather than later to censor journalists. It is the possession of the guns and bombs of terrorists which are to be feared and resisted. Their words are without popular support and can be effectively reflected or command a significant following and must be accommodated. Either way, the law and State must trust to the public's judgment.[105]

(e) Election controls

A closely related issue is the candidature in elections of terrorist prisoners or the political supporters of terrorists. Two legal attacks on these tactics have been made.[106]

After the election of Bobby Sands, an I.R.A. convict who later died on hunger-strike, as Member of Parliament for Fermanagh and South Tyrone in 1981, the speedy response was the passage of the Representation of the People Act 1981.[107] The Act disqualifies from nomination for, and membership of, the House of Commons anyone who has been convicted of an offence and is undergoing more than twelve months' imprisonment either in the United Kingdom or in the Republic of Ireland.

It is submitted that this reaction was wholly inappropriate.[108] In principle, the Act curtails political expression rather than violence. An election is a valuable opportunity for testing constitutionally the support for the political objectives behind terrorism. In practice also, bans are of dubious effect. An eligible surrogate candidate may be found to campaign on behalf of a terrorist prisoner with the same policies, including abstentionism, attendant publicity and costs to public funds. This in fact occurred when Owen Carron, Sands' election agent, was elected as his successor in August 1981 following his death.

The other relevant curtailment of free elections is the Elected Authorities (Northern Ireland) Act 1989.[109] The Act first demands that any candidate in Northern Ireland council or Assembly elections must declare that:[110]

... I will not by word or deed express support for or approval of
(a) any [proscribed] organisations ... or
(b) acts of terrorism. ...

Proof in court of a public breach of the promise will result in automatic disqualifications from office for five years.[111] Next, persons found guilty of offences in Northern Ireland or the British Islands and sentenced to imprisonment for three months or more are disqualified from council office not only during the period of disqualification (as under the 1981 Act) but also for five years thereafter.[112]

The 1989 Act, like the broadcasting ban, is mainly aimed at Sinn Fein politicians, whose activities are officially viewed as 'a total abuse of the democratic process'.[113] The arguments for and against the Act have been addressed elsewhere,[114] subject to one additional observation. The measure can hardly be justified in security terms, since local councillors have not suffered unduly from terrorist attacks,[115] nor has any Sinn Fein councillor since been excluded from office either by refusing to make, or breaching the declaration.

In conclusion, Parliament should learn the lesson of cases such as Wilkes, Bradlaugh and Benn and remember that the assessment of the fitness of a person to serve as a Member of Parliament is ultimately a matter for the electorate and not for itself.

2 Foreign terrorism[116]

Much of the legislation inspired mainly by foreign terrorism is based on international convention and follows a standard pattern. Accordingly, it first establishes new offences which are extraditable and have universal jurisdiction. Any offender should be considered for prosecution or extradited; the latter may often be ruled out by the political offence exception. The Acts also provide assistance for victims and law enforcement agencies. Most of the offences overlap with existing criminal law:[117]

The real value of these instruments is that they require State Parties actually to deal with offenders. ...

Nevertheless, the legislation has considerable weaknesses. It is piecemeal and lacks enforcement, especially at an international level. Even in the U.K. many of these exotic measures have been dormant.

(a) Aviation security
Some of the earliest and most important legislation against foreign terrorism combats hijacking and other attacks on aircraft and at airports and ports.[118]

The first such measure was the Tokyo Convention Act 1967[119] (now mostly consolidated as the Civil Aviation Act 1982, sections 92 to 96). This legislation is mainly aimed at 'offenders and trouble-makers'[120] rather than terrorists and so extends the jurisdiction of English criminal law to British-controlled aircraft wherever situated and confers powers on aircraft commanders to quell disturbances. More directed against terrorists were the Hijacking Act 1971,[121] the Protection of Aircraft Act 1973,[122] and the Policing of Airports Act 1974. These Acts have been incorporated within the Aviation Security Act 1982, which has in turn been amended by the Aviation and Maritime Security Act 1990.[123] The effects fall into three parts.

Firstly, Part I of the 1982 Act contains broad offences with wide jurisdiction dealing with hijacking, the destruction or endangerment of aircraft and the possession of dangerous articles.[124] These offences are supplemented by section 1 of the 1990 Act, which forbids the endangerment of life or property at aerodromes. The offences are extraditable, subject to the political offence exception.

Secondly, protective measures for aircraft and aerodromes may be required by directive from the Secretary of State for Transport or his Airport Security Inspectorate under Part II of the 1982 Act (as amended in 1990). The measures which may be imposed are comprehensive and include the supply of information, restrictions on access by persons to aircraft or sensitive areas, restrictions on flights, the provision of technical equipment, searches of persons and premises, alterations to buildings and powers to inspect and test. Security arrangements are considered by the National Aviation Security Committee, comprising governmental, police airport and airline representatives.[125] The Committee considers all aspects of aviation security, including the Department of Transport's National Aviation Security Programme and Handbook.[126] The guidelines are applied locally at each airport by an Airport Security Committee, whose plans must be approved by the Department of Transport.[127] It is an offence under section 5 of the 1990 Act to make false statements in response to baggage or identity checks or to enter restricted zones without authority. Most ominous of all, airport managers may be directed to inform the local Chief Officer of Police that the Secretary of State considers it appropriate that the police at airports should carry weapons.[128] They are routinely armed at Heathrow Airport.[129]

The policing of airports is implemented further by Part III of the 1982 Act. Airports may be 'designated' under section 25 so that the local force may freely enter what is otherwise private property and replace the allegedly under-resourced and inefficient airport constabularies which existed before 1974. Nine major British airports are designated.[130] Section 28 confers extra powers to stop and question, and by-laws under the Airports Authority Act 1972 can also restrict or prohibit access to airports.[131]

It would be difficult to devise on paper a more stringent security system, but there is room for doubt as to whether it has been implemented as vigorously as possible, despite the success which has been achieved in deterring or thwarting attacks.[132] The Government has sought to achieve voluntary cooperation and has therefore avoided use of formal, enforceable directives.[133] It has also shirked any responsibility for the funding of security measures and wound up an Aviation Security Fund in 1983.[134] The implementation of the legislation has been scrutinised by two Transport Select Committee reports[135] and many of its recommendations have since been implemented either administratively or by the 1990 Act.[136] In particular, access to aircraft and sensitive areas has been further restricted, extra checks are made on hold baggage, there is to be greater reliance upon directives and, perhaps most important of all, an Airport Security Inspectorate has been established. Nevertheless, some concerns about security remain. For example, worries about costs should not prevent the police being granted access at all times to all airports.[137] Next, it is surprising that the use of passenger profiling has only recently been seriously considered.[138] Thirdly, although a formal Aviation Security Fund may be unduly bureaucratic, security spending targets and financial reporting should be imposed.[139] Many other regulations could be devised, but it should be remembered that for air travel to grind to a halt because of security restrictions would itself be a victory for terrorism.

(b) Maritime security

Shocked by the *Achille Lauro* incident in 1985[140] and fearful that the law relating to piracy did not meet the challenge of terrorism to shipping,[141] the international community responded with the International Maritime Organisation's Convention for the Suppression of Unlawful Acts against the Safety of Maritime Navigation and Protocol for the Suppression of Unlawful Acts against the Safety of Fixed Platforms on the Continental Shelf.[142] These instruments were modelled on the air conventions and have been implemented by the Aviation and Maritime Security Act 1990, which is also concerned with the security of ships and harbours. The Act may be described in two parts.

Part II implements the Convention and Protocol. At its core are several extraditable offences with wide jurisdiction in sections 9 to 14, which deal with seizure, destruction damage, acts of violence or threats in relation to ships,[143] fixed platforms and navigational facilities.

Part III is concerned with the physical protection of ships and ports in the U.K. or U.K. ships anywhere against acts of violence.[144] As under the Aviation Security Act 1982, the Secretary of State is empowered, for example, to demand information, to designate 'restricted zones', to direct searches, to specify numbers of guards and security apparatus and to inspect and test.[145] These powers apply to ships and harbours but not to fixed platforms, though they have received some protection since the passage of the Continental Shelf Act 1964[146] (now the Oil and Gas (Enterprise) Act 1982),[147] by which a 'safety zone' may be imposed and platforms may not even be approached without authority. This measure does not, of course, address the danger of attacks by infiltrators.

Part III supplements security arrangements for ports under the Harbour, Docks and Piers (Causes) Act 1847[148] and the Port of London Act 1968,[149] by which special constables may be appointed and by-laws made. Indeed, such local forces[150] will continue to play a leading role, since enforcement under the 1990 Act is intended to be used only 'infrequently'.[151]

As with airport security, doubts persist concerning enforcement. In response, Directives were issued under the Act on 22 January 1991, demanding the appointment of a Port Security Committee and Officer at major ports, contingency plans, restricted zones, and the segregation and searching of passengers. In addition, seven Maritime Security Inspectors have been appointed within the Department of Transport, but they do not enjoy the same degree of independence and access to their Minister as their aviation brethren.[152]

As befits the unique status of the development, a separate legal regime has been created by the Channel Tunnel Act 1987. For policing purposes, the Tunnel is integrated within the Kent Constabulary, and its security is overseen by an Intergovernmental Commission and Safety Authority.[153] One of the reasons for choosing a tunnel was that it is inherently least vulnerable to terrorism,[154] but extensive by-laws of the type found at airports are nevertheless likely to be issued by the Concessionaires.[155]

(c) *Diplomats*

Diplomats have featured in contrasting legislative initiatives concerned with terrorism. One aspect is that, pursuant to a U.N. Convention,[156] the Internationally Protected Persons Act 1978 grants them special protection. Thus, section 1 creates wide offences with extra-territorial jurisdiction involving attacks on, or threats to, diplomats and governmental officials, and section 3 (now the Extradition Act 1989, section 22) allows extradition, subject to the political offence exception. This favoured treatment is said to be justified because diplomats 'by virtue of their duties are particularly susceptible to terrorist attacks'.[157] However, the legislation fosters no practical security measures.[158]

Diplomats are accorded many concessions in international and national law, some of which, as described in chapter 8, have been abused in the furtherance of terrorism. The reaction in the U.K. has mainly consisted of the tighter enforcement of sanctions already permitted under the Diplomatic

Privileges Act 1964, including limits on the size of missions and the expulsion or non-accreditation of diplomats.[159] In addition, the Diplomatic and Consular Premises Act 1987 attempts to curtail the improper use of diplomatic premises by preventing the siting of embassies in sensitive locations, by regulating the conferment of diplomatic status on outlying offices and by removing such status from transgressing missions.[160]

(d) Hostage-taking

In view of the scope of its protection and the common nature of the acts outlawed, the U.N.'s International Convention against the Taking of Hostages[161] has been described as 'the most significant' anti-terrorist agreement in international law.[162] However, the Convention suffers from substantive limits (for example, a demand must be made on a third party), and its enforcement may be hampered by exceptions for political offences or asylum, while sovereignty may block rescue missions. Furthermore, any hostage-takers in the U.K. will be processed under preexisting offences, such as kidnapping.[163] Consequently, the Taking of Hostages Act 1982, by which the Convention is implemented, is really designed to resolve jurisdictional and extradition problems.[164]

A rather different strategy sometimes suggested for discouraging hostage-taking is to prohibit compliance with the offenders' demands or any negotiations.[165] However, a 'flexible response' policy has successfully prevailed in the U.K. for sound reasons.[166] First, terrorists have divergent ideals and purposes, so a single policy is too rigid and of uncertain deterrent effect. Moreover, a refusal to treat will induce hostility in victims and their relatives and the temptation to undermine the State's policy.[167]

(e) Nuclear materials

The next legislation inspired by international concerns about terrorism[168] is the Nuclear Material (Offences) Act 1983. By section 1, it is an offence in the U.K. to commit abroad specified offences (including homicides, serious assaults, theft, extortion or damage) in relation to, or by means of, nuclear materials, or, by section 2, to engage anywhere in preparatory acts or threats. The main objective is to confer extraterritorial jurisdiction and allow for extradition,[169] but the Act has just been brought into force because of fears of a conflict with European Communities treaty requirements.[170] The Act may also be deficient in that it does not protect nuclear material held for foreign military purposes.[171]

The nuclear industry receives more effective protection from other sources, though some are so extensive as to create their own concerns.[172] In particular, restrictions may be placed on approaches to atomic installations,[173] and the Atomic Energy Authority (Special Constabulary) Act 1976 establishes an

K

armed guard at especially sensitive sites.[174] In the background, EURATOM and the I.A.E.A. demand high standards to prevent contamination and proliferation but have not promulgated binding rules on physical security at installations.[175]

(f) Conclusions

More ambitious plans for the combating of transnational terrorism[176] have generally not been acceptable to the international community,[177] but the more realistic piecemeal approach so far adopted inevitably entails lingering gaps.[178] Equally, the enforcement of existing codes suffers from limited ratifications, exceptions for political offences and obstacles to investigations and prosecutions. However, some of these barriers are now being removed, especially within Western Europe, and these reforms have the added attraction of applying not only to rarefied international offences but also to commonplace crimes.

Three measures should be mentioned (in outline only) in this connection. Two facilitate extradition. Thus, the Criminal Justice Act 1988 (now the Extradition Act 1989, Parts I and II) simplifies the procedures by which extradition may be obtained, as inspired by the European Convention on Extradition 1957.[179] Next, the Suppression of Terrorism Act 1978,[180] arising out of the European Convention of 1977,[181] substantially delimits the definition of 'political offence'. Thirdly, the Criminal Justice (International Cooperation) Act 1990[182] will allow ratification of the European Convention on Mutual Assistance 1959[183] so that court process may be served abroad and evidence by way of testimony, documents or searches obtained. In addition, section 32 of the Criminal Justice Act 1988 admits evidence by way of live T.V. links from witnesses overseas.

The coordination of police efforts against terrorism has also been aided by the reinterpretation in 1984 of Interpol's constitution so as to empower it to assist in terrorist cases.[184] However, dissatisfaction with its role and efficiency hitherto contributed to the establishment of an alternative European structure, TREVI. This body provides a forum for discussion and the exchange of information between Ministers and police chiefs[185] but has not yet developed a permanent bureaucracy and remains remote from operational detectives.[186]

In the light of the removal of border checks within the European Communities, there are proposals for more sweeping moves towards cooperation including transnational arrests, interrogation and surveillance (perhaps in situations of hot pursuit only), the conferment of extra-territorial jurisdiction over a wide range of offences and the harmonisation of criminal law.[187] Much has already been achieved in recent years to the extent that international cooperation is now a significant aspect of the U.K. anti-terrorism strategy.

Notes

1   See: H.C. Debs. Vol. 227 cols. 1505–6 5 April 1883, Sir W. Harcourt. See also: Explosives Acts 1875-1923; Emergency Laws (Miscellaneous Provisions Act 1953; Control of Explosives Order 1953 S.I. No. 1598; Explosives Act (N.I.) 1970; Explosives (N.I.) Order 1972 S.I. No. 730.

2   As amended by the Criminal Jurisdiction Act 1975 s. 7, Criminal Law Act 1977 s. 33 and Sched. 12, Criminal Law (Amendment) (N.I.) Order 1977 Art. 5.

3   Compare: Offences against the Person Act 1861 ss. 28–30.

4   Compare: Offences against the Person Act 1861 s. 4. See also Law Commission Report No. 29, Offences of Damage to Property (1970–71 H.C. 91) paras. 62–6, 97.

5   *R. v. O'Reilly* (1989) 4 B.N.I.L. n. 17.

6   The maximum penalty is fourteen years' imprisonment. See: *R. v. Hallam* [1957] 1 Q.B. 569.

7   S. 9. See: *R. v. Downey* [1971] N.I. 224; *R. v. Wheatley* [1979] 1 W.L.R. 144; *R. v. Bouch* [1982] 3 W.L.R. 673.

8   See: *R. v. Fegan* [1972] N.I. 80; *A.G.'s Reference (No. 2 of 1983)* [1984] 2 W.L.R. 465.

9   Compare: H.C. Debs. Vol. 227 col. 855 9 April 1883, Mr. Stansfield.

10   See: *R. v. Berry* [1985] A.C. 246. Compare: *R. v. El-Hakkaoui* [1975] 2 All E.R. 146.

11   Cmnd. 7031, 1977.

12   The Act applies in Northern Ireland and Scotland; Poyning's Law 1495; Treason Act (Ir.) 1537; Crown of Ireland Act 1542; Treason Act 1708.

13   See also: Treason Act 1842.

14   See: *R. v. Lynch* [1903] 1 K.B. 444; *R. v. Casement* [1917] 1 K.B. 98; A. Wharam, 'Casement and Joyce' (1978) 41 *M.L.R.* 681.

15   East, 1 P.C. 72. See also: *R. v. Dammaree* (1710) 15 St. Tr. 521; *R. v. Gordon* (1781) 21 St. Tr. 485. As the quotation implies, the levying of war can involve direct attacks on Crown forces or may be constructive.

16   J.W. Cecil Turner, *Kenny's Outlines of Criminal Law* (19th ed., 1966) para. 406. See: *R. v. Smith O'Brien* (1849) 3 Cox C.C. 360; *R. v. Burke* (1867) 10 Cox C.C. 519; *R. v. McCafferty* (1869) 10 Cox C.C. 603.

17   *R. v. Gallagher* (1883) 15 Cox C.C. 291 at p. 317 *per* Lord Coleridge. See also: *R. v. Deasey* (1883) 15 Cox C.C. 334. These were prosecutions for treason felony which, some claim, should not affect the interpretation of the 1351 Act: H.C. Debs. Vol. 882 col. 662 28 November 1974, Sir P. Rawlinson.

18   Compare: A. Wharam, 'Treason and the terrorist' (1976) 126 *N.L.J.* 428.

19   *S. v. Mange* 1980 (4) S.A. 613 (A.D.); *S. v. Lubisi and others* 1982 (3) S.A. 113 (A.D.); *S. v. Tsotsobe and others* 1983 (1) S.A. 856 (A.D.); *S. v. Gaba* 1985 (4) S.A. 734 (A.D.); *S. v. Ramgobin and others* 1986 (1) S.A. 68 (N.P.D.).

20   1983 (2) S.A. 46 (W.L.D.). See also: *S. v. Mayekiso* 1988 (4) S.A. 738 (W.L.D.).

21   But see now: Criminal Law Act 1967 s. 12(4).

22   See: *R. v. Mitchel* (1848) 3 Cox C.C. 2.

23   (1848) 3 Cox C.C. 509.

24   Reported in: J. Bowyer Bell, *The Secret Army* (revised ed., 1979) p. 125.

25   Reported in: J. Ll. J. Edwards, 'Special powers in Northern Ireland' [1956] Crim. L.R. 7 at p. 14.

26   (1973) *Times* 20 January p. 2.

27   (1986) 16 Cox C.C. 335 at p. 360. Sedition in Scotland is confined to attacks on the laws and constitution; see: G.H. Gordon, *The Criminal Law of Scotland* (2nd ed., 1978) paras. 39.01–39.08.

28   See: *O'Connell* v. *R.* (1844) 11 Cl. & Fin. 155; *R.* v. *Mitchel* (1848) 3 Cox C.C. 93; *R.* v. *Fussell* (1848) 3 Cox C.C. 291; *R.* v. *Gray* (1865) 10 Cox C.C. 185; *R.* v. *Sullivan* (1868) 11 Cox C.C. 424; *ex p. William O'Brien* (1883) 12 L.R. Ir. 29; *R.* v. *McHugh* [1901] 2 I.R. 569.

29   Reported in: T.P. Coogan, *The I.R.A.* (3rd ed., 1987) pp. 360–1.

30   See: *S.* v. *Twala* 1979 (3) S.A. 864 (T.); *S.* v. *Zwae* 1987 (4) S.A. 369 (W.L.D.).

31   [1990] 3 W.L.R. 986. See: Law Commission Working Paper No. 72, *Treason, Sedition and Allied Offences* (1977) paras. 70–3, 75; L.H. Leigh, 'Law reform and the law of treason and sedition' (1977) *P.L.* 128; M. Supperstone, *Brownlie's Law of Public Order and National Security* (2nd ed., 1981) pp. 238–40; J.C. Smith and B. Hogan, *Criminal Law* (6th ed., 1988) pp. 834–6.

32   See: Treachery Act 1940 (terminated by 1946 S.R. & O. No. 893); Criminal Code (Amendment) Law 1958 (No. 27) (Cyprus); Sedition Ordinance 1948 (No. 14) (Malaya); Sedition Law 1963 (No. 6) (South Arabia).

33   *Loc. cit.* paras. 57–66, 76–8. Compare: McDonald Commission, *2nd Report* Pt. IX ch. 4 para. 4; Rabie Report, para. 8.2.3.1; H.P. Lee, *Emergency Powers* (1984) p. 101.

34   See: Crimes Act 1914 (No. 12, as amended) ss. 24(1), 24 A-F (Australia); Criminal Code 1953–54 (c. 51) ss. 46–8, 60–1 (Canada); Penal Code 1860 (Act 1, as amended) ss. 121, 124, 124S (India); Sedition Act 1948 (No. 15) (Malaysia); Crimes Act 1961 (No. 43, as amended) ss. 73–6, 81–5 (N.Z.); U.S. Constitution Art. III, s. 3, 18 U.S.C. ss. 2381–5.

35   Constitution Art. 39; Treason Act 1939; Offences against the State Act 1939 ss. 6–9 (as amended). See P.V.L.I. pp. 257–9.

36   A.S. Mathews, *Freedom, State Security and the Rule of Law* (1988) p. 219.

37   *Loc. cit.*, para. 58.

38   H.C. Debs. Vol. 98 col. 14 19 May 1986.

39   See also: Criminal Law (Amendment) (N.I.) Order 1977 S.I. No. 1249 Art. 3; P.V.L.I. p. 148.

40   J.C. Smith and B. Hogan, *Criminal Law* (6th ed., 1988) p. 428.

41   *Ibid.*

42   See: case of Langstreath (*Times* 2 July 1985 p. 1).

43   See H.J. Yallop, *Protection against Terrorism* (1980) p. 47.

44   For example, *R.* v. *Browne* (1984) 6 Cr. App. R. (S) 5.

45   But see: *R.* v. *Dunbar and Johnson* (1988) 9 Cr. App. R. (S) 393 (twelve months' imprisonment for hoax on behalf of Animal Liberation Front).

46   H.C. Debs. Vol. 187 col. 514 w.a. 13 March 1991.

47   See: J. Marston, *Public Order* (1987) ch. 3: P. Thornton, *Public Order Law* (1987) ch. 3.

48   See: S. Watson, 'Consumer terrorism' (1987) 137 *N.L.J.* 84; D. Henshaw, *Animal Warfare* (1989) pp. 203–4.

49   See: I.S. Dickinson, 'Maintaining public order in the 1980s' 1987 *S.L.T.* 105. The law may be deficient in regard to preparatory offences and contamination involving one's own property.

50   See: S. Watson, 'Product contamination' (1987) 84 *L.S. Gaz.* 7 January p. 13; C. Parkes, 'Packaging to beat the poisoner' (1989) *Financial Times* 29 April, p. 3.

51   See: P. Schlesinger, G. Murdoch and P. Elliott, *Televising Television* (1983) chs. 1, 2; *The Protection of Military Information* (Cmnd. 9499, 1985) para. 10.

52   See: Campaign for Free Speech on Ireland (ed.), *The British Media and Ireland* (1979) pp. 21, 54 (hereafter cited as 'Campaign'); L. Curtis, *Ireland: The Propaganda War* (1984) chs. 1, 7, 8; P. Schlesinger, 'Terrorism, the media and the liberal–democratic State' in Y. Alexander and A. O'Day (eds.), *Terrorism in Ireland* (1984) p. 215; B. Rolston (ed.), *The Media and Northern Ireland* (1990); Y. Alexander and R. Latter (eds.), *Terrorism and the Media* (1990).

53   See: Campaign, *op. cit.* pp. 26, 35, 40–3; Curtis, *op. cit.*, chs. 3–6, 9; Article 19, *No Comment* (1989) Chs. 4, 5.

54   See: *Report of the Committee on the Future of Broadcasting* (Cmnd. 6783, 1977) para. 17.11 (the 'Annan Report'); Curtis, *op. cit.* pp. 9–20.

55   See: H.C. Debs. Vol. 939 col. 1735 24 November 1977, Mr. Mason; R. Cathcart, *The Most Contrary Region* (1984) ch. 8.

56   The restrictions thus extend to politicians sympathetic to terrorism: Curtis, *op. cit.* pp. 180–1; *Sunday Times* 25 August 1988 p. 2.

57   See: Cathcart, *op. cit.* App. IV.

58   B. Lapping (ed.), *The Bounds of Freedom* (1980) p. 216.

59   Curtis, *op. cit.* Appendix; 'Crossfire' (*Times*, 15 February 1987 p. 3); Article 19, *op. cit.* pp. 54–9.

60   *Times* 16 July 1985 pp. 1, 30.

61   The film was shown in October with a twenty second amendment: *Times* 3 August 1985 p. 1, 6 August p. 1, 7 August p. 1.

62   (1991) para. 5.2.

63   Lapping (ed.), *op.cit.* p. 214.

64   See n. 59 *supra*.

65   *Times* 29 April 1988 p. 1, 30 April pp. 1, 8.

66   'Death on the Rock' (1989). See also R. Boulton, *Death on the Rock* (1990).

67   See: Gardiner Report, para. 43; Baker Report, para. 39; R. Clutterbuck, *The Media and Political Violence* (2nd ed., 1983) ch. 15.

68   See: *R. v. Arrowsmith* [1975] Q.B. 687; *Arrowsmith* v. *U.K.* Appl. No. 7050/75, D.R. 19 p. 5; *X* v. *U.K.* Appl. No. 6084/73, D.R. 3 p. 62; T. Bunyan, *The History and Practice of the Political Police in Britain* (revised ed., 1983) pp. 34, 292–3.

69   H.C. Debs. Vol. 833 cols. 1497–8 22 March 1972.

70   See: Campaign, *op. cit.* pp. 45–6; Article 19, *op. cit.*; G. Marcus, 'Secret Witness' (1990) *P.L.* 207. But 'D' Notices have not been issued: *Third Report of the Select Committee on Defence* (1979–80 H.C. 773) Minutes of Evidence pp. 7, 15.

71 *Copy of Licence and Agreement dated the 2nd Day of April 1981 between H.M. Sec. of State for the Home Dept. and the B.B.C.* (Cmnd. 8233).

72 See: Annan Report, para. 5.11.

73 But an interview with Adrian Gallagher of Clann na h'Eireann on the Bristol Channel Cable T.V. in November 1974 was banned: Curtis, *op. cit.* p. 154.

74 See: J. Michael, 'Attacking the easy platform' (1988) 138 *N.L.J.* 786; R.L. Weaver and G. Bennett, 'The Northern Ireland broadcasting ban' (1989) 22 *Vanderbilt J. of Transnat. L.* 1119; Article 19, *op. cit.* ch. 3; S.A.C.H.R., *14th Report* (1988–89 H.C. 394) ch. 5.

75 The 1988 ban has been continued under the Broadcasting Act 1990 (see H.C. Debs. Vol. 183 col. 201 w.a. 19 December 1990).

76 Article 19, *op. cit.* p. 32.

77 *Ibid.* p. 65.

78 The I.B.A. interpretation was that all statements on public issues on behalf of Sinn Fein may be banned: Weaver and Bennett, *loc. cit.* p. 1126. See now: I.T.C., Programme Code, *op. cit.* para. 5.2(i).

79 *Ibid.* pp. 1127–8. Richard Stanton, a Labour Councillor in Brighton, was censured: *Times* 13 February 1989 p. 2.

80 See: Broadcasting Act 1990 ss. 44, 45; Michael, *loc. cit.* p. 787.

81 See: L. Henderson, D. Miller and J. Reilly, *Speak No Evil* (1990) pp. 20–2.

82 [1990] 1 All E.R. 469 (C.A.); [1991] 2 W.L.R. 588 (H.L.). See: B. de Smith, 'Broadcasting and Northern Ireland' (1989) 139 *N.L.J.* 1240; J. Jowell, 'Broadcasting, terrorism, human rights and proportionality' (1990) *P.L.* 149; B. Thompson, 'Broadcasting and terrorism' (1989) *P.L.* 527; E. Barendt, 'Broadcasting censorship' (1990) 106 *L.Q.R.* 354; C. Gearty, 'The media ban, the European Convention and the English judges' (1990) 49 *C.L.J.* 187.

83 The High Court doubted whether there was a breach of the Convention: (1989) *Times* 30 May. See also: *X and the Association of Z* v. *U.K.* Appl. No. 4515/70, 14 Y.B.E.C. 538 (1971); *Castells* v. *Spain* Appl. No. 11798/85. An application (No. 15404/89) is pending in regard to the Republic's broadcasting ban.

84 *Loc. cit.* at p. 481, echoed in the House of Lords, *loc. cit.* pp. 593, 603, 607.

85 *Ibid.* at p. 487, *loc. cit.* (H.L.) at p. 600.

86 *Ibid.* at p. 488 *per* McCowan L.J.

87 (1991) 1 B.N.I.L. n. 36. The additional ground raises two further arguments (one rejected, one left open). Firstly, s. 19 does not protect support for violence (*In re McCartney's Application* [1987] 11 N.I.J.B. 94), but the ban is not confined to expressions favouring violence. Secondly, s. 23 allows the Secretary of State to certify that derogations allowed by statute are necessary, but the B.B.C. ban is non-statutory.

88 See: Defence (Emergency) Regulations 1945 ss. 86–101 (Israel); Internal Security Act 1960 (No. 82) ss. 22–31 (Malaysia); Emergency Powers (Maintenance of Law and Order) Regulations 1983 S.I. No. 458 ss. 43, 44, 60 (Zimbabwe); Publications Act 1974 (No. 43), Internal Security Act 1982 ss. 5–12, 15, 56, 70 (No. 74) (South Africa); Public Emergency (Publications) Decree 1964 (No. 28)

(South Arabia); Prevention of Terrorism (Temporary Provisions) Act 1979 s. 14 (Sri Lanka); A.P. Schmid and J. de Graff, *Violence as Communication* (1982) ch. 4.

89 See: P.V.L.I. pp. 268–9.

90 See: *ibid.* pp. 267–8; Report of I.F.J. Mission, 'Censuring the Troubles' (1987); Article 19, *op. cit.* ch. 3.

91 H.C. Debs. Vol. 138 col. 885 19 October 1988, Mr. Hurd.

92 Henderson, Miller and Reilly, *op. cit.* p. 43.

93 P. Wilkinson, *Terrorism and the Liberal State* (2nd ed., 1986) pp. 176–7.

94 *Protection of Military Information* (Cmnd. 9499, 1985) para. 6.

95 Henderson, Miller and Reilly, *op. cit.* pp. 30, 37; I.F.J. Special Report, *Press Freedom under Attack in Britain* (1989) pp. 6–7. The same effect has been detected in the Republic: G. Adams, *The Politics of Irish Freedom* (1986) p. 156.

96 But this has not happened in the Republic: C. Cruise O'Brien, 'I.R.A. arsenal in bomb, gun and box', *Times* 6 April 1988 p. 14.

97 See: G. Wardlaw, *Political Terrorism* (2nd ed., 1989) pp. 78, 79.

98 A.H. Miller (ed.), *Terrorism, the Media and the Law* (1982) chs. 1, 4; R. Clutterbuck, *The Media and Political Violence* (2nd ed., 1983) chs. 12, 13.

99 Compare: McDonald Commission, *2nd Report* Pt. IX ch. 1 para. 88; Wardlaw, *op. cit.* ch. 9; International Terrorism (Emergency Powers) Act 1987 (No. 179) ss. 14, 15; K.J. Patterson, 'The spectre of censorship under the International Terrorism (E.P.) Act 1987' (1988) 18 *V.U.W.L.R.* 259 (New Zealand).

100 *Op. cit.* paras. 5.3, 5.6.

101 H.O. Circular, No. 128/1976 para. 3. See Miller (ed.), *op. cit.* ch. 6.

102 Miller (ed.), *op. cit.* p. 123.

103 (Cmnd. 9112, 1983) paras. 76, 164. Compare: *Report of the Commission of Enquiry into Reporting of Security Matters Regarding the S.A. Defence Force and the S.A. Police Force* (RP 52, 1980); P. G. Cassell, 'Reflections on press coverage of military operations' (1985) 73 *Georgetown L.J.* 931.

104 *Loc. cit.*, para. 10.

105 Compare: *Gitlow* v. *U.S.* 268 U.S. 652 at p. 673 *per* Holmes J. This conclusion does not exclude positive media campaigns: J.J. Paust, 'Private measures of sanction' in A.E. Evans and J.F. Murphy (eds.), *Legal Aspects of International Terrorism* (1978) p. 606; Campaign, *op. cit.* pp. 36–7; Curtis, *op. cit.* ch. 10. Clutterbuck, *op. cit.* ch. 10.

106 The Representation of the People Act 1985 seems more defensible because it does not disqualify anyone on grounds of belief (except perhaps anarchists).

107 See: Walker, 'Prisoners in Parliament' (1982) *P.L.* 389; P.V.L.I. pp. 158–9, 220; Internal Security Act 1982 s. 33 (South Africa).

108 Compare: S.A.C.H.R., *7th Report* (1981–82 H.C. 202) ch. 3.

109 See Walker, 'Political violence and democracy in Northern Ireland' (1988) 51 *M.L.R.* 605; S.A.C.H.R., *14th Report* (1988–89 H.C. 394) ch. 4 and Annex C; S.R. Chowdhury, *Rule of Law in a State of Emergency* (1989) pp. 249–59.

110 Ss. 3–5, Sched. 2.

111 Ss. 6–8.

112 S. 9.

113 H.C. Debs. Vol. 143 col. 44 5 December 1988 Mr. King.

114   See n. 109, *supra*.

115   See H.C. Debs. Standing Comm. A cols. 16–17 15 December 1988.

116   It is not intended to discuss the treatment of terrorism purely in international law, on which there exists a vast literature. For surveys, see: A. D. Sofaer, 'Terrorism and the law' (1986) 64 *Foreign Affairs* 901; G.M. Levitt, *Democracies against Terror* (1988); A. Cassesse, *Law and Violence in the Modern Age* (1988), 'The international community's "legal" response to terrorism' (1989) 38 *I.C.L.Q.* 589, *Terrorism, Politics and Law* (1989); J.F. Murphy, *State Support for International Terrorism* (1989); J.J. Lambert, *Terrorism and Hostages in International Law* (1990) Pt. I.

117   Lambert, *op. cit.* p. 55.

118   See: A.D. Evans, 'Aircraft hijacking' (1969) 63 *A.J.I.L.* 695, (1972) 66 *A.J.I.L.* 819; H.F. Van Panhuys, 'Aircraft hijacking and international law' (1970) 9 *Col. J. of Transnat. L.* 1; G. White, 'The Hague Convention for the Suppression of Unlawful Seizures of aircraft' (1971) 6 *Rev. of I.C.J.* 38; S.K. Agrawala, *Aircraft Hijacking and International Law* (1973); S. Shubber, *Jurisdiction over Crimes on Board Aircraft* (1973); E. McWhinney, *Aircraft Piracy and International Terrorism* (2nd ed., 1987).

119   See: Convention on Offences and Certain Other Acts Committed on board Aircraft (Cmnd. 2261, 1961).

120   H.C. Debs. Vol. 738 col. 885 16 December 1966, Mr. Maclennan.

121   See: Convention for the Suppression of Unlawful Seizures of Aircraft (Cmnd. 4577, 1971).

122   See: Convention for the Suppression of Unlawful Acts against the Safety of Civil Aviation (Cmnd. 4822, 1971).

123   See: Protocol for the Suppression of Unlawful Acts of Violence at Airports Serving International Civil Aviation (Cm. 378, 1988).

124   See: Smith and Hogan, *op. cit.* pp. 820–2; *R. v. Moussa Membar and others* [1983] Crim. L.R. 618, *Times* 26 November 1985 p. 1; *R. v. Hindawi* (1988) 10 Cr. App. R. (S) 104.

125   H.C. Debs. Vol. 854 col. 445 2 April 1973; Transport Select Committee, *Airport Security* (1985–86 H.C. 597) para. 41. Such arrangements are demanded by the I.C.A.O.: Evans and Murphy, *op. cit.* ch. 1; J.J. Finger, 'Security of international aviation' (1983–84) 6 *Terrorism J.* 519; S. Akwanda, 'Prevention of unlawful interference with aircraft' (1986) 35 *I.C.L.Q.* 436. Compare, in the U.S.A. 14 C.F.R. Pts. 107, 108, 129.

126   Transport Select Committee, *loc. cit.* para. 3.

127   *Ibid.* para. 8.

128   1990 Act s. 15(5). Compare 1982 Act s. 16(1).

129   *Times* 9 January 1986 p. 2, 10 January p. 3.

130   Home Affairs Committee, *Practical Police Cooperation in the European Communities* (1989–90 H.C. 363) Vol. II, Memo. from B.A.A. Aldergrove is policed by the Northern Ireland Airports Constabulary: Transport Select Committee, *loc. cit.* para. 48. Troops have sometimes been deployed: P. Rowe, *Defence: The Legal Implications* (1987) p. 61.

131   S. 9. See also Civil Aviation Act 1982 ss. 18, 27–40.

132   Incidents within the U.K. have been limited to a bomb on a flight from

Aldergrove in 1975 (C. Ryder, *The R.U.C.* (1989) pp. 134–5), the Hindawi case (n. 124 *supra*), and three attacks at Sydenham, Belfast (July and November 1989, February 1990). Charges for the Lockerbie bombing have yet to be brought.

133   Transport Select Committee, *loc. cit.* para. 32.

134   See: 1982 Act Pt. IV; 1978 S.I. No. 769, 1982 S.I. Nos. 220, 1065, 1983, S.I. Nos. 81, 1644.

135   *Airport Security* (1985–86 H.C. 597), (1988–89 H.C. 509). The Government replies are at 1985–86 H.C. 602, 1989–90 H.C. 52. The Lockerbie bombing also resulted in immediate changes: *Times* 17 January 1989 p. 1. See also Report of Sheriff Mowat, *Times* 23 March 1991 p. 6.

136   Government replies to the Reports of the Transport Select Committee, *Airport Security, loc. cit.*, H.C. Debs. Vol. 164 col. 958 10 January 1990.

137   Transport Select Committee, *loc. cit.* (1985–86 H.C. 597) para. 54; Colville Report, para. 10.22.

138   Government reply, *loc. cit.* (1989–90 H.C. 52) p. viii; McWhinney, *op. cit.* ch. 3.

139   Transport Select Committee, *loc. cit.* (1988–89 H.C. 509) para. 35.

140   See: Halberstram, 'Terrorism on the high seas' (1988) 82 *A.J.I.L.* 269; A. Cassesse, *Terrorism, Politics and Law* (1989). I.R.A. attacks on shipping include two bombs on Belfast ferries in 1972 and the sinking of two merchant ships in Lough Foyle in 1981 and 1982.

141   See: Smith and Hogan, *op. cit.* pp. 815–20; G.R. Constantinople, 'Towards a new definition of piracy' (1986) 26 *Va. J. of Int. L.* 723; A.P. Rubin, *The Law of Piracy* (1988).

142   (1988) 27 *I.L.M.* 672, 685. See: (1990) 39 *I.C.L.Q.* 27; N. Ronzitti (ed.), *Maritime Terrorism and International Law* (1990).

143   The Act applies to vessels of the security forces in certain circumstances: ss. 9(2), 11(5), 12(6).

144   Ss. 18(1), 26(5). The measures are supported by the Colville Report, para. 10.2.6.

145   Ss. 19–25, 28–32, 36–9, 41.

146   S. 2. See: Evans and Murphy (eds.), *op. cit.* ch. 3.

147   S. 21. See: Offshore Installations (Safety Zones) Orders. The criminal law is applied by s. 22: Criminal Jurisdiction (Offshore Activities) Order 1987 S.I. No. 2198.

148   Ss. 79, 83.

149   Ss. 154, 160, 170.

150   There are twelve forces: Home Affairs Committee, *Practical Police Cooperation in the European Communities* (1989–90 H.C. 363) Vol. II p. 72.

151   H.C. Debs. Vol. 168 col. 636 5 March 1990, Mr. Portillo. Voluntary guidelines already issued (see: *Prevention of Terrorism, Guidance Notes on the Protection of Shipping against Terrorism*, 1986) will continue: H.C. Debs. Vol. 110 cols. 537–8 w.a. 17 February 1987.

152   Letter from Department of Transport, 26 February 1991. Compare: Omnibus Diplomatic Security and Terrorism Act 1986 Title IX (32 U.S.C. s. 1226, 846 U.S.C. 2.1801); D. B. Fascell, 'Combating international terrorism' (1986) 16 *Ga. J. Int. L.* 655.

153   Ss. 14, 17. P. Hermitage, 'Light on the start of the Tunnel', (1989) 5 *Policing* 121.

154   *The Channel Fixed Link* (Cmnd. 9735, 1986) para. 23, Annex B.

155   S. 20. See ch. 9.

156   *Prevention and Punishment of Crimes against Internationally Protected Persons, Including Diplomatic Agents* (Cmnd. 6176, 1977). See: M.C. Wood, 'The Convention etc.' (1974) 23 *I.C.L.Q.* 791; L.L. Rozakis, 'Terrorism and the internationally protected person in the light of the I.L.C.'s draft articles' (1974) 23 *I.C.L.Q.* 32; L.M. Bloomfield and G. Fitzgerald, *Crimes against Internationally Protected Persons* (1975).

157   H.L. Debs. Vol. 392 col. 397 17 May 1928, Lord Garner.

158   Compare in the U.S.A.: Omnibus and Diplomatic Security and Anti-Terrorism Act 1986 (22 U.S.C. 54801 *et seq.*); 22 C.F.R. Pts. 2 and 2a.

159   See: *Diplomatic Privileges and Immunity* (Cmnd. 9497, 1985); G.M. Levitt, *Democracies against Terror* (1988) chs. 2, 3; J. Lodge, *The Threat of Terrorism* (1988) p. 247.

160   See: C. Islam, 'The inviolability of diplomatic and consular premises' (1988) 85 *L.S. Gaz.* 29 June p. 30.

161   Cmnd. 7893, 1979.

162   Lambert, *op. cit.* p. 6. See also: S. Shubber, 'The International Convention etc.' (1981) 52 *B.Y.I.L.* 205;, W.D. Verwey, 'The International Hostages Convention and national liberation movements' (1981) 75 *A.J.I.L.* 69; C.C. Aston, 'The U.N. Convention etc.' (1981) 5 *Terrorism J.* 139; J.W. McDonald Jr., 'The U.N. Convention etc.' (1983) 6 *Terrorism J.* 546.

163   H.C. Debs. Vol. 25 col. 573 11 June 1982.

164   As amended by the Extradition Act 1989 ss. 22, 25. The offence in s. 1 involving threats is unique.

165   See Evans and Murphy (eds.), *op. cit.* p. 454.

166   See: E. Evans, *Calling a Truce to Terrorism* (1979) chs. 6, 8; C.C. Aston, 'Political hostage-taking in Western Europe' in W. Gutteridge (ed.). *The New Terrorism* (1986) pp. 57, 62; G. Wardlaw, *Political Terrorism* (2nd ed., 1989) ch. 13.

167   See also: Council of Europe Committee of Ministers, *On Measures to be Taken in Cases of Kidnapping Followed by a Ransom Demand* (Recommendation R(82)14). On the London kidnap insurance market and Control Risks, see: R. Clutterbuck, 'Management of kidnap risk' in P. Wilkinson (ed.), *British Perspectives on Terrorism* (1981); J. Radcliffe, 'The insurance companies' response to terrorism' in Y. Alexander and R.A. Kilmarx (eds.), *Political Terrorism and Business* (1979).

168   Convention on the Physical Protection of Nuclear Material (Cmnd. 8112, 1983). The Royal Commission on Environmental Pollution (6th Report, *Nuclear Power and the Environment* (Cmnd. 6648, 1976) para. 34) considered the risk of terrorism to be slight, but compare: P. Leventhal and Y. Alexander (eds.), *Preventing Nuclear Terrorism* (1987). For commencement, see S.I. 1991 No. 1716.

169   As amended by Extradition Act 1989 s. 22.

170   H.L. Debs. Vol. 440 col. 990 21 March 1983; Ruling Delivered Pursuant to the Third Paragraph of Art. 103 of the E.A.E.C. Treaty [1978] E.C.R. 2151.

171   S. 6. See: H.C. Debs. Vol. 37 col. 905 22 February 1983.

172 See: D. Schiff, 'Reconstructing liberty in the nuclear age' in C. Harlow (ed.), *Public Law and Politics* (1986).

173 See: Official Secrets (Prohibited Places) Orders 1955 S.I. Nos. 1497, 1975, S.I. No. 182.

174 See H.C. Debs. Vol. 906 cols. 701–10 26 February 1976. But transportation may need greater protection; see: Radioactive Material (Road Transport) Act 1991.

175 See: Evans and Murphy (eds.), *op. cit.* ch. 2; D.A. Howlett, *EURATOM and Nuclear Safeguards* (1990).

176 See: T.M. Franck and B.B. Lockwood Jr., 'Preliminary thoughts towards an international convention on terrorism' (1974) 68 *A.J.I.L.* 89.

177 See: N. Galr-Or, *International Cooperation to Suppress Terrorism* (1985) ch. 4; Murphy, *op. cit.* ch. 1.

178 The protection of postal workers may be the next step; McWhinney, *op. cit.* p. 141; R. A. Friedlander, *Terrorism* Vol. V (1990) pp. 309–10.

179 E.T.S. No. 24.

180 See also Extradition Act 1989 s. 24.

181 Cmnd. 8031, 1977. See also: Agreement concerning the Application of the E.C.S.T. among Member States of the European Communities (Cmnd. 7823, 1979); P. Weis, 'Asylum and terrorism' (1977) 19 *I.C.J.* 37: A.L. Seager, 'The new terrorism legislation' 1978 S.L.T. 301; A.V. Lowe and J.R. Young, 'Suppressing terrorism under the European Convention' (1978) 25 *Neths. Int. L.R.* 305; J. Lodge (ed.), *Terrorism* (1981) chs. 7, 8. Similar arrangements have been agreed with the U.S.A.: 1986 S.I. No. 2146; B.G. Kulman, 'Eliminating the political offence exception for violent crime' (1986) 26 *Va. J. of Int. L.* 755.

182 The Act is not yet in force. See: Home Office, *International Mutual Assistance in Criminal Matters* (1988), I. Cameron, 'Mutual assistance in criminal matters' (1989) 38 *I.C.L.Q.* 954; W. Finnie, 'International cooperation against crime and Scots legislation' 1990 *S.L.T.* 205.

183 E.T.S. Nos. 30, 99. See also: S.M. Tigar and A. Doyle, 'International exchange of information in criminal cases' (1983) *Mich. Y.B. Int. L. Stud.* 61.

184 M. Fooner, *Interpol* (1989); M. Anderson, *Policing the World* (1989).

185 See: R. Clutterbuck, *The Future of Political Violence* (1986) ch. 18; C. Fijnaut and R. Hermans, *Police Cooperation in Europe* (1987); F. Geysels, 'Europe from the inside' (1990) 6 *Policing* 338.

186 See: Home Affairs Committee, *Practical Police Cooperation in the European Communities, loc. cit.* para. 61. There also exists a Police Working Group on Terrorism within Western Europe and the Metropolitan Special Branch has a European Liaison Section.

187 See: European Parliament Committee on Legal Affairs and Citizens' Rights, *Report on the European Judicial Area (Extradition)* (A1-318/82), *Report on Problems relating to Combating Terrorism* (A2-155/89). Compare: 18 U.S.C. s. 2331; P.L. Donnelly, 'Extra-territorial jurisdiction over acts of terrorism committed abroad' (1987) 72 *Cornell L.R.* 599.

Chapter 13

Anti-terrorism: a model code[1]

A Permanent provisions

1 *Introduction*

Two conceivable approaches to eradicating I.R.A. political violence were available in 1974. The one adopted was to enact special legislation to counteract what was viewed as a unique problem, distinguishable from ordinary crime by both the motives and the organisation of those concerned. The other would have been to rely on existing offences and police practices on the assumption that terrorism was essentially criminal activity and had already been suppressed as such.[2] Notwithstanding its advantages of familiarity and legitimacy, the role of the 'normal' law against terrorism has barely been considered by Parliament and was beyond the purview of the Shackleton and Jellicoe Reports.[3] Therefore, Part A of this Chapter attempts to redress this neglect and to examine those areas in which regular law could with minor adjustments be readily employed against political violence. Those already hinted at in previous chapters will be examined first.

2 *Permanent reforms directly relevant to the Prevention of Terrorism Act*

(a) *Proscription: public order aspects* The view has previously been rehearsed that the main aim of proscription in Britain is to prevent public outrage.[4] Yet the regular law already outlaws paramilitary organisations and could wholly replace proscription with the aid of some simple amendments. In particular, changes to section 2 of the Public Order Act 1936 could make redundant sections 2, 9 and 10 of the Prevention of Terrorism Act.[5] Accordingly, additions should include offences of being, or professing to be, a member and soliciting, inviting, collecting or giving any financial support, facilities, services or contributions. Fewer changes would be necessary in Northern Ireland, since mere membership is already penalised by section 7 of the Public Order (Amendment) Act (Northern Ireland) 1970.[6]

If the foregoing reforms were adopted, it would be possible to dispense with proscription in Britain. However, it may serve other purposes in Northern Ireland, and these will be considered later.

(b) *Permanent police powers: arrests*   Amongst the proposals, which were aired in chapter 8, are ones which suggest that more detailed legal guidance than section 3 of the Criminal Law Act 1967 should be available on the application of lethal force to effect an arrest or prevent crime, that the rules relating to self-defence and superior orders should also be clarified and that a qualified defence of excessive force should be instituted.[7] The use of lethal force also suffers from lack of accountability by way of inquests; a remedy by way of an additional, more open-ended inquiry in cases of public interest has been suggested.[8]

Another matter canvassed in chapter 8 concerned the treatment of terrorist suspects in police custody. In particular, it was argued that they should at least be accorded the normal safeguards, including routine tape-recording of interviews, stricter rules relating to the admissibility of confessions in Northern Ireland, police detention limited to ninety-six hours and access to lawyers in private after thirty-six hours. Moreover, it is advisable to institute extra protections for prisoners such as terrorists, since they are especially at risk from maltreatment. These measures could be activated by reference to certain serious suspected offences,[9] whereupon the extra arrangements prescribed by the Bennett Report,[10] especially routine medical checks, would then apply. Finally, the actual powers to arrest and detain now available in England and Wales via Parts III and IV of the Police and Criminal Evidence Act should be extended to Scotland.[11]

(c) *Permanent police powers: searches*   Aside from the extension of the Police and Criminal Evidence legislation to Scotland, perhaps the most pressing reform concerns the control of surreptitious surveillance by technical devices. The Interception of Communications Act 1985 ineffectively governs those methods of search within its purview and altogether ignores techniques such as electronic bugging. Telephone-tapping and other modern methods of search are important and justifiable techniques against terrorism, but visual and aural surveillance with the aid of special devices should in principle be conducted only under judicial warrant.[12] Covert surveillance unaided by intrusive techniques does not pose the same danger to liberty and should even be assisted by concessions (such as from certain road traffic licensing requirements) when a serious crime is being investigated.[13]

Amongst the secondary recommendations arising out of Chapter 8 is one that the police should be able to undertake searches under warrant covertly, provided the issuing judge agrees and there is disclosure after a specified delay.[14] In addition, the stop and search powers in section 1/ Article 3 of the Police and Criminal Evidence legislation should comprehend explosives, and bodily searches and sampling should be subject to prior judicial scrutiny. In addition, the May Inquiry's Interim Report on the Maguire case calls for greater care and independence from the police in the gathering and presentation of forensic evidence.[15] Next, the rather haphazard and secretive rules (so far as they exist)[16] governing police access to governmental information should be systemised and made subject to independent oversight. Finally, the storage and dissemination of police records should be subject to outside inspection both of data and of manual files.[17]

Further relevant policing powers will be considered in Part B of this chapter.

(*d*) *Financial controls*   It was argued in chapter 7 that the financial assistance offences and forfeiture measures in Part III and Schedule 4 of the Prevention of Terrorism Act could be consolidated with the Drug Trafficking Offences Act 1986, the Criminal Justice Act 1988, and the Criminal Justice (Confiscation) (Northern Ireland) Order 1990, subject to extension of such legislation to Scotland and some modifications. These include new powers to conduct actions *in rem* in certain situations and to issue monitoring orders, more generous rules as to compensation and the interests of third parties, the giving of notice of applications (subject to delay if obstruction is likely), increasing the amount recoverable to reflect increases in property values or interest on sums unpaid, the granting of charging orders and widening laundering offences to any form of evasion. It would also be prudent to allow forfeiture when a connection with a terrorist-type offence is established, even if no proof of benefit or benefit above a minimum amount can be established. Finally, branches of the Serious Fraud Office should be opened in Northern Ireland and Scotland.

3   *Other permanent reforms*
(*a*) *Offences*   The archaic offences against the State discussed in chapter 12 urgently need reform – but not for the sake of the criminalisation of terrorists. Whether treason should be activated in order to apply the death penalty will be considered later. Amongst other measures described in chapter 12, it was noted that those relating to bomb hoaxes and food contamination do not extend to Scotland.

Turning to relevant offences against the person, one serious uncertainty is whether or not a terrorist who plants a bomb which results in fatalities is guilty of murder. As the law stands at present,[18] a bomber who realises that the probability of causing death or grievous injury is little short of overwhelming, even if the device was not aimed at the persons in fact killed, commits murder. Consequently, those who plant explosives in places of public resort without giving a substantial, clear warning can be liable,[19] but the verdict may be different if the target is remote and unoccupied or if a timely and explicit warning was provided.[20] This distinction was accepted by the Criminal Law Revision Committee (and later official studies), which advocated that the *mens rea* of murder should be confined to an intention to kill or to cause serious bodily harm in the knowledge that there is a risk of death.[21] However, recognising that Parliament might wish to condemn as murder all acts of terrorism which take life, the Committee outlined an additional possible heading, namely, unlawful acts intended to cause fear of death or serious injury and known to the defendant to involve a risk of causing death.[22] This wider version may be welcomed in so far as it marks society's repudiation of terrorism. On the other hand, such explicit condemnation is unnecessary, since manslaughter will take care of those who escape murder charges, and the enactment of rules designed to take account of terrorism will be perceived as marking out as special those convicted under them. Thus, the balance of arguments probably weighs against the supplemental formulation,[23] and the subsequent House of Lords Select Committee on Murder and Life Imprisonment concluded likewise.[24]

Amongst other proposals of interest by the Criminal Law Revision Committee was one that, just as it is an offence to threaten to kill another or destroy property,[25] so it should be unlawful to threaten serious injury, such as by 'knee-capping'.[26] Intimidation of this kind is already an offence in Northern Ireland and Scotland,[27] and it is also criminal to threaten 'protected persons' (meaning members of foreign governments, diplomats and their accompanying families) under section 1(3) of the Internationally Protected Persons Act 1978.

(b)   The control of explosives and firearms   Extensive regulations already exist under the Explosives Act 1875, the Explosive Substances Act 1883 and the Firearms Acts 1968–88[28] in order to prevent the supply and use of weapons for unlawful purposes such as terrorism. Unfortunately, these controls are not perfect, and the following improvements might be considered.

The first would be the delimitation of the suspicious circumstances relevant to section 4 of the 1883 Act, the reformulation of the extra-territorial effects of sections 2 to 4, and the removal (to Part B) of section 6. Another change would be the institution on a permanent basis of an offence along the lines of section 32 of the Northern Ireland (Emergency Provisions) Act 1991, which penalises the giving of training in the manufacture or utilisation of firearms or explosives except for lawful purposes. Section 32 overlaps to some extent with existing offences relating to the unlawful possession of munitions but will be indispensable when the instruction involves mere models or is confined to theory.[29]

Further controls in regard to explosives could include the compulsory 'coding' of detonators and explosive ingredients.[30] Coding is already undertaken by most manufacturers in the British Isles and involves the insertion of material which survives an explosion, thereby aiding forensic investigations. Consideration might also be given to the adoption in Britain of the extra restrictions operating in Northern Ireland. These include the prohibition of materials commonly incorporated into home-made bombs (such as certain weed-killers and fertilisers), stricter controls over the keeping of registers and amounts of explosives stored, a ban on the movement of explosives without the police's consent and the licensing of shot-firers.[31] The desirability of each of these regulations depends on practicability, technical considerations and the bomb-making practices of terrorists.[32] Even tighter controls are imaginable and will be discussed later as possible temporary provisions.

Turning to firearms, restrictions have tightened pursuant to the Firearms Act 1982, which circumscribes imitation firearms,[33] and the Firearms (Amendment) Act 1988.[34] The latter increased the categories of prohibited weapons, increased the controls over shotguns and established a consultative committee to give advice to the Home Office. However, other important suggestions, some outlined as long ago as 1973,[35] such as national numbering and record-keeping and more detailed criteria for the issuance of certificates, have not been implemented. Furthermore, there is a strong lobby against restrictions both on grounds of individual and sporting interests[36] and to achieve greater harmonisation with other European Community States,[37] whose codes are almost all laxer.[38]

One should be as sceptical about the utility of a more elaborate firearms control system as about one for explosives, since many terrorist weapons are imported illegally or are self-produced.[39] Nevertheless some of the suggestions made hitherto may prove marginally helpful.

(c)   *Other matters*   Remaining issues demanding permanent reform will not be examined in depth, since all involve repercussions beyond the combating of terrorism. Such matters include the legislative regulation of the secret services,[40] the revision of the common law and administrative arrangements governing military aid to the civil power[41] and the establishment of institutions to ensure the coordination of security activities and intelligence[42] and to formulate contingency plans.[43] Progress has been made in some of these areas. For example, following the Brighton bombing in 1984, a Committee for Terrorist Information Gathering, Evaluation and Review ('TIGER') was established, comprising Home Office, police, security services and Army representatives.[44] Further, the Metropolitan Police Special Branch has long held a national responsibility for intelligence-gathering against Republican terrorism in Britain. This role has recently been supplemented by conferring a similar roving commission to control operations on the Head of the Metropolitan Police's Anti-Terrorist Branch, and a committee of chief police officers has been appointed to ensure that Metropolitan Police expertise is readily available elsewhere.[45] Next, the Security Service Act 1989 has provided a legal constitution for a small part of the U.K.'s security apparatus but does not effectively impose controls or accountability,[46] so it is not surprising that disquiet persists. [47]

B Temporary provisions

1 *Structure*

Even if reformed as outlined, the regular law might still fail to dissipate a major terroristic challenge to a democratic State and the rights of its citizens.[48] One problem is that arrests and convictions after the event do little to prevent political violence from the outset, but delay until the infliction of some catastrophic attack might be unacceptable. Next, the collection of sufficient evidence against clandestine, armed conspiracies, which may command community support as well as fear, could place undue burdens on police capabilities. Another complication arises from the need to preserve the secrecy of police detection methods, so that under-cover agents or techniques might be reactivated. Finally, those prosecutions which can be mounted might be defeated by intimidation of, or assaults upon, the participants in the proceedings. For all these reasons, temporary supplements should be made available.

In order to avoid the manifold shortcomings of 'panic' legislation,[49] it is suggested that, though the measures in Part B are to operate temporarily, the proposed 'Anti-Terrorism Act' by which they are to be implemented should be permanent along the lines advocated by the Colville Report and others before it.[50] This structure should bolster public and parliamentary scrutiny of the initial drafting and enactment and of any later invocation or renewal.[51] The Emergency Powers Act 1920 operates in a similar fashion,[52] but it is envisaged that the substance as well as framework of the anti-terrorism legislation should appear in the Act itself rather than subsidiary regulations,[53] so as to facilitate full discussion.[54] This model has long been basically followed by the Republic of Ireland's Offences against the State Acts 1939–85 (though some parts are permanently in force and there is no review or monitoring system).[55] A more recent elaborate version of permanent legislation is the Emergencies Act 1988 in Canada,[56] which deals with various levels of crisis ranging from public disorder to war, though with an over-reliance upon unspecified regulations. Another example is

New Zealand's International Terrorism (Emergency Powers) Act 1987 and Defence Act 1990,[57] which further suggest that the enterprise of devising a British code is not as utopian as some believe.

The main danger associated with the permanent availability of special laws is overuse and 'normalising the extraordinary'.[58] Therefore, three safeguards should be incorporated.[59]

The first is to formulate explicit criteria on which to judge the necessity of each provision in the proposed Act. In essence, these should ensure that resort to the regular law is an insufficient remedy for the affected area (which could be defined by counties) and that the special measures adopted are proportionate to the emergency.[60] Criteria have already been delineated in chapter 2, and those should in turn be judged against the European Convention on Human Rights and Fundamental Freedoms and the Paris Minimum Standards of Human Rights Norms in a State of Emergency.[61]

The next safeguard is to enforce observance of these preconditions. This vigilance should be undertaken not simply by Parliament, whose record in emergencies is uninspiring,[62] but also by an independent standing committee,[63] which would investigate and report on any proposed institution of the legislation, its working whilst in force, its renewal and its compatibility with international obligations. To some extent, the Standing Advisory Commission on Human Rights in Northern Ireland[64] performs a similar role but is greatly handicapped by its restrictive terms of reference, limited resources, and the absence of triggering criteria in the current emergency legislation and lack of information from security sources.[65]

The third restriction is that, once invoked, the actual application of each special law should be subjected to judicial control so far as possible.[66] Some commentators have additionally proposed that the courts should deliberate upon the prior questions of the existence of the emergency and the proportionality of the counter-measures invoked.[67] However, such issues would fall well outside the experience of British judges[68] and would involve unmanageable excursions into security and political, as well as legal, issues, a frolic which would often prove unpalatable both to Parliament and to the electorate.[69] Moreover, the judiciary has usually proved no more solicitous of individual rights during past emergencies than politicians.[70] These arguments are less applicable to judges in the European Court of Human Rights, who have provided a valuable longstop.

2 Measures to provide information
According to the counter-terrorism strategy delineated in chapter 2, the collection of information is vital for the eradication of terrorism. Consequently, the following devices attempt to increase its supply. The suggested justifying standards for each are as follows. First, is it reasonably likely to increase significantly the information available to the security forces about

relevant offences in a way which cannot reasonably be achieved under the existing law? Second, is it reasonably necessary in view of the threat of terrorism, as evidenced by the frequency of certain types of offences (which might be grouped together as 'scheduled offences')? It should be noted at the outset that this (and any other) resort to scheduling in Britain has been deprecated because, unlike in Northern Ireland, most homicides and munitions offences are not perpetrated by terrorists.[71] However, this pertinent observation should usefully serve to guard against the premature listing of any crime until it is predominantly committed by terrorists, thereby further precluding the excessive use of temporary provisions.

(*a*) *An offence of withholding information* It was concluded in chapter 7 that section 18 of the Prevention of Terrorism Act[72] is justifiable but of limited value. Therefore, provided it is applied with restraint, there should be a special offence[73] of withholding information known or suspected to relate to scheduled offences, subject to the insertion of more carefully drawn privileges for the suspect, lawyers and journalists.[74]

As well as an offence directed against the individual suppression of information, community failures to cooperate have sometimes been punished by reprisals, as under the Emergency Powers (Collective Punishments) Regulations 1955 in Cyprus.[75] However, this sanction was quickly removed in 1956.[76] Those inhabitants affected were mostly in no position to control the terrorists or to avoid their retribution if they did inform, so the main effect was alienation from the authorities imposing the punishments.

(*b*) *Informers and agents* The shadowy evidence available suggests that informers and agents are a prime weapon against terrorism.[77] Accordingly, anonymous information is encouraged in Northern Ireland by the provision of a confidential telephone number,[78] and more traditional forms of treason to the cause are also fostered. Three such mechanisms for promoting informers will now be evaluated. The first measure is the ability to interrogate a person in police custody for long periods. This affords the police an opportunity to investigate not only criminal involvement but also any willingness to supply evidence against others.[79] How far there should be special detention powers will be discussed in the next section.

Another way of eliciting information is by offers of rewards. The police are reticent about their practices in this field,[80] but some examples have surfaced. Thus, the Irish Government offered a substantial reward following the assassination of Lord Mountbatten,[81] and money has been offered for information about Welsh arson attacks in 1989 and I.R.A. activities in Britain in 1990.[82] Though these instances betoken the value of payments for information, there is at present insufficient control over police discretion. The suggested remedy is not an intricate statutory scheme,[83] since

standing rewards are thought to encourage irrelevant or misleading disclosures.[84] Rather, internal police rules should, and to some extent do,
ensure that substantial payments are authorised at a senior level and are
not excessive.[85]

A third tactic designed to encourage informers is the offer of concessions
in regard to prosecution or sentence. Bargains with Irish rebels have an
infamous lineage,[86] but there occurred a marked change of policy in
Northern Ireland from 1981 to 1984, since it was then decided to require
informers to testify in court rather than merely to supply details in confidence to the police. In short, the 'supergrass' system was born and produced
about three dozen Loyalist and Republican defectors, who implicated
hundreds of others.[87] The results were mixed. Relatively few convictions
were sustained, but the fear of betrayal disrupted terrorist groups to such
an extent that the R.U.C. claimed that they were 'reeling from the blows
inflicted upon them . . .'.[88] Further telling evidence of their impact is that
suspected informers have been murdered, their relatives kidnapped and
threatened and 'amnesties' offered. Despite its benefits in providing detailed,
inside information, and the sowing of discord in closed societies, the
arrangement suffered not only from the obvious practical danger of reprisals[89] but also from serious legal problems, which all contributed to its
demise after 1983.

One is the inherent risk that an offer of immunity or leniency might
motivate an informer falsely to implicate as many persons as possible to
improve the terms of the bargain. Furthermore, the trial forum in Northern
Ireland will be a non-jury court, whose quality of decision as to the reliability
of evidence has been compared unfavourably to the collective and fresher
verdict of a jury.[90] In response, the courts have for many years warned
juries that it is dangerous to rely upon the evidence of an accomplice
unless corroborated, though such corroboration is only to be taken into
account if the accomplice is otherwise credible.[91] As for special courts in
Northern Ireland, the normal common law rules have been scrupulously
applied, but they were formulated with a full jury trial in mind. Therefore,
further restrictions should apply in special courts, and these have in practice
taken the form of two extra barriers.[92] Firstly, a judge should direct
(himself in a 'Diplock' court) that it is highly dangerous to convict in the
absence of corroboration, unless the witness is exceptionally credible.
Secondly, if any part of the accomplice's statement is found to be false, any
other uncorroborated part should automatically be disregarded unless his
possible reasons for mendacity cannot equally contaminate his remaining
remarks. The cumulative effect is that virtually no conviction has been
sustained without corroboration, and this hostile legal climate has largely
terminated any reliance at trial upon supergrasses. Some critics have advocated stronger barriers – that convictions should never be returned solely

on the basis of uncorroborated accomplice evidence.[93] However, this rather inflexible proposal would exclude the testimony of totally credible witnesses.[94] Equally, the removal of any requirement of corroboration[95] not only underplays its protective benefits but also ignores the moral qualms about reliance upon this source of evidence.[96]

Problems also surround the mechanics of the bargaining between police and informer. It was settled in practice (though not in law) following *R. v. Turner*[97] that undertakings of immunity should only be given by the Directors of Public Prosecution after consultation with the Law Officers. As for the substance of the offer, large financial payments, partial, and even full, immunities have all been held out. However, to avoid providing overwhelming incentives to lie, total immunity should be tendered 'most sparingly',[98] and no inducement should be conditional upon the giving of evidence or sustaining a conviction.[99] At least, the terms of the deal should, as the Attorney General has now directed, be revealed to the court.[100] As was suggested in regard to financial rewards, offers of immunity by way of standing legislation have disadvantages. In any event, foreign laws encouraging 'repentant terrorists' have had a limited impact and mixed results.[101]

Several procedural difficulties have been experienced in Northern Ireland in connection with supergrasses. Firstly, to avoid straining unduly their star deponents, the prosecuting authorities have sometimes circumvented the usual preliminary inquiry (committal) by introducing a Voluntary Bill of Indictment. This is undesirable; such a vital witness should be 'put through his paces' as soon as possible, and intimidation could be reduced by expelling hostile spectators.[102] Other problems arising are the size of trials and delay. Cases have regularly involved dozens of defendants and so demand prolonged preparation and make it difficult to isolate relevant evidence against each defendant in turn. The Baker Report[103] recommended in response statutory deadlines on remand periods (the power to impose which was taken by the Northern Ireland (Emergency Provisions) Act 1987 section 3 (now the 1991 Act section 8) but remains unactivated) and limits on the number of defendants per trial.

The final problem associated with informers concerns their employment as police agents. The courts have accepted that: 'in these days of terrorism the police must be entitled to use the effective weapon of infiltration . . .'[104] as in the Lennon and Littlejohn cases.[105] However, there is a danger that infiltrators will act as *agents provocateurs* by instigating offences rather than simply reporting them. Consequently, a Home Office Circular[106] advises, *inter alia*, that senior officers should supervise agents, that no crimes are to be incited or procured and that courts should not be misled in order to protect agents. To strengthen these controls, the Law Commission has usefully suggested that it should be unlawful to take the initiative in persuading another to commit a crime even with the intention of preventing or nullifying the offence.[107]

(c) *Special police powers: arrests* Provided the permanent reforms suggested in Part A of this chapter were realised, most of the extra powers to arrest or detain so commonly encountered in emergency codes throughout the world need not be replicated.[108] However, some additional measures are worthy of consideration.

First, a special power to detain for questioning without warrant or reasonable suspicion should be available in three situations: in the vicinity of an attack (within, say, twenty-four hours)[109] involving scheduled offences; in areas which are likely targets for such attacks; and in the proximity of the Irish border.[110] Since powers of this nature cause inconvenience to innocent bystanders, their use should be confined in various ways.[111] Thus, a short maximum period of detention should be specified,[112] and the measure should be activated only when a judge is satisfied (retrospectively in an emergency) that ordinary police methods are insufficient to protect against attacks which are reasonably likely to happen. Applications should be *ex parte*, but after a public notice and an invitation to make representations have been issued. Judicial authorisation should expire after a fixed period. In practice, this provision would operate almost continuously in cities and border areas in Northern Ireland but would rarely be justifiable in Britain.

A detention power of a rather different kind is section 6 of the Explosive Substances Act 1883, by which the Attorney General can order the judicial examination of persons when it is reasonably suspected that any offence under that Act has been committed. Witnesses have no privilege against self-incrimination but are granted immunity from prosecution based on their evidence. Similar 'Star Chamber' provisions had been used with some success in Ireland,[113] which implies that they might be an advantageous temporary device for extracting information about terrorist offences generally.

One final extraordinary power sometimes advocated is that the security forces should be allowed to inflict brutality or even torture in order to obtain information from terrorists. The most recent officially sanctioned experiment in the U.K. was 'interrogation in depth', which operated in Northern Ireland during 1971.[114] This 'highly sophisticated and clinical' procedure[115] involved the questioning of selected suspects over several days while subjecting them to loud noise, forced standing at a wall, sleep deprivation and a strict diet. These techniques had been developed in earlier colonial campaigns[116] and were envisaged by the Joint Directive on Military Interrogation in Internal Security Operations Overseas.[117] The Compton Report concluded in November 1971 that the regime constituted 'physical ill-treatment' but not 'brutality'.[118] The following year, the majority in the Parker Report boldly asserted that any ban on such behaviour was 'unrealistic and . . . unfair both to the State and law-abiding citizens', provided there were safeguards.[119] Only Lord Gardiner demurred, but his dissent convinced the Government to terminate its flirtation with torture in March 1972.[120] By contrast, similar techniques were acceptable to the Landau Commission in Israel.[121]

The principal practical argument for ill-treatment is that it may secure evidence. For example, it has been said that torture in parts of South America 'provides the most important sources of information for the authorities'.[122] The Parker Committee also pointed to successes in Northern Ireland, though Lord Gardiner responded that ordinary methods might have been equally productive.[123]

The drawbacks of official torture arise at various levels. There will inevitably be condemnation in morality and international law.[124] Both are beyond the scope of this book,[125] save to note that they may also undermine public support for the security forces, thereby reducing the overall flow of information.[126] Amongst other practical disadvantages are that any statement so obtained will not only be inadmissible but will also be unreliable for any purpose.[127] Finally, since such techniques are probably unlawful as criminal assaults[128] and have been forbidden expressly by section 134 of the Criminal Justice Act 1988, the vague guidance in the Joint Directive would have to be translated into carefully drawn legislation. Yet the Parker Committee itself could produce no manual,[129] and drafting would be complicated by the needs to account for the varying degrees of tolerance to maltreatment and to ensure that the prescribed parameters are not transgressed. The Landau Commission claimed to have prepared a suitable code of practice,[130] but, as it remains confidential, it is impossible to comment further.

Even disregarding the moral revulsion which should greet any legal sanction of torture, the difficulties of control, the alienation generated and the uncertain quality of the product almost certainly outweigh any practical benefits which torture might procure.

(*d*) *Special police powers: searches* If the law of search and seizure were reformulated in accordance with Part A of this chapter, only the following limited additions might remain worthwhile. Firstly, there should be a power to stop and search pedestrians and vehicles without warrant or reasonable suspicion on the same basis as, and possibly in concert with, the detention for questioning provisions outlined above.[131] Secondly, it was noted in chapter 8 that Schedule 7 of the Prevention of Terrorism Act enables the police to obtain 'excluded material' and is therefore more extensive than Schedule 1 of the Police and Criminal Evidence legislation. In principle, evidence relevant to terrorism provided by confidential personal records held by doctors or social workers, confidential journalistic documents and human bodily samples should be accessible, though judicial scrutiny should be applied in all cases so as to protect individual privacy.[132] Furthermore, as suggested in Part A, State agencies should be forbidden from entering informal arrangements with the police which could avoid these restrictions.

(e) *Powers to monitor travellers* The port controls under section 16 of the Prevention of Terrorism Act illustrate that the monitoring of movements provides a further means of gathering intelligence, albeit of a lowly grade. A similar view has been taken in other jurisdictions, where the main terrorist threat originates from outsiders.[133] Therefore, temporary surveillance should be facilitated of traffic between Britain and Ireland, subject to the restraints of European Community law, as described in chapter 9. Enforcement problems render controls pointless within Britain, but the maintenance of hotel registers, however imperfectly, may have some value, as evidenced by Magee's case.[134]

(f) *Identity cards* Identity cards could prove helpful in various contexts in United Kingdom security law. Firstly, their availability would have avoided the disruptive and possibly unlawful subversion of special powers in Northern Ireland for population 'screening' and 'head checking' purposes.[135] Secondly, identity cards would reinforce the port controls. Thirdly, their production could also combine well with temporary powers of detention for questioning and summary searches.

The institution of an identification system has occasionally been raised in Parliament, most recently by the National Identity Card Bill 1988–89,[136] which had general application. Amongst the many objections is that cards would generate a vast amount of administrative work, which would divert police attention from prime suspects.[137] However, this criticism seems to be founded upon the misconception that checking would be obligatory on all conceivable occasions. In any event, any scheme could be confined to the most disturbed areas, such as Northern Ireland. Other practical problems are said to be forgery, theft and evasion.[138] Evasion or active resistance may be countered by making governmental services conditional upon registration.[139] Forgery and theft may not be wholly avoidable, but both involve a risk of detection which does not exist at present.[140] There is finally concern that cards 'give the State an opportunity to index and control the life of a citizen which is objectionable on grounds of liberty'.[141] However, it might be argued that, as Northern Ireland experience shows, they could obviate even more unpalatable infringements of personal freedom caused by the abuse of police powers.[142]

The Government currently rejects a compulsory scheme because of administrative burdens and the absence of difficulties with identification of individuals in Northern Ireland; it also fears that a voluntary scheme would fail since it would not be comprehensive.[143] Nevertheless, a statutory reserve power seems advisable, especially as remaining parts of the U.K. have not been so closely catalogued. Implementation should broadly follow the wartime National Registration Act 1939, except that production should only be necessary when other normal or special policing powers are being exercised.[144]

3 Measures to aid the administration of justice

The provisions considered hereafter are designed to aid the administration of justice and should be invoked on the following criteria: that the ordinary criminal laws and procedures are not reasonably adequate, even assuming the aid of measures already described, owing to the commission of scheduled offences, and that special measures are reasonably necessary in view of their effects.[145] Even with these safeguards, departures from traditional rules should be minimised, since all 'undermine the value of ... judicial authentication ...'[146] and strengthen claims to 'political' status.[147]

(a) *Special courts* If terrorists would not obtain a proper trial because of intimidation or bias on the part of the jury or witnesses, various modifications can be envisaged. Perhaps the most common riposte is to dispense with the jury.[148] If it can be demonstrated that the jury has become an unreliable arbiter of fact, temporary abrogation is acceptable,[149] though as many traditional features as possible should be retained in order to maintain trust in the independence and objectivity of the legal system.[150] In this light, the replacement of the jury by a single judge or even a bench of them is undesirable.[151] A *fortiori*, military courts should not be considered, despite their appearance in the Republic of Ireland as recently as 1962.[152] The most acceptable system would be to employ a judge to deal with legal issues accompanied by three lay assessors of fact, who would retain the elements of common sense and freshness normally imparted by a jury.[153] Thus, the assessors should be selected and act in the same way as a jury and would of course have to receive police protection, which rules out a larger panel or indeed a full jury. The court thus constituted should try cases involving scheduled offences which are expressly referred to it by a Law Officer.[154]

Before a special court is activated, attention should be given to alternative steps which might preserve the jury system. In Britain, such measures have included the vetting of juries.[155] However, protection along these lines is undesirable. On the one hand, the intimidation of some jurors should be dealt with by the law of contempt and security arrangements. On the other hand, some bias must be accepted as part of the charm of selecting a random cross-section of society, and, unless so endemic that a fair trial would be impossible, can be nullified by majority verdicts or powers to challenge the panel.[156] More acceptable protective measures,[157] including postponements, the suppression of the identities of jurors or witnesses or of publicity concerning the trial[158] and a change of venue,[159] are already possible without resort to special laws.

Extraordinary procedures may finally be necessary to cope with disruption by, or the absence of, the defendant or collusion in offences by defence lawyers.[160]

(*b*) *Special evidential rules*   The operation of both regular and special courts may be boosted by certain evidential rule changes which take due account of the dangerous and intimidating nature of terrorism. Indeed, these might even avoid resort to special courts and should, therefore, be considered a priority.

One current example is section 11 of the Northern Ireland (Emergency Provisions) Act 1991, which provides that confessions are inadmissible in proceedings for a scheduled offence only on *prima facie* evidence that the accused was 'subjected to torture or to inhuman or degrading treatment'.[161] Evidence obtained through interrogation is often vital against terrorist conspiracies, but such relaxed rules suffer from two considerable drawbacks. The first is that they provide some inducement to mistreat suspects, with costs in terms of damning allegations against the police, judicial backsliding and the necessity for expensive and complicated safeguards.[162] The second problem is that a special rule as to admissibility distinguishes the defendant from ordinary criminals, thereby defeating the objective of prosecution.

Proceedings may alternatively be assisted by altering the burden or level of proof. This may be achieved to some extent by imposing a presumption relating to some constituent part of the offence. For example, under section 12 of the Northern Ireland (Emergency Provisions) Act, proof that a firearm was found in premises where the defendant was or of which he was the occupier is sufficient evidence of his possession, unless he proves otherwise.[163] Another illustration is section 3(1) of the Offences against the State (Amendment) Act 1972,[164] by which acting as a spokesman for an unlawful organisation becomes evidence of membership. In both Irish jurisdictions, the possession of documents relating to a proscribed group likewise imputes membership.[165] Rules like these should be endorsed only when there is a rational connection between the facts proved and the facts presumed[166] and when the presumption is not conclusive[167] and can therefore be supported as a genuine attempt to elicit evidence rather than condemnation by legislative fiat.[168] Applying these considerations, the presumptions concerning firearms and the possession of documents are unobjectionable, though the latter has previously been rejected because of the fear that evidence would be planted.[169] However, section 3(1) of the Offences against the State (Amendment) Act links the expression of support for a cause with its furtherance by criminal acts, a dangerous leap in a democracy.

Remaining aids which have been employed against terrorist suspects include modifications to the privilege against self-incrimination. The prime example is the Criminal Evidence (Northern Ireland) Order 1988[170] which, as described in chapter 7, allows evidential weight to be derived from silence in certain situations. The Order has been criticised because of its wide application to all suspects, the summary way in which it was introduced,[171] the lack of demonstrable need for such a change,[172] and its uncertain effect in practice.[173] In principle, the Order seems to clash with such fundamental tenets as adversarial trials and the presumption of innocence[174] and has not been balanced by corresponding safeguards, such as tape-recording, legal advice, disclosure by the police of the incriminating evidence and questioning by an independent judge.[175] Other tactics have included the admission of hearsay evidence[176] and the removal of rights to cross-examine witnesses.[177] These ideas have been reflected in Northern Ireland by court orders which have suppressed the identity of witnesses[178] and by Article 81 of the Police and Criminal Evidence Order, under which witnesses who will not appear in court through fear may give evidence via a live television link.[179] Measures of this kind have the potential to undermine the proper scrutiny of evidence and so should be applied with restraint and not extended further.[180] Rather than 'imperiling the whole concept of a fair trial' in these vital ways,[181] executive measures such as internment might even be preferable so as to preserve the courts for those cases where due process remains viable.

Special evidential rules protective of suspects should also be considered. In particular, experience of the Prevention of Terrorism Act suggests that uncorroborated confessions should not be relied upon (at least without warning) to convict persons held in isolation for special detention periods.

(c) *Special offences* The advantages of generic proscription in the field of public order have already been considered in Part A. It was further accepted in chapter 5 that proscription of named groups may also act as justifiable alleviation of the prosecutor's burden by avoiding the repeated proof of the criminal nature of the organisation in question or a defendant's precise role in it, provided that condemnation is based on fact, challengeable in court and reviewable regularly.[182]

The kind of judicially based procedure envisaged could involve an annual application to the Divisional Court by the Attorney General, with any member or officer of the impugned group having the right to be heard at the original hearing. The issue should turn on proof that one or more of its adherents has committed scheduled offences on its behalf and that it officially supports such violence.[183] If a declaration is granted, the effects should be the same as those pursuant to section 2 of the Public Order Act 1936. Thus, 'active' participation should be forbidden,[184] but speaking on the group's behalf should remain lawful. Wider offences and effects[185] (save for the extra financial controls discussed earlier) should likewise be rejected as too far divorced from the basic idea of participation in criminal actions.

As there have been extremely few prosecutions in Britain in connection with proscribed organisations, there would be no real hardship in having to prove afresh the nature of the groups prohibited under section 2 of the Public Order Act. Only in Northern Ireland would it be really useful to have more specific powers of proscription.

A rather more direct step towards criminalisation would be an offence of terrorism. For example,[186] section 54(1) of the Internal Security Act 1982 in South Africa forbids the commission of, or conspiracy or incitement to commit, any act or threat of violence with intent to overthrow or endanger the State, to achieve constitutional, political, industrial, social or economic change, to induce the Government to do or abstain from doing anything, or to put in fear or demoralise the public or any section of it.[187]

The most important proposal along these lines in the United Kingdom was made by the Gardiner Report,[188] which suggested an offence of being 'concerned in the commission or attempted commission of any act of terrorism or in directing, organising, training or recruiting persons for the purposes of terrorism'. It was believed that this recommendation would ensnare terrorist leaders, who avoid participation in specific acts of violence. However, this justification was correctly rejected. For its part, the Government was opposed to vague 'catch-all' measures.[189] In any event, the reason why organisers escape prosecution is not a lack of appropriate and serious charges but a dearth of evidence, which the proposal cannot remedy.[190] Other claims on behalf of the offence can likewise be rejected. For example, arguments that it avoids charges of treason or sedition and yet emphasises society's special displeasure are self-defeating.[191] The main reason for avoiding offences against the State, namely their political nature, militates equally against terrorism charges, which would not even be justified by history. The offence is alternatively supported because existing special crimes and powers already exist by reference to the term 'terrorism', despite the anomaly that it is not *per se* unlawful.[192] However, the preferred remedy for this confusion, which has been followed throughout this work, is to avoid all legislative mention of 'terrorism'. Finally, it has been asserted that a terrorism offence might prove valuable because:[193]

if there is a resolution of the political issues ... the declaration of an amnesty for all those convicted ... is made administratively and psychologically easier....

However, this reasoning amply reveals the inherent contradictory and unsatisfactory nature of the offence in terms of the advancement of criminalisation.

Amongst the disadvantages of outlawing terrorism directly are those of vagueness[194] and its inevitable emphasis upon motives,[195] which will result in convictions not only grounded on a special crime but also by express reference to the political context of the deed.[196] Ultimately for this reason, the Criminal Law Revision Committee has rejected the notion of an offence of terrorism,[197] a verdict clearly favoured by the balance of the arguments. These arguments apply with even greater force against proposals to outlaw preparatory acts, such as, under section 30 of the Northern Ireland (Emergency Provisions) Act 1991, by the possession of materials which might be used for terrorism.[198] Such equivocal actions as the possession of rubber gloves, wire and batteries could occur quite innocently, especially at home, so the danger arises of premature police reaction and harassment. The offence might be more acceptable if confined to public places and if the articles had to be adapted or held in combination.

(*d*) *Special penalties* Special penalties are already applied to terrorists as a matter of judicial sentencing policy. For example, it has been held that the 'deterrent aspect of the sentence . . . shall be made clear' when terrorists are convicted of explosives offences.[199] Similarly, those who murder for political motives are often recommended for periods of imprisonment for longer than average,[200] and this judicial reaction has been reinforced by the adoption of the licensing policy by the Home Secretary in 1983 that at least twenty years must normally be served by terrorist murderers.[201] Finally, as noted in chapter 10, sections 22 and 23 of the Prevention of Terrorism Act increased the term served by terrorist offenders.

If it is assumed that terrorism can to some extent be deterred by savage penalties, how could that effect be enhanced? Some of the possibilities include minimum sentences,[202] an increase in maximum penalties[203] and corporal punishment.[204] However, it is the death penalty which has attracted most attention,[205] and its advisability will now be assessed.

The first reason advanced in its favour is that it is a unique deterrent. Unfortunately, hard evidence for or against this assertion is difficult to find,[206] but there must be scepticism concerning its potency over terrorists, who already risk death at the hands of the security forces. By comparison, the remote possibility of judicial execution will not greatly affect their calculations.[207] A second argument for capital punishment is that it effectively prevents any repetition of terrorist involvement by the convict. However, lengthy imprisonment is almost as effective in securing the public's safety, provided lapses in prison security can be avoided.[208] The death penalty is finally claimed to satisfy the public's desire for retribution, thereby avoiding unofficial reprisals.[209] However, similar arguments advanced on behalf of proscription were doubted because the handful of people prone to indulge in retaliation are the least likely to be satisfied by vicarious and tardy legal sanctions. Amongst the factors weighing against the judicial killing of terrorists is that it would depict them as special offenders (albeit a transitory problem in any individual case). Furthermore, there would be the recurrent problem of clarifying who is a 'terrorist',[210] which would inevitably focus attention on the political motives of the offender. Next, execution may engender sympathy for the plight of the condemned terrorist and his cause. The liquidation of rebels in Dublin in 1916 is a salutary reminder of this process, and various benefits could accrue to the terrorist cause, including 'martyrs, publicity, and a greater degree of approval within [its] community . . .'[211] on a scale which would even surpass that obtained by the self-inflicted hunger-strikes in Northern Ireland in 1981.[212] More specifically, the threat of death may reduce public cooperation with the police and the willingness of juries to convict,[213] especially in the light of miscarriages of justice in Irish terrorist trials.[214] The death penalty would also discourage cooperation by suspects, whose confessions are a major source of evidence.[215] Lastly, there are various practical difficulties associated with reviving the death penalty. First, it would be illogical not to extend it to Northern Ireland if it is truly of assistance against terrorism. However, until impartial, unintimidated juries can be restored, it would be unfair and unwise to refer capital trials to 'Diplock' courts.[216] Secondly, majority jury verdicts would surely be unacceptable in capital cases, but their removal would decrease the chances of conviction. Thirdly, the terrorists might be encouraged to increase reliance upon juveniles, who would presumably not be subjected to the death penalty. Subject to the overriding moral considerations on the issue (which are beyond the scope of this book),[217] a rational counter-terrorism strategy should not include the death penalty, and its abolition in Northern Ireland in 1973 was the correct policy.[218]

Other issues affecting the treatment of terrorist prisoners, including political status and prison regimes, the transfer of prisoners, strip-searching, and the release of life-sentence prisoners, have been discussed in P.V.L.I.[219]

4 Alternatives to the administration of justice

The following preventive measures offer alternatives to prosecution in the wake of political violence. These should arise only when Parliament and the proposed advisory committee are convinced that, even assuming the aid of special measures, criminal procedures are inadequate and that any of the following is necessary in view of the threat of terrorism, as evidenced by the commission of scheduled offences.[220]

(*a*) *Exclusion* Exclusion under the Prevention of Terrorism Act 1984 has been criticised in chapter 6 because it demands insufficient proof that suspects are likely to engage in terrorism or that their removal will decrease the chances of doing so. It was further suggested that the system should minimise derogations from normal rights, which entails evidence that the police cannot ensure that the person abstains from terrorism by normal investigative methods. The application of these criteria would require substantial changes to the system in the 1989 Act. For instance, the second consideration should mean that removal to Ireland becomes less common, though immunity after a period of short residence would be maintained. The first and third points should produce a more formal system of verification. Thus, following the making of an interim order by a Secretary of State, there should be proof on the balance of probabilities of all three criteria before an inquisitorial 'Security Tribunal' with features as described in chapter 6 and itself subject to judicial review. As at present, there should be periodic reviews of orders, though annually and automatically, and restrictions on residence should not be applied within Great Britain owing to enforcement difficulties.[221]

(*b*) *Other non-custodial restrictions* Confining a suspect to Northern Ireland or Britain is hardly conducive to monitoring his activities closely. Therefore, more direct restraints should be contemplated. Registration presents itself as a leading candidate in this field and was included in the Prevention of Violence (Temporary Provisions) Act 1939.[222] It has the advantages of leaving suspects in their known haunts and furnishing additional evidence about them as part of the registration process (which might involve photography, fingerprinting and regular reporting to the police),[223] whilst curtailing their liberty to a lesser degree than exclusion. The last point means that registration should always be considered in priority to other security orders (and perhaps in combination with them). Otherwise the criteria and procedures should be adapted from those for exclusion.

Far more drastic controls than registration can be devised. For example, 'banning orders' under the South African Internal Security Act 1982 can limit rights of expression, association, assembly and movement even to the extent of imposing house-arrest.[224] Limited measures along these lines may be justifiable as offering an intermediate degree of control between exclusion and internment. Thus, there should be powers to specify the area or place of residence of a suspect and to restrict his departure therefrom, subject to proof before a 'Security Tribunal'.

(*c*) *Internment* Internment is amongst the world's favourite security devices though it is one which should be employed with great reluctance.

Being such a radical departure from normal procedural rights, detention will be viewed as lacking legitimacy and risks manipulation for political, rather than security, purposes.[225] The criteria under which it operates should be broadly consistent with those for exclusion, though it should be specified that internment is a last resort. Given these preconditions, executive detention should be invoked only when terrorism is widespread. Even then, it should be treated as a short-term palliative, to be taken only while the security forces are being strengthened so that they may revert to the more painstaking, but ultimately more effective and acceptable, due process methods of criminal detection and prosecution.[226] Given the current formidable capabilities of the security forces, the institution of even selective internment in Britain or Northern Ireland is at present unsupportable.[227]

Internment procedures in most countries have tended to be wholly 'executive' in character,[228] including those in the now dormant Schedule 3 of the Northern Ireland (Emergency Provisions) Act 1991[229] and those in wartime Britain.[230] Nevertheless, it has been argued in chapter 6 that inquisitorial and judicial security procedures are preferable, and this view applies equally to internment,[231] so the proposed 'Security Tribunal' should again operate. Systems of this nature have sometimes prevailed[232] in Northern Ireland,[233] the Republic of Ireland,[234] India[235] and Israel.[236] Moreover, judicial review in the normal way has occasionally provided further protection and so should not be excluded.[237]

Finally, since internment is to be preventive rather than punitive, the custodial regime adopted should be distinct from that in prisons.[238]

5   Other measures

(a)   *Equipment controls*   The permanent restrictions on munitions described in Part A of this chapter should be supplemented by extra temporary provisions. The governing criteria to be applied by Parliament and the advisory commission would be whether they are reasonably likely to decrease significantly supplies or equipment which might be used in the commission of scheduled offences, whether this cannot reasonably be achieved by existing controls and whether they are necessary in view of the commission of such offences.[239]

The most drastic step would be to ban the private possession of firearms and explosives in whole or part.[240] Total prohibition would cause great inconvenience and expense and would necessitate the establishment of a system of official possessors available for hire. Stringent restrictions governing the ingredients of home-made explosives might be more acceptable as a temporary expedient, depending on evidence as to terrorist practices in relation to weapons.[241]

Equipment controls in two further directions might also be valuable. Firstly, electronic and transmitting equipment, which can be employed, for example, to detonate bombs[242] or to gather intelligence,[243] should be denied to terrorists by way of special prohibitions and licensing requirements. Secondly, the taking of a vehicle has been a preparatory step to many attacks in Northern Ireland. A modest step, which hinders the plotters and increases the possibility of detection, is the Northern Ireland (Emergency Provisions) Regulations 1975,[244] which provide that it is a summary offence not to ensure that an unattended vehicle is properly secured.

(*b*) *Target controls* If terrorism is to be prevented *ab initio*, attention should be paid to its potential victims or objects of attack so as to remove them from the firing-line. Some vulnerable categories, such as diplomats, nuclear materials, oil rigs, ports and airports, have been the subject of legislation described in the previous chapter. 'Target-hardening'[245] does, however, incur many problems, including increased costs, police intrusion and displacement to softer targets. Consequently, further protection should be confined to persons and property most at risk and should operate under criteria similar to those for equipment controls.

Temporary measures may first be invoked to defend vulnerable persons, such as the security forces. For example, it was an offence in Palestine to trespass in, or loiter near, or enter, vehicles used by the police or soldiers.[246] However, the regular arrest and search powers in the U.K. (especially if further reformed and strengthened as outlined) are already sufficiently wide to deal with such suspicious behaviour. More appropriate is section 31 of the Northern Ireland (Emergency Provisions) Act 1991, which penalises the gathering of information likely to be useful to terrorists concerning the security forces, judges, court officials and prison officers.[247] The precision of this offence reduces substantially the danger of harassment, and it might even be expanded to cover police, Army and court premises, police authorities and Members of Parliament and diplomats. A much longer list is conceivable but may invite police over-reaction.[248]

The safety of vulnerable physical locations as well as persons can also be improved. This has partly occurred on an *ad hoc* basis by increasing security levels, such as at Parliament,[249] political conferences[250] and military bases,[251] and warning targets in response to specific threats. Defences in Northern Ireland have been more systematic and include restrictions on parking,[252] control-gates around city centres, manned by civilian search units,[253] and (until 1986)[254] a Security Staff Grants Scheme for the payment of grants for security guards in certain premises open to the public. Construction planning and design have also been important, with such features as limited access and blast deflectors being incorporated on the advice of the security forces.[255]

In the light of these examples, protective measures for premises should

L

appear in five legislative forms. First, the special powers of detention for questioning and stop and search already outlined would be of great assistance. Secondly, a statutory scheme of security grants should be available. Thirdly, traffic regulations should be issuable on grounds of security. Next the temporary offence of gathering information could be extended to public utilities such as railways, roads, water and power equipment and broadcasting stations.[256] Finally, security regulations might demand the filing with the security forces of layouts, the implementation of security measures (such as cameras, bag searches and the removal of hazards) and the drawing of contingency plans for evacuation in respect of categories of buildings to which the public has regular access.[257] These additions would strengthen the legal armoury already available.[258] For example, it is an offence to trespass in railway, dockland premises and explosives factories and magazines[259] or, following a proclamation under the Emergency Powers Act 1920, in any installations used in connection with essential services.[260]

Next, more extensive security measures to protect targets, such as the evacuation of whole areas or the declaration of special zones have been employed abroad[261] but are probably not feasible against terrorism in the U.K.[262] However, more limited interference with property rights, such as the closure of roads, the installation of monitoring cameras in public places or the demolition of structures which might provide cover for attacks, could be acceptable.[263] Such intrusions should be permitted after proof in court (and subject to compensation) that such interference is reasonably likely to increase significantly protection from attacks involving scheduled offences in a way which cannot reasonably be achieved by existing means and which is necessary in view of the threat of such attacks.

(*c*) *Compensation* As well as compensation for interferences with private property on security grounds, reimbursement against damage caused by terrorism should also be considered. Such payments would reflect the State's responsibility for order and would also ensure that economic dislocation is minimised and spread as thinly as possible.[264] Compensation is available for criminal injuries in Britain,[265] but both personal injury and property losses are recoverable in Northern Ireland[266] and elsewhere.[267]

C Conclusions

Given its attractions for politically and militarily weak causes, terrorism is likely to persist for the foreseeable future. This prediction should trigger two results. One is that there should be more officially backed studies into the phenomenon of terrorism and related issues. The other is that a comprehensive and permanent legal code should be constructed. This chapter has attempted the second task, and the results would be a modest improvement on emergency legislation current in the U.K. for three reasons. Firstly, they are based on a coherent anti-terrorism strategy and comparative investigations rather than on chance events, outrage or the legacy of past rancour. Secondly, they are comprehensive and therefore able to combat various forms and degrees of terrorism. Thirdly, the proposals attempt to incorporate far more safeguards for democracy and individual rights than presently observed (with the result that very few special measures would be currently justifiable in Britain).

Even if the model legislation were adopted, it would have a limited impact. Like the Prevention of Terrorism Act 1989 it should replace,[268] its effect would be to control terrorists already active as much as to prevent political violence. Whatever its benefits, security legislation can never provide the entire response to terrorism, especially in regard to its prevention, and there are many extraneous factors to consider. These include the size, nature, accountability and efficiency of the security and intelligence agencies, the manner of disposal of terrorist convicts[269] and, most important of all, political reactions. In this way:[270]

there can be no such thing as a purely military solution because insurgency is not primarily a military activity. At the same time, there is no such thing as a wholly political solution either, short of surrender, because the very fact that a state of insurgency exists implies that violence is involved which will have to be countered to some extent at least by the use of force. . . . the overall plan of campaign should not be regarded as an operational matter, but . . . as a major function of government. . . .

Taking all these complications into account, the process of defeating a substantial terrorist movement will often be a protracted,[271] expensive and perhaps politically impossible[272] undertaking. Nevertheless, there is room for hope. Most terrorist groups lack significant support, technical capabilities or both. In addition, counter-measures can prevent or reduce the injury and damage they can inflict. Assuming that moral and political scruples are satisfied, lawyers can contribute to this enterprise by arguing for a legislative framework most appropriate not only to the defeat of terrorism but also to the achievement of justice in that strategy and in society generally.[273] In this pursuit, it should be remembered that the rule of law has more often been injured by overweening governments than by terrorist bombs. The suggestions produced in this study are offered as part of the answer to avoiding both calamities.

Notes

1   In drafting terms, the envisaged Code was set out in P.T.B.L. (1st ed.) App. 2.

2   See: Conference on the Defence of Democracy against Terrorism in Europe:

Tasks and Problems (Clutterbuck) (Council of Europe AS/POL/COLL/Terr 32(2) (1980).

3   See ch. 4.

4   See: ch. 5; P.V.L.I. p. 143.

5   As explained in ch. 5, the Prevention of Terrorism Act s. 3 is largely otiose.

6   Compare: Internal Security Act 1960 (No. 82) s. 5 (Malaysia); Internal Security Act 1970 (c. 115) s. 5(1) (Singapore); Criminal Code ss. 129, 129a (F.R.G.).

7   See: ch. 8; P.V.L.I. pp. 64–9. Compare: Internal Security Act 1960 s. 74 (Malaysia); Internal Security Act 1982 (No. 74) s. 49 (South Africa); Model Penal Code s. 3.07(2)(6), *Tennessee* v. *Garner* 471 U.S. 1 (1985) (U.S.A.); Paris Minimum Standards, Section C Art 4 (see S.R. Chowdhury, *State of Law in a State of Emergency* (1989) pp. 155–71); U.N.G.A., Code of Conduct for Law Enforcement Officials (1979) Art. 3 (see N.S. Rodley, *The Treatment of Prisoners in International Law* (1987) ch. 6).

8   See ch. 8 n. 74.

9   A workable list is provided in the Police and Criminal Evidence Act 1984 and (Northern Ireland) Order 1989 S.I. No. 1341 Sched. 5

10   Compare: Landau Report, ch. 4; Rabie Report, ch. 10. Exclusionary sanctions are suggested by the McDonald Commission (*2nd Report* Pt. X ch. 5 paras. 44, 71).

11   The Scottish police have suggested a twenty-four-hour detention power, but even this has been rejected by the Government: Home Affairs Committee, *Practical Police Cooperation in the European Communities* (1989–90 H.C. 363) para. 127 and *Government Reply* (Cm. 1367, 1991) p. 9.

12   Compare: Royal Commission on Criminal Procedure (Cmnd. 8092, 1981) paras. 3.53–3.60; Hope Report, Pt. C and Appendix K, Australian Security Intelligence Organisation Act 1979 (No. 113) s. 26, Telecommunications (Interception) Act 1979 (No. 114) (Australia); McDonald Commission, *2nd Report*, Pt. III ch. 3, Pt. V ch. 4 para. 127, Pt. X ch. 5 para. 15 (Canada); Report by the Chief Ombudsman on the Security Intelligence Service (1976) pp. 57–60 (hereafter cited as the 'Powles Report'), N.Z. Security Intelligence Service (Amendment) Act 1977 s. 4 (New Zealand); Post Office Act 1958 (No. 44) s. 118A (as amended) (South Africa); Organic Law No. 4/1988 (Spain); Omnibus Crime Control and Safe Streets Act 1968 (18 U.S.C. ss. 2510–20), Foreign Surveillance Act 1978 (ss. 2521–8) (U.S.A.).

13   See: McDonald Commission, *2nd Report*, Pt. III ch. 8, Pt. V ch. 4 para. 57, Pt. X ch. 5 para. 34; *Buckoke* v. *G.L.C.* [1971] Ch. 657; *Johnson* v. *Phillips* [1975] 3 All E.R. 682; Road Traffic Regulations Act 1984 ss. 67, 87.

14   See: McDonald Commission, *2nd Report*, Pt. III ch. 2, Pt. V ch. 4 para. 137, Pt. X ch. 5 para. 7; Final Report of the Select Committee to Study Governmental Operations with Respect to Intelligence Activities (U.S. Senate, 94th Cong. 2d Sess. Report, No. 94-755, 1976) Book II p. 328 (hereafter cited as the 'Church Committee'). This power might again be linked to the Police and Criminal Evidence legislation Sched. 5.

15   Compare Chief Constable, R.U.C., *Annual Report for 1989* (1990) p. 11.

16   See, for example: H.C. Debs. Vol. 167 cols. 495–696 w.a. 20 February 1990; Land Registration Act 1988.

17   A.C.P.O.'s Code of Practice for Police Computer Systems (1987) provides
for no independent scrutiny nor does it apply to manual records, and the Data
Protection Act 1984 contains wide exemptions for records relating to national
security.
18   See: *R.* v. *Moloney* [1985] A.C. 905; J. D. Jackson, 'Mens rea of murder
in Northern Ireland' (1981) 32 *N.I.L.Q.* 173. An intention merely to frighten resulting in death is not murder in Scotland: G.H. Gordon, *The Criminal Law of
Scotland* (2nd ed., 1978) para. 23.15.
19   See: *R.* v. *Louden* [1980] N.I. 1. Compare: *R.* v. *Bateson and others* (1980)
9 N.I.J.B.
20   See: *R.* v. *McFeeley* [1977] N.I. 149.
21   14th Report, *Offences against the Person* (Cmnd. 7844, 1980) para. 30. See
also: Law Commission Report No. 177, Criminal Code (1988–89 H.C. 299) cl.
54(1); H.L. Select Committee on Murder and Life Imprisonment (1988–89 H.L.
78) para. 76.
22   *Ibid.* para. 31.
23   The same applies to special offences involving the death of judges, policemen or politicians, as in the Prevention of Terrorism (Temporary Provisions) Act
1979 (No. 48) ss. 2(1)(a), 31 (Sri Lanka).
24   *Loc. cit.* para. 76.
25   Offences against the Person Act 1861 s. 16 (as amended by Criminal Law
Act 1977 Sched. 12; Criminal Law (Amendment) (N.I.) Order 1977 Art. 4); Criminal
Damage Act 1971 s. 2.
26   *Loc. cit.* para. 217. Compare: Conspiracy and Protection of Property Act
1875 s. 7.
27   Protection of Persons and Property Act (N.I.) 1969 s. 1 (see: P.V.L.I. p.
145). There is a common law offence of threatening grievous harm in Scotland:
Gordon, *op. cit.* para. 29.61. Compare: Law and Order (Maintenance) Act 1960
(c. 65, as amended) ss. 27, 30 (Rhodesia/Zimbabwe); Intimidation Act 1982 (No.
72) (South Africa); B. Smith, 'State anti-terrorism legislation in the U.S.' in R.M.
Ward and H.E. Smith (eds.), *International Terrorism* (1987).
28   See also: Firearms Rules 1969 S.I. No. 1219; Firearms (N.I.) Order 1981
S.I. No. 155.
29   See P.V.L.I. p. 143. Compare: Emergency Powers (Maintenance of Law and
Order) Regulations 1983 S.I. No. 458 s. 45 (Zimbabwe). There would also be
overlap with the Public Order Act 1936 s. 2 and the dormant Unlawful Drilling
Act 1819. The latter should be repealed, but the Review of Public Order Law
(Cmnd. 9510, 1985 para. 6.2) proposes its retention. Compare: J. Baker, *The Law
of Political Uniforms, Public Meetings and Private Armies* (1937) p. 115; A.T.H.
Smith, *Offences against Public Order* (1987) p. 250; Internal Security Act 1960
s. 6 (Malaysia).
30   See: National Advisory Committee on Criminal Justice Standards and Goals,
Disorders and Terrorism (1976) p. 89; P. Wilkinson, *Terrorism and the Liberal
State* (2nd ed., 1986) p. 175.
31   See: 1970 S.I. Nos. 110, 332, 1972 S.I. Nos. 432, 1164, 1973 S.I. Nos. 171,
463, 474, 1974 S.I. No. 32, 1976 S.I. Nos. 51, 562, 1977 S.I. No. 28, 1981 S.I.
No. 31. Some reforms were implemented by 1991 S.I. No. 1531.

32   See: Hope J., *Protective Security Review: Report* (1979) ch. 6 (Australia);
C. Dobson and R. Payne, *The Weapons of Terror* (1979) ch. 7; P. Bishop and
E. Mallie, *The Provisional I.R.A.* (1987) ch. 17. The movement of firearms can be
strictly controlled; see: Firearms Act 1968 s. 6; Firearms (Removal to N.I.) Order
1975 S.I. No. 760; Firearms (N.I.) Order 1981 Art. 7; Firearms (Amendment) Act
1988 s. 20. A secret governmental review has been held, and tighter controls are
envisaged: H.C. Debs. Vol. 187 col. 25 4 March 1991.
33   See also: Firearms (N.I.) Order 1983 S.I. No. 1899. This followed the case
of *R.* v. *Sarjeant* (1981) *Sunday Times* 14 June p. 1.
34   See: *Firearms Act 1968: Proposals for Reform* (Cm. 261, 1987).
35   *Control of Firearms in Great Britain* (Cmnd. 5297). See also: H.L. Select
Committee, *1992*, *loc. cit.* Minutes of Evidence p. 186.
36   See: Firearms Consultative Committee, *1st Report* (1989–90 H.C. 543)
para. 3.8.
37   See: Council of Europe Committee of Ministers, Recommendation on the
Harmonisation of National Legislation Relating to Firearms (R(84)23; Draft E.C.
Council Directive on the control of the acquisition and possession of firearms
(8356/8; COM. (87) 383 Final), E.C. Council Common Position (10946/1/90).
38   See: H.L. Select Committee, *1992* (1988–89 H.L. 90) paras. 31, 86, Minutes of Evidence pp. 184–6; D. Lanfer, 'The evolution of Belgian terrorism' in J.
Lodge (ed.), *The Threat of Terrorism* (1988).
39   See: C. Greenwood, *Firearms Controls* (1972) pp. 247, 253–4; Dobson and
Payne, *op. cit.* ch. 6; H.L. Select Committee, *1992*, *loc. cit.* pp. 184–6.
40   See: D. Leigh, *The Frontiers of Secrecy* (1980) ch. 5; J. Bloch and P. Fitzgerald,
British Intelligence and Covert Actions (1983); R. Norton-Taylor, *In Defence of
the Realm* (1990); W. Finnie, 'The smile on the face of the tiger' (1990) 41 *N.I.L.Q.*
64; Hope Report; Landau Report, para. 4.19; McDonald Commission; Powles
Report; Bureau for State Security Act 1978 (No. 104) (South Africa); Church
Committee.
41   See: Walker, 'The role and powers of the Army in Northern Ireland' in
B. Hadfield (ed.), *Northern Ireland and the Constitution* (forthcoming); Emergency
Provisions Act 1991 s. 60.
42   See: K.G. Robertson, *1992* (1989) pp. 38, 40.
43   See: Hope J., *op. cit.* chs. 7, 8; State Counter-Disaster Organisation Act
1975 (No. 40) (Queensland); Security Intelligence and State Security Council Act
1972 (No. 64) (South Africa); J.B. Wolf, *Fear of Fear* (1981) ch. 6; National Advisory
Committee on Criminal Justice Standards and Goals, *loc. cit.* pp. 137–8.
44   See: H.C. Debs. Vol. 65 col. 440 22 October 1984, Mr. Brittan; G. Davidson-
Smith, *Combating Terrorism* (1990)
45   H.C. Debs. Vol. 187 col. 27 4 March 1991. The arrangements were made
in August and October 1990.
46   See: D. Bonner, *Emergency Powers in Peacetime* (1985) ch. 2; K.G.
Robertson, 'Intelligence, terrorism and civil liberties' (1987) 7.2. Conflict Q. 43;
I. Leigh and L. Lustgarten, 'The Security Servict Act 1989' (1989) 52 *M.L.R.* 801;
Norton-Taylor, *op. cit.*
47   See especially: K. Lindsay, *The British Intelligence Services in Action* (1980);
A. Verrier, *Through the Looking Glass* (1983); A. McArdle, *The Secret War*

(1984); R. Faligot, *Britain's Military Strategy in Ireland* (1983); J. Stalker, *Stalker* (1988); P. Wright, *Spycatcher* (1988); P. Foot, *Who Framed Colin Wallace?* (1989); F. Holroyd, *War without Honour* (1989); R. Murray, *The S.A.S. in Ireland* (1990); M. Dillon, *The Dirty War* (1990).

48 See: National Advisory Committee on Criminal Justice Standards and Goals, *loc. cit.* pp. 78, 95; Rabie Report, paras. 7.45–7.49, 11.1.7–11.1.12; Robertson, *loc. cit.*

49 Compare: National Advisory Committee on Criminal Justice Standards and Goals, *loc. cit.* pp. 77–9; D.O'Donnell, 'States of exception' (1978) 21 *Rev. of I.C.J.* 52; McDonald Commission, *2nd Report*, Pt. IX ch. 1; Rabie Report, para. 8.2.4.2. It follows that retrospective indemnity Acts are also to be deprecated.

50 See: ch. 4; A.J. Dicey, *England's Case against Home Rule* (1886) p. 113.

51 Compare: Lord MacDermott, 'Law and order in times of emergency' (1972) *J.R.* 1 at p. 21.

52 See: G.S. Morris, 'The Emergency Powers Act 1920' (1979) *P.L.* 317; K. Jeffrey and P. Hennessy, *States of Emergency* (1983). Compare: Air Raid Precautions Act 1937; Civil Defence Act 1939.

53 Compare: Fabian Tract No. 416, *Emergency Powers: A Fresh State* (1972); Standing Advisory Commission on Human Rights, *8th Report* (1982–83 H.C. 230) para. 8, *10th Report* (1984–85 H.C. 175) para. 49; McDonald Commission, *2nd Report*, Pt. IX ch. 1 para. 43; J. Hatchard, 'The implementation of safeguards on the use of emergency powers' (1989) 9 *Ox. J.L.S.* 116.

54 By contrast, wartime contingency plans are almost always drafted in secret: P. Gillman and L. Gillman, *Collar the Lot* (1980) pp. 119, 1220; N. Stammers, *Civil Liberties in Britain during the Second World War* (1983) chap. 1; D. Campbell, 'Secret laws for wartime Britain' (1985) *New Statesman* 6 September p. 8. The Paris Minimum Standards Section (b) Art. 4(b) also requires advance formulation (see Chowdhury, *op. cit.* p. 129).

55 See P.V.L.I. pp. 182–3.

56 35-57 Eliz. II c. 29. This 'umbrella' approach, covering all emergencies, obviously differs from the 'sectoral' Anti-Terrorism Act envisaged in this chapter. See: H.P. Lee, *Emergency Powers* (1984) p. 129.

57 Nos. 179 (1987), 28 (1990). See: Walker, 'The role and powers of the Army in Northern Ireland', *loc. cit.*

58 J. Sim and P. Thomas, 'The Prevention of Terrorism Act: normalising the politics of repression' (1984) 10 *J. of L. & S.* 71 at p. 72. See also: Lee, *op. cit.* p. 6; Stammers, *op. cit.* p. 222.

59 Compare: 'The national security interest and civil liberties' (1972) 85 *Harv. L.R.* 1130 at Pt. V; C. Townshend, *Britain's Civil Wars* (1986) pp. 69, 72. These matters have also been discussed in ch. 4.

60 See: R. Higgins, 'Derogations under human rights treaties' (1976) 48 *B.Y.I.L.* 281; J.F. Hartman, 'Derogations from human rights treaties in public emergencies' (1981) 22 *Harv. Int. L.J.* 1. Renewal periods of six or twelve months should be adopted, as appropriate.

61 Historical evidence does not support the lasting efficacy of unrestrained responses. Compare: T. Wilson, *Ulster* (1989) p. 245.

62 Compare: C.L. Rossiter, *Constitutional Dictatorship* (1948); J. Eaves

Jr., *Emergency Powers and the Parliamentary Watchdog* (1957); C.E.S. Franks, *Parliament and Security Matters* (1979); O.G. Lomas, 'The executive and the anti-terrorist legislation of 1939' (1980) *P.L.* 16; Stammers, *op. cit.* p. 233. Problems include turnover of members, overwork, partisanship and lack of confidentiality: H.P. Lee, 'The A.S.I.O' (1989) 38 *I.C.L.Q.* 890. Despite this record, both New Zealand's International Terrorism (Emergency Powers) Act 1987 ss. 7, 8 and Canada's Emergencies Act 1988 ss. 7, 18, 29, 39, 58, 59, 61, 62 place great faith in parliamentary scrutiny (and the latter envisages a Parliamentary Review Committee).

63 Compare: M.P. O'Boyle, 'Emergency situations and the protection of human rights' (1977) 28 *N.I.L.Q.* 160 at p. 186; Rabie Report, para. 8.2.5.

64 See: Northern Ireland Constitution Act 1973 s. 20; P.R. Maguire, 'Standing Advisory Commission on Human Rights' 1973–80 (1981) 32 *N.I.L.Q.* 31.

65 As an example of some of these difficulties, see the passage of the Criminal Evidence (N.I.) Order 1988. Annual reports on the threat of terrorism are required by 22 U.S.C. s. 2656f; 46 U.S.C. s. 1802.

66 See: Paris Minimum Standards Section B Art. 5 (see: Chowdhury, *op. cit.* pp. 131–40); Lord Lowry, *Civil Proceedings in a Beleaguered Society* (1987).

67 See: O'Boyle, *loc. cit.* p. 186; 'The national security interest and civil liberties', *loc. cit.* p. 1296; Lee, *op. cit.* ch. 7; S.A.C.H.R., *13th Report* (1987–88 H.C. 298) App. D. para 68.

68 But these questions are justifiable when martial law is declared. See: *R. v. Allen* [1921] 2 I.R. 317.

69 Compare: 'The national security interest and civil liberties', *loc. cit.* pp. 1294–1301; H.L. Debs. Vol. 396 col. 1366 29 November 1978, Lord Diplock; M.L. Friedland, *National Security: The Legal Dimensions* (1980) pp. 118, 120.

70 See: J. Jaconelli, *Enacting a Bill of Rights* (1980) p. 239; G.J. Alexander, 'The illusory protection of human rights by national courts during periods of emergency' (1984) 5 *H.R.L.J.* 1.

71 See: Jellicoe Report, para. 74.

72 See also: Law on Terrorism (21.4.78) Art. 3 (Greece); Internal Security Act 1960 s. 60 (Malaysia); Law and Order (Maintenance) Act 1960 s. 51 (Rhodesia/ Zimbabwe); Penal Code Art. 386bis (Spain); Prevention of Terrorism (Temporary Provisions) Act 1979 s. 5 (Sri Lanka).

73 The Criminal Law Act (N.I.) 1967 s. 5(1) should be repealed, but the Baker Report (para. 253) proposes its retention for non-scheduled arrestable offences.

74 Compare: Privacy Protection Act 1980 (42 U.S.C. s. 2000aa), 28 C.F.R. 59 (1980) (U.S.A.).

75 No. 232. Compare: Emergency (Amendment) (No. 3) Regulations 1952 (G.N. 1253) (Kenya); Emergency Regulations 1951 (L.N. 569) s. 17D, 17DA (Malaya); C. Townshend, *The British Campaign in Ireland 1919–1921* (1975) p. 149. Unofficial reprisals are more common; see for example: *Report of the Nyasaland Commission of Inquiry* (Cmnd. 814, 1959) paras. 275–6.

76 No. 239. For an example of its operation, see: *Ross-Clunis v. Papadopoullos* [1958] 1 W.L.R. 546; C. Hewitt, *The Effectiveness of Anti-Terrorist Politics* (1989) pp. 56, 58.

77 See: R. Allason, *The Branch* (1983) pp. 94, 95; R. H. Ward and H.E. Smith, *International Terrorism* (1987) p. 69; Dillon, *op. cit.* chs 3, 10, 12–14.

78   10 per cent of callers have relevant information: *Times* 19 June 1987 p. 2.
79   See: Evelegh, *op. cit.* ch. 2, 7.
80   See: H.C. Debs. Vol. 901 col. 583 w.a. 3 December 1975.
81   See: *Irish Times* 30 August 1979. See also: *R.* v. *Governor of Winson Green Prison, ex p. Littlejohn* [1975] 3 All E.R. 208; cases of Mr and Mrs Hayde (*Times* 12 October 1983 p. 2).
82   *Times* 23 June 1989 p. 2, 21 September 1990 p. 1.
83   Compare: Law on Terrorism 1979 Art. 5(2) (Greece); 1984 Act to Combat International Terrorism (18 U.S.C. ss. 3071–7), Omnibus Diplomatic Security and Anti-Terrorism Act 1986 (22 U.S.C. ss. 2708, 2711) (U.S.A.).
84   See: H.C. Debs. Vol. 901 cols. 985–6 26 November 1975, Mr. Crowder; col. 1021 27 November 1975, Mr. Jenkins. The emphasis in organised crime cases in the U.S.A. is likewise on the protection and relocation of the witnesses rather than rewards: M.H. Graham, *Witness Intimidation* (1985).
85   See: D. Campbell, 'Whisper who dares' (1991) 91 *Police Rev.* 532.
86   See: K.R.M. Short, *The Dynamite War* (1979); case of James Carey (1882); case of Henri Le Caron (see: J.A. Cole, *Prince of Spies* (1984); case of Kenneth Lennon (see: *Report to the Home Secretary from the Commissioner of Police of the Metropolis on the Actions of Police Officers concerned with the case of Kenneth Joseph Lennon* (1974 H.C. 351); G. Robertson, *Reluctant Judas* (1976); A. Boyd, *The Informers* (1984); Belfast Bulletin No. 11, *Supergrasses* (1984).
87   See: Baker Report, paras 163–72; T. Gifford, *Supergrasses* (1984). S. Greer, 'Supergrasses and the legal system in Britain and Northern Ireland' (1986) 102 *L.Q.R.* 189; D. Bonner, 'Combating terrorism: supergrass trials in Northern Ireland' (1988) 51 *M.L.R.* 23; Amnesty International, *Northern Ireland: Killings by Security Forces and 'Supergrass' Trials* (1988); PVLI pp. 123–6.
88   *Times* 25 March 1982 p. 1.
89   To avoid coaching in evidence, the informer should not be housed in police premises; see: Gifford, *op. cit.* paras. 16, 81. Compare: Internal Security Act 1982 s. 31 (South Africa); Witness Security Reform Act 1984 (18 U.S.C. ss. 3521–8) (U.S.A.).
90   See P.V.L.I. ch. 4.
91   See Law Commission Working Paper No. 115, *Corroboration of Evidence in Criminal Trials* (1990) pp. 11–22.
92   P.V.L.I. pp. 124–6.
93   See: Gifford, *op. cit.* para. 99; A. Jennings, 'Supergrasses and the Northern Ireland legal system' (1983) 133 *N.L.J.* 1043; Walsh, *op. cit.* p. 128; S.A.C.H.R., *10th Report, loc. cit.* Appendix B para. 74, Appendix C paras. 18–30. Supporting evidence is demanded in Scotland: *Sinclair* v. *Clark* 1962 J.C. 57. The Government has rejected such proposals: H.C. Debs. Vol. 80 cols. 1009–10 13 June 1985.
94   Informer evidence was upheld as a fair basis for conviction in *X* v. *U.K.* Appl. No. 7306/75, D.R. 7 p. 45.
95   See: Law Commission, Working Paper No. 115, *loc. cit.* para. 4:42, Compare: Essential (Security Cases) (Amendment) Regulations 1975 (P.U.(A)362) r. 21(2) (Malaysia).
96   See: J.D. Jackson, 'Credibility, morality and the corroboration warning' (1989) 47 *C.L.J.* 428.
97   *Loc. cit.* at p. 80. The Attorney General has directed accordingly: H.C.

Debs. Vol. 12 col. 12 9 November 1981; Vol. 47 cols. 3–5 w.a. 24 October 1983.

98   R. v. *Turner, loc. cit.* at p. 80. For the Attorney General's response, see *supra.* Compare: Law on Terrorism 1978 Art. 5(1) (Greece); S.A.C.H.R., *10th Report, loc. cit.* Appendix C paras. 5–13.

99   R.U.C. policy reflects both points. See: S.A.C.H.R, *10th Report, loc. cit.* Appendix C paras. 5, 8. Immunity should be confined to crimes expressly or implicitly disclosed, as in 18 U.S.C. s. 6002 (U.S.A.).

100   See n. 97 *supra*; R. v. *Graham, loc. cit.* at p. 23; S.A.C.H.R., *10th Report, loc. cit.* Appendix B. para. 66, Appendix C paras. 14–17. But insufficient details are often given: Bonner, *loc. cit.* pp. 41–2; Amnesty International, *op. cit.* ch. 4.

101   Art. 86-1020 (France); Criminal Code s. 129 (5) (F.R.G.); Decrees of 21 March 1978, 15 December 1979, 15 February 1980, 29 May 1982, 29 November 1989 (see: A. Grassi, 'Terrorism in Italy and the Government's response' in R.H. Ward and H.E. Smith (eds.), *International Terrorism* (1987) (Italy); Organic Law 4/1984 Art. 6, Organic Law 3/1988, inserting Penal Code Arts. 57 bis (b), 98 bis (see: B. Pollock and G. Hunter, 'Dictatorship, democracy and terrorism in Spain' in Lodge (ed.), *op. cit.*) (Spain).

102   Baker Report, para. 59. See also: *ibid.* para. 57, 58; S.A.C.H.R., *9th Report* (1982–83 H.C. 262) ch. 4, Appendix A, *10th Report, loc. cit.* Appendix B para. 65; Colville Report on the E.P. Acts, para. 7.1; Practice Direction (Crime: Voluntary Bills) [1990] 1 W.L.R. 1630. The procedure may be liable to attack under the European Convention, Art. 6. Compare: Re R. *and Arviv* (1985) 20 D.L.R. (4th) 422 (Ont. C.A.).

103   Paras. 172, 185. See now: Emergency Provisions Act 1991 s. 8. Compare: S.A.C.H.R., *10th Report, loc. cit.* Appendix C paras. 36–42; Amnesty International, *op. cit.* ch. 11; *Wilson and others* v. *U.K.* Appl. no. 13004/87; Internal Security Act 1982 s. 67 (South Africa).

104   R. v. *Mealey and Sheridan* (1974) 60 Cr. App. R. 59 at p. 61 *per* Lawton L.J. Entrapment is no defence: R. v. *Murphy* [1965] N.I. 138; R. v. *Sang* [1980] A.C. 402; D. Lanham, 'Entrapment, qualified defences and codification' (1984) 4 *Ox. J.L.S.* 437; M.J. Allen, 'Entrapment' (1984) 13(4) *Anglo Am. L.R.* 57.

105   See Faligot, *op. cit.* ch. 6.

106   See: 'Police use of informants' (1969) 119 *N.L.J.* 513. Compare: Presidential Executive Order No. 12333 of 1981 (U.S.A.); J.B. Wolf, *op. cit.* ch. 9; Church Committee, Book II pp. 328–9; The McDonald Commission, *2nd Report*, Pt. III ch. 9 paras. 33, 93, Pt. X ch. 5 para. 38.

107   Report No. 83, *Defences of General Application* (1976–77 H.C. 556) para. 5.48. Persons who merely assist with such an intention may be excused: Law Com. Report No. 177, *A Criminal Code for England and Wales* (1988–89 H.C. 299) para. 9.33. See further: E. Oscapella, 'A study of informers' [1980] Crim. L.R. 136; A. Choo, 'A defence of entrapment' (1990) 53 *M.L.R.* 453; McDonald Commission, *2nd Report*, Pt. X para. 92; Powles Report, p. 32.

108   See: for example: Public Order (Temporary Measures) Act 1970 (c. 2) s. 9 (seven days' detention), McDonald Commission, *2nd Report*, Pt. IX ch. 1 para. 52 (seven days' detention) (Canada); Act 86-1020 (four days) (France); Emergency Regulations 1952 (G.N. 1103) r. 3 (ten days) (Kenya); Internal Security Act 1960 ss. 45, 64 (unlimited) (Malaysia); Internal Security Act 1982 ss. 29, 44, 45 (unlimited), 34 (six months) (South Africa); Public Emergency Decree 1963 (as amended) (F.L.N. 21/63, 42/64 24/66) s. 3 (twenty-eight days) (South Arabia); Organic Law 9/1984 Art. 13 (ten days); Organic Law 4/1988 Art. 520A (five days) (Spain); Prevention of Terrorism (Temporary Provisions) Act 1979 ss. 6, 7 (seventy-two hours) (Sri Lanka); Emergency Powers (Maintenance of Law and Order) Regulations 1983 s. 53 (thirty days) (Zimbabwe).

109 Compare: Baker Report, paras 382–4; Criminal Procedure Code s. 111 (F.R.G.).

110 Compare: Public Emergency Decree 1963 s. 4 (South Arabia); Hope J., *op. cit.* paras. 3.53–3.74. Special powers of detention and stop and search (see *infra*) should be available to soldiers, though their deployment would be a last resort and preferably on the request, and in the presence, of the police. Compare: Hope Report, Protective Security Review, *loc. cit.* p. 171; Lee *op. cit.* pp. 248–50; International Terrorism (Emergency Powers) Act 1987 s. 12 (New Zealand).

111 Nevertheless, special powers of detention and stop and search (see *infra*) may breach the European Convention on Human Rights Art. 5. See chs. 8, 9.

112 Compare: S.A.C.H.R., *9th Report, loc. cit.* para. 12; Baker Report, para. 394; Criminal Justice (Scotland) Act 1980 s. 1(2).

113 See especially: Prevention of Crime (Ireland) Act 1882 s. 16. See also: Defence (Emergency) Regulations (Gazette No. 1442 Supp. No. 2 27.9.45) (Palestine).

114 See: Compton Report; J. McGuffin, *The Guinea Pigs* (1974); P. Watson, *War on the Mind* (1978).

115 M. Dewar, *The British Army in Northern Ireland* (1985) p. 55.

116 See: Bowen Report; D. Hamill, *Pig in the Middle* (1985) pp. 65–6.

117 See: Parker Report, Appendix.

118 Paras. 92–6, 105.

119 Paras. 32, 34 (majority).

120 See: I. Brownlie, 'Interrogation in depth' (1972) 35 *M.L.R.* 501. The Diplock Report (para. 86) concurred with this reaction.

121 Pt. I paras. 3.15, 3.16, 4.7. See: I. Zamir, 'The rule of law and the control of terrorism' (1988) 8 *Tel Aviv Univ. Studies in Law* 81.

122 J. Kohl and J. Litt, *Urban Guerrilla Warfare in Latin America* (1974) p. 21. Torture is as often used for purposes of deterrence, intimidation and the assertion of authority: Amnesty International, *Torture in the Eighties* (1984) p. 5.

123 Paras. 20, 21, 26 (majority); 14 (minority).

124 Interrogation in depth amounted to inhuman and degrading treatment contrary to the European Convention Art. 3: *Ireland* v. *U.K., loc. cit.* See also: *Denmark and others* v. *Greece* Appl. Nos. 3321, 3322, 3323, 3344/67, 12 Y.B.E.C. Pt. II; *Donnelly and others* v. *U.K.,* Appl. Nos. 5577–83/72, Coll. 43 p. 124; K. Boyle and H. Hannum, 'Ireland in Strasbourg' (1972) 7 *Ir. Jur.* 329, (1976) 11 *Ir. Jur.* 243; H. Hannum and K. Boyle, 'Individual applications under the E.C.H.R. and the concept of administrative practice' (1974) 68 *A.J.I.L.* 440, 'The Donnelly case, administrative practice and domestic remedies under the European Convention' (1977) 71 *A.J.I.L.* 316; R.J. Spjut, 'Torture under the E.C.H.R.' (1979) 73 *A.J.I.L.*; U.N. Convention against Torture and Other Cruel, Inhuman or Degrading Treatment or Punishment (Cmnd. 9593, 1985); Council of Europe Convention for the Prevention of Torture and Inhuman or Degrading Treatment or Punishment (Cm. 339, 1988); Paris Minimum Standards, Section B Art. 1, Section C Art. 6 (see: Chowdhury, *op. cit.* pp. 187–203).

125   But see: N.S. Rodley, *The Treatment of Prisoners under International Law* (1987).

126   Parker Report, para. 15 (minority).

127   The Landau Report accepts inadmissibility as a consequence (para. 2.54) but equally wishes to discourage false or misleading evidence by the security forces to cover up the use of torture (para. 4.15). Its findings suggest that the two objectives may be incompatible.

128   See: Felton's Case (1628) 3 St. Tr. 367; Parker Report, paras. 2, 38 (majority), 8, 10 (minority): K. Boyle, T. Hadden and P. Hillyard, *Law and State: The Case of Northern Ireland* (1975) pp. 135–8.

129   Paras. 35–42 (majority). Compare: H. Rudolph, *Security, Terrorism and Torture* (1984) ch. 6; A.S. Mathews, *Review* (1985) 102 *S.A.L.J.* 341 at p. 343.

130   Paras. 3.16, 4.8.

131   The Defence Act 1952 s. 99A and Police Act 1958 s. 6(4) (South Africa) allow searches without warrant within ten miles of the border.

132   Compare: Internal Security Act 1960 s. 65, Essential (Security Cases) (Amendment) Regulations 1975 (P.U.(A.) 362) rr. 22, 23 (Malaysia); Internal Security Act 1970 s. 77 (Singapore); Organic Law (4/1988) Art. 553 (Spain).

133   See: J. Sundberg, 'The anti-terrorist legislation in Sweden' in R.D. Crelinsten, D. Laberge-Altmejd and D. Szabo (eds.), *Terrorism and Criminal Justice* (1979). See also: Temporary Immigration Security Act 1976 (c. 91) (passed at the time of the Montreal Olympics).

134   No special measure is needed as there is authority under the Immigration (Hotel Records) Order 1972 S.I. No. 1689. See: Home Affairs Committee, *Practical Police Cooperation in the European Community* (1989–90 H.C. 363) para. 130 and *Government Reply* (Cm. 1367) p. 10. Record-keeping has been applied as a special measure to lodging houses; see: Civil Authorities (Special Powers) Regulations (N.I.) 1922 S.R. & O. 56.

135   Boyle, Hadden and Hillyard, *op. cit.*, pp. 42–3; *Ten Years on in Northern Ireland* (1980) p. 27; Baker Report, para. 392; *Murray v. M.O.D.* [1988] 1 W.L.R. 692.

136   H.C. No. 16. See also: Colville Report on the E.P. Acts, para. 1.12.

137   See: Shackleton Report para. 152; H.C. Debs. Vol. 146 col. 1272 10 February 1989.

138   *Ibid.*, col. 1316.

139   Compare: Emergency (Registration Areas) Regulations 1948 (G.N. No. 2033) (Malaya).

140   H.C. Debs. Vol. 146 col. 1327 10 February 1989.

141   *Times* 23 November 1974 p. 15.

142   See: N.C.C.L., *Identity Cards and the Threat to Civil Liberties* (1990). Many Western European countries operate identity cards; see: (1980) Vol. VIII *E.L.D.* 161. See also: Council of Europe Committee of Ministers' Resolution (77) 26, *On the Establishment and Harmonisation of National Identity Cards.*

143 H.C. Debs. Vol. 187 cols. 337, 338 6 March 1991; *Government Reply* (Cm. 1367, 1991) p. 10.

144 See: 1939 Act s. 6(4); *Willcock v. Muckle* [1951] 2 K.B. 844; A.V. Bradley, 'Why National Registration had to go' (1985) 65 *Public Admin.* 209 (and see (1986) 64, p. 59, (1987) 65, p. 466).

145 Judicial review of such a multifaceted issue would not be appropriate. Compare: S. Pye, 'Judicial review of the discretionary powers under Part V of the Offences against the State Act 1939' (1985) 3 *I.L.T.* 65.

146 J. Dugard, *Human Rights and the South African Legal Order* (1978) p. 274. Compare: 'Crime is crime is crime. It is not political' (Mrs. M. Thatcher, *Times* 22 April 1981 p. 1).

147 See: O. Kirchheimer, *Political Justice* (1961); F.A. Allen, *Crimes of Politics* (1974); B. Ingraham, *Political Crime in Europe* (1979); A.T. Turk, *Political Criminality* (1982).

148 Compare: Criminal Procedure Ordinance (G.N. 114/1967) (Aden); Special Court Law 195 (No. 55) (Cyprus); Law 86-1322 (France); Terrorist Affected Areas (Special Courts) Act 1984 (No. 6), Terrorist and Disruptive Activities (Prevention) Act 1987 (No. 28) (India); Emergency Regulations 1948 r. 32 (Malaya); Essential (Security Cases) (Amendment) Regulations 1975 r. 7 (Malaysia); Prevention of Terrorism (Temporary Provisions) Act 1979 ss. 15, 22 (Sri Lanka).

149 Special Courts do not infringe the European Convention Art. 6(1) provided they remain independent and impartial. See: F.G. Jacobs, *The European Convention on Human Rights* (1975) pp. 104–7. 12839/87 v. *Ireland*; 1254/86 v. *Netherlands*, 10 E.H.R.R. 161. *Barbera and others* v. *Spain* Appl. No. 10588, 10589, 10590/83, 11 E.H.R.R. 360. See also: Paris Minimum Standards 1984 Section C Art. 7 (Chowdhury, *op. cit.* pp. 203–19).

150 See Diplock Report, para. 13.

151 As in the Northern Ireland (Emergency Provisions) Act 1991 s. 9, Offences against the State Act 1939 Pt. V. See: P.V.L.I. pp. 101–9, ch. 10. The three-judge model was rejected in *Northern Ireland: Anglo-Irish Agreement, Review of the Working of the Conference* (1989) para. 16; Colville Report on the E.P. Acts, ch. 9.

152 See: P.V.L.I. p. 238; Defence (Emergency) Regulations 1945 (Gen. No. 1442) rr. 10–22, 46–8, 55–6 (Palestine).

153 Compare: Defence (War Zone Courts) Regulations 1940 S.R. & O. No. 1444 (judge plus two J.P.s). The various alternatives are discussed in the following: M.T.W. Robinson, *The Special Criminal Court* (1974), Pt. III; K. Boyle, T. Hadden and P. Hillyard, *Ten Years on in Northern Ireland* (1980) pp. 80–1; S.C. Greer and A. White, *Abolishing the Diplock Courts* (1986); S.A.C.H.R., *14th Report*, *loc. cit.* Annex F, p. 102; Baker Report, paras. 108–29.

154 Compare the present overuse in Northern Ireland: P.V.L.I. pp. 107–9.

155 See: Attorney General's Guidelines (1989) 88 Cr. App. R. 123 paras. 4, 5.

156 See: *R. v. Pennington* [1985] Crim. L.R. 394; H. Harman and J. Griffith, *Justice Deserted: The Subversion of the Jury* (1979); P. Duff and M. Findlay, 'Jury vetting' (1983) 3 *L.S.* 159. Special unrepresentative juries are equally unacceptable. Compare: Prevention of Crime (Ireland) Act 1882 s. 4; Criminal Law and Procedure (Ireland) Act 1887 s. 3. Majority verdicts should not apply in special courts.

See generally: National Advisory Committee on Criminal Justice Standards and Goals, *op. cit.* p. 107; Greer and White, *op. cit.* ch. 7.

157 See generally: National Advisory Committee on Criminal Justice Standards and Goals, *op. cit.* p. 107; Greer and White, *op. cit.* ch. 7.

158 See: Contempt of Court Act 1981 ss. 4, 11; H.O. Circular 18/1990, Exclusion of Addresses from Witness Statements. Compare: Juries Protection Act 1929 (No. 33), Special Criminal Court Rules 1975 S.I. No. 234, rr. 7, 8 (Ireland): Internal Security Act 1982 s. 65 (South Africa); E. Wertheim, 'Anonymous juries' (1986) 54 *Fordham L.Rev.* 981. These measures should not interfere with the defendant's right of cross-examination: G. Marcus, 'Secret witnesses' (1990) *P.L.* 207.

159 Compare: Act 86-1020 (France): Peace Preservation (Ireland) Act 1870 s. 29, Prevention of Crime (Ireland) Act 1882 s. 6, Criminal Law and Procedure (Ireland Act 1887 s. 4, Public Safety (Emergency Provisions) Act No. 2) 1923 (No. 29) s. 12, Public Safety (Punishment of Offences) Temporary Act 1924 (No. 15) s. 8 (Ireland); Internal Security Act 1982 s. 68 (South Africa); Organic Law 4/1988 (Spain); Emergency Powers (Maintenance of Law and Order) Regulations 1983 s. 58 (Zimbabwe).

160 See Criminal Code ss. 31, 137, 138a, 146, 231, 255 (F.R.G.). Any procedural changes must take account of the European Convention Art. 6: *Barbera and others* v. *Spain, loc. cit.*

161 See: P.V.L.I. pp. 109–14. Compare: Terrorist and Disruptive Activities (Prevention) Act 1987 s. 15 (India); Emergency Regulations 1948 (G.N. No. 1953) r. 33 (Malaya); Internal Security Art. 1960 s. 75, Essential (Security Cases) (Amendment) Regulations 1975 r. 21(1) (Malaysia); Public Emergency Decree 1963 r. 16 (South Arabia); Prevention of Terrorism (Temporary Provisions) Act 1979 ss. 16(2), 23 (Sri Lanka).

162 See ch. 8. Despite any greater safeguards, amendments which increase incentives for obtaining confessions are contrary to the Paris Minimum Standards 1984, Section C Art. 6.4. (see Chowdhury, *op. cit.* pp. 187–203).

163 See P.V.L.I. pp. 114–15. There is no breach of the European Convention Art. 6(2). See: Diplock Report, para. 61; *X* v. *U.K.* Appl. No. 5124/71, Coll. 42 p. 135. But a more general switch of the burden would be condemned under Art. 6(2) (and under the Paris Minimum Standards 1984, Section C Art. 7.5 (Chowdhury, *op. cit.* pp. 203–19).

164 P.V.L.I. p. 248.

165 Northern Ireland (Emergency Provisions) Act 1991 s. 28(5); Offences against the State Act 1939 s. 24; P.V.L.I. pp. 139, 248; Compare: Internal Security Act 1982 s. 69(1) (South Africa).

166 See: *R.* v. *Vaillancourt* (1987) 47 D.L.R. (4th) 399, *R.* v. *Whyte* (1988) 51 D.L.R. (4th) 481 (S.C.C.) (Canada); Rabie Report, para. 9.3.4.2 (South Africa); *Tot* v. *U.S.* 319 U.S. 463 (1943), *U.S.* v. *Gainey* 380 U.S. 63 (1965), *U.S.* v. *Romano* 382 U.S. 136 (1965), *Leary* v. *U.S.* 395 U.S. 6 (1969), *Turner* v. *U.S.* 396 U.S. 398 (1970), *Barnes* v. *U.S.* 412 U.S. 837 (1973), *County Court of Ulster County, N.Y.* v. *Allen* 442 U.S. 140 (1979) (U.S.A.).

167 See: *Ong Ah Chuen* v. *Public Prosecutor* [1981] A.C. 651; *R.* v. *Stanger* (1984) 2 D.L.R. 4th 121 (Alberta C.A.); *S.* v. *Marwane* 1982 (3) S.A. 717 (A.D.), Internal Security Act 1982 s. 69 (5), (6) (South Africa); *Heiner* v. *Donman* 285 U.S. 312 (1932), *U.S.* v. *Fleischman* 339 U.S. 349 (1950) (U.S.A.).

168   See C. Collier, 'The improper use of presumptions in recent criminal law adjudications' (1986) 38 *Stan. L. Rev.* 423.

169   See ch. 5.

170   S.I. No. 1987. Compare: Anarchical and Revolutionary Crimes Act 1919 (No.1) s. 12, Terrorist and Disruptive Activities (Prevention) Act 1987 s. 21 (India).

171   S.A.C.H.R., *14th Report, loc. cit.* ch. 3. There had been previous indications of interest, especially in the Colville Report (paras. 15.1.5, 15.1.6), but the Government conducted its discussions in secret: H.L. Debs. Vol. 501 col. 776 10 November 1988.

172   Scanty evidence is provided in the *Report of the Working Group on the Right of Silence* (1989).

173   See: J.D. Jackson, 'Recent developments in criminal evidence' (1989) 40 *N.I.L.Q.* 105; *Alexander* v. *H.M. Advocate* 1989 S.L.T. 193.

174   See: Paris Minimum Standards Section C Art. 7.5.

175   See: S.A.C.H.R., *14th Report, loc. cit.* Annex B p. 78; 'How silently, how silently' [1989] Crim. L.R. 1.

176   See: Offences against the State (Amendment) Act 1972 s. 3(2); P.V.L.I. pp. 248–9; Essential (Security Cases) (Amendment) Regulations 1975 rr. 17, 21 (Malaysia).

177   See: Northern Ireland (Emergency Provisions) Act 1973 s. 5 (repealed in 1975); P.V.L.I. pp. 109–10.

178   Compare: Essential (Security Cases) (Amendment) Regulations 1975 r. 19 (Malaysia).

179   Written depositions of missing witnesses may also be admitted in certain circumstances: P.V.L.I. p. 130 n. 85; Criminal Justice (Evidence etc.) (N.I.) Order 1988; M.H. Graham, *Witness Intimidation* (1985).

180   Compare: *Kostovski* v. *Netherlands* Appl. No. 11454/85, Judgment of Court Ser. A. Vol. 166.

181   Gardiner Report, paras. 55–6.

182   Compare: Public Order (Temporary Measures) Act 1970 s. 3 (Canada); Defence (Emergency) Regulations 1945 r. 84 (Palestine); Unlawful Organisations Act 1971 (c. 91) (Rhodesia/Zimbabwe). Codes which do incorporate full or partial review are as follows: Crimes Act 1914 s. 30AA (compare the alternatives in *Adelaide Company of Jehovah's Witnesses Inc.* v. *Commonwealth* [1943] 67 C.L.R. 116, *Australian Communist Party* v. *Commonwealth* [1950–51] 83 C.L.R. 1) (Australia); Prevention of Terrorism Ordinance 1948 (No. 33) (Israel); Internal Security Act 1982 ss. 7–11 (South Africa). Judicial scrutiny should ensure that proscription is justifiable under the European Convention Arts. 9–11; compare: Baker Report, para. 416.

183   Compare: Prevention of Terrorism Ordinance 1948 s. 7 (Israel).

184   Fabian Tract No. 416, *op. cit.* p. 20.

185   See: Public Order (Temporary Measures) Act 1970 ss. 4, 8 (Canada); Prevention of Terrorism Ordinance 1948 s. 4(g) (Israel); Unlawful Organisations Act 1971 ss. 6, 11 (Rhodesia/Zimbabwe); Internal Security Act 1982 ss. 4, 13, 14, 16, 22, 33. 34, 56 (South Africa).

186   See: A.S. Mathews, *Freedom, State Security and the Rule of Law* (1988) ch. 6. See also: Restoration of Order in Ireland Regulations 1920 S.R. & O. No. 1.530 r. 50; Civil Authorities (Special Powers) Act (N.I.) 1922 s. 2(4); Emergency

Regulations 1965 (L.N. Nos. 7–10) r. 16 (Aden); Terrorist and Disruptive Activities (Prevention) Act 1987 ss. 3, 4 (India); Law and Order Maintenance Act 1960 s. 50 (Rhodesia/Zimbabwe).

187   See also: s. 69(5), (6); Rabie Report, paras. 8.3.5, 9.2.1–9.2.2.3.

188   Para. 70.

189   H.C. Debs. Vol. 893 col. 891 27 June 1975, Mr. Rees.

190   But see: Northern Ireland (Emergency Provisions) (Amendment) Act 1975 ss. 12, 15.

191   See: Fabian Tract No. 416, *op. cit.* p. 19.

192   Even Lord Fraser was confused in *D.P.P. for N.I.* v. *Maxwell* ([1978] 3 All. E.R. 1140 at p. 1149).

193   Fabian Tract No. 416, *op. cit.* p. 18.

194   See: ch. 2; A.S. Mathews, 'The Terrors of Terrorism' (1974) 91 *S.A.L.J.* 381.

195   But see: A.E. Evans and J.F. Murphy, *Legal Aspects of International Terrorism* (1978) p. 349.

196   Compare: *R.* v. *Governor of Durham Prison, ex p. Carlisle* [1979] Crim. L.R. 175.

197   14th Report, *Offences against the Person, loc. cit.* para. 125.

198   Colville Report on the E.P. Acts, para. 2.9; S.A.C.H.R., *15th Report* (1989– 90 H.C. 459) ch. 5 para. 17. Compare: Internal Security Act 1960 s. 43 (Malaysia).

199   *R.* v. *Byrne and others* (1976) 62 Cr. App. R. 159 at p. 163 *per* Lawton L.J. See also: *R.* v. *Al-Mograbi*; *R.* v. *Cull* (1979) 70 Cr. App. R. 24; *R.* v. *Relf* (1979) 1 Cr. App. R. (S) 111; *R.* v. *Gerald and others* (1981) 3 Cr. App. R. (S) 162. *R.* v. *Al-Banna (Marwan)* (1984) 6. Cr. App. R. (S) 426; *R.* v. *Hindawi* (1988) 10 Cr. App. R. (S) 104. The same trend occurs in Northern Ireland: P.V.L.I. pp. 154–6; *R.* v. *O'Reilly* (1990) 6 B.N.I.L. n. 71; *R.* v. *Payne* (1990) 6 B.N.I.L. n. 72; *R.* v. *Breslin and Forbes* (1990) 10 B.N.I.L. n. 58. Compare: *S.* v. *Maseko* 1988 (4) S.A. 1 (A.A.) (South Africa).

200   See: Criminal Law Revision Committee, *14th Report, loc. cit.* Annex 5. Their prison regime is also extraordinarily harsh: Irish Freedom Movement, *The Irish War* (3rd ed., 1987) pp. 180–8.

201   See: *In re Findlay* [1984] 3 W.L.R. 1159. The policy does not apply in Northern Ireland (P.V.L.I. p. 155) and has been criticised in the *Report of the Select Committee on Murder and Life Imprisonment* (1988–89 H.L. 78) para. 184. Related restrictions are criticised in the Report of the Review Committee, *The Parole System in England and Wales* (Cm. 532, 1988) para. 190. However, special restrictions are to continue: *Crime, Justice and Protecting the Public* (Cm. 965, 1990) para. 6.11.

202   See: Criminal Justice (Temporary Provisions) Act (N.I.) 1970 (amended in 1970 and repealed in 1973), K. Boyle, 'The Minimum Sentences Act' (1970) 21 *N.I.L.Q.* 425; Terrorist and Disruptive Activities (Prevention) Act 1987 ss. 3–6 (India); Law and Order (Maintenance) Act 1960 s. 38 (Rhodesia/Zimbabwe); Rabie Report, para. 8.4.6.2 (South Africa).

203   See: Explosive Substances Act 1883 s. 3 as amended in 1977 (see ch. 12 *supra*); Civil Authorities (Special Powers) Act (N.I.) 1922 s. 6, Criminal Law Act 1976 (No. 32) s. 2, Criminal Justice Act 1984 (No. 22) s. 14 (Ireland); Internal Security Act 1982 s. 58 (South Africa); Act 3/1988 (Spain).

204   See: Civil Authorities (Special Powers) Act (N.I.) 1922 s. 5; Emergency (Criminal Trials) Regulations 1948 (G.N. 1961) (Malaya); Defence (Emergency) Regulations 1945 r. 32 (Palestine); Law and Order (Maintenance) Act 1960 s. 64 (Rhodesia/Zimbabwe). Corporal punishment would probably breach the European Convention Art. 3 (see: *Tyrer* v. *U.K.* Appl. No. 5856/72, Judgment of Court Ser. A. Vol. 26) and other international safeguards (see Rodley, *op. cit.* ch. 10).

205   See H.C. Debs Vol. 833 cols. 518–640 11 December 1974 (hereafter cited as the '1974 Debate'); Vol. 902 cols. 633–728 11 December 1975 (the '1975 Debate'); Vol. 970 cols. 2019–166 19 July 1979 (the '1979 Debate'); Vol. 23 cols 608–701 11 May 1982 (the '1982 Debate'); Vol. 45 cols. 892–997 13 July 1983 (the '1983 Debate'); H.C. Debs. Vol. 113 cols. 1115–90 1 April 1987 (the '1987 Debate'); H.C. Debs. Vol. 134 col. 734 7 June 1988 (the '1988 Debate'); H.C. Debs. Vol. 183 cols. 22–127 17 December 1990 (the '1990 Debate'). For its use abroad, see: Amnesty International Report, *The Death Penalty* (1979) pp. 52–5, 58, 89–91; Rodley *op. cit.* chap 7; R. Hood, *The Death Penalty* (1989); Internal Security Act 1960 s. 57 (Malaysia); Law and Order (Maintenance) Act 1960 ss. 214, 37, 38, 50 (Rhodesia/Zimbabwe); Internal Security Act 1982 s. 54(1) (South Africa). The death penalty should not be restored in an emergency: Paris Minimum Standards 1984, Section C Art. 4 (see Chowdhury, *op. cit.* pp. 155–71).

206   See: Hood, *op. cit.*; 1990 Debate col. 35.

207   1975 Debate col. 717, Mr. Jenkins; 1979 Debate col. 2050, Mr. Whitelaw.

208   In December 1980, Gerard Tuite escaped from Brixton Prison, as did Quinlivan and McAuley in July 1991. In June 1981, eight remand prisoners escaped from Crumlin Road Prison, Belfast. In September 1983, nineteen Republicans fled from the Maze Prison. See: *Report of an Inquiry by H.M. Chief Inspector of Prisons into the Security Arrangements at H.M. Prison, Maze* (1983–84 H.C. 203).

209   1975 Debate col. 672, Mr. Lawrence.

210   1983 Debate col. 904, Mr. Hattersley. This problem would not arise if the death penalty were revived for all murders. However, a separate motion relating purely to terrorist killers was proposed (amongst others) in the 1982, 1983, 1988 and 1990 debates.

211   1974 Debate col. 523, Mr. Walden; 1988 Debate col. 768, Mr. Mallon.

212   1982 Debate col. 616, Mr. Jenkins.

213   See: J.H.J. Edwards, 'Capital punishment in Northern Ireland' [1956] Crim. L.R. 750.

214   1988 Debate col. 786, Mr. Mullin.

215   N.I.A. Debs. Vol. 4 p. 47 22 November 1982, Mr. McCartney.

216   P.V.L.I. p. 154. But see: 1983 Debate cols. 913, 956, Mr. Brittan. A transfer of venue to Britain should also be unacceptable in such vital litigation.

217   The U.K. has not signed the 6th Protocol to the European Convention on Human Rights.

218   P.V.L.I. p. 154. See: Northern Ireland (Emergency Provisions) Act 1973 s. 1. Compare: Criminal Justice Act 1964 (No. 5) (Ireland). The latter has not been applied since 1954. The Law Commission has been asked to consider the death penalty for treason: 1990 Debate col. 42.

219   See: P.V.L.I. pp. 157–8.

220   Though exclusion probably does not breach the European Convention

Art. 5 (see ch. 6), there is some doubt about more restrictive forms of security orders. Internment certainly contravenes Art. 5; see: *Lawless* v. *Ireland* Appl. No. 332/56, Judgment of Court Ser. A. Vol. 3; *Ireland* v. *U.K. loc. cit.*; A.H. Robertson, '*Lawless* v. *Government of Ireland* (Second Phase)' (1961) 37 B.Y.I.L. 536; P. O'Higgins, 'The Lawless Case' (1962) C.L.J. 234; E. Rauch, 'The compatibility of the Detention of Terrorists Order (N.I.) with the European Convention for the protection of Human Rights' (1973) 6 *N.Y.U.L.J. Int. L. and P. 1.*

221 Compare: Act 86-1020 (France).

222 S. 1(3). Compare: Internal Security Act 1982 s. 21 (South Africa).

223 Compare: Immigration (Registration with the Police) Regulations 1972 S.I. No. 1758 (as amended).

224 Ss. 18–21, 22–27, 35–43, 56, 70. See: Rabie Report, paras. 11.3.2.1–11.3.2.31. See also: Special Districts (Administration) Ordinance 1952 (No. 36) (Kenya); Restricted Residence (Amendment) Ordinance 1948 (No. 13), Emergency Regulations 1948 (G.N. 3632) rr. 17B, 17C (Malaya); Emergency (Transitional Provisions) Ordinance 1956 (No. 38) s. 8 (N. Rhodesia); Defence (Emergency) Regulations 1945 rr. 109, 110 (Israel); Law and Order (Maintenance) Act 1960 s. 55 (Rhodesia/Zimbabwe); Prevention of Terrorism (Temporary Provision) Act 1979 s. 11 (Sri Lanka); Emergency Powers/Maintenance of Law and Order) Regulations 1983 s. 47 (Zimbabwe).

225 See: M. Rees, *Northern Ireland: A Personal Perspective* (1985) pp. 212, 243; R.J. Spjut, 'Internment and detention without trial in Northern Ireland 1971–75' (1986) 49 *M.L.R.* 712.

226 Compare: Gardiner Report, para. 148; Baker Report, ch. 6; Hewitt, *op. cit.* p. 86.

227 Compare: P. Wilkinson, *Terrorism and the Liberal State* (2nd ed., 1986) p. 169; T. Wilson, *Ulster* (1989) pp. 245, 247–8; H.C. Debs. Vol. 169 col. 51 12 March 1990, Mr. Maginnis.

228 See: International Commission of Jurists, *States of Emergency: Their Impact on Human Rights* (1983); Emergency Regulations 1965 r. 4 (Aden); Detention of Persons Law 195 (No. 26) (Cyprus); Emergency Regulations 1952 r. 2 (Kenya); Emergency Regulations 1948 rr. 17, 18 (Malaya); Constitution Art. 151 and Internal Security Act 1960 ss. 8–21, 73 (Malaysia); Defence (Emergency) Regulations 1945 r. 111 (Palestine); Law and Order (Maintenance) Act 1960 ss. 55–7 (Rhodesia/Zimbabwe); Internal Security Act 1970 ch. II (Singapore); Internal Security Act 1982 ss. 28, 35–43, 50, 50A (South Africa); Public Emergency Decree 1963 s. 7 (South Arabia): Prevention of Terrorism (Temporary Provisions) Act 1979 ss. 9, 10, 13 (Sri Lanka).

229 See: P.V.L.I. ch. 3; Colville Report on the E.P. Acts, para. 11.10.

230 Defence (General) Regulations 1939 S.R. & O. No. 1681 r. 18B, 1940 S.R. & O. No. 770 r. 18 (1A). See: *Liversidge* v. *Anderson* [1942] A.C. 206; C.P. Cotter, 'Emergency detention in wartime: the British experience' (1954) 6 *Stan. L.R.* 238; P. Gillman and L. Gillman, *Collar the Lot* (1980).

231 But reviews should be six-monthly. Compare: McDonald Commission, *2nd Report*, Pt. IX ch. 1 para. 65; Rabie Report, paras. 11.3.1.22–11.3.1.47. The Paris Minimum Standards 1984 Section C Arts. 4, 5 require judicial or quasi-judicial review, a register of detainees, procedural safeguards and humane conditions. See: Chowdhury, *op. cit.* pp. 155–86; Rodley, *op. cit.* ch. 8.

232 See also: Emergency Detention Act 1950 (18 U.S.C. ss. 811–26, repealed by 1971 P.L. 92-128) (U.S.A.); Emergency Powers (Maintenance of Law and Order) Regulations 1983 Pts. II and III (Zimbabwe).

233 See: Detention of Terrorists (N.I.) Order 1972 S.I. No. 1632, Northern Ireland (Emergency Provisions) Act 1973 s. 10, Sched. 1. But these were adversarial in nature; see: Diplock Report, paras. 27–34; Gardiner Report, ch. 6; P.V.L.I. ch. 3.

234 See: P.V.L.I. pp. 216–19.

235 Constitution Art 22(4); Preventive Detention Act 1950 (as amended); Maintenance of Internal Security Acts 1971–75 (No. 26) (as amended); National Security Act 1980 (No. 65, as amended).

236 Emergency Powers (Detention) Law 1979 (No. 33 as amended). See Rudolph, *op. cit.* chs. 3, 4.

237 Compare: *Re McElduff* [1972] N.I.; *Re Mackey* (1972) 23 N.I.L.Q. 113; *Kelly* v. *Faulkner* [1973] N.I. 31; *In re Art. 26 and the Offences against the State (Amendment) Bill 1940* [1940] I.R. 470; *The State (O'Laighleis)* v. *O'Sullivan and Minister for Justice* [1960] I.R. 9; I.C.J. *op. cit.* pp. 185–8.

238 See: Report of the Sedition Committee (Rowlatt J.) 1918 p. 206 (India); Fabian Tract No. 416, *op. cit.* pp. 24–5; Rodley, *op. cit.* ch. 9.

239 As a result, these measures should always be justifiable under the European Convention Art. 8 and Art. 1 of Protocol 1.

240 See, for example: Emergency Powers (Public Safety and Order) Regulations 1955 (Orders nos. 795, 806, 825) r. 51 (Cyprus); Public Emergency Decree 1963 s. 14 (South Africa); Emergency (Maintenance of Law and Order) Regulations 1983 ss. 7, 8 (Zimbabwe).

241 See: Hope J., *op. cit.* paras. 6.11–6.30. Most evidence suggested that the I.R.A. has external suppliers for firearms, but a proportion of explosives is homemade: J. Adams, *The Financing of Terrorism* (1986) ch. 6; J. Holland, *The American Connection* (1989) chs. 2, 3; H.L. Select Committee on the European Communities, *1992* (1989–90 H.L. 90) Minutes of Evidence pp. 184, 186.

242 See: D. Barzilay, *The British Army in Ulster* (1978) Vol. 3 pp. 226–7; *McAfee* v. *Smyth and Quigley* [1981] 1 C.M.L.R. 410; Northern Ireland (Emergency Provisions) Act 1991 s. 19, P.V.L.I. pp. 60–3. Sophisticated radio-coding equipment and scanning and listening devices are widely used: *Times* 15 July 1989 p. 3.

243 See: C. Ryder, *The R.U.C.* (1989) p. 218; S. Tendler, 'Who is listening?' (1989) 97 *Police Rev.* 599.

244 S.I. 2213; P.V.L.I. p. 74. Compare: Civil Authorities (Special Powers) Regulations (N.I.) 1956 S.R. & O. No. 199 r. 32.

245 See: Crelinsten, Laberge-Altmejd and Szabo, *op. cit.* p. 16; R.V.G. Clarke and P. Mayhew (eds.), *Designing Out Crime* (1980). Non-legal, internal security arrangements should also be encouraged. See: Hope J., *op. cit.* ch. 11; Y. Alexander and R. A. Kilmarx, *Political Terrorism and Business: The Threat and Response* (1979).

246 Defence (General) Regulations 1945 r. 127.

247 P.V.L.I. pp. 146–7. Compare: Criminal Law Act 1976 s. 10 (Ireland, see P.V.L.I. p. 254); Emergency Powers (Maintenance of Law and Order) Regulations 1983 ss. 43, 44 (Zimbabwe). Ironically, most recent charges have been against soldiers pursuant to the Stevens inquiry: *Times* 18 May 1990 pp. 1, 4, 16 October p. 5, 11 October pp. 1, 2.

248   See: Hope J., *op. cit.* ch. 9, Baker Report, para. 432; Colville Report on the E.P. Acts, para. 14.2.

249   There is security vetting of staff as well as checks on entry: Select Committee on House of Commons Services, *Access to the Precincts of the House* (1987–88 H.C. 580).

250   See: Byford Report in P. Wilkinson, 'British policy on terrorism' in J. Lodge (ed.), *The Threat of Terrorism* (1988).

251   See: H.C. Defence Committee (two reports), *The Physical Security of Military Installations in the U.K.* (1983–84 H.C. 397) and *Government Reply* (Cmnd. 942, 1985), (1989–90 H.C. 171).

252   Northern Ireland (Emergency Provisions) Regulations 1991 S.I. No. 1759; P.V.L.I. p. 74.

253   See: Chief Constable of R.U.C., *Annual Report for 1983*, p. 20.

254   See P.V.L.I. p. 160.

255   See: Metropolitan Police Commissioner, *Report for 1984* (Cmnd. 9541, 1985) p. 20; Chief Constable of R.U.C., *Annual Report for 1987* (1988) p. 12; P. Hillyard, 'The normalisation of special powers' in P. Scraton (ed.), *Law, Order and the Authoritarian State* (1987) p. 291.

256   See the restrictions on disclosure by employees in Atomic Energy Act 1946 ss. 11, 13; Official Secrets Act 1989. Compare: National Key Points Act 1980 (No. 102) s. 10(2)(c), Rabie Report, para. 12.9.12, Protection of Information Act 1982 (No. 84) ss. 3, 4 (South Africa).

257   Compare: National Advisory Committee on Criminal Justice Standards and Goals, *op. cit.* pp. 58, 170–1; H.J. Yallop, *Protection against Terrorism* (1980); National Key Points Act 1980 ss. 3, 11 (South Africa).

258   Review of these is advisable: Hope J., *op. cit.* para. 6.58.

259   See: Railway Regulation Act 1840 s. 16 (as amended); Harbours Docks and Piers Clauses Act 1847 s. 83; Port of London Act 1968 s. 161; Explosives Act 1875 s. 77. Compare: Defence Act 1957 (No. 44) s. 99; Railways and Harbours Control and Management (Consolidation) Act 1957 (No. 90) s. 57A (South Africa).

260   See: Emergency (No. 3) Regulations 1974 S.I. No. 350 Art. 31.

261   See: Terrorist and Disruptive Activities (Prevention) Rules 1987 G.S.R.843(E) (India); Protected Areas Ordinance 1949 (No. 28) (Kenya); Emergency Regulations 1948 (G.N. 1953) r. 10, (G.N. 3679) r. 10A, 1951 (L.N.569) r. 17F, 1952 (L.N.29) r. 19A (Malaya); Internal Security Act 1960 ss. 47, 48, 49, 50, 52, 71 (Malaysia); Protected Places and Areas Act 1959 (c. 89, as amended) (see: C.K. Cilliers, *Counter-Insurgency in Rhodesia* (1980) ch. 3) (Rhodesia/Zimbabwe); Emergency Powers (Maintenance of Law and Order) Regulations 1983 ss. 10, 11 (Zimbabwe).

262   The sealing of the Northern Ireland border would be neither practicable nor politically desirable: M. Dewar, *The British Army in Northern Ireland* (1985) p. 123; ch. 9.

263   See: Northern Ireland (Emergency Provisions) Act 1991 ss. 24, 25, 63, 64; Emergency Provisions (Compensation) (N.I.) Rules 1982–91; P.V.L.I. pp. 69–71; Internal Security Act 1960 ss. 53–5 (Malaysia); International Terrorism (Emer-

gency Powers) Act 1987 ss. 10, 11, 13 (New Zealand); Emergency Powers (Maintenance of Law and Order) Regulations 1983 s. 16 (Zimbabwe); Emergencies Act 1988 s. 48 (Canada). Trespassers in an emergency (for example, by taking cover in private land when under fire) are probably covered by the defence of necessity.

264 See: P. Wilkinson, *Terrorism and the Liberal State* (2nd ed., 1986) pp. 300–1.

265 Criminal Justice Act 1988 Pt. VII.

266 Criminal Injuries (Compensation) (N.I.) Order 1988 S.I. No. 793; Criminal Damage (Compensation) (N.I.) Order 1977 S.I. No. 1247.

267 Art. 86-1020 (France); Royal Decrees 24 January 1986, 28 October 1988 (Spain); 37 U.S.C. s. 1013, Exec. Order 12598 (1987) (U.S.A.).

268 The Northern Ireland (Emergency Provisions) Act 1991 should likewise largely be replaced.

269 See: Walker, 'Irish Republican prisoners' (1984) 19 *Ir. Jur.* 189.

270 F. Kitson, *Bunch of Five* (1977) pp. 283–4. Compare: Bonner, *op. cit.* p. 97, Mathews, *op. cit.* p. 273; A. Guelke, *Northern Ireland* (1988) pp. 202–3. For assessments of reforms in Northern Ireland, see: K. Boyle and T. Hadden, *Ireland: A Positive Proposal* (1985) pp. 67–9; F. Wright, *Northern Ireland* (1987) p. 206.

271 See: Hewitt, *op. cit.* pp. 52, 67.

272 'Every act of murder and violence makes a just solution more difficult to achieve' (New Ireland Forum, *Report* (1984) para. 3.20).

273 The two aims are not incompatible. Compare: Belfast Bulletin No. 10, *Rough Justice* (1982) p. 10; P. Hillyard, 'Political and social dimensions of emergency law' in A. Jennings (ed.), *Justice under Fire* (2nd ed., 1990) p. 207.

Bibliography

1 Terrorism in general

The following works describe the phenomenon of terrorism, especially as experienced in the British Isles.

Adams, G., *The Politics of Irish Freedom* (Brandon Books, Dingle) 1986

Adams, J., *The Financing of Terrorism* (New English Library, London) 1986

Adams, J., Morgan, R. and Bambridge, A., *Ambush* (Pan, London) 1988

Alexander, Y. (ed.), *International Terrorism: National, Regional and Global Perspectives* (Praeger, New York) 1976

Alexander, Y. and O'Day, A. (eds.), *Terrorism in Ireland* (Croom Helm, London) 1984

— *Ireland's Terrorist Dilemma* (Nijhoff, The Hague) 1986

Arthur, M., *Northern Ireland Soldiers Talking* (Sidgwick & Jackson, London) 1987

Bishop, P. and Mallie, E., *The Provisional I.R.A.* (Heinemann, London) 1987

Bowyer Bell, J., *On Revolt* (Harvard University Press) 1976

— *The Secret Army: the I.R.A. 1916–1979* (Academy Press, Dublin) 1979

Boyd, A., *Holy War in Belfast* (3rd ed., Pretani Press, Belfast) 1987

Burton, A.M., *Urban Terrorism* (Leo Cooper, London) 1975

Cairns, E., *Caught in the Crossfire* (Appletree Press, Belfast) 1987

Carlton, D. and Schaerf, C., *International Terrorism and World Security* (Croom Helm, London) 1975

Clutterbuck, R. *Britain in Agony: The Growth of Political Violence* (Faber & Faber, London) 1978

— *The Future of Political Violence* (Macmillan, London) 1986

Conroy, J., *War as a Way of Life: A Belfast Diary* (Heinemann, London) 1987

Coogan, T.P., *The I.R.A.* (3rd ed., Fontana Books, Isle of Man) 1987

Council of Europe, *Conference on the Defence of Democracy against Terrorism in Europe: Tasks and Problems* (AS/POL/COLL/Terr 32) (Strasbourg) 1980

Cronin, S., *Irish Nationalism: A History of its Roots and Ideology* (Academy Press, Dublin) 1980

Darby, J., (ed.), *Northern Ireland: The Background to the Conflict* (Appletree Press, Belfast) 1983

Dillon, M., *The Shankill Butchers* (Hutchinson, London) 1989
— *The Dirty War* (Hutchinson, London) 1990
Eckstein, H., (ed.), *Internal War: Problems and Approaches* (Free Press of Glencoe, New York) 1964
Elliott, J.D. and Gibson, L.K., (eds.) *Contemporary Terrorism: Selected Readings* (I.A.C.P., Maryland) 1978
Evans, E., *Calling a Truce to Terror* (Greenwood Press, Connecticut) 1979
Faligot, R., *Britain's Military Strategy in Ireland: The Kitson Experiment* (Zed Press, London) 1983
Friedlander, R.A., *Terrorism: Documents of International and Local Control*, Vols. I–V (Oceana Publications, New York) 1979–90
Galliher, J.F. and Degregory, J.L., *Violence in Northern Ireland: Understanding the Protestant Perspective* (Gill & MacMillan, Dublin) 1985
Grivas-Dighensis, G., *Guerrilla Warfare* (Longmans, London) 1962
Guelke, A., *Northern Ireland: The International Perspective* (Gill & MacMillan, Dublin) 1988
Guevara, C., *Guerrilla Warfare* (M.R. Press, New York) 1961
Gurr, T.R., *Why Men Rebel* (Princeton University Press) 1970
Henshaw, D., *Animal Warfare* (Fontana, London) 1989
Holland, J., *The American Connection* (Poolbeg, Belfast) 1989
Kelly, K., *The Longest War: Northern Ireland and the I.R.A.* (Brandon, Dingle) 1982
Kitson, F., *Low-Intensity Operations* (Faber & Faber, London) 1971
Laqueur, W., *Guerrilla* (Weidenfeld & Nicolson, London) 1977
Lee, A.M., *Terrorism in Northern Ireland* (General Hall, New York) 1983
Livingston, M.H., (ed.), *International Terrorism in the Contemporary World* (Greenwood Press, Connecticut) 1978
Mao Tse-tung, *Selected Military Writings* (Foreign Language Press, Peking) 1968
Marighella, C., *For the Liberation of Brazil* (Penguin, London) 1971
Morton, P., *Emergency Tour: 3 Para in South Armagh* (William Kimber, Wellingborough) 1989
Nelson, S., *Ulster's Uncertain Defenders* (Appletree Press, Belfast) 1984
O'Malley, P., *The Uncivil Wars: Ireland Today* (Houghton Mifflin Boston) 1983
Royal United Services Institute for Defence Studies, *Ten Years of Terrorism* (London) 1979
Ryder, C., *The R.U.C.: A Force under Fire* (Methuen, London) 1989
Townshend, C., *Political Violence in Ireland* (Oxford University Press) 1983
— *Britain's Civil Wars* (Faber & Faber, London) 1986
Wardlaw, G., *Political Terrorism* (2nd ed., Cambridge University Press) 1989
Wilkinson, P., *Terrorism and the Liberal State* (2nd ed., Macmillan, London) 1986
Wilkinson, P., (ed.), *British Perspectives on Terrorism* (George Allen & Unwin, London) 1981
Wilkinson, P. and Stewart, A.M., (eds.) *Contemporary Research on Terrorism* (Aberdeen University Press) 1987
Wilson, T., *Ulster: Conflict and Consent* (Basil Blackwell, London) 1989
Wolf, J.B., *Fear of Fear* (Plenum Press, New York) 1981

2   Law and terrorism

The following describe or comment upon domestic legal and security measures in response to terrorism, especially those in Britain.

Alexander, Y. and Nanes, A.S., (eds.), *Legislative Responses to Terrorism* (Nijhoff, The Hague) 1986

Amnesty International, *Political killings by Governments* (1983)
— *Torture in the Eighties* (1984)
— *Northern Ireland: Killings by Security Forces and Supergrass Trials* (1988)
— *Investigating Lethal Shootings: The Gibraltar Inquests* (1989)

Article 19, *No Comment: Censorship, Secrecy and the Irish Troubles* (1989)

Bates, T. St. J.N., 'The Shackleton Report on Terrorism' (1979) *Scottish Law Times* 205

Belfast Workers' Research Unit, Bulletin No. 10: *Rough Justice* (1982)
— Bulletin No. 11: *Supergrasses* (1984)

Bishop Jr., J.W., 'Law in the control of terrorism and insurrection' (1978) 42 *Law and Contemporary Problems* 140

Bloch, J. and Fitzgerald, P., *British Intelligence and Covert Action* (Brandon, Dingle) 1983

Bonner, D. 'Combating terrorism in Great Britain: the role of exclusion orders' (1982) *Public Law* 262
— 'Combating terrorism: the Jellicoe approach' (1983) *Public Law* 224
— 'The Baker Review of the Northern Ireland (Emergency Provisions) Act 1978' (1984) *Public Law* 348
— *Emergency Powers in Peacetime* (Sweet & Maxwell, London) 1985
— 'Combating terrorism: Supergrass trials in Northern Ireland' (1988) 51 *Modern Law Review* 23
— 'Combating terrorism in the 1990s' (1989) *Public Law* 440

Boyle, K., Hadden, T. and Hillyard, P., *Law and State: The Case of Northern Ireland* (Martin Robertson, London) 1975
— *Ten Years on in Northern Ireland* (Cobden Trust, London) 1980

Chowdhury, S.R., *Rule of Law in a State of Emergency* (Pinter, London) 1989

Committee on the Administration of Justice, *Just News* (monthly) and several pamphlets (Belfast)

Curtis, L., *Ireland: the Propaganda War* (Pluto Press, London) 1984

Crelinsten, R.D., Laberge-Altmejd, D. and Szabo, D., (eds.) *Terrorism and Criminal Justice* (D.C. Heath, Massachusetts) 1978

Dash, S., *Justice Denied: A Challenge to Lord Widgery's Report on Bloody Sunday* (N.C.C.L., London) 1972

Dewar, M., *The British Army in Northern Ireland* (Arms and Armour Press, London) 1985

Dickson, B., 'The Prevention of Terrorism (Temporary Provisions) Act 1989' (1989) 40 *Northern Ireland Legal Quarterly* 250

Evelegh, R., *Peacekeeping in a Democratic Society* (C. Hurst, London) 1978

Fabian Tract No. 416, *Emergency Powers: A Fresh Start* (London) 1972

Finnie, W., 'Fourth bite at the cherry' (1989) *Scottish Law Times* 329

— 'Old wine in new bottles?' 1990 *Juridical Review* 1
— 'Anti-terrorist legislation and the European Convention on Human Rights' (1991) 54 *Modern Law Review* 288
Gifford, T., *Supergrass: The Use of Acomplice Evidence in Northern Ireland* (Cobden Trust, London) 1984
Greer, S., 'Supergrasses and the legal system in Britain and Northern Ireland' (1986) 102 *Law Quarterly Review* 189
Greer, S.C. and White A., *Abolishing the Diplock Courts* (Cobden Trust, London) 1986
Hamill, D., *Pig in the Middle: The Army in Northern Ireland 1969–84* (Methuen, London) 1985
Hayes, J. and O'Higgins, P. (eds.), *Lessons from Northern Ireland* (S.L.S., Belfast) 1990
Henderson, L., Miller, D. and Reilly, J., *Speak No Evil: The British Broadcasting Ban, the Media and the Conflict in Ireland* (Glasgow University Media Group) 1990
Hewitt, C., *The Effectiveness of Anti-Terrorist Policies* (University of America Press) 1984
Hillyard, P., 'The normalisation of special powers' in Scraton, P. (ed.), *Law, Order and the Authoritarian State* (Open University Press) 1987
Hogan, G. and Walker C., *Political Violence and the Law in Ireland* (Manchester University Press) 1989
Holroyd, F. and Burbridge, N., *War without Honour* (Medium, Hull) 1989
International Commission of Jurists, *States of Emergency: Their Impact on Human Rights* (1983)
Irish Freedom Movement, *An Anti-Imperialist's Guide to the Irish War* (3rd ed., Junius, London) 1987
Jackson, J.R., 'Recent developments in criminal evidence' (1989) 40 *Northern Ireland Legal Quarterly* 105
Jennings, A., (ed.), *Justice under Fire* (2nd ed., Pluto Press, London) 1990
Kitchen, H., *The Gibraltar Report* (N.C.C.L., London) 1989
Lee, H.P., *Emergency Powers* (Law Book Co., Sydney) 1984
Leigh, L.H., 'Comment' (1975) *Public Law* 1
Lowry, D.R., 'Terrorism and human rights' (1977) 53 *Notre Dame Lawyer* 49
— 'Draconian powers' (1976–77) 8–9 *Columbia Human Rights Law Review* 185
Lowry, Lord, *Civil Proceedings in a Beleaguered Society* (Child & Co. Lecture), 1987
Mathews, A.S., *Freedom, State Security and the Rule of Law* (Sweet & Maxwell, London) 1988
Michael, J., 'Attacking the easy platform' (1988) 138 *New Law Journal* 786
Miller, A.H. (ed.), *Terrorism, the Media and the Law* (Wesleyan University Press, Connecticut) 1982
Morison, J. and Geary, R., 'Crime conflict and community' (1989) 28 *Howard Journal* 9
Mosesson, L., 'Prevention of Terrorism' (1975–76) *Polytechnic Law Review* 45
Mullin, C., *Error of Judgment* (revised ed., Poolbeg Press, Dublin) 1987
Murray, R., *The S.A.S. in Ireland* (Mercier, Dublin) 1990

Narain, B.J., *Public Law in Northern Ireland* (Shanway Services, Northern Ireland) 1975

National Advisory Committee on Criminal Justice Standards and Goals, *Disorders and Terrorism* (Department of Justice, Washington D.C.) 1976

O'Boyle, M.P., 'Emergency situations and the protection of human rights' (1977) 28 *Northern Ireland Legal Quarterly* 160

Reports from official sources: (See Glossary after Preface)

Robertson, K.G., 'Intelligence, terrorism and civil liberties' (1987) 7.2 *Conflict Quarterly* 43

— *1992: The Security Implications* (Institute for Defence and Strategic Studies, London) 1989

Rolston, B., (ed.), *The Media and Northern Ireland* (Macmillan, London) 1990

Rose-Smith, B., 'Police powers and the terrorism legislation' in Hain, P., (ed.), *Policing the Police* Vol. I (John Calder, London) 1979

Rudolph, H., *Security, Terrorism and Torture* (Juta, Cape Town) 1984

Samuels, A., 'The legal response to terrorism: the Prevention of Terrorism (Temporary Provisions) Act 1984' (1984) *Public Law* 365

Schiff, D.N., 'The Shackleton Review of the Operation of the Prevention of Terrorism Act' (1978) *Public Law* 352

— 'Law and order – the British response to terrorism' (1979) 9 *Kingston Law Review* 121

Scorer, C., *The Prevention of Terrorism Acts 1974–1976: A Report on the Operation of the Law* (Cobden Trust, London) 1976

Scorer, C. and Hewitt, P., *The Prevention of Terrorism Act: The Case for Repeal* (Cobden Trust, London) 1981

Scorer, C., Spencer, S. and Hewitt, P., *The New Prevention of Terrorism Act: The Case for Repeal* (N.C.C.L., London) 1985

Sim, J. and Thomas, P.A., 'The Prevention of Terrorism Act: normalising the politics of repression' (1983) 10 *Journal of Law and Society* 71.

Spjut, R.J., 'Internment and detention without trial in Northern Ireland 1971–75' (1986) 49 *Modern Law Review* 712.

Stalker, J., *Stalker* (Harrap, London) 1988

Street, H., 'The Prevention of Terrorism (Temporary Provisions) Act' (1975) *Criminal Law Review* 192

Taylor, P., *Beating the Terrorists?* (Penguin, London) 1980

Twining, W.L., 'Emergency powers and the criminal process: the Diplock Report' (1973) *Criminal Law Review* 406

Walker, C.P., 'Shoot to Kill' (1980) 43 *Modern Law Review* 591

— 'The Jellicoe Report on the Prevention of Terrorism (Temporary Provisions) Act 1976' (1983) 46 *Modern Law Review* 484

— 'Members of Parliament and executive security measures' (1983) *Public Law* 537

— 'Arrest and rearrest' (1984) 35 *Northern Ireland Legal Quarterly* 1

— 'Prevention of Terrorism (Temporary Provisions) Act 1984' (1984) 47 *Modern Law Review* 704

—'Irish Republic prisoners, political detainees, prisoners of war or common criminals?' (1984) *Irish Jurist* 189

— 'Emergency arrest powers' (1985) 36 *Northern Ireland Legal Quarterly* 145

— 'Political violence and democracy in Northern Ireland' (1988) 51 *Modern Law Review* 605
— 'Army special powers on parade' (1989) 40 *Northern Ireland Legal Quarterly* 1
— 'Police and community in Northern Ireland' (1990) 41 *Northern Ireland Legal Quarterly* 105
— 'The role and powers of the Army in Northern Ireland' in Hadfield, B., (ed.), *Northern Ireland and the Constitution* (Open University Press, forthcoming)
Walsh, D.P.J., *The Use and Abuse of Emergency Legislation in Northern Ireland* (Cobden Trust, London) 1983
Warbrick, C., 'The protection of human rights in national emergencies' in Dowrick, F.E., (ed.), *Human Rights* (Saxon House, Farnborough) 1979
— 'The European Convention on Human Rights and the prevention of terrorism' (1983) 32 *International and Comparative Law Quarterly* 82
— 'The Prevention of Terrorism (Temporary Provisions) Act 1976 and the European Convention on Human Rights' (1983) 32 *International and Comparative Law Quarterly* 757
Ward, R.H. and Smith, H.E., (eds.), *International Terrorism: Operational Issues* (O.I.C.J., Chicago) 1987
— *International Terrorism: The Domestic Response* (O.I.C.J., Chicago) 1987
Watson, S., 'Consumer terrorism – the impracticability of legislation' (1987) 137 *New Law Journal* 84
— 'Product contamination' (1987) 84 *Law Society Gazette* 7 January p. 13.
Weaver, R.L. and Bennett, G.J., 'The Northern Ireland broadcasting ban: some reflections on judicial review' (1989) 22 *Vanderbilt Journal of Transnational Law* 1119
Wharam, A. 'Treason and the terrorist' (1976) 126 *New Law Journal* 428
Wheatley, D., 'Guilty . . . said the Red Queen?' (1989) 139 *New Law Journal* 499
Woffinden, B., *Miscarriages of Justice* (Hodder & Stoughton, London) 1989
Zamir, I., 'The rule of law and the control of terrorism' (1988) 8 *Tel Aviv University Studies in Law* 81.

Table of cases

Table of statutes

Table of subordinate legislation

United Kingdom
Channel Tunnel (Fire Services, Immigration and Prevention of Terrorism) Order 1990 (S.I. No. 2227) 214
Criminal Evidence (Northern Ireland) Order 1988 (S.I. No. 1987) 137–8, 171, 257, 303
Criminal Justice (Confiscation) (Northern Ireland) Order 1990 (S.I. No. 2588) 120, 130, 290
Criminal Justice (Northern Ireland) Order 1991 (S.I. No. 1711) 170
Defence (General) Regulation 18(2) (1939 S.R.& O. No. 927) 81
Defence of the Realm Regulation 14E (1916 S.R.& O. No. 561) 81
Northern Ireland (Emergency Provisions) Regulations (1975 S.I. No. 2213) 309
Police and Criminal Evidence (Northern Ireland) Order 1989 (S.I. No. 1341) 162–3, 165, 170, 173, 187–9, 191–5, 197, 217, 220, 257, 290, 299, 303, *see also Table of Statutes; General Index*
Treatment of Offenders (Northern Ireland) Order 1976 (S.I. No. 226) 241

Cyprus
Emergency Powers (Collective Punishments) Regulations 1955 (No. 232) 295

Index